# QUESTIONING RAMAYANAS

D1557027

# QUESTIONING RAMAYANAS
## A South Asian Tradition

Edited by
Paula Richman

UNIVERSITY OF CALIFORNIA PRESS
Berkeley Los Angeles London

University of California Press
Berkeley and Los Angeles, California

University of California Press, Ltd.
London, England

Published by arrangement with Oxford University Press

© 2001 by
The Regents of the University of California

Library of Congress Cataloging-in-Publication Data

Questioning Ramayanas : a South Asian tradition / edited by Paula Richman.
p. cm.
Includes bibliographical references and index.
ISBN 0-520-22073-0 (cloth : alk. paper)—ISBN 0-520-22074-9 (pbk. : alk. paper)
1. Indic literature—History and criticism. 2. Råma (Hindu deity) in literature. 3. Vålmåki. Råmåyaòa. 4. Tulasådåsa, 1532–1623 Råmacaritamånasa. I. Richman, Paula.

PK2907.R25 Q83 2001
891.4—dc21 00-046706

Printed in the United States of America

08 07 06 05 04 03 02 01
10 9 8 7 6 5 4 3 2 1

The paper used in this publication is both acid-free and totally chlorine-free (TCF). It meets the minimum requirements of ANSI/NISO Z39.48-1992 (R 1997) (*Permanence of Paper*). ∞

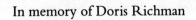

In memory of Doris Richman

*Fiction has only one form. True story inevitably has many.*

Velcheru Narayana Rao, in oral narrative

# Foreword

ROMILA THAPAR

I have been told that the poet Intizar Hussain, speaking at a gathering of authors at Kathmandu, stated that he had never known that Ayodhya actually exists on a map of the world. It had always been for him a fabulous kingdom, a sound, a resonance. After the demolition of the Babri Masjid, he was compelled to remap his geography as a writer.

In a sense, remapping the location of the *kathā,* or the story, of Rama has been a constant feature of Indian civilization. This was made quite apparent in the earlier companion volume edited by Paula Richman, *Many Rāmāyaṇas,* which added to our awareness of the range of variants and versions, an awareness which has led to much discussion on these in recent times. The Valmiki *Rāmāyaṇa* should not necessarily be taken as a fixed text and the others necessarily as variants of this fixed text, for the latter often contextualized the differing worldviews of particular segments of Indian society. Each variant is better seen in its own specific context before it is juxtaposed with the authoritative versions.

The range of variants—now generally recognized and part of the discussion on the story of Rama—includes those previously ignored or neglected, as for example from the regional languages, or even the dialects of these; tribal versions; and some composed by and for the lower castes. The collecting of these, which has revealed a new discourse on the *kathā* of Rama, is of course not a sufficient point at which to stop, for they too must be analysed. Questioning the Ramayana is therefore questioning that which is seen as the norm, but it also involves an explanation of why variant versions were composed and why they retain a vitality different from that of the authoritative versions. The variants point to the richness of a narrative which has been appropriated by a vast number of people in diverse ways. To reduce it to a received version would be to rob it of its richness. Even a national culture has to be nourished on variants. Investigating these would involve investigating authorship, audience, location and purpose. These are in part the explanations sought in the present book.

The questioning process also raises the related issue of whether the Valmiki and Tulsidas versions can be described as the authoritative ones, and the others as oppositional. The authoritative versions should not be treated as somehow chronos-free and without a historical context. From a social and historical point of view this treatment reduces the meaning of the texts, however much such an approach may add to their philosophical connotations. My intention is not to suggest that their historicity must be established if their historical context is to be known: this would be uncalled for. But even a fictional account relates to a moment or moments of time and to a socio-political niche, which provided it with a historical context but not necessarily with historicity. In the history of the *kathā* of Rama two occasions when the historicity of the story was crucial to the argument of its identity were in the earliest Jaina version, the *Paumacariyam,* which insisted that its retelling was not the version told by the Brahmins but was instead the historically true version of the story, and was recited in the presence of the king, Bimbisara; and the equal insistence of the Vishva Hindu Parishad on the authenticity of the location of the Ramjanmabhoomi and the historicity of the events of the Ramayana, even if both differed from the Jain version. Are there similarities in both these concerns? One may well ask who and what was being mobilized through such insistence.

In contemporary India, the *kathā* of Rama, quite apart from its enduring symbolism in the Vaishnava and in some bhakti traditions, has taken on a political role. This role draws largely from Valmiki's *Rāmāyaṇa* as well as the *Rāmacaritamānas* of Tulsidas. These were the inspiration both for the television version of the serial *Rāmāyaṇa* as well as in the debate on the location of the Babri Masjid as the Ramjanmabhoomi. It would be worth investigating whether the story has always been used as a metaphor in Indian politics. How often and in what ways has the *kathā* of Rama been used to negotiate power and status, and to claim access to knowledge? Can it be that we have not recognized its role as such because we have not viewed it in juxtaposition with the variants? Some attempts have been made to suggest a rather obvious form of its political role by arguing that the appellation of Ravana was given to the Muslim enemy. But this argument is questionable when one knows that the same appellation was applied to Hindu kings as well. One can reverse this argument and ask whether Ravana was not actually the personification of "the other"—any threatening "other", and could therefore be extended to a multiplicity of persons. Nor was this a simplistic or restricted "otherness." Michael Madhusudan Dutt's *Meghanādavada kāvya* empathizes with the family of Ravana. As a political and literary statement it had a powerful appeal in the nineteenth century, but in the Hindutva society of today, it would in all likelihood be rejected, assuming that an attempt could even be made to give it visibility.

The received version, whether it be of Valmiki or Tulsidas, can be used for political purposes, for projecting an upper-caste dominance or a lower-caste opposition where there is an identity of lower castes with Ravana; or it can be used to assert Hindu dominance over the Muslim, as in the Ramjanmabhoomi–Babri Masjid issue. But where the presence of variant versions is made visible, there the political use of the dominant version becomes more complicated. There is a need to recognize that a range of social groups adapted the story or fragments of the story to express their worldviews.

A more subtle argument is implicit in this volume, raising the question of why the variants were composed. The multiple forms of questioning within the tradition of the Rama story range across norms of rulership, of social obligations and relationships, of gender constructions, of the ethics of behaviour, of demons and deities—in effect of every aspect of human activity.

Perhaps the one most evident feature of these studies, and some others which pertain to the variants of a folk and tribal nature, is the revelation of the diversity in treatment of the story. This diversity not only adds to the richness of the versions that we are already familiar with, but also demonstrates the ways in which the story has been contextualised. Such multiple contextualisations come into confrontation with the current attempts—often politically motivated—to legitimize a single version as the "authentic" one. If even today the "authentic" version is not that which is telecast but that which is sung, recited or performed by groups of people in different parts of the country, such renderings would have been even more characteristic of the past.

This is quite logical considering that the worship of Rama is not uniformly observed throughout India. There are some areas, such as the Hindi-speaking regions, where it is more widespread, whereas elsewhere the rituals associated with other deities such as Durga take precedence at the time of Dussehra. So too with caste appreciations of the story. For the upper castes Rama may be the *maryādā puruṣottam*—the man to be venerated—but would the same be true of the lower castes, who would be familiar with the story of Rama killing a Shudra because he had dared to perform rituals permitted only to the upper castes?

Religious narratives have multiple versions. Each version is also a cultural item and should be viewed as such. Each has a social clientele which gives it legitimacy and the recognition of this social clientele is essential. The question then is, which particular version does a particular ideology appropriate and why? The recent attempt in the politics of Hindu nationalism to homogenize the story and present a single version is antithetical to the tradition of how the story was perceived in Indian culture.

The competition between the televised presentation of the dominant version and the traditional recitation and presentation of the local versions becomes acute these days since television has such a strong appeal. Can the local versions survive or will they be brushed aside? This is of course not merely a matter of maintaining a local version, for it is also tied to the concept of status and participation in national culture. As long as national culture is something which is devised and imposed it will remain somewhat alien, but will need to be appropriated by those aspiring to status and power. What one hopes will actually happen is that the sentiments of the local versions will be reflected in the continuing multiplicity of retellings. Will television have the courage to project the versions not only of the regional languages but even the diversities in the dialects of the regional languages, or the equivalent versions from local poets, or the songs of women, many of which are contestations of what are taken to be the authoritative versions? With the growth of greater consciousness of gender status, for example, there will have to be some reflection of the way in which the story is presented from the songs of women, songs which project the emotions of Sita or any other woman from the story in a different light from that with which we have been familiar in the homogenized version. These may be seen as degrees of unravelling the authoritative version and therefore innocuous. But they also represent a diversity of worldviews. This makes them culturally viable and therefore threatening to the dominant culture.

Other kinds of non-conformities may also become visible. It is often argued that the Rama story embodies the tension between Sanskritic, Brahmanical culture and values, and those of other groups, collectively treated as *rākṣasas* (demons). But there are other tensions which have also been addressed and continue to be addressed in divergent ways. For example, consider the contestation between monarchies and chiefdoms, where Ayodhya and the concept of Ramraj assumes the ascendency of monarchical systems over all others, but where the depiction of the lifestyle of the *rākṣasas* indicates an alternative society, closer in form to the *gaṇa-saṅghas,* the chiefdoms or republics as they have been called, which were prominent in the early period of Indian history.

Another major dichotomy is that between the *grāma* or *kṣetra* (the settlement)—and the *araṇya* or *vana* (the forest.) This dichotomy goes back to the Vedic corpus and, as it has been said, the duality is not just one of space or of ecology for it underlines a perception of the activities in each area and implicit in this is their relationship to concepts of dharma. If the settlement is the ordered, the disciplined and the known, the forest is that which lacks order or discipline and is therefore wild—and above all it is the unknown. Symbolically the forest is the reversal of the settlement. Epic events in the stories of both the Ramayana and the Mahabharata move between the settlement and the forest, and the symbolism of each governs many facets of the stories.

The voicing of these tensions remains closer to silence than to speech in many presentations of the homogenized versions. The symbolism too tends to fade or is given a particular coloring through the insensitivities of the political treatment of the epic. Those that wish to explore the richness of the diversities are silenced, as happened in the case of the Sahmat Exhibition on Ayodhya. This carried a panel describing the version of the *Dasaratha Jātaka;* and because some politicians were unaware of the role of *jātaka* stories in Indian civilization, and could not comprehend the symbolic meaning of this particular *jātaka,* the panel was objected to and had to be removed, and there was a demand that the exhibition be closed. Unfortunately such demands, claiming to uphold the values of Indian culture and tradition, generally come from those who do not understand these values. This was not a variant of the Valmiki version nor a questioning of a sacred story, since the *kathā* of Rama was not regarded as sacrosanct at the time when the *jātaka* story was composed. It was an independent telling of the story from the perspective of Buddhist origin myths.

Narratives acquire historical encrustations. It is insufficient therefore to merely examine the text believed to be the original and see it only from the perspective of the present. Focusing on the nature of the encrustations and the process by which these change our perceptions of the original provides an insightful study. Sometimes these encrustations are the result of the political use of a text. The political role of the Ramayana in the twentieth century would have to be seen as forming the front for at least two major situations of political confrontations: as part of the anti-Brahmin movement in South India, where Rama was counterposed to Ravana and the identity of an anti-Brahmin movement endorsed Ravana instead of Rama; and the Ramjanmabhoomi agitation, where the glorification of Rama in effect projected an upper-caste, Hindutva attempt at paring down the rights of Muslims as Indian citizens.

Today, at the beginning of the millennium, one wonders what forms these cultural symbols will take in the future. Will there be a need to create counter myths? Will new myths reverse the status of the characters and provide them with different roles, resonant with social and historical change? The discussions on variant versions and on questionings signal the dangers inherent in insisting on a single version as authentic. This will also signal a need for sensitivity to the creations of those who seek in the story an articulation of their own anguish and aspirations.

# Preface

The edited volume *Many Rāmāyaṇas: The Diversity of a Narrative Tradition in South Asia* appeared in print before the religious violence of 1992–3 that centered around the North Indian city of Ayodhya. As a result of those events, debates about the nature and boundaries of *Rāmkathā* (Rama's story) acquired new urgency. In the discussion following the destruction of the Babri Masjid, some scholars and journalists implied that the problem lay with *Rāmkathā* itself, as if it were a story that necessarily led to religious intolerance. Our edited volume titled *Questioning Ramayanas, A South Asian Tradition* suggests that a condemnation of the story itself ignores the centuries of questioning carried on within the Ramayana tradition—questioning of authoritative values, interrogating notions of the ideal polity, challenging the rationale for ways in which various characters behaved, querying the gender norms depicted, and criticizing the ways in which members of particular castes have been portrayed. Such questions have helped to perpetuate a tradition of openness and generated a range of tellings of *Rāmkathā* which have kept the Ramayana tradition vital, fluid, and multi-faceted. This volume highlights the process of questioning and brings to the fore the multiplicity of tellings and perspectives included in the Ramayana tradition, both in the past and in the present.

My thanks goes first and foremost to the contributors for their generosity of spirit, capacity to adapt to the temporal and spatial constraints that our project required, and willingness to revise their papers to ensure the overall coherence of the volume. Second, I appreciate the thoughtful responses of the following people to my introductory essay: an anonymous reviewer, Michael Fisher, Sally Sutherland Goldman, Linda Hess, Mary McGee, Velcheru Narayana Rao, Augusta Rohrbach, David Shulman, Romila Thapar, and Sandra Zagarell, as well as audiences at talks given at the Nehru Memorial Library in Delhi and the History Department of Delhi University, the Bookpoint in Chennai, Utkal University in Bhubaneshwar, and the Dhvanyaloka Center in Manasagangotri. My two editors, Lynne Withey at University of California Press in Berkeley and Rukun Advani at Oxford University Press in Delhi, dealt efficiently with the complexities of co-publication in order to make the volume available simultaneously in India and the United States. I am especially grateful to Rimli Borooah and Anupama Arora for their patience and care. To all of these people I express my gratitude, but I alone am responsible for any errors that remain.

# Contents

# A Note on Transliteration

That it has been harder to decide upon a transliteration policy for this volume than to solve any other editorial problems bespeaks much about the boundaries between discourse communities within the field of South Asian Studies. In the end, we settled on two transliteration systems. The one used by Sanskritists and linguistic anthropologists necessitates the full set of standard diacritical marks used by Indologists; the essays by Shulman, Aklujkar, Goldman, Freeman, Sutherland Goldman, Stewart and Dimock adhere to this system of transliteration. The remaining essays use diacritical marks much more sparingly, reserving them primarily for words given in italics to provide the exact equivalent for a word presented in English translation. This system seems especially appropriate for studies of a more ethnographic nature, and well as ones dealing with recent or current events. In this transliteration system, authors generally employ the Anglicized spellings of Indian names and terms that have become familiar in the English discourse of India. In the endnotes, of course, full diacritical marks are provided for all non-English sources.

Authors whose papers deal primarily with Hindi materials drop the final short a of syllables in Devanagari in order to reflect Hindi usage most faithfully. Thus, for example, the reader will encounter both Rama and Ram over the course of the volume. Place names, such as Lanka and Ayodhya, and Indian terms widely recognized in English, such as dharma, varna, kaliyuga, and bhakti, are used without diacritical marks. When "Ramayana" appears in italics with diacritical marks, it indicates the title (or part of the title) of a particular text. Without italics and diacritics, it refers to the Ramayana story in general.

ONE

# Questioning and Multiplicity Within the Ramayana Tradition

PAULA RICHMAN

As part of the 1993 celebration of Indian Independence Day (August 15), a group of artists, actors, musicians, and dancers mounted an arts festival. It included an eighty-three panel exhibit of texts, photographs, and archaeological reports that documented the long and varied cultural history of Ayodhya. One panel represented many tellings of Rama's story including Buddhist versions. Among them was a well-known early Pali narrative, *Dasaratha Jātaka*, one of more than five hundred stories of the previous lives of the Buddha. Each *jātaka* depicts a main character who practises virtuous act that will cause him to be reborn in his next life closer to nirvana. In *Dasaratha Jātaka* the Buddha takes birth as Rama and goes into exile at his father's request, accompanied by his sister, Sita, and his brother, Lakshmana. When the three learn that their father, King Dasaratha, has passed away, Sita and Lakshmana grieve mightily, but Rama—like the Buddha figure he will become many births later—refuses to let sorrow overwhelm him, noting that all lives are characterized by impermanence. By thus cultivating detachment, he teaches his siblings the transience of all things. Later, all three return to the kingdom, where Rama rules justly alongside his queen-consort, Sita.[1]

On August 12, 1993 about fifteen members of the VHP (Vishva

Hindu Parishad, literally World Hindu Organization), along with its youth affiliate organization, destroyed the exhibit to protest against references to this Buddhist telling. Later, members of the BJP (Bharatiya Janata Party, literally Indian People's Party) filed charges of criminal conspiracy against the organizers of the cultural festival because it depicted Rama and Sita as brother and sister. One could raise many questions about the BJP's charges. For example, many among the BJP and the VHP claim that Buddhism belongs to the "Hindu" family, possessing the quality of Hindutva, or essential "Hinduness" that distinguishes ancient Indian religions from "foreign" religions. How, then, can they be so distressed about a story of the Buddha's past birth told and revered in Buddhist communities?[2] Leaving such specific issues aside, let us turn to the more general implications of declaring an ancient and well-attested telling of Rama's story part of a criminal conspiracy. In so declaring, the BJP leadership betrayed the Ramayana tradition they claimed to be protecting, since they ignored two key characteristics at the heart of the Ramayana tradition in South Asia: its multiplicity and its ability to accommodate questioning within its boundaries.

Questioning Rama's story has played a generative role in sustaining the Ramayana tradition over centuries, across regions, and among different communities. In looking at tellings of Rama's story, contributors to this volume do not assume that only one "right" version of Rama's story exists. Instead, they take multiplicity as a starting point for their inquiry into ways that various tellings reflect, subvert, legitimate, undermine, or reject certain relations of power and religious claims. In emphasizing the multiplicity of the Ramayana tradition, however, this volume does more than confirm what we already know—namely that there are many Ramayanas.[3] It also explores the consequences of such extensive diversity in a narrative tradition. The essays here show that the Ramayana tradition has been broad enough and responsive enough to encompass within its borders tellings of Rama's story that question its contents and emphases.

In this introductory essay, first I assess the ways in which the diversity of the Ramayana tradition has been conceptualized in the past, and then propose an alternative framework. Next I demonstrate how the ordering of the sixteen contributions to this volume elucidates the value of this framework. When read together as a single work, these essays reveal the range of creativity and power inherent in questioning Rama's story.

## Two Past Models of "the Ramayana"

Hundreds of tellings of Rama's story exist in India. They range over time from the *Rāmāyaṇa* attributed to Valmiki, the oldest full literary telling of the story (as manifested in several regional recensions),[4] to the most familiar telling at this moment, the production by Ramanand Sagar for Indian national television.[5] How can one best articulate the relationships among the many tellings of Rama's story?

Although scholars often speak loosely of "the Ramayana," the complexity of the issues explored in this volume calls for more precision. I thus employ the terms "story of Rama" or "Rama's story" (a translation of *Rāmkathā*)[6] to refer in general to a narrative that recounts or takes for granted most of the following: Rama's birth and youth in Ayodhya, his marriage to Sita and subsequent exile to the forest, the abduction of his wife by the demon Ravana, Rama's search for her with the aid of an army of monkeys, and Rama's defeat of Ravana. When I discuss particular tellings of Rama's story, such as Bhavabhuti's *Uttararāmacarita,* the *Rāmāyaṇa* attributed to Valmiki, or a Ramlila performance in Fiji, I refer to the specific name of the text, author, and/or performance. When referring to the diverse set of tellings that present the story of Rama in different styles, languages, and media, I use, as a collective term, "the Ramayana tradition." This phrase indicates a set of tellings rather than some abstract summary or synthesis of many tellings.

Two major models of the Ramayana tradition have been articulated in scholarly literature. The older model developed within the academic discipline of philology. Philologists specializing in Sanskrit literature and concerning themselves with the transmission of manuscripts have viewed the *Rāmāyaṇa* attributed to Valmiki as the "*ur*" or "original" text, and, by extension, as the authoritative telling of Rama's story.[7] Such a view identifies all other tellings in terms of how they diverge from Valmiki's *Rāmāyaṇa.* This model generates several benefits. It rightly recognizes the status of Valmiki's poem as the oldest extant rendition of Rama's story in a highly ornate literary genre (*kāvya*).[8] The model also takes into account the text's long history of transmission, primarily by Brahmin literati. Most significant, this view accurately reflects the extent to which Valmiki's *Rāmāyaṇa* has influenced the many tellings of Rama's story that developed over the centuries.

This philological model applies the metaphor of a family lineage to a collection of manuscripts. Genealogy remains the model's central concern, so it focuses upon discovering which text developed out of which previous text(s). The lineage metaphor serves us well if we seek to determine how earlier texts have influenced later texts within the Ramayana tradition. Valmiki is the trunk, but limbs branch off in various directions and then bear their own smaller limbs. For example, we can see how Tulsidas relates back to Valmiki, through the mediation of the anonymous Sanskrit *Adhyātma Rāmāyaṇa.*[9] The genealogical model also illustrates the relationship between a text and multiple performances, such as that between the Hindi *Rāmcaritmānas* by Tulsidas and the Ramlilas performed in Banaras, as well as in Fiji.

Yet many problems arise when we use this genealogical framework. For example, some scholars have argued that the Buddhist *Dasaratha Jātaka* may have preceded Valmiki's text chronologically, while others have wondered whether the kernel-like story of Rama within the *Mahābhārata* might pre-date Valmiki's telling.[10] Chronological controversies aside, however, the genealogical model contains implicit judgments that oversimplify the complexity of the Ramayana tradition. It implies that one should view all subsequent tellings of Rama's story as deviations from Valmiki. Supposedly, therefore, these later versions possess less authority. Because this view creates a hierarchy of tellings that tends to induce comparison of all others to Valmiki's text, it might be labeled the "Valmiki and Others" model.

By locating the best and most "authentic" telling in Valmiki's elite Sanskrit text, this approach perpetuates a narrow view incommensurate with the amazing popularity of Rama's story. The vast majority of Hindus today cannot read Sanskrit, nor could they in the past; knowledge of Sanskrit remained primarily the intellectual property of the upper three varnas in society, and of Brahmin males in particular. In contrast, most Hindus learned the story of Rama by hearing it in their local or regional language. The first model thus privileges a telling that excludes the majority of Hindus.

Responding to the limitations of this model, A.K. Ramanujan developed an alternative way to conceptualize the Ramayana tradition. A specialist in folklore who was familiar with the creativity, scope, and diversity of oral tellings in India, he argued that we should abandon the binary notion of "the Ramayana" and "its variants." Instead, Ramanujan likened the Ramayana tradition to a pool of signifiers, arguing that each author (or performer) "dips into it and brings out a unique crystallization, a new text with a unique texture and a fresh context." Ramanujan concluded: "In this sense, no text is original, yet no telling is a mere retelling."[11] His perspective pushes us to view each text as a telling rather than a variant, since "variant" implies divergence from the "real" one. This view could be called the "Many Ramayanas" approach.

The "Many Ramayanas" model assumes that each telling of Rama's story is valid in its own right: Tulsidas, the [Original] Southall Black Sisters in Greater London, the domestic servants singing in Bhojpuri dialect, Valmiki, the artisan priests of northern Kerala, and the anonymous author of *Ānanda Rāmāyāṇa* all recount Rama's story, but they do so in their own ways. Ramanujan's model emphasizes the many different tellings of Rama's story—oral and written, read and performed, recited and depicted in visual forms—*without* representing each one primarily in terms of its relationship to Valmiki's telling. His model envisions a non-hierarchical set of relationships between various tellings within the Ramayana tradition. It also encourages us to consider how certain tellings are in consonance with religious affiliation, region, language, historical period, literary conventions, and the teller's social location and experiences.

Although the second model does not provide the chronological sequencing of the first model, it presents more accurately the varied impacts of different tellings across India, including places where people have never heard a word of Valmiki's Sanskrit text. The "Many Ramayanas" approach encourages us to consider the unique characteristics of each telling we encounter. It moves beyond the earlier geneaological model, but there is more work to do before we can account for the complexity of the tradition.

## Politics, Propriety and Questioning

Although the "Many Ramayanas" model fosters appreciation of multiple tellings on their own, instead of in relation to Valmiki's telling, it does not pay adequate attention to the different degrees and kinds of political power that particular tellings wield. "Political" here indicates the set of negotiations about power, status, and access to information and/or knowledge that take place among groups that possess differing amounts and kinds of influence in a society based on ranked status. A telling of Rama's story always carries political messages, whether they are explicitly stated or not, and whether listeners perceive *Rāmkathā* as a political text or not.

Rama's story is inherently political for at least three reasons. First, the Ramayana tradition elevates the ideal of "Ramraj," a polity whose king practises absolute justice, maintains order, preserves stability, and ensures the prosperity of the kingdom, as these functions are set out in *dharmaśāstras* (religious treatises that specify one's code for conduct, or dharma, in specific situations). Thus, the text articulates clear standards for leadership of the polity. Second, because devotees praise Rama as *maryādā puruṣottama* (exemplar of social propriety), Rama's story presents ideal behavior not only for ruler and citizen, but in relation to family, caste, and gender hierarchy as well. Thus, Rama's story sets out socially normative ideals that bear upon negotiations among group with differing levels of power in society, explicity linking the realization of these ideals with the reign of a just king. Third, the vision of Ramraj is utopian; utopian visions tend to encourage people to achieve the perfect society here on earth, a project that often mobilizes elite, courtly, state, and/or electoral intitutions to do so.

A starting point for controversies about power, propriety, and kingship within the Ramayana tradition is the set of Rama's actions which, at least without the benefit of legitimation through exegesis, appear to indicate that he himself has deviated from the path of dharma. Depending upon one's interpretation, these incidents may include: Rama's shooting of Vali in the back, thereby violating the warrior code; Rama's mutilation of Shurpanakha even though she is a female; Rama's willingness to eat pre-tasted fruit offered to him by the tribal woman Shabari; the killing of the Shudra, Shambuka, because he performed ascetic practices reserved for his social superiors; Rama's demand that Sita prove her purity through a fire ordeal; and his banishment of pregnant Sita to the forest. Since Rama should act as an exemplar of dharmic action and propriety, many remain troubled by these seeming deviations from dharma. It should come as no surprise, therefore, that a number of essays in this volume deal with questions raised by these incidents, and others like them.

Questioning occurs both within the story and as listeners or readers respond to *Rāmkathā*. Right in the narrative itself, characters express doubts about the morality of certain actions Rama performs. For example, as early as in Valmiki's *Rāmāyaṇa,* as Vali lies dying, he castigates Rama for his departure from the warrior code.[12] Devotees of Rama have found themselves forced to cope with ambiguities and seeming inconsistencies of their Lord's behavior. Ironically, sometimes the closeness with which devotees examine accounts of Rama's greatness leads them into doubt. Changes in reading practices among devotees and literati, introduced by new print technology, have also raised new kinds of questions in the discourse about Rama's story. Both the consequences of close reading and the results of new kinds of readings are explored in the essays that follow. Exegesis, resourceful glossing, interpretation, and commentary are mobilized in attempts to justify, rationalize, or excuse some of the lapses of propriety in *Rāmkathā*.

Those authors who wrote after Valmiki's time dealt with seemingly problematic behavior in a number of ways. For example, the anonymous author of *Ānanda Rāmāyaṇa* (*c.* fifteenth century) transforms the story of Shambuka so that it illustrates Rama's compassion and generosity, while in his sixteenth-century *Rāmcaritmānas,* Tulsidas explains troubling issues by the fact that Rama is the Supreme Lord who came to earth on a special mission, so he needs to perform certain acts that ordinary mortals might not consider appropriate. In contrast, other tellings, such as Krttibasa's Bengali telling of the *Uttarakāṇḍa* of Rama's story (which took its present form *c.* the late eighteenth or early nineteenth century), depicts the abandonment of Sita in ways that imply a condemnation of Rama's deeds. All three texts, analyzed in this volume, reflect the fact that certain incidents continue to trouble authors of *Rāmkathā*. Extensive reinterpretation of the story, addition of new incidents and characters, reframing of particular incidents—all these indicate a continuing uneasiness with which authors continue to grapple in relation to problematical deeds.

As tellings of Rama's story generated more and more varied narratives over the centuries, the Ramayana tradition's sheer multiplicity raised another set of questions. For example, if one telling is considered the true story of the Lord's acts and another telling contradicts the earlier one, is one to be abandoned and the other retained? Or, since the bhakti tradition suggests multiple ways to relate to God, should multiple accounts of *Rāmkathā* flourish, each with its own emphasis? And why do certain tellings come to be deeply identified with certain *sampradāyas* (religious movements or sects) or regions? Because *Rāmkathā* has been told in so many ways, as different tellings compete for adherents, enter print culture, or take on electoral consequences, the process of questioning may intensify and the stakes for answers to questions may rise. This volume explores how—in combination with each other—factors of gender, social location and regional identity shape decisions about which telling of *Rāmkathā* one chooses as one's "own."

Academic scholars of *Rāmkathā* too interrogate the narrative, according to their own distinctive methodologies. For example, many in the discipline of Cultural Studies are attempting to understand the processes by which hegemony is constituted and whether it can be subverted: do subaltern groups have the agency to oppose regimes of power or are they mere victims of domination? Within such a context of discussion, close examination of multiplicity within the Ramayana tradition proves fruitful because, although certain tellings of *Rāmkathā* have dominated Indian culture for centuries, questioning tellings have existed for nearly as long. Questions from the academy, as well as those of characters within the story, devotees, textual specialists, and authors are rarely answered in ways that completely resolve them; an examination of the process of questioning, within the context of multiple tellings, stands at the center of this volume.

Who can ask the questions, and who is allowed to frame the answers? Let us return to the two previous models of the Ramayana tradition. On the one hand, if we adopt the "Valmiki and Others" model, the only authoritative text is Valmiki; all other questions and answers are "derivative." Yet such a position ignores centuries of generative queries and creative retellings of the story. On the other hand, if we adopt the "Many Ramayanas" model, anyone can legitimately ask questions or respond to questions. Each response would be equally valid. Yet it would be naive and misleading to ignore that, in practical terms, some questioners speak with enormous weight and authority, while others are barely heard.

## Authoritative and Oppositional Tellings

Certain tellings have achieved a level of acceptance and legitimacy greater than most other tellings of Rama's story. Although other labels have been given to such tellings, the term "authoritative" seems most helpful for our discussion.[13] An authoritative text might warrant its status due to any, or a combination, of several factors such as the religious prestige of the language in which it is written, the number of people who know it, its links with a revered literary tradition, or the extent to which people can experience its telling simultaneously. Whatever factors generate a text's status, authoritative tellings of *Rāmkathā* share certain characteristics.

Most people familiar with Hindu texts today would probably name

Valmiki's ancient Sanskrit poem as the most important telling of Rama's story. Because Brahmins carried Valmiki's story to farflung parts of the subcontinent, it became a pan-Indian telling. Recited by bards patronized by kings or other wealthy notables, Valmiki's telling has usually been supported by the elite structures of power in Indian society. In addition, since Valmiki is credited with creating the versatile Sanskrit poetic meter called the *śloka,* his telling wields linguistic and aesthetic, as well as religious and political, authority.

The other text most often mentioned as pre-eminent is the Hindi *Rāmcaritmānas* by Tulsidas. During the last one and a half centuries, some have even titled it "the Hindu Bible."[14] While Valmiki's influence was broad, it did not penetrate equally through all social layers, since the use of Sanskrit was limited largely to the highest groups in society. In contrast, Tulsidas composed in a vernacular language spoken throughout large parts of North India. Many Hindi speakers would claim that the telling of Tulsidas has surpassed Valmiki's status in parts of North India.

In Tamil Nadu, in contrast, relatively few people would know even a few verses of *Rāmcaritmānas.* Instead, those familiar with Tamil literary tradition would claim Kamban's *Irāmāvatāram* (*c.* twelfth century) as the most significant account of Rama. They might even consider offensive the idea that Tulsidas has more than regional significance, since the Hindi language that endears Tulsidas to North Indians is often seen as a liability in Tamil Nadu, which boasts its own "classical" telling of Rama's story.

The newest entrant, Ramanand Sagar's serial production of Rama's story, gained its authoritative status largely in relation to its medium of presentation and the magnitude of audience response. This serialized rendition of *Rāmkathā* simultaneously reached an unprecedented number of viewers throughout India, and did so on a weekly basis. Video-cassette versions for sale allowed viewers to rewatch favorite episodes and also served as gifts presented to friends and relatives abroad. Thus, this telling's availability and packaging bring it a unique form of authority.

Authoritative tellings usually share several characteristics, including a link with normative ideologies or contents. Elites with extensive power in society tend to embrace authoritative tellings, praising them as a source of models for dharmic action. On the whole—although of course there will be qualifications and differences—authoritative tellings tend to affirm the values of the existing social order; they help to ungird institutionalized power. These tellings often affirm the need to perform one's brahmanically defined dharma, even at great social or personal cost. Much exegesis within the Ramayana tradition emphasizes that one must perform one's duties in relation to one's husband, wife, parents, elder brother, family, master, lineage (*kula*), caste, ruler, and kingdom—all behavior that upholds the status quo.

Second, authoritative texts have usually expanded beyond their limited historical local context and continue to be respected, studied, and transmitted centuries after their composition. People read or hear them in places beyond the region and community within which they were composed. Thus, Valmiki experts can be found in Andhra Pradesh; people chant Tulsidas in Gujarat and Fiji; Kamban's poem proved influential in much of South India and today *Irāmāvatāram* experts flourish among Sri Lankan Tamil refugee communities in London, while Ramanand Sagar's television Ramayana, with subtitles, has traveled way beyond the Indian subcontinent. These texts transcend merely local boundaries.

Third, authoritative texts of Rama's story have gained recognition as privileged tellings. They can be said to function as literary monuments or, to put it another way, as textual products from which it is difficult to escape. One can negotiate, reject, or be in conversation with them, but one can seldom ignore them. Traveling performers, schoolbooks, and satellite-powered television transmissions that disseminate authoritative tellings are likely to reach even the remotest village. Not only the telling itself, but the author or producer gains the status of a cultural icon. For example, Valmiki is widely venerated as the Preeminent Poet, legend tells us that God himself approved the decision of Tulsidas to make *Rāmkathā* accessible in Hindi, while Ramanand Sagar has been hailed as enhancing "national integration." In sum, authoritative tellings tend to affirm normative behavior, cross geographical barriers, and win privileged status.

Nonetheless, even within authoritative texts, questioning and contestation occur in a variety of ways. A recited or enacted version of a text is often more fluid than a printed one, and more likely to allow room for different points of view. A playwright can modify the narrative, while an actor can bring to the surface certain nuances not previously recognized. Exegesis of authoritative texts can provide an opportunity for asking questions. Highly selective appropriation of certain sections of a text can transform the social consequences of the story. Thus, even authoritative tellings contain—in recitation, in performance, in political appropriation—some room for questioning.

Still, it is useful to distinguish, in general terms, between authoritative and oppositional tellings. First and foremost, oppositional texts tend to be more involved in telling Rama's story in ways that leave room to question selected aspects of normative behavior and conventional interpretation. Oppositional tellings often provide alternative perspectives on characters, incidents, or ethical issues, thereby enriching the diversity of the Ramayana tradition. How can one question fundamental tenets expounded in authoritative tellings within the Ramayana tradition without divorcing oneself from the text altogether? No text is entirely oppositional; if it were, it would lie outside the boundaries of the Ramayana tradition. Instead, a particular telling may question, reframe, modify, or debate specific incidents as they occur in authoritative tellings.

In contrast to authoritative tellings, oppositional tellings tend to have a somewhat limited area of influence. Sometimes they circulate only in a particular locality or area. Others are known among certain religious communities but not others, so that two groups might live nearby but each have their own interpretation about *Rāmkathā*. For example, in the Karnataka region, both Jain and Hindu tellings of Rama's story flourished side by side. In other cases, even in a single household, women may have different traditions of *Rāmkathā,* due to their social location. Only upper-caste women sing certain songs about Rama, while only members of castes considered low by upper castes sing other songs (see Nilsson).

Furthermore, most oppositional tellings are selectively oppositional. For example, some women's tellings of Rama's story remain silent about ethical issues arising from Rama's destruction of the monkey Vali, focusing almost entirely on characters such as Kausalya or topics such as Sita's dowry. A text may have particular oppositional tendencies in its treatment of certain issues, but reaffirm dominant norms in other areas. For example, a performance by artisans in northern Kerala may function oppositionally by questioning Rama's destruction of Vali (see Freeman), but may not question gender relations as they are acted out between Rama and Sita or Vali, Sugriva, and Tara.

Oppositional tellings do not have a privileged pan-Indian status, and thus, there is a tendency to overlook the significance of their presence in the Ramayana tradition. On the one hand, since they are usually limited to certain groups, they are not widely disseminated. On the other hand, an extraordinary number of oppositional tellings exist. One has to step back, however, and look at oppositional telling as a whole, in order to realize the magnitude of their collective presence within the Ramayana tradition. By looking at them as a category, we can best see the influence they wield in people's everyday lives.

Even as we enumerate the components of authoritative tellings and oppositonal tellings, we must avoid the tendency to reify their power or treat them as monolithic in their effects. "Authoritative" and "oppositional" can only function as relative and partial descriptors. Any particular telling of Rama's story falls largely—but not completely—into one characterization, rather than the other. On the one hand, while *Rāmcaritmānas* functions primarily as an authoritative telling, that fact does not entirely pre-empt other kinds of social uses. For example, Baba Ramchandra enlisted sections of *Rāmcaritmānas* to inspire a peasant movement agitating for lower rents and fairer treatment from absentee landlords who collaborated with the British.[15] On the other hand, even the most radically oppositional tellings are never completely independent of authoritative tellings. For example, E.V. Ramasami, a South Indian ideologue who made his attack on Rama's story the centerpiece of his anti-Aryan polemic, depended upon the audience's knowledge of authoritative tellings (those of Valmiki and Kamban) in order to critique them.[16]

The Ramayana tradition's ability to support both authoritative and oppositional tellings remains one of its most astonishing features. Negotiations between authoritative and oppositional tellings provide much of the liveliness within the Ramayana tradition; the process of questioning provides the impetus for those negotiations. The four sections in this volume each demonstrate ways in which texts, performances, and exegesis pose questions while remaining within the broad boundaries of the Ramayana tradition.

## Forms of Questioning

Four authors in this volume focus upon generic and literary resources that foster the questioning of problematic incidents in authoritative tellings of Rama's story. In "Lovers' Doubts: Questioning the Tulsi *Rāmāyan*," Linda Hess examines an entire exegetical genre based on questioning passages in the Hindi *Rāmcaritmānas*. David Shulman's "Bhavabhuti on Cruelty and Compassion" considers how embedded frames within an eighth-century Sanskrit play provide opportunities for Rama to question his own actions. Vidyut Aklujkar's "Crying Dogs and Laughing Trees" analyses how a return visit by Valmiki authorizes questions and the inclusion of new stories that advocate equality and compassion, rather than arbitrary use of power. In "Ravana's Kitchen," Robert Goldman shows how the dichotomous portrayal of demonic behavior illustrates what happens when questions go too far, leading to shocking transgressions of proper conduct appropriate only for demons. Together, the four essays identify formal means that foster, and at times constrain, interrogations of authoritative texts.

Hess sets to rest the misconception that those who question dominant tellings necessarily place themselves outside the devotional tradition. Her analysis focuses upon a genre called *shankāvalī* (Collection of Doubts), which consists of anthologies of questions in which devotees have asked a *Rāmcaritmānas* expert to resolve some confusion, ambiguity, or apparent inconsistency in the text. Although their questions rarely express a lapse of faith in the ultimate goodness of Lord Rama or Tulsidas, the range and keenness of their queries demonstrate the centrality of questioning in the discourse about one of the most influential stories of Rama. These collections of doubts reveal a mode of dialogue whose nature, protocol, and results simultaneously enhance devotion to Lord Rama and provide regular opportunities to interrogate the story's events, characters, and moral values.

Interrogation sometimes arises from exegetical dialogue; at other times, nested tellings of Rama's story may prompt it. Shulman's analysis of Bhavabhuti's Sanskrit *Uttararāmacarita* demonstrates the extent to which the playwright incorporates multiple tellings of Rama's story into the framework of his drama. The play open with Lakshmana's recounting of Rama's story, as Lakshmana leads Rama and Sita past a set of paintings depicting its key events. In the middle section Rama listens to a recitation of his deeds by two boys who are (unbeknownst to him) his own sons. Bhavabhuti's play culminates with the dramatization of a play (within the play) attended by Rama, who watches his own story enacted. Valmiki's telling, known to Bhavabhuti and his audience, tends to justify Rama's banishment of his wife and neglect of his sons, whereas Bhavabhuti depicts Rama's encounters with multiple tellings of his story as causing him to question his past choices and attain wisdom through the self-knowledge he thus gains.

Authors sometimes use Valmiki himself to question the authority of the text attributed to him, as Aklujkar demonstrates in her analysis of *Ānanda Rāmāyaṇa*, an anonymous fifteenth-century Sanskrit work dealing primarily with Rama's rule in Ayodhya after Ravana's defeat. Although the text indicates its knowledge of many other Valmiki and post-Valmiki tellings of Rama's story, it also depicts Valmiki declaring to Rama that he created all tellings and that *Ānanda Rāmāyaṇa* conveys the essence of the story most perfectly. This self-reflexivity, in which the text comments on itself in relation to other texts, enables its anonymous author to incorporate new stories into the text that portray Rama as more just and less caste-bound than Valmiki's telling, while claiming authorization from Valmiki himself.[17]

In the context of this volume's overall argument about the centrality of questioning within the Ramayana tradition, Goldman's paper reminds us that Rama's story also illustrates the results if one passes too far beyond the bounds of propriety into the realm of the Other.[18] Goldman demonstrates how Valmiki's portrayal of Lanka foregrounds dichotomized portrayals of the sexual life and food habits of the demons. The highly eroticized beauties in King Ravana's harem are at the opposite end of the spectrum from the ugly demon hags who stand guard over captive Sita. In a similarly sharp contrast, demons either feast on elegant foods and fine liquors or gorge on raw human flesh. Such portrayals mirror disgust, but also desire. Such extremes suggest that too much questioning may entail danger: deviating from norms would lead to revolting, e.g. demonic, behavior. Yet along with disgust comes a desire to trespass bounds. Thus this depiction of Ravana poses for its audience irresistible, yet frightening, issues about how far questions can go.

## Assertions about Social Rank

Among the many kinds of questioning, interrogation of caste hierarchy plays a prominent role in the Ramayana tradition–especially in relation to incidents concerning people who do not belong to the upper three varnas, as defined by brahmanical texts. Four essays in this volume show how Rama's story becomes a medium for expressing tensions or assertions about caste interactions. Philip Lutgendorf's "Dining Out at Lake Pampa" focuses upon the boundary between tribal women and high-caste men. In "Grinding Millet but Singing of Sita," Nilsson shows the complexity of the rift between high-caste female employers and their lower-caste domestic servants. Velcheru

Narayana Rao considers the tensions between Brahmins and non-Brahmins in "The Politics of Telugu Ramayanas." [John] Rich[ard] Freeman's "Thereupon Hangs a Tail" examines how the liturgies of artisans in Kerala depict Monkey King Vali as a way to express resentment about exploitation by high castes.

Lutgendorf traces the depiction of Rama's meeting with Shabari, a tribal woman who offers him fruits which she has pre-tasted to ensure that he receives only the sweetest ones. Because Shabari is low born and Rama a prince, social convention prohibits his acceptance of food from her, doubly tainted by contact with her saliva, a polluting substance, yet Rama eats Shabari's offering in recognition of her intense devotion to him. Lutgendorf highlights the inherent ambivalence and tensions that charge the first full telling of the story in the eighteenth century, showing their traces in today's tellings as well, as writers continue to balance Rama's role as protector of social hierarchy with his love for all devotees.

Nilsson examines three kinds of Awadhi and Bhojpuri songs about Rama and Sita that both unite and separate women: 1) those sung together by all the women of the house, 2) those sung separately by lower-caste domestic servants, and 3) those sung separately by their high-caste employers. When women sing together about how Rama mistreats Sita, tensions over unequal power relations are masked. In contrast, when women sing within their own caste, differing assessments of characters in Rama's story emerge. Consider, for example, the song in which a doe's buck is killed for a feast held to celebrate Rama's birth. Domestic servants singing the song emphasize how the doe suffers, so the royal couple can celebrate. In contrast, when employers sing the song, their version downplays the doe's anguish by having the buck tell the doe that if he sacrifices his body to Rama, he will gain merit and a good rebirth. Thus, even within a single household, singing about the story of Rama and Sita asserts differing models of domestic relations, each with its own charged questions.

Another social faultline, that between Brahmins and non-Brahmins, has produced notable heterogeneity within the South Indian Ramayana tradition. Although precolonial Telugu Ramayanas were numerous and diverse, during the colonial period Brahmin-dominated publishing firms promoted Valmiki's text as "the" proper telling, helping to submerge other Telugu tellings. Narayana Rao traces how, as people first began to read Valmiki's *Rāmāyaṇa* in written form from beginning to end, they subjected it to intense questioning, critiquing the relationship between the narrative and brahmanical authority. The plays, novels, and poetry of such critics recast the story in consonance with intellectual movements such as romanticism, realism, marxism, and feminism, thereby questioning the hegemony of Valmiki's text and restoring heterogeneity to the Telugu Ramayana tradition.

Interrogation of caste oppression emerges in a particularly striking form in Malayalam liturgies of praise to Vali in *teyyāṭṭam,* a ritual mode of worshipping ancestors and local folk deities through spirit-possessed dancers in northern Kerala. Vali, king of monkeys in Kishkindha, appears only briefly in authoritative tellings of Rama's story, but the dubious manner in which Rama kills him has generated much controvesy about the "perfect" king's morality. Most teyyams celebrate deified forms of low-caste warriors slain either in the service of, or by members of, higher castes. Freeman demonstrates how Vali's social ambiguity as a human-like simian, his victimization by higher-ups, and his essential nobility function as an implicit critique of high-caste society by these artisan communities.

## Modalities of Speaking

In recent years literary and cultural critics have devoted increasing attention to the vexed issue of voice. Some scholars have explored ways to recover voices of silenced and/or marginalized groups, searching for vestiges in texts. Others have theorized about who has the right to speak on behalf of a particular group, debating whether a speaker must be from within the group in order to have a say. Four pieces in the volume consider varied modes of speaking. In "The Voice of Sītā in Vālmīki's *Sundarakāṇḍa,*" Sally Sutherland Goldman argues that we can recover traces of Sita's voice, but only in muffled form. Bina Agarwal's two original poems exemplify the complexity of imagining how Sita would speak if she could, and voice questions about how to interpret Sita's actions. "Kṛttibāsa's Apophatic Critique of Rama's Kingship," by Tony K. Stewart and Edward C. Dimock, examines how an author can raise questions about the morality of Rama's behavior without being accused of doing so. In "The Tamil Ramayana and Its Muslim Interpreters," Vasudha Narayanan shows that generations of Muslim exegetes had an appreciative audience for their say about a Tamil Hindu telling of Rama's story.

Seldom in Valmiki's telling do we hear Sita's voice without the mediation of males who surround and protect her. In order to examine Sita separately from her male spokesmen, Sutherland Goldman focuses on Valmiki's depiction of Sita's confrontation with Ravana in his palace pleasure garden, where he usually sports with members of his harem. When confronted by Ravana, Sita defends herself by upholding the patriarchal notion that her sexuality belongs to her husband alone. After Ravana leaves, however, as Sita despairs because Rama has not yet rescued her, she comes to realize how wretched her dependence upon men is, thereby opening up a small crack in the ideological structure of Valmiki's narrative. Sutherland Goldman suggests that Sita's interactions with Ravana and their aftermath awaken Sita to the terrors of female dependence upon men's power.

Negotiations about what, and how much, Sita can say emerge not only by examining ancient texts, but from Indian feminist discourse today as well. Consider, for example, the fate of the first poem included in this section, called "Sita Speak" by Bina Agarwal, one of India's foremost economists. First published in 1985 in *The Indian Express*, a leading English-language newspaper, this poem sparked many responses. The newspaper received a number of angry letters to the editor written by men. At the same time, several South Asian women's groups embraced the poem, translating it into Hindi in India and into Bengali in Bangladesh, thus making it accessible to readers beyond English-speaking elites. Activists have also used it as the basis of skits performed to resist oppression of women. Agarwal's second (unpublished 1985) poem on Sita, also included in this section, demonstrates another way that Sita can be conceived—as a force of nature. Agarwal imagines Sita not as imprisoned but as able to undergo constant renewal. The first poem questions Sita as if in a conversation; the second answers questions by rethinking the meaning of Sita.

In situations where everyone knows that certain questions should not be asked, one sometimes needs to hedge queries or distance oneself from them. Dimock and Stewart show how stories in the Bengali *Uttarakāṇḍa* by Krttibasa display apophasis, the technique of mentioning something by saying that it will not be mentioned or should not be said. These stories consistently include negative comments about Rama's character and motives, judging him a coward, an inadequate warrior, or a cruel husband. Just as consistently, as soon as characters voice such judgments, they dismiss the comments or shift the blame to fate. Yet the recurrent critique of Rama's rule undercuts the inviolability of the perfect king and highlights how he has wronged his wife. The strategy of apophasis enables the author to interrogate certain norms while seeming to remain within the bounds of propriety.

In addition to constraints about what can be said, limits on who can speak also generate questions. Much recent Ramayana discourse in the Indian political sphere has presented Rama's story as an exclusively Hindu text, yet this view does not reflect the social reality of the renowned *Irāmāvātaram*, the Tamil telling of Rama's story by Kamban. Vasudha Narayanan demonstrates how Muslim and Hindu poets from Kamban's time shared literary assumptions, as well as how Kamban's poem has remained a literary domain in which Muslim exegetes have excelled for generations. Both in the twelfth century and in today's Tamil Nadu, poets and commentators of differing religious persuasions eloquently share poetic motifs and common understandings of ultimate concerns. These two moments encourage us to question recent political claims about the exclusively "Hindu" nature of Rama's story, especially in light of the increasing polarization between Hindu and Muslim communities.

## Applied Ramayanas

In the aftermath of the Ayodhya conflict, many people bemoaned the fact that Hindutva groups had "politicized the Ramayana," claiming that such groups had brought a text previously lodged safely in the religious sphere into the political arena. Yet, as Sheldon Pollock shows, Rama's story has been perceived as deeply political for many centuries.[19] Throughout Indian history kings and would-be kings have used language from various tellings to make claims upon, justify, legitimate, or destabilize political power. In this century, many have told Rama's story in explicitly political ways, from nationalist leader Jawaharlal Nehru to "Dravidian" separatist E.V. Ramasami. Because some critics have responded to the Ayodhya conflict by equating the political use of Rama's story with jingoism and fascism, it is crucial to highlight other kinds of ideological stances that have close links with *Rāmkathā*. The final section of this volume presents three examples of recourse to Rama's story by women activists, anti-racism coalitions, and indentured servants abroad. Madhu Kishwar's "Yes to Sita, No to Rama" shows how women use stories and songs of Sita to strive for dignity and self-respect. Paula Richman's "The Ramlila Migrates to Southall" looks at a drama presented by a feminist group of South Asian and African Caribbean women in the late 1970s to combat British racism. John Kelly's "Fiji's Fifth Veda" examines political uses of Tulsidas among indentured laborers in Fiji. Each essay demonstrates that Rama's story is not inherently oppressive; those who tell the story can bring out its power to liberate.

As the editor of *Manushi*, a journal concerned with women and society in India, Kishwar sought to understand widespread admiration for Sita, rather than simply dismiss it as a function of male domination. Her interviews with women from varied caste and regional backgrounds reveal that they respect Sita because she maintained the moral upper hand, never stooping to Rama's level of pettiness or moral myopia. Such views are also shared by male religious reformers, prominent among whom is Sharad Joshi, who uses the story of Sita's banishment as a central narrative for his campaign to register family lands in one's wife's name to protect her from destitution. Songs and ritual from Mithila, Sita's childhood home, also attest to wide admiration for Sita's courage. Kishwar argues that admiration for Sita indicates not acceptance of female slavery but a respect for her loyalty, dignity, and keen moral sense.

The tradition of seeing one's politics through the story of Rama and Sita became pivotal for women of South Asian and African Caribbean descent who united to combat racism in Southall, a working-class neighborhood in Greater London. In 1979 they staged a Ramlila performance as a fund-raiser for Southall citizens arrested during a notorious confrontation where riot police, armed with truncheons and other riot gear, injured many unarmed people. The performers framed and periodically interrupted their rendition of the play with humorous bilingual commentary by jesters, who critiqued repressive ideas about women's frailty and submissiveness, while simultaneously identifying Ravana as an embodiment of British racism. Ravana sported ten heads, including those of Margaret Thatcher, several neo-Nazi leaders, and the insignia of the riot police. The Ramlila culminated with the burning of an effigy with this ten-headed mask. Here a ritual rooted in South Asian tradition has become a symbol for the evils of anti-migration policies and prejudice in the United Kingdom.

The final essay in this volume examines political uses of Rama's story among South Asians who went to Fiji. Mostly indentured laborers from the North Indian Hindi belt who worked on plantations, many interpreted their lives within the framework of Rama's exile to the forest. Early in the indenture period, Tulsi's *Rāmcaritmānas* earned the status of a holy book upon which Indians had to swear before giving testimony in Fijian colonial courts. The book also provided imagery to protest against plantation officials abusing Indian women, to express the suffering of exile, and to seek destruction of evil. The burning of huge effigies of Ravana served as a way to question the morality of indentured servitude and hasten its abolition. Both Kelly and Richman demonstrate how the political imagination of Rama's story has played a major role for South Asian communities in the diaspora.

## Conclusions

The essays in this volume demonstrate how the Ramayana tradition encompasses within its boundaries opportunities for questioning incidents, characterization, and ideals of authoritative tellings of Rama's story. "Within its boundaries" means that multiple and competing tellings continue to be seen as part of *Rāmkathā*. Those who have doubts about the telling of Tulsidas continue to be seen as lovers of Tulsidas. Women who taunt Sita's father-in-law continue to think of Sita as one of them. The Southall Black Sisters chose the Ramlila as a way to express their ultimate concerns and affirm their links with their community, even while their performance critiqued traditional notions of Sita's relation to Rama. Tellings from different historical periods and social strata are valid parts of Rama's story, even if they do not say the same things that earlier authors or performers said, or tell their story in the way that earlier authors or performers did. The Ramayana tradition of South Asia is spacious enough to maintain room within its borders for tellings of Rama's story that provide alternatives to authoritative tellings.

The essays in this volume do not provide a comprehensive account of how questioning occurs within the Ramayana tradition. Such a task is impossible because interrogation has occurred in so many ways and among so many communities. The ubiquity of questioning within the Ramayana tradition, however, points to a key feature of Rama's story: the centrality of questioning within a single narrative tradition. The essays do, however, suggest patterns of questioning that appear within that enormous tradition. Sometimes it is a genre, a framing device, a commentarial tradition, the mediation of a jester, or the sudden return of Valmiki that facilitates questioning. At other times, we find that the complexity or ambiguity of a particular problematic incident in the narrative fosters new interpretations. In yet other cases the political circumstances of the tellers send them back to Rama's story to find ways of understanding new experiences—such as immigration or indenture—that generate questioning and multiplicity.

The Ramayana tradition contains authoritative tellings of Rama's story, yet maintains an open-endedness rarely found in religious traditions that venerate certain sacred texts. The capacious nature of the Ramayana tradition is precious. The BJP's criminal charges against a Buddhist telling of Rama's story go against the basic nature of the Ramayana tradition. When a single group argues that it possesses the only "correct" version of Rama's story, that group has misunderstood the Ramayana tradition. This volume confirms that questioning and multiple tellings of Rama's story have been major forms of practice within the Ramayana tradition. Ideologues who claim exclusive rights to *Rāmkathā* have departed from the very Ramayana tradition they claim to be saving. Who has authority over the Ramayana tradition? No single group ever has complete authority over what can and cannot be said about Rama's story. No single group ever should.

# FORMS OF QUESTIONING

TWO

# Lovers' Doubts: Questioning the Tulsi *Rāmāyaṇ*

LINDA HESS

*Why did Kaikeyi ask for exactly fourteen years of exile for Ram?*

*"When Sita set foot in the arena, men and women were entranced by her beauty," Tulsidas says. But Kak Bhushundi says to Garuda, "Women are not entranced by women's beauty." Why this inconsistency?*

*When Lakshman became angry at the Bow Contest, he vowed to pick up the universe like a ball and smash it down like a clay pot. If he picked up the whole universe, where would he stand? If he dashed it down, where would it burst?*

*Did Vibhishan really rule for a whole* kalpa *(eon)? The* kalpa *has not ended yet. If he were living in any part of the ocean, in Ceylon or anywhere, wouldn't we know it?*

*Instead of lamenting over not having sons in his old age, why didn't Dasharath just adopt a child of his own caste?*

*Shiva and Parvati worshiped Ganapati at their wedding. Is this the same Ganapati who later became their son? What is the reality here?*

*Savitri, a true* satī *wife, restored her dead husband to life. Why didn't Dasharath's wives restore him? Why did they not become* satī *(widows who immolate themselves on their husband's funeral pyre)? Were they not* pativratā *(ideal wives devoted to their husband as God)?*

*Why did Ravan call Vibhishan a barley worm? If he wanted to call him some kind of grain worm, why not a worm in a fine grain like rice, wheat,* urad, masur, kesari, *or the like? Why did he call him a worm in a base, common class of grain?*

*"Drum, rustic, Shudra, animal, woman: one has the right to beat all these." Does this line mean that Tulsidas had a bad attitude toward women and Shudras?*[1]

If you were a scholar studying *Rāmcaritmānas* (henceforth *Mānas*), would you direct your research to any of the above matters? Undoubtedly there are some questions here that would not appear on your scholarly agenda. The people who asked these questions, in their turn, would find some of the preoccupations of professional academics strange.

A primary act of scholarly imagination is to decide what questions are worth asking. Imposing questions on the material can also be seen as an act of domination: We carve up the territory, name categories, declare what is important, and subordinate the rest. We often call our questions "problems," which implies quasi-scientific precision.

This paper began as I tried to imagine ways of asking questions different from the ones that "naturally" occurred to me. I was delighted to discover that there is a special genre within the *Mānas* commentarial tradition that selectively questions the text to bring out what is troubling, perplexing, intriguing to its primary audiences. That genre is called the *Shankāvalī* or "Garland of Doubts." Collecting and studying *Shankāvalīs*, I formulated the following questions, which the present essay tries to answer:

1) What can we learn from the form, content, and process of these questions and answers?
2) Who are the people whose questions we are studying? Where do they stand socially and historically?
3) In the 140 years spanned by the texts studied here, are there changes in the kinds of questions asked?
4) Is this questioning genre primarily subversive or conservative? In the terms of Richman's introduction to this volume, will the *Shankāvalīs* tend to line up more with authoritative or with oppositional tellings of Ram's story?

## Scholars and Lovers

Beyond the content of these "Garlands of Doubts" there is a context, a social fabric, that comes into view if we are attentive. People asking questions, someone giving answers: It amounts to a scene, a dialogic community. In the case of bhakti texts and performances in North India, that community is often called *satsang*. *Satsang* is good company, holy company, the fellowship of devotees. The power of *satsang* is extolled in the *Mānas*, as in devotional discourse of all sectarian persuasions. People have often told me that I am very fortunate as a scholar of bhakti texts and practices, because my work brings me into contact with holy persons, holy places, the atmosphere of devotion. I may think something else is the point of my research—intellectual inquiry or professional publication; but in the view of many people I work with, all that is beside the point.[2] For them, the work calls me toward God; toward love.[3]

Pandit Ramkumar Das, author of a four-volume *Mānas shankā samādhān ratnāvalī* (Jewel-Garland of Solutions to *Mānas* Doubts), explains that he has received questions about the *Mānas* and published answers in magazines for decades. The questioners are styled as lovers (*premī*): "The lovers' doubts would come; I would provide solutions."[4]

Jayram Das "Din," author of the popular *Mānas shankā samādhān* (Solutions to *Mānas* Doubts), dedicates his efforts on a difficult question to lovers of the *Mānas*: "In order to remove this doubt from the hearts of lover-readers, with the Lord's gracious inspiration, and according to my own poor wit, this heartfelt interpretation is dedicated to the service of *Mānas* lovers."[5]

Scholars have problems, lovers have doubts. In the fellowship of *kathā* (oral telling of and commenting on the text), devotees may pose questions to specialists, or the specialists may pose the questions to give themselves a chance to answer. Inquirers are called doubt-makers (*shankākārs*) as well as lovers. Over generations some questions come up repeatedly. Others may be peculiar to individuals or historical moments. Specialists often refer to *shankās* in the regular course of their oral and written commentary. The assumed context for the discussion is *satsang*—the circle of believers, of sharers, of *bhaktas* or devotees, who love the text, the gods, the poetry, the stories, the emotions they call forth. Within this circle of devotion and affection, doubts arise and resolutions are offered.

A doubt is an obstacle to faith, a disturbance that needs to be cleared up. But the questioning process is not just a means of getting answers. Those who question are already assumed to be lovers, and the process enacts the love that exists. It is a way of lingering in the text, enjoying *satsang*, savoring the endless possibilities of wisdom and pleasure that text and community afford.

This emphasis on love and devotion should not lead readers to expect merely tedious repetitions of piety. Love relationships are full of tussles. As devotees follow Tulsidas in believing the whole world to be *sīyārāmamaya*—permeated with Sita-Ram—the *Shankāvalīs* reflect the world in microcosm, with its curiosities, idiosyncrasies, quarrels, marks of personality and ego, sociopolitical conditions, and historical changes.[6]

## The *Shankā* Tradition

I have collected four written *Shankāvalīs* whose publication dates range from 1847 to 1987. The earliest, the *Mānas shankāvalī* of Vandan Pathak (*c.* 1815–1909) was published in Banaras in the 1840s and contains 120 doubts.[7] Next in chronological order is the *Mānas shankā mochan* (Remover of *Mānas* Doubts), self-published by Babu Jang Bahadur Sinha, with 185 doubts. While the dates of two printed instalments are given as 1918–19, Sinha says in a preface that he wrote the entire work in 1899.[8]

In 1942 Gita Press, Gorakhpur—a major North Indian publisher of Hindu religious texts which mass produces books and sells them very inexpensively—published the *Mānas shankā samādhān* of Jayram Das "Din." This is the shortest of the four collections, containing 39 *shankā*s and solutions. Reprinted many times, it has sold well over a million copies. Din had died by the time this collection was published, so we can imagine him flourishing as a commentator in the 1930s. The selection of questions may reveal as much about Hanuman Prasad Poddar, who edited the volume, as about Din (see n. 9 below).

Finally, the longest collection—and the richest for the purpose of studying reception—is a four-volume work by Pandit Ramkumar Das, published by the author with the help of supporters: three volumes from Ayodhya and one from Madhya Pradesh, appearing respectively in 1962, 1972, 1981, and 1987. These volumes contain more than 400 doubts and solutions, most of them published previously in magazines. Das refers to *shankās* that he published as early as 1932 and to publications by others as early as 1912.

The small number of published collections should not suggest that the format of *shankā-samādhān*—doubts and solutions—is rare. In fact it is a standard form of discourse among appreciators of the *Mānas*. Introducing Din's work, editor Hanuman Prasad Poddar says:

> The readers of *Shrī Rāmcaritmānas* pose many kinds of doubts about the different parts of the story, and various solutions are given by commentators, writers, scholars. The late Shri Dinji used to give very beautiful solutions to such doubts, and listeners and readers received great satisfaction. In this collection the solutions to some specially important doubts are published. We hope readers will find satisfaction.[9]

One of Ramkumar Das's preface writers indicates that published discussions of *shankās* are easy to find, though usually poor in quality: "Many people go on publishing solutions to *Mānas* doubts . . . [but] most have given solutions from their intellectual cleverness (Das 1972: 6)."[10] The writer reminds us that Tulsidas's textual knowledge was vast; his poetry cannot be explicated simply by reference to itself. True exegesis requires rare scholarly knowledge, along with devotion, spiritual discipline, and God's grace, all of which distinguish Mr Das.

Das says that he has read many *shankās*, and where he found the solutions good he did not bother to publish his own versions (Das 1972: 7).[11] Sometimes he refers to an earlier *shankā* tradition in an answer:

> Your doubt is a very old one. I know because Bharatendu Babu Shri Harishchandra asked it of the great *Mānas* exponent Shri Vandan Pathak. I read this in Bharatenduji's biography, but Shri Pathakji's solution was not published, so with God's grace I will try to give a solution according to my understanding (Das 1962: 36).

Evidence of the widespread presence of *shankā* as a category for studying the Ramayana appears in unexpected places. In 1989 I acquired a small sheaf of letters that had been written to Doordarshan (the Indian national television channel) in response to the televised Ramayana serial.[12] One reads:

> (1) Please remove my doubts about the establishment of Rameshvaram. Who was really the priest during that *pūjā*? I have heard some say that Ravan was the priest, which is not true. (2) When Hanuman went to

get the life-giving herb, was there some connection between him and the sun god? (3) The third doubt is about the killing of Meghnad. Indrajit was always victorious because of his *tapasya*. When that was disturbed, Ram could not protect him. If you had shown this correctly, we would have been full of praise for your serial. However, it is still good. Hari Adhikari, June 14, 1988 (my translation from Hindi).

The written *Shankāvalī* adumbrates a much more widespread oral activity. This is true of *Mānas* commentary in general: hundreds of oral *kathā* sessions form the background of any manuscript or print commentary by a prominent exegete. The editor of *Mānas pīyūsh*, a massive anthology of nineteenth- and early-twentieth-century commentators, describes a *ṭīkā* of the 1820s as strikingly original in the way it presents *shankā-samādhān*.[13] Lutgendorf also mentions much older traditions of "living commentary" in which audience members participate: "A passage in the *Padma Purāṇa* depicts a recitation program beneath a street-corner *mandap* in which a listener closely questions a *paurāṇikā*, who is then obliged to elaborate on his commentary."[14]

Written *Shankāvalīs* bear the marks of the oral practices in which they are grounded. Each *shankā* may begin or end with a mantra, an oral marking of a ritualized space.[15] The solutions, though purged of most signs of conversation, still occasionally evoke the spontaneity and interchange of the *satsang* circle: "This is a good doubt, an excellent doubt," Din sometimes says. Das completes an explanation, then adds, "Oh yes, there's one more point . . ." A questioner poses his doubt, then adds, "Please don't get angry with me and say 'Why is he asking this?' I want to know, that's why I ask. Forgive my impudence" (Das 1962: 185). Or: "Please excuse me, I'm not asking out of any bad intention but out of the playful curiosity of my restless mind" (Das 1962: 75). The Vandan Pathak manuscript has strong oral markers: Each doubt in the handwritten version ends with, "Please speak [of this]" (*so kaho*), and each solution begins with, "Listen to the answer" (*uttar suno*). Interestingly, these formulas are absent in the printed version.

The whole structure of a *Shankāvalī* is one of dialog. This structure replicates the dialog between Shiva and Parvati that constitutes the largest narrative frame of the *Mānas*. Shiva tells the story of Ram's deeds and discourses on questions posed by his consort. In two other mythic narrative frames as well, tellers respond to listeners' doubts.

One narrator, the crow Bhushundi, not only answers a devotee's general doubt by telling Ram's story, but also takes a set of particular questions and responds as commentator and teacher.[16] The frame of questions by Parvati and answers by Shiva is typical of the Agamas or tantric texts that were of great importance in the millenium preceding Tulsidas.[17] By adopting such a frame, Tulsi links his text with the broad stream of Shaivite Agamas—part of a general intention to link the worship of Shiva with that of Vishnu-Ram that is evident throughout the *Mānas*.[18] A Patna University professor writing a preface for Das explicitly identifies the *Ratnāvalī*'s readers with Parvati and its author with Shiva:

> It is my firm belief that on reading "Shrī mānas samādhān ratnāvalī," even the most formidable logicians and the most obdurate opponents will attain the state of Parvati, Mother of the Universe—"when she heard Shiva's words, which shatter delusion, the whole structure of false arguments dissolved" (1.118.7).[19]

## Audiences and Authors

*Shankāvalīs* have always been used as specialist handbooks by expounders wishing to sharpen their expertise, but they also have wider popularity. The collections studied here show both kinds of constituency. While Das's *Ratnāvalī* caters to many specialists, questions also come from nonspecialists. Din's *Shankā samādhān* is intended for and has reached a mass audience. Pathak, part of a lineage patronized by the Maharajas of Banaras, seems to assume a very knowledgeable audience; in the 1840s he would not have imagined reaching millions or even thousands of readers.

We know more about Ramkumar Das than about the others because he writes about himself in introductions and reveals a vivid personality throughout his work. Das explains that he began to write a *shankā-samādhān* column at the request of the publisher of *Mānas Maṇi* magazine. Then other periodicals adopted the column. As time went on, people increasingly sent in previously published doubts. Not enjoying "hackneyed repetition," the author decided to collect the doubts and solutions in book form.

Since these doubts were originally posed in writing, often the questioners' names, towns, and titles are recorded. Many use titles like Pandit, Ramayani, *Mānas* Kovid, Pujari, Mahant, and Jyotishi (Brahmin scholar, Ramayana expounder, *Mānas* specialist, priest, head of temple, and astrologer). Some indicate sectarian affiliations: Shri Vaishnav and Rasik. Some mention secular professions, including doctor, teacher, lawyer, advocate, postmaster, engineer, and editor.[20] Some use terms indicating that they are Vaishyas and businessmen: Seth, Dalal, Sahu. A few attach B.A. or M.A. to their names. Among hundreds of correspondents, only one names a relatively humble occupation: Mr Chandrikaprasad Gupta of Kavardha is a *pānvālā*, or betel-seller.

The geographic spread of the writers is impressive. While most come from the Hindi heartland, especially Uttar Pradesh, Madhya Pradesh, and Bihar, there are also letters from Bengal, Rajasthan, the Himalayan foothills, and South India. Some maintain an ongoing correspondence, having questions in all four volumes. This constituency is obviously literate, educated, largely upper-caste. Not only upper-caste, the questioners are predominantly Brahmin and close to 100 per cent male (only one name among more than 100 is clearly that of a woman).[21]

Ramkumar Das himself seems to be a colorful and abrasive character. He is very scholarly; technical and textual discussions seem to claim his attention more than pious sentiments. He does not hesitate to express contempt for ignorance, misguided viewpoints, and institutions. When one writer suggests that Tulsidas lifted an inauthentic passage from another source, Das gets angry:

> Today we are forced to do our work from the level of mud. In 1912 this question—this mud thrown up on the sun, Gosvami Tulsidasji, in the sky of literature—was asked by the same man and answered in the magazine *Sarasvati*. Today he is again throwing up this mud that has been rotting for 30 years.

One questioner is impressed with titles and with the authority of a famous British scholar:

> [Regarding a verse in which Tulsi says he began to compose the *Mānas* on Tuesday, the ninth of the bright half of Chaitra.] Dr Grierson and his follower Mata Prasad Gupta have said this date is wrong, that in 1631 the bright ninth of Chaitra is a Wednesday. Dr Gupta is a professor at Prayag University. He has written a book on Tulsidas for which he got a D.Litt.
>
> —Rajajyotishi (master astrologer) Pandit Chandrasekhar Shastri (Das 1962: 30–1)

Das's response is withering:

> The condition of western scholars is like that of the fool to whom someone said, "The crow just snatched your ear!" Immediately he started running after the crow. It never occurred to him to check his ear. The Indian followers of those western scholars are also blind. What is surprising is that a master astrologer has fallen into this confusion.

In most instances Das answers his questioners earnestly and with all the erudition at his command. The picture I get of this man is similar in many respects to that of a university scholar. He reads widely and constantly in Sanskrit and in medieval and modern Hindi. He keeps up with and contributes to professional journals, passes his days in discussion with those who share his interests, mentors younger scholars, has a spirited attachment to his own views and methods, doesn't hesitate to attack those he disagrees with, shows defensiveness and a sharp streak of resentment toward well-endowed seats of Tulsidas scholarship. Where he differs from many university scholars is in his habit of rising at 2 a.m. to perform prayers and rituals—in short, in worshiping the protagonist of the book he studies (Das 1987: 8).[22]

## Sampling the Doubts and Solutions

It is difficult to select a few "representative doubts" from the 700 or so questions and answers I have surveyed. In fact, part of the expe rience of studying the doubts for me has been a growing appreciation of their endlessness. It is like swimming in the ocean. Beyond the large features that one can observe, there is no end to small differences in currents, the way the light strikes the surface, the formations and movements beneath the surface. A vast curiosity flows. Seeing the questions—even when I myself would never have thought of such questions—arouses a desire to know the answers.

To make it easier to think about the material, I created a rough set of categories. The headings (though many questions can fit under more than one) give some idea of the directions in which doubts and solutions can go.

1. Maryādā/*proper conduct.* As Ram has always been called *maryādā puruṣottam*, the supreme exemplar of good conduct, many questioners

inquire about morality and propriety. This category highlights people's interest in the text as a source of ideals and models. Questions touch on personal morality, family relations, social order, political norms, ritual correctness, fate and responsibility. Ram, his family members, and his close associates, become reference points. Bad characters are used as negative examples. Episodes and verses are probed for their capacity to give guidance in everyday life. Did Angad lie in Ravan's court when he said Hanuman was a puny messenger and was frightened after burning Lanka? Why did Ram tell Shurpanakha that Lakshman was a bachelor? Ram says one should worship a bad Brahmin but not a good Shudra. Why shouldn't a good Shudra be honored, and why should an unworthy Brahmin be honored? Why were Bharat and Shatrughna not informed that Ram was being made regent? Did Dasharath have any deception in mind? Why did Ram and the Janakpur queens bow to each other's feet at the time of departure? Is the mother-in-law supposed to touch the son-in-law's feet or vice versa? How was it right for Ram to kill Bali? Angad said to Ravan, "If you can move my foot, fool, then Ram will go home and Sita will be lost in the gamble." Does anyone have the right to lose anyone's wife gambling? Why use such a word?

2. *Bhakti/devotion.* Under this heading we place questions on the nature of divinity and *līlā* (divine play), relations between the gods, the experience of bhakti and the ways of practicing to attain true devotion. For example, a question mentions many means of attaining bhakti, then asks: Which practice is most correct? Which is not correct? If all are correct, how can we reconcile the differences? Several questions inquire about the mystery of worshiping Ram and Shiva: are they equal, or does one take precedence over the other? One *shankā* asks how to recognize the true guru. Another refers to Ram asking Valmiki where in the forest he should dwell. Why does Valmiki say he should dwell in the temple of the heart? Did Sita meditate on the soles of Ram's feet, which were the last sight she had of him when he went after the false deer?

3. *Inconsistencies and incongruities.* It is popular to juxtapose two pieces of text that seem to contradict each other and to ask the commentator to reconcile them. The question about women entrancing women (at the beginning of this essay) is an example. Another: After saying that Ram is never angry, why does the text say that he became very angry?

4. *Formal and scholarly details.* Some questioners are interested in

matters that are linguistic and literary, technical and scholarly. They inquire about poetic devices, rhyme and meter, synonyms and redundancy, composition, sources, author's intentions, and narrative structure.

5. *Literal details.* With this broad category, I refer to the kind of interest that comes from directly engaging with the story as historical fact and religious truth. For the lovers who ask questions and the lovers who give answers, the Ram narrative is true, and every detail is interesting and potentially meaningful. The characters (in the forms of gods, demons, humans, animals) lived out the events in historical time. Questioners ask about their thoughts, feelings, and motives. They ask what certain characters were doing when not on the scene, or before they got into the story. They suggest alternative courses of action and scrutinize the passage of time, seeking to clarify what happened when and why. People look realistically at time, wanting to know how long activities took, how sequences fit together, what the characters' ages were in certain episodes. Since the story mingles conventional narrative time with mythic time, questions arise about apparent anomalies. Shiva went into deep meditation for 87,000 years after Sita's abduction, but he also appeared on the battlefield at Lanka. How is this possible? Is Vibhishan still alive, as he is said to have ruled for a *kalpa*, and the *kalpa* is not yet over?

There is no end of particular, irreducibly literal questions. The poet does not say that Ram got blisters on the forest journey, but he says that Bharat got blisters. Why this difference? When Hanuman, taking Ram's ring to Sita, reduced himself to the size of a mosquito, where did he keep the ring? How could 10,000 kings try to pick up the bow all at once? Were the kings of that time mice or ants, that 20,000 hands could touch the bow? When Hanuman burned Lanka, all the houses were destroyed except Vibhishan's. Kumbhakarna was asleep, so why didn't he burn up?

I have been fascinated with the literal-mindedness of attention to every conceivable aspect and detail of the narrative. The fact that I speak of this "literal-mindedness" as fascinating indicates a gulf between me and the community that shares the questions and answers. To them, these inquiries are natural. Close attention to many such questions has led me to appreciate them as the road to intimacy in a devotional practice. Many books, articles, and translations of Hindu bhakti poetry have illuminated this practice of intimacy.[23] There is an interesting Christian parallel. When Ignatius of Loyola devised his

*Spiritual Exercises*, he realized the psychological power of imagining the physical details of a scene in Christ's life, entering the situation emotionally, seeing the tears on Mary's face, or having a colloquy, an intimate conversation, with Jesus or Mary in a concretely imagined setting. *Saguṇ* bhakti in Hinduism goes much farther than the *Spiritual Exercises* in making intimate involvement with the details of a sacred narrative part of one's own psychological makeup and everyday life.

## Continuities and Changes over Time

What the *Shankāvalīs* all have in common, to begin with, is bhakti: devotion to Ram and to other divine protagonists of the Ramayana story, and veneration of Tulsidas as the divinely inspired poet of the *Rāmcaritmānas*. This bhakti suffuses the authors' expressions, influences their questions, colors their answers. They are lovers. They are, in addition, learned men, professional specialists who expound on Tulsidas in oral and written forms.

Many questions appear repeatedly across the 140-year period. Beyond the reappearance of particular questions, all collections share interest in the large categories of subject matter discussed above—social propriety, forms of devotion and ritual, relations between human and mythic time scales, apparent inconsistencies in the text, interpretations of divine teaching, and infinite varieties of literal detail. On the whole, one is more impressed with similarity than with difference.

Differences can, however, be noted and correlated to different personalities, settings, and moments. Vandan Pathak, a specialist's specialist in the 1840s, is less concerned with popular interests than Jayram Das "Din," published by Gita Press a century later. Pathak begins with dozens of questions on matters that are relatively technical (meters, the order of *vandanas* or homages in Tulsi's prologue), and he regularly returns to such questions. The Din volume spends no time on technical matters and dwells on certain issues that would seem to concern twentieth-century audiences—for example, meat eating and the tensions between divine will and human agency (both discussed below). In the nineteenth century, there is not a single question on meat-eating and the killing of animals; in the twentieth, there are eight. Also in the mid-twentieth century, we can detect a faint hint of approaching concerns about gender and caste. Both Das and Din discuss the now notorious line about "drum, rustic, Shudra, animal, woman" (see the beginning of this essay); the line is not mentioned by Pathak or Sinha.

If *Shankāvalīs* reveal the community created by bhakti, they also reveal feuds and fissures in that community. Ramkumar Das, through sheer volume of questions and through a quirky, assertive personality, provides more local color than the rest. He attacks the biggest institutions involved in the dissemination and interpretation of the *Mānas.* The following passages show that intellectual passions and professional resentments burn just as hot in devotional worlds as they do in academic ones:

> Don't ask me to explain changes in the text, ask the helmsmen of the Gita Press. It is true that in our time no one has done more to spread the *Mānas* than Gita Press. It is also supremely true that no one has done more than Gita Press to defile the *Mānas* text and destroy the truth, except maybe the *Mānas pīyūsh* (1987: 17–18).

> The Gita Press helmsmen spun like tops after English degrees. The degree-holders, instead of doing the labor themselves, prepared their patchwork from the twisted readings of the *Mānas pīyūsh.* The *Mānas pīyūsh* editor is a good scholar of English, Persian, and Urdu, but not of Hindi or Sanskrit, and he doesn't even know the ABCs of Avadhi. Proper knowledge of Avadhi is found in the countryside near Ayodhya, not in colleges and Sanskrit universities. The Gita Press has accepted more or less all the errors of the *Mānas pīyūsh* textual whirlings (Das 1962: 158).

## How Questions Reflect Historical Controversies: Did Ram Eat Meat?

Many questions in the *Shankāvalīs* illuminate historical contexts and changes. History is reflected in subtle as well as broad ways. The question that refers to the adoption of a son by a king (see beginning of essay) is associated not only with cases in the ancient epics, but with recent predicaments in the Banaras court. The last ruling Maharaja of Banaras, Shri Vibhuti Narain Singh, was adopted by his predecessor as the latter lacked an heir. Another question maps colonial bureaucracies onto Ram's world: Being a renunciant, why did Ram himself administer justice to Jayant? He could have had it done by some nearby justice officer (*dandādhikārī*) or district magistrate, or he could have had Bharat do it (Das 1981: 14).

To illustrate one longstanding controversy, I have selected a set of questions that relate to meat-eating and animal-killing. These issues and the relevant *Mānas* passages do not come up at all in the two nineteenth-century *Shankāvalīs*. But eight questions in the twentieth-century collections are related to episodes in which Ram hunts deer; Brahmins are served meat by an evil character; Bharat is served fish by good forest dwellers; roosters are heard crowing in Janakpur; and Kaushalya is said to make sacrifices to village goddesses.

Questioners want to know what is morally right, with implications for their own behavior. They wonder about Ram's perfection, ever anxious to be reassured that there is no stain on his character. Questions reflect changes in moral standards and social practices over different historical periods. They reflect tensions between Kshatriya and Brahmin codes. And they contain indications of the way meat-eating functions as an index of status between high and low, pure and impure castes. Selections from questions and answers follow.

1. *Did Brahmins in ancient times eat meat?*[24] Din strongly affirms that there is no way Brahmins of that time could even dream of eating meat, and that absolutely nothing in the text supports such an idea.

Das goes on at greater length. After describing the four types of living creatures that emerged in the creation of the universe, he divides them into meat-eaters and grass-eaters (vegetarians). He lists eighteen points on which the two classes differ from each other, including shape of teeth, longevity, odor, and so on. He cites Muslim hadiths according to which Adam received ten punishments and Eve fifteen for eating meat. All the punishments are listed. He discusses further the sin and unwholesomeness of eating meat and killing animals, and the certainty of hell for offenders, with supporting quotations from the Rig and Atharva Vedas. Kautilya's *Arthaśāstra* is quoted: feeding meat or wine to a Brahmin incurs 432 units of punishment; to a Kshatriya 216; to a vaishya 108; and to a Shudra 64.[25] Finally he gets to the episode in question and gives the same answer as Din, concluding, "It is clear that neither in that time nor in any other dharmic time was it socially acceptable for humans to eat meat or drink wine."

2. *The Nishad king presents Bharat with a big fish. In the Rāmāyaṇa*

*age, did Kshatriya kings eat fish?* (Din 1942: 27–8) By quoting further lines around the statement that the forest people brought Bharat a fish, Din demonstrates that Guha, the forest chief, was consciously testing Bharat's character and motives in seeking Ram in the forest. Guha placed before Bharat roots and fruits, animals and birds, and fish—*sāttvik* (pure), *rājasik* (passionate), and *tāmasik* (dark, heavy) foods. Bharat more than passed the test. Not only did he not eat the animal foods, but on learning from his guru that Guha was an intimate devotee of Ram, he became lost in love, embraced the tribal chief, and ignored all the food. Thus Din upholds the conviction that Kshatriyas of that age—especially Ram and his family—did not eat fish or any other nonvegetarian food.

Din's interpretation assumes the inferiority of the tribal people's way of life to that of the pure upper castes. The forest people hunt and fish for food. Presumably their chief does too. But he knows that this is a bad, polluted way of life, and he tests Bharat in such a way as to prove that Bharat is indeed better and purer than he and his people. We can infer that bhakti for the tribals, as presented by Tulsidas and affirmed by commentators, is a form of Brahminization.[26] This notion accords with the fact that low-born people in the *Mānas* refer to themselves as vile beings who can be purified only by contact with Ram.

3. *Blood sacrifice by Ram's mother?* When Kaushalya hears of the imminent installation of her son as regent, she worships village goddesses, gods, and nagas, promising further sacrifices (*bali*) if they will give the boon of ensuring Ram's welfare (*Mānas* 2.7.5). In what appears to be the only question in Das's *Ratnāvalī* submitted by a woman, the word *bali*, sacrificial offering, arouses concern (Das 1972: 20–1).[27] Can it be proper to do violence to living beings for the purpose of sacrifice? This section of Tulsi's narrative is explicitly about women's activities. Besides mentioning Kaushalya's rituals, it refers to women's observances on this special occasion: preparing ceremonial pots, making rice-flour diagrams on the floor, giving gifts, and singing songs. Das dismisses the issue of Kaushalya's sacrifice by citing definitions of *bali* that include vegetable offerings as well as figurative self-sacrifice to God.

The questions about meat-eating and animal slaughter point to a historic tension that goes back to the Vedas. The Vedic people were not vegetarian and did not hold *ahimsa* (nonviolence) as a major ideal. Around the eighth to fifth centuries BCE, profound changes in

Brahminical beliefs and values broke through the surface, as evidenced by the Upanishads and the emergence of Buddhism and Jainism. In the course of these changes, vegetarianism and *ahimsa* did become mainstream ideals in all three traditions. Large-scale Vedic sacrifices, entailing the killing of diverse animals from chickens to horses, were curtailed and gradually rejected in principle. The ideology of *varṇa* hardened, with the purity of twice-born *varṇas*—above all Brahmins—being linked to their vegetarianism and lack of contact with killing. Yet throughout the centuries in which these changes took place, up to the present day, the Vedas remained the most prestigious of Hindu texts, the putative foundation of the eternal dharma. Their authority could not be challenged, even if many of their old practices were reinterpreted, forgotten, or rejected. Simultaneously to keep and to displace the Vedas became one of the ordinary juggling acts of Hindu tradition.[28]

Even as vegetarianism became the norm for the twice-born, an exception was widely granted to Kshatriyas; there was (and still is) an understanding that warriors need meat. This exception did not sit comfortably with those in the tradition who insisted that purity was inseparable from *ahimsa*. As princes, Ram and his brothers are touched by the expectation that Kshatriyas may hunt, sacrifice animals, and eat meat. At the same time, as the spiritualized king who combines the Kshatriya's valor with the Brahmin's renunciation and purity, Ram also tends to repel impure associations.[29] He cannot, however, be separated cleanly from these unsavory Kshatriya habits. Sheldon Pollock reports commentarial debate over a verse in Valmiki's *Ayodhyākāṇḍa*, just after Ram, Sita, and Lakshman cross the Ganga:

> On the further bank the brothers killed four large animals—a boar, an antelope, a gazelle, and a great black buck. They were famished and took meat hurriedly.[30]

The Valmiki *Rāmāyaṇa* gives a detailed account of Ram's performance of the Vedic *ashvamedha* or horse sacrifice, which lasts a year and culminates, as its name implies, in the sacrifice of a horse. Tulsidas does not describe performance of the *ashvamedha*, but a reference makes it clear that he has not effaced its memory (*Mānas* 7.24.1). Similarly, the young princes' sport of hunting demonstrates how the vestiges of early epochs intersect with, mingle with, and subtly alter the colors of later ones. The twentieth-century *shankākārs'* worries and the expounders' replies reflect the long history of ambivalence and shifting standards on these matters.

In all the *shankās* on hunting and meat-eating, we get "party-line" answers that reflect orthodox standards of today: no meat or fish eating for Brahmins or Kshatriyas, indeed for any Aryan Hindu or any decent human being; no game-killing except in the absolutely unique case of Ram, the supreme being, performing a *līlā* in which he compassionately releases certain chosen animals, who are pure and ready, into a new life in his own heavenly realm.[31] This official line is maintained in the face of much historical evidence to the contrary and much ambivalence among Hindus today—all further complicated, of course, by the last 500 years of political and cultural involvement with two meat-eating, non-Hindu societies, the Muslims from West and Central Asia and the Christians from Europe.

Another tension to which these questions point is the discontinuity between Brahminical norms and old indigenous practices still common in certain regions, among certain ethnic groups, and in many rural areas. Despite disapproval from various sectors, goddesses throughout the subcontinent continue to be fond of blood sacrifice, and these goddesses are often propitiated by women to ensure family welfare. So when the woman questioner worries that Kaushalya's *bali* (sacrifice) to the *grāmdevī* (village goddess) may involve the death of animals, her worry is not based merely on an ignorant fantasy, as the commentator implies.

## Courtesy and Costume

During Ram's forest exile, when he was supposed to dress and behave as a renunciant, why did he carry his bow and arrow, ride a chariot, make war? (Din 1942: 64–5; Das 1972: 142–4;, Pathak 1847: 49–50)

Bharat saw golden spangles on the ground where Sita had slept. How could she have been wearing these if she was dressed as a renunciant? (Das 1972: 103–6)

Why did ideal *devī* Sita tell Hanuman to grasp the feet of the Lord and his younger brother on her behalf? It seems fitting for the Lord but not the younger brother. (Das 1987: 68–70)

When Hanuman was in the form of a Brahmin, was it right for him to do obeisance to Ram, a Kshatriya? (Pathak 1847: 69–70)

> Anasuya gave Sita *rājasī* clothes and jewels. How could she have such things in her hut in the forest? (Sinha 1899b: 60–7)

Throughout the collections, questioners address matters of etiquette: who touches whose feet, who gives and takes permission, what titles of address are used, who stands in deference to whom, and what forms of dress are suitable for what figures and circumstances. The word "etiquette" should not suggest triviality. These are the bodily forms of culture—sites of pleasure, power, affection, nostalgia. They shed light in diverse realms: hierarchy and emotion in the family, political struggles in history, the experience of devotion.

A world of experience lies behind questions about touching and washing feet as a sign of respect. In everyday life, these acts can be perfunctory or highly charged rites. They can be understood as enactments of power and subordination or of love and intimacy. While watching the television Ramayana, I noticed many scenes in which the touching of a parent's, guru's, or elder brother's feet was associated with positive and strongly evocative feelings. There would be emotional glances; the superior person would quickly raise the kneeling inferior, and a tearful embrace would often follow. Some observers will focus on the negative implications of such ritualization of hierarchy, seeing it as socially stifling, politically inhibiting, or just distastefully obsequious. But it is also worthwhile to attend to the pleasure and warmth, and to the far-reaching net of meanings, that these forms convey.

In *saguṇ* bhakti, especially in Vaishnava traditions, outward forms have great importance. Dressing one's part and playing one's role are often seen as essential to spiritual practice. Vishnu himself takes on a body, a role, and a costume when he enters his earthly *līlā*. Devotees are urged to participate in the *līlā* by identifying emotionally with it and taking parts in the drama. Form is not separate from substance. A *sadhu* at the Ramlila once tried to explain to me how the devotees at that annual performance could believe that the brilliantly costumed Ram was God incarnate even while they understood that the wearer of the costume was also a schoolboy of Banaras. At one point he said emphatically, with some exasperation at my failure to understand, "Form! Form! We believe in the form, the dress" (Hess 1983:183). A similar import was conveyed by the Maharaja's explanation of why, in his Ramlila, Ram and Lakshman continue to wear crowns during the forest exile. Some have criticized this choice by the Ramnagar producers—a choice the latter justify by referring to Tulsidas's term *jaṭā mukuṭ*, or matted-hair crown. The princes in exile wear smaller but still quite kingly golden crowns, with a line of black symbolizing the matted hair of renunciants. The Maharaja explained that they retained the crowns in the interests of bhakti. Devotees needed to see a stable physical image of the Lord, whose *darshan* has such power to evoke a devotional experience. There is also a tradition that the crowns embody the power of the transformation from Banaras schoolboy to God. In an hour-long daily process of costuming and makeup, the last touch is placing the crowns on the heads; at that moment, the five actors are considered to have become the gods.[32]

The *shankā* about whether Ram should carry weapons while dressed as a *sadhu* is not merely iconographic. Peter Van der Veer writes of "a long tradition of organized ascetic violence in India which began even before the Muslim conquest of the twelfth century" and provides details on the Ramdal (army of Ram), "the military arm of the four Vishnuite sampradayas," which developed formidable power in the eighteenth and nineteenth centuries.[33] Though three of those sampradayas were Krishnaite, it was the Ramanandis who predominated in the Ramdal. The image of Ram dressed as a *sadhu*, bearing arms and fighting with righteous violence against evil enemies, remains potent in late-twentieth-century India.[34]

## Divine and Human Agency

Din (or more likely H.P. Poddar, who edited Din's posthumous collection) shows a special interest in the conflicting claims of fate, divine will, ritual prescriptions, individual moral responsibility, and justice. In an often quoted line about *karma*, he suggests that our actions determine what happens to us: "In this world *karma* prevails; according to one's actions, one tastes the fruit." But other lines indicate that God controls us like puppets, that fate can overrule good *karma*, that devotion or pilgrimage can bring liberation to sinful people, that astrological influences can outweigh good or bad *karma*. Din's *Shankāvalī* devotes five out of 39 questions to these issues. One *shankā* bears the heading, "Knowing destiny to be irrevocable, should we give up trying to do our duty?"

> "Only that happens which Ram makes happen. Who ever made a branch grow by arguing?"

> "Uma, like a puppeteer the master Ram makes everyone dance."
>
> "Like a street performer with his monkey, Ram makes everyone dance. Thus sing the Vedas, O king of birds."
>
> Seeing and hearing these words, why do people get embroiled in the confusion of sin and merit? Why not sit tight and stop worrying? Yet how could one stop worrying on the basis of these lines when Lakshmanji cuts these lines to bits by saying, "Lord, what's the point of relying on gods?" and "Lazy people cry out to the gods." Please clarify all this.

The answers to questions like this show a pattern. First, Din contextualizes each quoted line to show that it has a special and limited meaning. The first line above is not meant to apply to ordinary people in normal circumstances, but only to Sati on this occasion. Next he argues that, even though some events are clearly beyond human control, it is still appropriate to try to do one's duty and to perform meritorious acts like charitable offerings (*dān*), Vedic rituals (*yajña*) and austerity (*tap*).[35] Recognizing that some things are in God's hands simply encourages us to cultivate detachment. Finally, he says that the last two statements about Ram's transcendent power do not contradict Lakshman's cutting remarks. The interpretation rides on the particular context of each speech.

Another doubt asks how the following words of Shiva to Parvati can be consistent with the statement that we all taste the fruits of our own actions:

> Then Mahesh said, smiling, no one's wise or a fool.
> Whatever, however, whenever Ram wants you,
> at that moment you become.

Din resolves the apparent contradiction by saying that God does not turn a wise man into a fool just on a whim. For ordinary people the rule of karma operates. But for those who are God's loving servants, who have taken refuge in him alone, he may perform strange-seeming *līlās* for the devotee's ultimate benefit. This is illustrated by a story about the humbling of sage Narad. Din concludes:

> In the *Mānas*, such words occur in distinct connection with certain worthy characters. Often people try to use these lines . . . as a screen, to make their own wicked activities look clean . . . . Such people

> should remember that the lines are connected to Naradji and Kak Bhushundi. How can [ordinary] beings, bound to the world, be equated to such intimate *bhaktas*? If they want to participate in such joy, they should keep before them the examples of these guru-*bhaktas*.

In these discussions about fate and divine will on one hand, human agency and justice on the other, insights emerge from both questions and answers. In the answers, first we may note the invariable confirmation of the authority of the text, the smoothing over of apparent contradictions. Every line is true, if understood correctly. Second is the resort to contextual interpretation. Place, time, character, and situation crucially affect the meaning of any statement.[36] Third is the unwillingness to let go of any rules or conventions associated with the Brahminical ethos. Rituals should be performed, ritual boundaries in space and time should be respected, meritorious offerings should be made. Ordinary devotees should believe in and strive for transcendent experience (bhakti) but should not presume to put themselves in the same category with great devotees like Narad and Bhushundi.

While the answers are conservative, the existence of the questions demonstrates that audience members are restive. They are looking for connections between the text and life. Concerned with the problem of inconsistency, they want guidelines for living based on the text. The commentator in most cases dissolves inconsistencies into contextual distinctions. Doubters are urged to cultivate bhakti, but with a great humility that precludes questioning of traditional authority.

## The Scope and Limits of Doubt

The written *Shankāvalī* as well as the wider practice of *shankā-samādhān* is a dialogical form that leaves scope for discussion of enormously diverse questions. Political, social, spiritual, moral, rhetorical, text-critical, and other issues arise freely. Interests change from one time, place, and person to another. Is doubt then valorized in these collections? Is this marvelously open system infinitely open? Or is the openness an optical illusion, diverting us from noticing how the system is contained, capped, closed? This is my concluding doubt.

I begin my solution by referring again to the structure of the

*Mānas*, which has four major narrative levels, each featuring a teller and an audience, with the listener often posing questions to the teller. The *Shankāvalīs* and the *Mānas* reflect each other not only in their dialogical structure but also in the centrality and power of doubt. At three of the four narrative levels, the telling of Ram's story begins because one partner in the dialog has a great doubt. And the doubt remains the same through all the frames: How could the *nirguṇ* Ram be the *saguṇ* Ram? How could the indescribable, unreachable ultimate reality, *parabrahma*, be a child playing in Dasharath's courtyard, a man weeping for the loss of his wife, and so on?

The form is dialogical; the range of questions is vast. Yet in both the *Mānas* and the *shankā* tradition, there is a limit to acceptable doubt: One must affirm the ultimate importance of faith in and love for Ram, a personal God experienced through these forms. All the doubt, the exploring, the delight, the tears, the community, the courtesy, find their consummation in the dissolution of doubt, its disappearance at last. Through the medium of *kathā* and *satsang*, doubt ends in an expansive experience of love that opens the heart, melts fear and tension, and enables the lover to see the whole world as suffused with Sita-Ram, partaking of that same love.

Doubt is certainly valorized in this tradition; but at the fundamental level of doubting Ram's divine nature, it is not. Shiva gets downright abusive in his language when he speaks of those who doubt Ram's full *nirguṇ-saguṇ* divinity.[37] Shiva's wife Sati pays a dire price for acting out her doubt. The commentators often affirm that there should be no doubt about Ram's ultimate nature. All the layers of doubt in the *Mānas* narrative structure lead at last to the liberation of doubters into moments of joyful, flowing love.[38]

This resolution of doubt in an experience of love contributes to both the openness and the closedness of the system. Faith is expected and even enforced by a series of male figures from Shiva to the local oral expounder. Nonetheless, the resolving experience is described in passionate terms. It dissolves boundaries and liberates tension. Such experiences are always potentially subversive. They suggest that someone will push for further openness and that the exploration will continue to be wide-ranging and unpredictable.

The system of *shankā-samādhān* as seen in these published collections helps to maintain structures of male Brahminical authority. The expert resolvers-of-doubt are Brahmin men, and the solutions reliably reflect their values and uphold their authority. The questioners who have voices in these records are also overwhelmingly high-caste men. Thus, in significant ways, the system is bounded.

Yet we can imagine that it will not always be bounded in the same way. The pervasive presence of doubt as a mode of discourse can be liberating. The process of doubting can be carried to nonconventional forums. For instance, in recent years we have seen activists in women's causes in India raising fresh and creative questions about the Ramayana.[39] Women are great doubters when they attain inner and outer freedom of expression. In the *Rāmcaritmānas* the most inveterate, audacious, and persistent doubter is Parvati-Sati—the only female in the frame structure. Over and over she claims to have been "cured" of her doubt, to have understood Shiva's teaching about devotion to Ram as the supreme being. Then suddenly she will say, "But still, Lord, I have this doubt," and they will be off again. Shiva gets the last word in the *Mānas* dialog, as high-caste men dominate the *Shankāvalīs*. But I can imagine the goddess's succession of questions continuing beyond the boundaries of these texts; and I can imagine different solutions arising in locations where diverse voices speak freely.

Some scholars are interested in rhapsodic descriptions of religious love; others decidedly not. We can learn a great deal about more worldly matters from *Shankāvalīs*: historical debates, sectarian turf wars, gender ideologies, Brahmin self-interest, and so on. But taking the lover's view, at least temporarily, may transform our sense of what *Mānas* audiences want, see, and feel as they use and live in their text.

THREE

# Bhavabhūti on Cruelty and Compassion

DAVID SHULMAN

## When Two Become One

Sanskrit poets often sing of love, in many modes and names—*sneha*, *anurāga*, *preman*, *prīti*, *prīti-yoga*—but who among them has ventured to define this most refractory and compelling of human states? What we call desire fares, it seems, a little better in this respect, neither demanding nor resisting definitive formulations—though here too the animating structures and subtleties of texture deserve, and receive, attention. Desire—or is it love?—bears, among other titles, that of *smara*, i.e. memory;[1] and remembering, the grammarians tell us, is what follows upon longing (*utkaṇṭhā-pūrvakaṃ smaraṇam*). This triple nexus is richly explored in the classical texts, including, of course, the Ramayana literature from Valmiki onwards: Sītā and Rāma love, desire, and mostly long for one another throughout a narrative saturated with painful forms of separation, some of them self-induced. As we know, these paradigmatic, or ideal, lovers move through isolation, loss, war and reunion to the harsh events of the *Uttara-kāṇḍa*, when Rāma sends his pregnant wife to permanent exile in the wilderness. It is his choice; he claims his duty as a king demands it, for his subjects have been slandering the innocent Sītā; the king cannot let his personal feelings endanger the integrity of his perceived perfection. But is this love?

At least one highly unusual voice in the classical Sanskrit tradition offers an answer to our (possibly somewhat exotic) question, at the same time boldly setting out not one but several potential definitions and addressing, or, better, questioning, the inner meaning and experience of loving. The voice is that of Bhavabhūti, probably belonging to the first half of the eighth century, and to the Gangetic plain—perhaps to Kanauj at the time of Yaśovarman, though he links himself to a site known as Padmapura, probably in Vidarbha.[2] Here is Bhavabhūti's first formulation, put in the mouth of Rāma himself, as Sītā lies asleep on his lap:

That state when two become one
in joy as in sorrow,
where you find rest together
and feelings never age
but deepen and ripen as you move
through the layers of time,
that rare state of human fullness
is real. You *may* find it, once,
in life. (1.39)[3]

It is an optimistic statement, hardly meant to be exhaustive, certainly rooted in experience. Love exists, and when found or attained—somehow or other (*katham api*), and apparently only once (*ekam*)—abrogates duality in a continuous way. There is stability in it, and restfulness. Temporality infuses it, at least on a certain level, in which there is a gradual peeling away of veils (*āvaraṇa*) but also an apparently crucial aspect of "ripening" or self-transformation (*pariṇāma*), that affects the very core of this emotion. And all of this belongs to being human, perhaps even constitutes humanity at its fullest (*sumānuṣa*).[4] Hence its place in the awareness of Rāma, the god who has chosen to become a man.

So much for definitions: this one is, after all, placed within a certain dramatic context, in the first act of Bhavabhūti's play known as the *Uttara-Rāma-Carita*—"The End of Rāma's Story." What is set out at different points in the text as a declarative statement is elaborated and also problematized by the work as a whole. We will attempt, in what follows, to test the deeper meanings and understandings of this theme in the hands of one of the master-poets of the Sanskrit literary tradition, as embodied in this work of remarkable lyrical precision.

## Paintings, Reflections, and a Play-within-a-Play

Let me fill in the initial context of the verse I have quoted, and then briefly summarize the rest of the narrative structure of this play and outline the context of performance. The verse comes toward the end of the first act: the great war in Laṅkā is over, and Rāma has been crowned king in Ayodhyā; the palace has, however, been emptied out, for the queen-mothers have gone off to the ashram of Ṛṣyaśṛṅga to take part in a long sacrificial ritual, and Janaka, Rāma's father-in-law, has returned home to Videha. Sītā, heavy with child, is saddened by all these departures and, unwittingly and with moving simplicity, strikes at the very outset one of the central notes of the entire play: "It is painful," she says to Rāma, "when people you love go away." He agrees: Such is life in the world, a series of states which pierce the heart (*ete hi hṛdaya-marma-cchidaḥ saṃsāra-bhāvāḥ*); that is why so many people renounce all desires and seek fulfilment in the wilderness. Lakṣmaṇa enters, happy to announce that a series of paintings on the Ramayana story, which he has recently commissioned for the walls of one of the royal galleries, has been completed. Perhaps they will divert the attention of the melancholy Sītā? Thus the same threesome that had once, long ago, left together for the forest now begins to inspect the newly painted gallery.

The early scenes are relatively happy. A painting of the divine weapons that Rāma inherited from Viśvāmitra leads Rāma, recalling this moment, to utter a blessing to the effect that these same weapons will some day serve Sītā's children. These are weighty words, already charged with potential reality. Then comes the breaking of the bow at Mithilā and the joyful multiple wedding that followed. The painting must be powerful and real, for Sītā, overwhelmed, says that she is, as it were, back at that very moment, experiencing again the first touch of her bridegroom's hand.

Soon, however, the pictures draw the spectators toward the traumatic events of exile, the journey to the forest, and then the torment of separation. Rāma, solicitous of his wife's emotional state, tries to spare her the worst of these memories; he also dwells lovingly on the joyful memories of the nights they spent in the Pañcavaṭī forest,

Whispering wonderful whatevers
in any which order,
cheek touching cheek,
arms totally enmeshed
from so much loving,

we never knew the hours passing
when suddenly night itself
was over.[5] (1.27)

But as the three advance along the course of the murals, the memory of loss and suffering becomes too much for them; it has all come flooding back, in the present; in a poignant intervention Rāma cuts into the middle of a verse that Lakṣmaṇa—the museum guide at this exhibition—is singing about Mount Mālyavant (in Kiṣkindhā) and begs his brother,

"Stop, stop, I can bear no more.
The whole loss is happening to me again!" (1.33)

Lakṣmaṇa sees that Sītā is exhausted and suggests that she rest. First, however, she has a request—and the wishes of a pregnant woman are not to be denied: "I would like to bathe again in the limpid waters of the Ganga and delight in the profound and peaceful landscapes of the forest." Rāma immediately orders Lakṣmaṇa to prepare a chariot for this expedition. "You are coming with me, aren't you?" asks the queen. "Is there any need to answer that?" he innocently replies.

Lakṣmaṇa leaves, and Rāma and Sītā seat themselves within the wide space of a window-well (*vātāyanopakaṇṭha*). Soon Sītā, resting upon Rāma's body, is fast asleep. He sings, as she sleeps, of the unique texture of her touch, resistant to simple articulation:

Is it happiness, or sorrow?
How can I know?
A wildness, a sleep,
the creeping numbness
of poison, or a maddening joy?
Each time I touch you, my body
is bewildered, and awareness
wanders, lost in itself. (1.35)

Soon he utters the verse with which we began, defining love.

It is the penultimate moment, the last taste of happiness before disaster occurs. Even as she sleeps restlessly, murmuring in her dreams, Rāma sings another verse of love, ending with a break and the asyndetic phrase: "Separation from you would be unbearable" (*asahyas tu virahaḥ*). Suddenly the doorkeeper, unconsciously revealing the future unfolding from this point, from these very words, announces: "Lord, it [something, someone] has come."[6] The transition is focused, heavy with suggestion, unbearable.

Durmukha, the king's spy, has arrived to inform Rāma of the state of affairs in the city. After a little prodding, he reveals the terrible truth that Rāma's subjects have not accepted the proof of Sītā's innocence during the course of her nine-month sojourn in Rāvaṇa's captivity. Rāma is pierced to the quick, as if by a lightning bolt made of language (*vāg-vajra*). Suddenly he is facing a tragic conflict: as dharmic king, scion of the Ikṣvākus, he has, he thinks, no choice but to send Sītā away forever; but as a man, a husband and lover, he knows that she is completely innocent. He takes the decision in a flash, sacrificing her, and his own happiness; he orders Durmukha to inform Lakṣmaṇa that the queen is to be abandoned, alone, in the forest. Rāma assumes that this means Sītā will die, the prey of wild beasts. Guilt floods him: in a second, he says, he has been transformed into a loathsome demon. The world is upside down (*viparyastaḥ samprati jīva-lokaḥ*), emptied out like a wasteland (*śūnyam adhunā jīrṇâraṇyaṃ jagat*), and there is no further meaning to his life; it is, moreover, all his fault; he is polluted and polluting, a kind of untouchable who should not even speak the names of his former friends and benefactors. He bows, touching the sleeping Sītā's feet with his head, for one last time; he begs the earth to care for his beloved wife, her daughter. Fortunately, at this point news arrives of a demon who is tormenting the sages on the bank of the Yamunā, so Rāma can rush off to take care of this external threat—leaving Sītā to awake, from a nightmare, without him. Although she does not yet know this, her nightmare of separation is about to be realized in fact.

*Act II.* Twelve years pass between this moment and the opening of Act Two. Vāsantī, goddess of the Dandaka Forest, meets Ātreyī, who has left Vālmīki's ashram, where she was studying, largely because the sage has been too busy composing poetry—the *Rāmāyaṇa*. In passing, she also tells the famous tale of Vālmīki's transformation into a poet and his inspired utterance of the first *śloka*.[7] We also learn from this conversation that Rāma has commenced an *aśvamedha* sacrifice, performing the ritual with a golden image of Sītā in lieu of the living person beside him, and that Lakṣmaṇa's son, Candraketu, is following the sacrificial horse as it roams the world.

Soon Rāma himself enters: he has gone in search of a Śūdra who had the temerity to engage in *tapas*; he attacks this impudent Yogi, Śambūka, with his sword, releasing him from his low-caste body and sending him off to heavenly realms. Before he leaves on this astral journey, Śambūka informs Rāma that he has unintentionally arrived at Janasthāna-Pañcavaṭī, where, before the kidnapping, Rāma had lived the unencumbered forest life with Sītā—perhaps the happiest moment in all of Rāma's experience. The king, still guilty and tormented, is overcome with longing and grief upon re-encountering the familiar sights and sounds of this idyllic wilderness—which the departing Śambūka describes for him with Pisarro-like verve and penetration, in a series of elevated and alliterative verses.

*Act III*, "The Shadow/Reflection" (*Chāyā*). Rāma continues his nostalgic tour of Pañcavaṭī, on his way to Agastya's ashram. He is in danger: the sites of his former happiness trigger an overwhelming sadness; at nearly every step he falls or swoons. Having anticipated this eventuality, the river Ganga has brought Sītā to this same spot, also rendering her completely invisible; her task will be to revive the weakened hero by her touch. With her is another, smaller river, the Tamasā (on whose banks Rāma, Lakṣmaṇa, and Sītā spent their first night in the forest, in the distant past).[8] Meanwhile, Rāma is joined by Vāsantī, the goddess of the forest. In a series of intimate confessions, he speaks of his burden of guilt, and of his love for the wife he wronged; all this is overheard by the hidden Sītā who, in her heart, now forgives him. Rāma, palpably feeling her touch, sensing her presence, is both restored and bewildered: Sītā must be right there, but he cannot see her; he has every reason to assume that she is dead; he is amazed, and rather angry, that he himself is still alive after all this suffering. Was Sītā's touch a dream? But then mental torment never allows him to sleep. Yet he knows she is there, and his heart is breaking. His present state is truly unendurable: before, when she was in Rāvaṇa's power, he had a goal, and a plan to put an end to this state of separation; but this unbounded present-future, without hope, is of a different order altogether. Sītā is gone, lost in some domain which even Lakṣmaṇa's arrows, or the indomitable Hanuman, can never reach.

Through all this the audience can see Sītā visibly before them. In fact, the stage is as if split in two: a shadow-half, where Sītā and Tamasā are hidden, and the overt, illuminated half, where Rāma and Vāsantī walk, weep, converse. The symmetry is palpable and evocative, even as the shadows wander among their mirror-like reflections, invisible to them but fully and audibly present to us. As the act ends, these mutual reflections converge in a surprising movement of integration. Rāma climbs into his flying chariot, the Puṣpaka-vimāna, in order to leave Pañcavaṭī; now the two secondary characters—both divine interlocuters and eavesdroppers, that is, the Tamasā River and the goddess Vāsantī—join in singing a single verse of blessing: may the earth and the Ganga, the first poet (Vālmīki), Vasiṣṭha and Arundhatī, all bring goodness to *you*, that is, to Rāma or to Sītā, as the case may be, but also implicitly to each spectator at the play (48).

It is perhaps worth mentioning, at least, that the rich emotional tone of this act slowly intensifies to an almost unimaginable pitch (surely resistant to translation). Within this swelling tide of feeling, each of the characters, in turn, approaches the limits of consciousness and needs to be cooled down and restored. The audience, or any sensitive reader, undoubtedly undergoes a similarly moving experience, perhaps akin only to the slow culmination of a musical performance in the state of cognitive and emotional melt-down that the texts call *laya*.

*Act IV*: Vālmīki's ashram in the wilderness is celebrating another holiday from study, for honored guests have arrived—Arundhatī and Vasiṣṭha, Janaka (Sītā's bereft father), and the Ayodhyā queens, who have refused to return to the unhappy capital after the completion of Ṛṣyaśṛṅga's twelve-year rite. The meeting of Janaka and Kausalyā, Rāma's mother, after so many years is heavy with bitterness and tears; since Sītā's exile and presumed death, life itself, says Janaka, has become hell (*ghore 'smin mama jīva-loka-narake pāpasya dhig jīvitam*, 17). Kausalyā confirms this: she, too, would rather be dead, but some cursed, dogged quality keeps her going. So dreadful is the lachrymose atmosphere that Arundhatī, who is present during the conversation, actually advises the queen: "My Lady, maybe you should take a short break from weeping" (*rājaputri bāṣpa-pariśramo'py antare kartavya eva*). In the midst of all this misery, they catch sight of the young boy Lava, one of Rāma's two sons, whom they have never seen or known. They call him over: something about this child uncannily reminds them all of both Rāma and Sītā, and Janaka begins to toy with the wild notion that the child might even be his grandson; Kausalyā, too, thinks her heart is going mad, murmuring to her something incredible, but of enormous import. She asks the child if he has a mother, and if he remembers his father. "No," he replies, to both questions. So whose child is he? Vālmīki's. That is as much as he knows.

Suddenly a horse appears in the ashram—the ritually consecrated horse protected by Candraketu, Lakṣmaṇa's son, whom we know about from Act II. Lava (like his playmates) is fascinated at the sight of this animal, and even more so when he learns the identity of Candraketu—for he knows of Lakṣmaṇa and Rāma from the *Rāmāyaṇa*, the text that Vālmīki has composed and taught the twins. His evident familiarity with this text prompts Janaka to ask him about the existence and fate of other children of Rāma and Lakṣmaṇa, but Lava can only say: "This is as far as the story is known." "But has not the poet composed the rest of it?" asks Janaka. Indeed he has, Lava announces, but he has so far not published it (*praṇīto na prakāśitaḥ* [*kathā-vibhāgaḥ*]; Vālmīki has, however, sent a copy of this concluding section of the *Rāmāyaṇa*, written by his own hand, to the sage Bharata, who will perform it on stage with *apsaras*-actresses. So precious is the text that Kuśa, Lava's twin, has been sent, armed with bow and arrow, to protect it from mishap on this journey. All this arouses intense interest on the part of Janaka, who also wants to know just how far the story goes. Lava can answer this question: it breaks off when Lakṣmaṇa has abandoned Sītā, about to give birth, in the wilderness. No sooner does he mention this tragic moment (the end of the text as known to him) than both Janaka and Kausalyā are, once again, swept away by violent feelings, as if they were witnessing, or re-experiencing, the actual events of Sītā's exile.

*Act V*: Meanwhile, a violent combat has developed: Lava, insulted by the challenge that Candraketu's soldiers have rudely announced—"This horse is the indomitable banner of Rāma, hero of all seven worlds" (4.27)—pits himself, alone and on foot, against the whole of Candraketu's army. After massacring most of the latter, including vast numbers of elephants and horses, the young child finds himself facing Candraketu himself. The two cousins, who do not, of course, know one another, feel a powerful but inexplicable attraction to each other, which they express in three stunning verses, sung together as a duet—as if both contain, within their hearts, this pre-existing text. They sing of love, and a mysterious connection (*nijo vā sambandhaḥ*), unconscious but rooted in the structure of reality (*vidhi-vaśāt*); their bodies are literally thrilling in the presence of one another; still, as warriors they are driven to battle, for the violent "taste" (*dāruṇa-rasa*) of heroism overrules affection (5.16, 18–19). Sumantra, Candraketu's driver and counsellor (*sūta*), sees what is happening and sings of love, that "thread of feeling that weaves together the innermost, hidden parts" (*sa hi snehâtmakas tantur antar-marmāṇi sīvyati*, 5.17). Despite their hesitation, the two young heroes rouse themselves to battle; Lava is still seething from the initial insult, and when Candraketu tells him that what is at stake is Rāma's extraordinary prowess, which is in a class of its own, Lava responds with mockery: "Do you think there is anyone who does not know Rāma's story? I could, if I wanted to, say something more about it . . . . But perhaps it is best not to investigate too deeply the deeds of old men. After all, we all know about how he killed a woman [Tāṭakā], and about the three steps he retreated when faced with Khara, and about that splendid feat of destroying Vālin . . . ." (5.35).[9] Once again, the story of the Ramayana surges up from within the text, which is somehow meant to complete it; and in this case what emerges is the all-too-familiar and embarrassing series of Rāma's less-than-heroic moments, rather brutally enunciated by Rāma's own son. This passage alone would place Bhavabhūti firmly in the tradition of "questioning Ramayanas"—though it would, perhaps, be closer to the mark to say that the Ramayana tradition in itself is nearly always, by definition, self-questioning. In any case, Lava and Candraketu are now set on a collision course.

*Act VI.* Their ferocious battle is described in richly onomatopoeic language as seen from the air: a flying Vidyādhara couple watches the two evenly-matched cousins hurl missiles at one another in a close approximation to Doomsday. At this point Rāma himself—still, as we know, in the forest, on his way back from Pañcavaṭī—arrives and intervenes; both boys desist out of deference to this authoritative presence. This means that Lava has to call back the divine weapons he has been using, with remarkable success; Rāma, watching him do so, is surprised: he himself received these same weapons, with their associated mantras, from Viśvāmitra; how did they come into the possession of this young boy? He asks Lava about this, and the boy says that the weapons spontaneously revealed themselves to him and his twin brother, Kuśa. At this very moment, Kuśa arrives (returned from his mission guarding Vālmīki's text on its way to production by Bharata); Lava introduces him to Rāma, the hero of the story both boys know so well, and tells him to behave himself in Rāma's presence. As Rāma embraces Kuśa, he feels a mysterious sense of kinship and joy—as if his consciousness (*cetana-dhātu*) had somehow emerged from his body and taken shape outside him, in the body of this twelve-year-old child.

But Rāma also notices that the boys look remarkably like Sītā. Those blue eyes (mixed with red, a touch of heroic volatility), those lips—it is almost as if he were seeing her again, in the flesh. By now Rāma is beginning to suspect the truth. The boys are right here, in the same part of the forest where Sītā was abandoned; there is the stunning physical resemblance; they have control of the divine weapons with which, he suddenly remembers, he blessed Sītā's still unborn children (while viewing the paintings in Act I)—and these weapons have never served anyone except those who received them through the direct line of transmission in which he, Rāma, is the final link. He also remembers, suddenly, that he was the first to notice that Sītā was pregnant with twins (he describes this almost forgotten discovery in a tender verse of exceptional lyricism, 6.28). So he probes a little further, asking the boys to recite a verse or two from this book everyone is talking about, the *Rāmāyaṇa*, Vālmīki's history of the Dynasty of the Sun. They do so, to overwhelming effect: Rāma is paralyzed, adrift in feeling, reliving within himself the truth captured in the verses they have sung; visualizing Sītā in his mind, he dreads, above all, the terrible moment when this text-induced hallucination will be dispelled, when the world will, again, become a desert. His heart is burning, "cooked," as it were, in a slow fire of dry husks. Suddenly Vālmīki, Vasiṣṭha and Arundhatī, Janaka, and the queen-mothers are upon him, curious at the news of the battle that has just taken place, and shocked at the sight of Rāma—after twelve years of absence—in his pale and forlorn state. For his part, he can barely face them; he wonders why he does not explode into a thousand fragments under the pressure of his horrendous guilt; somehow he pulls himself together, for, as he says bitterly, "there seems to be nothing that Rāma is incapable of doing" (*athavā rāmeṇa kiṃ duṣkaram*).

*Act VII:* A play is about to be performed on the banks of the Ganga—Vālmīki's composition, enacted by celestial dancers; the whole world has been invited to this drama. Lakṣmaṇa has seen to the seating arrangements; he now takes his place beside Rāma. The stage manager (*sūtradhāra*) begins: Let the audience pay heed to this work, richly flavored by compassion (*karuṇâdbhutarasam*), which Vālmīki has composed through his divine insight. In the audience, Rāma whispers to Lakṣmaṇa: "It is true, great sages can make reality visible."

A voice announces from behind the curtain that Sītā, about to give birth, has, in despair, cast herself into the river. Rāma cries out from his seat: "My love, stay a moment!"[10] Lakṣmaṇa rebukes, or reassures, him: "It is only a play." Rāma replies: "I am entering a dark place, with no foothold or support." Now Sītā appears on stage, supported by her mother, the goddess Earth, and the Ganga, who tell her that she has given birth to twins within the river. This is the first news that Rāma (in the audience!) has of the birth of his sons, and he begins to weep. The goddesses comfort Sītā, who wants only to die; she can no longer bear the vicissitudes of life in this world (*na sakkamhi īdisaṃ jīa-loa-parivattaṃ aṇubhavidum*); she begs her mother to reabsorb her, finally, melting her body into earth. Earth has some angry words to say about her son-in-law, the "noble" Rāma, as she sarcastically calls him, who gave no weight to anything or anyone—the hand he had taken in marriage, the Earth, his father-in-law Janaka, Sītā's goodness and perseverance, the future of his line—when he rejected Sītā. From his seat, Rāma fully agrees with this judgment: "Such, indeed, am I" (*īdṛsó'smi*). Ganga, however, defends him: What was he to do, given the Ikṣvākus' commitment to keep the entire world content? But there is also a practical problem: What of the new-born twins? Who will teach them the Kṣatriya lore? Ganga puts Sītā's mind at rest: as soon as the boys are weaned, she will hand them over to Vālmīki. Meanwhile, part of the problem is already solved, for the divine weapons—which Rāma inherited from Viśvāmitra, and which he had directed to Sītā's children by a blessing during the tour of the painted pavilion in Act I—suddenly appear and offer themselves to Kuśa and Lava.

All this floods Rāma with waves of feeling (*karuṇôrmayaḥ*), which include amazement (*vismaya*) and joy (*ānanda*)—altogether some strange, miraculous state (*kām api dáśām*, 12).[11] But at this point Sītā again asks her mother to enfold her, forever, in her depths. As she disappears from the stage, Rāma faints: "You are gone forever, lost in another world!" Lakṣmaṇa, alarmed, cries out to Vālmīki for help: "So this is the point of your poem!" (*eṣa te kāvyârthaḥ*). Rāma has stopped breathing. And suddenly another voice announces, from behind the curtain: "Clear the orchestra. Vālmīki has produced something surpassingly strange." Now Sītā herself is there, with the same two goddesses beside her. She touches Rāma—as she did, hidden and invisible, in the forest scene—and now, as then, he revives. He opens his eyes and sees her, Arundhatī, and the queen mothers. As he gropes for consciousness, both the Ganga and the Earth remind him of the blessings he spoke while viewing the paintings, committing Sītā to their care; they are now free of this debt. He is amazed that, despite his terrible guilt, they have shown him compassion. And, as husband and wife are reunited, and united for the first time with their two sons (formally introduced to their parents by Vālmīki, poet and magician), Rāma literally comes out of the text to conclude the drama with a blessing:

> This story purifies from evil and enhances all that is good,
> like the Earth—mother of the world—
> and Gaṅgā, who charms the mind.
> Connoisseurs may ponder it, for, as enacted,
> it embodies the voice of the poet
> who has ripened into wisdom,
> tying truth to words.

Such is the conclusion to Rama's story, the "ultimate tale"—*Uttara-rāma-carita*—about this hero, so tragically torn between love and a totalitarian notion of duty, or responsibility, or whatever else might fit into the elastic but binding notion of a king's *dharma*. Bhavabhūti has completely transformed the story as we find it in the *Uttara-kāṇḍa* of Vālmīki's *Rāmāyaṇa*: there the final moment of re-encounter between Rāma and Sītā ends with an irreversible, bitter separation of the lovers, as Sītā is swallowed up by her mother, the Earth. Rāma survives for another 60,000 years, ruling the earth in a state of unbearable loneliness and grief, with only the golden statue of Sītā to comfort him. Bhavabhūti's text contains other innovations, as well—for example, the theme of Sītā's attempted suicide in the river, nowhere hinted at by Vālmīki; the temporal sequencing of the *Uttara-kāṇḍa* has also been altered (the Śambūka episode, Rāma's revisit to Pañcavaṭī, the *aśvamedha* battle—all now deftly interrelated). But these details, like the question of Bhavabhuti's "sources,"[12] matter much less than the nature of the aesthetic transformation achieved by the poet: it is this issue that will primarily occupy us here. I may remark, in passing, that I do not share the common thesis that would remove the *Uttara-kāṇḍa*, or its essential narrative elements, from the allegedly earlier core of the epic (a core in which Rāma would be "merely" human, not yet an avatar of the god). As I have argued elsewhere,[13] the problem of Rāma's composite identity, with the related themes of inner conflict and epistemic wavering, is central to the whole of Vālmīki's text; and these themes continue to be worked through in the *Uttara-kāṇḍa* as integral parts of the heroes' evolving presence and personal fate.

Another major element should be taken into account as we begin our exploration of this text. The *Uttara-rāma-carita*, like Bhavabhūti's other two dramas, was, as the prologue informs us, performed at the festival (*yātrā*) of Śiva in his guise as Kāla-priyā-nātha (or Kāla-priya-nātha),[14] "Husband to the Bride of Time [or Death]," i.e. husband to his wife, Pārvatī—since Kāla is Śiva himself. Leaving aside the suggestive name for the god, and the tantalizing question of the location of his shrine,[15] we need to bear this performance context in mind as we read through the play. Many Sanskrit dramas are explicitly linked to ritual settings, and such contexts always need to be imagined in relation to the verbal text which is, after all, only a kind of "score." Whatever happens to Rāma and to Sītā, or to the audience watching their story, is part of a wider ritual scenario, now lost beyond reconstruction, though not without leaving behind traces relevant to our analysis.

## The Structure of Embedding

We have no record of the original ritual context; we know nothing of the specific progression of the *yātrā* to Kāla-priyā-nātha, or of its meanings for the spectator-participants; yet there is reason to believe that this context moulded the dramatic work in critical ways. For example, we may wish to think of Śiva in his temple as the first listener to our text.[16] In other respects, we may need to extrapolate from what we know of other, still living ritualized performances in India. One way to approach an understanding of the determining forces at work in the ritual frame specific to this text is to examine the resonance, or replication, of structure, texture, and theme. These levels, once defined, turn out to be mutually reinforcing to an astonishing degree.

Look, first, at a single micro-unit, particularly revealing in terms of structure. We are at the subtle moment of semi-recognition in

Act VI, where Rāma is facing his two sons. He does not yet know, for certain, who they are (or, for that matter, who he is). But he is deeply moved, and also full of despair: "Life," he says, "always ends up in some terrible, illogical inversion, and in separation." This is followed by another of his attempts to formulate the experience of love, in a way that echoes, somewhat eerily, the earlier definition:

Where is it,
that immense happiness, rooted in perfect trust?
Where is the mutuality of loving, the profound
curiosity about one another, the unity of hearts
in joy as in sorrow? Where has it gone
while I go on breathing? (6.33)

Love has fled, leaving him only technically alive. But this unhappy awareness has been triggered by an encounter with the text of Rāma's story, existing in some seemingly objectified form. Rāma has asked Kuśa to recite some small portion of this text:

RAMA: Everyone keeps talking about this *Rāmāyaṇa* book by Vālmīki, that tells the genealogy of the royal dynasty of the Sun. I am really curious to hear some piece of that work.

So the boy, who does not know that he is singing to his own father about that father's own story, brings up two rather pointed verses on love, that somehow spring to his mind (*smṛti-pratyupasthitau*), from the end of what he calls the *Bāla-carita* [= *Bāla-kāṇḍa*]:

Rāma loved Sītā—just like that,
naturally, without cause,
but she nourished that love
by all that was hers.

And just like that, Sītā loved Rāma,
more than life itself.
Only the heart knows the bond
that joins two lovers to each other. [6.31–2]

These verses pierce Rāma to the heart, galvanizing memory in the conscious mind. He tells us this, in a variation on a phrase that is repeated almost incessantly in this play: the words "wound the innermost recesses of the heart" (*hṛdaya-marmôdghātāḥ*). As the verses themselves suggest, and the hero now confirms, love is a matter of some deep and hidden innerness. Notice the sense of a potential veil within the mind, dividing active from latent memory—and the hurt that comes from penetrating the veil.

Somehow all of this is densely interwoven with the state that is named "desire" (*madana*, 6.35). Memory clearly plays a role: in a sense, this play is all about the composition, modes, and dynamic processes of memory, as a component of loving, seen in relation to temporal states that are not necessarily linear or sequential. In fact, the very notion of linear progression is frequently challenged in surprising ways as the play proceeds. In this respect, the *Uttara-rāma-carita* is situated firmly within the Ramayana tradition, where the "story," or the text that embodies it, always has an autonomous quality superseding any external reality;[17] at critical points, the overt reality of the narrative tends to fuse mysteriously into its own frame, which thereby swallows up sequential notions of time. We can see this defining feature of the tradition at work even in the small passage we have been following: Rāma hears, or overhears, his own story, which brings to the fore a partly forgotten fragment of his own experience as embedded in a text both internal to, but also encompassing and framing, the reality he inhabits; inside the play, he recalls the existence of a Ramayana and asks to hear a piece of it, almost as if he were recalling the existence of a person named Rāma, whom he has, amazingly, forgotten. Seemingly framed by a more external level—that is, by Bhavabhūti's play, where he is both actor and spectator—he actually embeds himself within the embedded inset of his own story, where once again he will appear as both actor and spectator, embedding himself still deeper . . . . and so on until infinity. The Ramayana frame evokes the Russellian paradox of the set that is a member of itself.

It is thus no wonder that Bhavabhūti's text will end with a play-within-a-play, in which the boundary between play and some external reality, or between play-time and present time, will ultimately vanish. The great English psychoanalyst Donald Winnicott once claimed that Hamlet's true misfortune was that he could not go to watch *Hamlet*: "Shakespeare had the clue [to Hamlet's distress], but Hamlet could not go to Shakespeare's play."[18] Rāma, by way of contrast, must always, or ever again, watch himself be re-enacted in one form or another of the Ramayana.

## Coinciding with Self

Already we can abstract two central structural features of this play: a tendency toward non-concentric, asymmetrical embeddedment, with unsettling transitions between levels (the frame merged in with what it purports to frame); and an astonishing drive towards repetition, as elements of the text consistently echo or reflect or engage one another, or even repeat themselves verbatim.[19] These two processes are themselves intertwined—since pointed repetitions often enact the embeddedment and the dizzying interconnection of levels. For example, in Act III Rāma comes to a rocky slab on which, long ago, he would lie with Sītā; the forest fawns always haunted this spot, where she used to feed them (3.21). In Act VI, in the passage we have discussed (6.36), Lava, as if by chance, recalls a *śloka* from the *Rāmāyaṇa* about just such a stone slab (this one on the banks of the Mandākinī), where the lovers lay together.[20] The young boy is, perhaps, innocent of the erotic atmosphere attached to this "object;"[21] but for us, eavesdroppers on the play, there is a strong and immediate resonance with the earlier mention in Act III. Of course, the stone of Act III is itself embedded in Rāma's memory of another time, and only as such brought forward into the outer action of the present moment. But it then turns up again, as it were, in a poetic fragment supposedly extracted from the master-text of the Ramayana, the all-encompassing frame submerged and then rediscovered from within the action of this scene. In this manner, various fragments of the story—often unconscious memory-pieces or half-known, half-recalled experiences—keep floating up to center stage, as the drama unrolls itself like a convoluted scroll.

It is also striking that the particular instance just cited comes at the moment when father and sons are beginning to recognize one another for the first time. Such encounters in the embedded-repetitive mode occur regularly. One might generalize from this pattern a wider statement about personal recognition (*pratyabhijñāna*, a term no less crucial for Bhavabhūti than for Kālidāsa):[22] to identify or to know another (intimately related) person is to experience that person through the multiple embedded, and recurring, fragments of his or her presence, including those fragments embedded in the mind or memory of the experiencing subject. But these fragments have to be loosened or activated in a certain way, as we shall see.

The problem of recognition goes still deeper in our play, to the point where it begins to seem like the central axis of the heroes' consciousness, as a subtle and powerful example from Act III makes clear. Rāma is hallucinating; he thinks he sees Sītā everywhere, though she continues to elude him; still, he *knows* she is near; his agony is cruelly intensified by the forest-goddess Vāsantī, who keeps pointing out the signposts and traces of the joyful period in Pañcavaṭī, now alive only in memory. There is a fire burning inside him, and outside everything is scorched and desolate:

My heart is cracking, my body will soon
fall apart. The whole world
is a wilderness, and inside I burn
without cease. The deepest part
of me is sinking, blind,
in darkness. Vision veiled,
I know despair, and know not
what to do. (3.38)

Soon he cannot breathe, until the invisible Sītā touches him with her hand, which brings both inner and outer domains back to life. Now he is sure she is there beside him, as he asserts to the doubting Vāsantī: "Can't you see, she is right in front of us?" "These are the ravings (*pralāpa*) of a madman," says Vāsantī, pouting, but Rāma indignantly mocks her and begins a verse, which is interrupted in the middle by Sītā:

RĀMA: Ravings? What ravings?

Held, long ago,
covered with bangles,
at the wedding, and always
cool as flooding moonlight—

SĪTĀ: My love, now you are, at last, yourself (*so jevva dāṇiṃ si tumam*).

RĀMA:
or gleaming snow,
slight as the Lavalī vine,
your hand is now, again,
in mine.

He grasps it, alarming Sītā. He, too, is completely out of control (*paravān*) with mixed delight and panic (*ānanda, sādhvasa*)—so much so that he asks Vāsantī to hold "her," the transparent Sītā, for a moment. Now Vāsantī is certain that Rāma is truly insane (*kaṣṭam unmāda eva*)—and Sītā, in a flurry, withdraws her hand, thereby at once generating an even more serious attack of despair in her forlorn husband, who sings a pointed and poignant verse about the tragedy of one hand slipping out of another (41). In a striking reversal of the overt reality of his own story, he even pleads with his lost wife not to abandon him; she sadly notes this ironic inversion (*vipratīpam*), one of a series of strange twists and shifts which seem to be endemic to consciousness in Bhavabhūti's world.

Indeed, the unveiling of this inner structure of ironic reversal in thought and feeling proves integral to the poet's art. Once again, we find repetition: for the bifurcated verse about Sītā's hand closely echoes an earlier verse, from Act I, spoken by Rāma to Sītā in front of a painting of their wedding:

> That moment is happening again,
> when your hand, with ringing bangles,
> festive, fully alive,
> was placed by Gautama,
> the priest, in mine. (1.18)

Past wholly merges into present, as it does, in a sense, in the forest scene, when Sītā truly touches her lover in the same external setting as before—though he cannot see her. At the moment of contact, in the very middle of a verse whose grammatical subject has not yet even been mentioned, she interrupts to tell him (in a whisper he cannot hear) that he is now, once again, himself. Perhaps the mere fact that he has broken into poetry of a complex, elevated character and staggered syntax (and in the richly emotional *śikhariṇī* meter) is reassuring to Sītā, who takes it as a sign that a more familiar presence is re-emerging; in her relief and joy, she cuts into the still unfinished, still incomprehensible poem.

Bhavabhūti has a certain penchant for such divided verses, which always reflect some inner dynamic (as, for example, when one character begins a verse and stops, and another then concludes it):[23] it is as if the open space flowing out of the hidden center of the verse creates something new and unexpected, which then molds its conclusion in a fresh pattern. This same rich transitional space at the center produces Sītā's paradoxical statement of Rāma's self-coincidence at this point, rather as if until this moment, in her eyes at least, he was not fully himself, or somehow out of focus.[24] The cooling, healing touch, a reassertion of connection across an empty gap, brings this subject into a transient state of full self-possession. He will soon lose this sensation once again, under the force of renewed loss and separation, so that, toward the end of this act, Sītā will need to repeat her statement: Rāma tells Vāsantī he wants to go back to the ritual performance of the *aśvamedha*, for which he has, after all, produced a substitute-wife; Sītā, alarmed, wonders aloud who this might be, Rāma completes his sentence—he is referring to the golden image of Sītā that he has commissioned, and that he now wishes to see again, in lieu of the lost, living woman. Relieved, in tears, Sītā says (again): "My lord, you are now truly yourself" (*ajjautta dāṇīṃ si tumam*). She also tells us that the barb of shame, tormenting her heart ever since her banishment, has been removed.

In this process of recognition, Rāma sees through the veil, mysteriously reconnecting him to his hidden wife; Sītā finds, again, the genuine goodness and faithfulness of her husband, as if watching a blurred photograph slowly emerging into focus. She also seems to find herself, or some part of herself, in the process, for as she now praises this same golden image "which offers hope for continued existence (*āsā-ṇibandhaṇaṃ jādā jīa-loassa*)," she is—as her companion Tamasā immediately notes—in fact praising herself (*ayi vatse evam ātmā stūyate*). None of this could happen without the recurrent structures of repetition—always, in fact, a kind of re-experiencing in present time of a pre-existing paradigm of feeling or cognition. Bhavabhūti's language itself iconically reproduces this pattern: the *Uttara-rāma-carita* abounds in what Sanskrit grammarians call *āmreḍita*, the literal repetition of a word to express either a continuous and permanent state, or the quality of pervasiveness (*nitya-vīpsayoḥ*, Pāṇini 8.1.4).[25] Language repeats, feeling repeats, touch re-touches and reconnects, the mind recognizes its remembered realities, and re-enacts them; within these parallel processes and homologous levels, one can also see the persistent workings of an entropic blurring or forgetting, a falling away from self or self-possession and, at moments, a sharp break or twist that reverses entropy and creates the condition for what might be seen as "healing."

Before we attempt to examine this process analytically, we need to look again at the theme of self in relation to memory, as it crystallizes in Act III. This time Sītā states the theme with eloquent pathos. Here, in Pañcavaṭī, with Rāma in front of her eyes, memories flood her heart; but she feels as if something is dreadfully unreal in these circumstances:

SĪTĀ: This is my husband; I am in the Pañcavaṭī forest; here is Vāsantī, my same old friend; I am seeing the same wooded banks of the Godāvarī, that witnessed so many intimate moments; the animals and birds and trees are no different than they were, just like my own children; and here am I, the very same me. And yet, though I can see it all plainly, it is as if none of it really exists for me any more. The world has been transformed.

The term she chooses for transformation—*pariṇāma*,[26] a kind of "ripening" or "cooking"—might characterize the entire ritual-dramatic process. What is it that drives a person, in particular a suffering person, to insist that "I am (still) me"? Clearly, there is a sense of a latent and unending fluidity of experience, that alters the world, and perhaps the self, even as one experiences life anew through familiar patterns; a painful gap thus opens up between the remembered self/world and its re-encountered contours.

But Sītā's words go still deeper, resuming one of the classic problems in Indian religion and resonating with an ancient formula. In *Brāhmaṇa* sacrificial rituals such as the *darśa-pūrṇa-māsa* offering (the new and full moon sacrifices), the ritual subject undertakes a vow (*vrata*) which entails a far-reaching existential transformation; in effect, he moves from a human identity to a divine one (complete with a divine body, *daivâtman*, created through the performance). Another way to describe the process is to think of an ascent to the world of the gods, followed by descent and re-entry into human life. In any case, a delicate boundary must be crossed, and much attention is given to the transition *out of* the heightened ritual mode. How does one release oneself (*vi-sṛjate*) from the transformed state achieved through the ritual? There is a formula to be uttered: *idam aham ya evâsmi so 'smi*, "I am just who I am."[27] There is something deeply paradoxical about this statement, which resembles Epimenides' paradox ("All Cretans are liars, and I am a Cretan");[28] for the formula is meant to substitute for a statement to the effect that "I," the ritualist, have now returned from the dimension of truth (*satya*) to a dimension of untruth (*anṛta*). To state the latter fact baldly is felt to be inappropriate;[29] one therefore makes the above identity statement, but from within a world ruled by untruth, in which every utterance must, apparently, be untrue. "I am just who I am" must also, therefore, be untrue.

I would like, again, to insist on the ritual frame within which Bhavabhūti composed his play. We might also consider that the *Brāhmaṇa* problematic just outlined is at the heart of the entire Ramayana literature (perhaps of *kāvya* generally, exemplified by this "first *kāvya*"): Rāma is, after all, a god who has made the transition to being human, and who has, in the course of this transition, *forgotten* his divine identity.[30] The root problem that our text, like so many Ramayana texts, sets out to address, or even to solve, is precisely this awareness of the gap embedded within the experience of self in time (or of language in time, which amounts to much the same thing)—the gap that makes Sītā claim that the familiar Pañcavaṭī world does not really exist for her, and that makes Rāma habitually amnesiac. Longing, and perhaps a certain empathic imagination or compassion—*karuṇā*, another term central to our text—inhabit this space, where memory also comes into play. We could also argue that this gap gives rise to the problem of loving, which seems, in the context of this drama, to encompass a dimension of cruelty, inner conflict, and a loss of focus, or of presence, on the part of the loving subjects. Why, after all, has Rāma acted as he has, in a manner that engenders such massive guilt—more, perhaps, than in any other consciousness within the whole of Sanskrit literature? And what is the truth—emotional, epistemic, existential—working itself outward toward concrete expression through this volatile mixture of sensations, in which the identity of the suffering subject is continually slipping away from awareness?

## Remembering the Present: On *Karuṇā*

There is a deep music in Bhavabhūti's text, perhaps a richer and more evocative musicality than in any other Sanskrit poet, some of it highly structured, like the internal processes undergone by the protagonists, in lucid and repeated patterns. We might isolate a "fugue" comprised of the haunting alternation of *śikhariṇī* and *mālinī* meters;[31] the fugue creates an eery familiarity and an insistent rhythm of discovery, or, perhaps, recovery (in more senses than one)[32]—a recognition, inexorably fulfilling itself, for example, in Rāma's slow identification of his sons and the subsequent recovery of Sītā from within the play-within-the-play.[33] This gentle and moving rhythm is itself a form of memory; and memory (*smṛti*), in relation to love, is, as I have said, the mainspring of the dramatic action.

Throughout the play—beginning in the first lines of dialogue after the Stage-manager's prologue—we keep hearing the anxiety of forgetting, just as we witness the tensions implicit in remembering. "Does he [Ṛṣyaśṛṅga] still remember us?" Sītā asks at the outset. "Do you, my love, remember those places?"—this is Sītā again, to Rāma, as they study the paintings of their life in the forest. Rāma throws the question back at her, this time repeating the verb *smarasi*—"Do you remember?'—three times in four lines:

Do you remember, my dear,
how Lakṣmaṇa cared for us
all those days on the mountain,
and how happy we were?
Do you remember the pure taste
of Godāvarī water?
Do you remember how we played there
on its shores? (1.26)[34]

The danger of forgetting always hovers over these characters; to counteract it, they resort to a remarkable range of experiential and literary/artistic devices—the paintings in the royal pavilion, the text composed by Vālmīki and memorized by Kuśa and Lava, the return-visits to Pañcavaṭī, the mirror-like physiognomies of the two boys, the play-within-a-play. All of these modes trigger some sort of memory, usually painful and burdened with longing. In most of them there is a directionality that may seem surprising, given the rhetoric of retrospection that fills the surface level of their statements. In general, the movement is toward a present or future moment, in which the remembered experience is relived or, even more surprisingly, anticipated.

In a way, it begins with the stage director (*sūtradhāra*), who first tells of being translated to another time unfolding in present-future: "I have become a citizen of Ayodhyā, from *that* time," he tells us, setting the stage for the play that is about to appear.[35] Then as Sītā gazes at the paintings, she confesses: "I seem to be in that very place, and in that time" (*ammo jāṇāmi tassiṃ jevva padese tassiṃ jevva kāle vattāmi*). Then Rāma repeats the thought: "All the events of Janasthāna seem to be taking place in the present moment" (*hanta vartamāna iva janasthāna-vṛttântaḥ pratibhāti*). So vivid is this feeling that, as we have seen, Rāma interrupts Lakṣmaṇa's verse, describing the period on Mount Mālyavant, in the middle:

"Stop, stop, I can bear no more.
The whole loss is happening to me again!" (1.33)

So memory, for the characters in this play—and what of its spectators?—happens now, making present, in the present moment, some previously experienced state or event, perhaps blocked or veiled by normal consciousness. Something—the play, the painting, the story—tears away the veil, and the effect is overwhelming. Memory of this type is not "about" absence or loss; if anything, it is about an overriding presence. Neither a question of recollection, nor a narrativized abstraction, it involves the actual reliving of an emotional reality, though sometimes with a jarring note of temporal or cognitive disparity.[36] Often, however, the entire experience unfolds again, as if an embedded capsule, patterned along condensed, paradigmatic lines, were detonated within the mind.

Very similar to this mode is proleptic memory, oriented toward future events that are already, it seems, known to the subject. Sītā, weary, troubled by the paintings of her history, says to her husband: "I would like to bathe again in the limpid waters of the Ganges and delight in the profound and peaceful landscapes of the forest." She uses the simple future: *viharissam*, *ogāhissam*, "I *will* delight, I *will* bathe . . . . " The idiomatic expression of the wish proves ironic, for Sītā is about to be cruelly exiled to those landscapes; she seems somehow to know this, unconsciously, in advance, just as the doorkeeper in the palace unconsciously announces the onset of separation while Sītā still lies sleeping in Rāma's lap, and just as Rāma himself seems to sense, in advance, something of the tragedy that is in store. There is good reason to think of this knowledge as a kind of remembering, exotic as the idea may seem to us, for such memories of the future are, in fact, one of the forms that memory takes in the epistemic universe of ancient India.[37] And although this type is not predominant in Bhavabhūti's play, it is of a piece with the notion of the unpublished part of the text—actually, the ending of the Rāma story—that Vālmīki has already composed and sent ahead to be performed in the presence of the very characters whose story it portrays. The story, in other words, could be said to exist before its characters, as latent potential, slowly externalizing itself through their consciousness and their deeds. In this sense it can also be remembered in advance.

It is this same sort of knowing that activates the recognition scenes, especially Act VI, when Rāma feels the unexpected rush of love for the sons he does not fully, or consciously, know as his. Here memory appears not as a cognitive act proper, in which both knowledge and the knowledge of knowing tend to be intimately combined,[38] but as a more opaque and sometimes doubt-ridden intuiting of a felt presence. Thus Sītā, in a flurry of mixed sensations in the Pañcavaṭī forest, at once angry at the grief-stricken Rāma and ready to forgive him for everything, terrified both of revealing herself to him and of letting him go, can still proudly assert to her friend Tamasā: "I know his heart, and he knows mine" (*aham edassa hiaam jāṇāmi mamāvi eso*, after 3.12). This deep innerness, utterly without reason or cause, is what Bhavabhūti identifies as love, extending his earlier definition ("when two become one") in the direction of a mutuality of knowing of this kind. It can be more closely characterized:

> This is a major part of being alive, this liquid love that someone suddenly has for someone else. People may speak of "love at first sight," or of a match that was "in the stars," but what they mean is that loving feeling that cannot be quantified or explained,
>
> that has neither reason nor remedy,
> this thread of feeling that weaves together
> the innermost, hidden parts. (5.17)

So speaks Sumantra, the charioteer, in Act V, referring to the suddenly apparent affection of the two cousins, Lava and Candraketu. We should notice the motif of weaving or sewing together the inner parts (*marmāṇi*); it is precisely these vulnerable inner parts that are constantly being cut, punctured, wounded, poisoned, or burnt, throughout the whole drama, as the characters repeatedly complain. Memory of the type we are exploring, active in the present or future, encompassing the liquid sensation of love and what we have called "recognition," has this healing power to reconnect the severed or discontinuous flux of inner feeling.

Certain other features are dependably linked with this experience. Sītā, in the passage just quoted, prefaces her statement about the knowledge of the heart with a self-reproach: she is, she says, hard as diamond (*vajra-mayī*), and without compassion (*nir-anukrośā*). This solid-state, rocky and blocked, melts when she sees, or, rather, empathically imagines, her husband. Sītā's riverine friend eloquently formulates this complex process at this same juncture:

TAMASĀ: I know, I know, my friend.

Numb with despair, yet still aching,
stirred by this sudden meeting
within an endless separation,
naturally lucid and kind, but feeling deeply
the sorrow your lover must feel,
this heart of yours, in a second,
has turned to water in your love. (3.13.)

This is, again, the mournful *śikhariṇī* meter, iconically melting down the listener—like broken-hearted Sītā—with its innate pathos. Hurt, sad, numb, Sītā is still, above all, capable of empathic imagination and a shared universe of feeling: the verse, moving toward a crescendo in the third line, uses the loaded term *karuṇā* (more often translated as "compassion" or "pity") for this notion.[39] As a considerable secondary literature on Bhavabhūti rightly insists, *karuṇā* provides the leitmotif of this play. This verse makes at least one of its components very clear—because of *karuṇā*, triggered at the sight of Rāma, and mixed with other emotions, Sītā's heart is now fluid, "turned to water" (*dravī-bhūtam*), freed, it seems, from the encrusted, adamantine state she earlier describes.

"Even a stone would weep," says Lakṣmaṇa, remembering Rāma's travails in the wilderness as vividly portrayed in the palace paintings (1.28). Throughout this play, as in so many Indian texts (especially from the deep south), we find a preference, even a powerful yearning, for states of melting, flowing, flooding, heating, softening, depetrifying, weeping, bathing, soaking through a frozen or calcified surface. "What a gift it is," says Tamasā, referring to Rāma, "to be able to cry!" (*nanu lābho hi ruditam*).[40] The real danger lies in the drift, within consciousness, toward rockiness, or, more abstractly, toward various forms of self-objectification and externalization—for "melting" always, in these texts, implies a movement inwards or from within.[41] Such are the preconditions for *karuṇā*, the underlying, internal state of fluid empathy.

This state is also closely linked with images of "ripening" or "cooking." In a striking verse at the opening of Act III, Rāma's own potential for *karuṇā* is likened to a process of preparing medicines through prolonged "cooking":

Too profound to be revealed,
unbroken, dense with suffering,
and deeply hidden,
Rāma's capacity for compassion
is like a compress of healing herbs
cooked in a clay oven. (3.1)[42]

The clay oven appears in medical texts of *Āyurveda*; *puṭa-pāka* is "a particular method of preparing drugs, in which the various ingredients are put in a vessel covered with a plaster of clay or wrapped up in the leaves of some tree which are then covered with a plaster of clay and the whole is then roasted in fire."[43] So this ability to flow with compassionate feeling, or with empathy, must mature within a person through the painful and fiery stages of suffering; the physical body serves as the oven, containing and cooking the compacted emotional, non-solidified stuff of selfhood; the healing end-product is deep, continuous, unbroken, unblocked, and unimaginably dense.

It must also be, in a profound sense, unitary and whole, as Bhavabhūti tells us in a much-quoted verse:

The flow of compassion is always one,
though it seems, for many reasons,
to break into distinct and separate
formations, just as whirlpools,
waves, and bubbles are, in the end,
all water. (3.47)

A whole literature of modern commentaries sees a kind of aesthetic theology in this statement about *karuṇā-rasa*, the "taste" or "flavor" of compassion, supposedly transcending or completing the series of other *rasas*;[44] but it would perhaps be closer to Bhavabhūti's vision to think of a ripening faculty of empathy which is the necessary substratum for all other forms of emotional or aesthetic experience, and for understanding other people, including those closest and most loved.

We began this section by speaking of memory, which led us to "recognition" and, then, to "empathy;" all three concepts are bound together by the imagery of flow and maturation and tied to the soft internal organs referred to as *marmāṇi*, the secret and vulnerable parts of our being, susceptible to all kinds of verbal, cognitive, and emotional assaults. These images are differentiated and complex;

"ripening," in particular, can also mean, for Bhavabhūti, the slow poisoning of the inner subject by suppressed, unhealed forms of grief. Rāma speaks in the first act of a fiery sorrow "cooking in the mind" (*manasi punar vipacyamānaḥ*, 1.30)—referring to the kidnapping of Sītā—long after the occasion of its first appearance, when it could, more or less, be endured because of the need to act and the hope of revenge. Bhavabhūti uses the analogous image of a wound or sore still festering inside the hardened scar-tissue that has grown up around it (2.26; 1.30). This is, perhaps, the difference between what is called "bad ripening/cooking" (*dur-vipāka*, often *daiva-dur-vipāka*, the unhappy ripening of divine fate)[45] and the often positive notion of ripening generally (*vipāka, vipakti*).[46] Such "cooking" includes a divine aspect as well, a structured process of maturation through suffering that is located deep inside the individual: as the goddess Gaṅgā asks in the play-within-the-play, "Who can close the doors to fate (*daivasya dvārāṇi*) for the creature who is beginning to ripen?" (*pākâbhimukhasya jantor*, 7.4). But rather than attempting a further mapping of these notions, we can sum up what we have learnt by examining one more verse. Here is Arundhatī explaining to Janaka why Kausalyā, Rāma's mother, is so distressed at meeting him again:

> That king—that happiness—
> that child—those days—
> it has all come back to her,
> visible in memory,
> on seeing you again.
> Things ripen and go wrong: no wonder
> your friend is in distress.
> Awareness, in a woman, is fragile
> as a flower. (4.12)

"Things ripen and go wrong"—sorrow has cooked Kausalyā, as it has nearly everyone else in this play, to the point where awareness is now soft, pliant, vulnerable to deep feeling. Memory allows this to happen; or, more precisely, memory here seems like a mirror, somewhere in the mind, in which objects and sensations are made present again, though not, or not primarily, through retrospection. The mirror discloses a state of feeling that exists now, or in the future, but one fashioned in the mould of an earlier, structured paradigm. Within this paradigm, gaps may emerge as a result of the ripening subject's internal evolution, or of the processes of displacement inherent in consciousness or in the world—as we can see from the rather unintegrated, dangling series with which this verse begins ("that king—that happiness—that child—those days . . . ."). The halting syntax enacts Arundhatī's rather conventional conclusion. At this juncture, very close to the spatial mid-point of our play, memory animates an unfocused, not wholly continuous subject very much in need of healing.

## Guilt, Dispersion, and the Meaning of Love

We can now turn to the moment of ultimate healing. Bhavabhūti is by no means the only Sanskrit poet to create a play-within-a-play (*garbhâṅka*),[47] but nowhere is the device more powerfully expressive of an entire semantic universe encompassing each of the major characters and moving them towards the full flowering of the seeds they carry in their minds. As so often, confusion about boundaries dominates the scene: Lakṣmaṇa has to remind Rāma, who is stricken at the dramatization of Sītā's fate, that he is "only" watching a play. The profound irony of this statement is almost immediately apparent. For in the end the "real" Sītā turns up on the stage and proceeds "really" to revive the unconscious Rāma. The embedded play becomes fully congruent with its external setting which, for want of a better word, we might call "reality." This moment clearly echoes another instance of congruence or, better, confluence, when the unfocused contours of Rāma's own "self" suddenly coincide, again under Sītā's benign touch, in the forest.

At such moments, apparently discontinuous and incongruent levels or domains come into alignment. Once again we are dealing with a classical restatement of a very ancient problem.[48] Imagine the world, including the emotional world of lovers and the psychic universe of the self, as inherently entropic, with a tendency to split and separate into disconnected realms and disparate experiences. Imagine dispersal of this sort to be constant, and to be translated constantly, experientially, into sensations of rocky encrustration, crystallization, blocking, and the fragmenting of presence. As we have already seen, the counter-movement requires melting, a restoration of flux, and the birth of that empathic imagination that we have been calling *karuṇā*. In formal terms, to reverse dispersion and disconnection is the real function of dynamic embeddedment, as Bhavabhūti so lucidly reveals to us. The play-within-a-play is an embedded piece of reality; and embedded in it are references to other, less deeply embedded levels—to the divine weapons, for example, that Rāma has seen and commanded at the time of the exhibition of paintings, explicitly mentioned in the text of the encapsulated play; and also to Vālmīki, the poet-author of the spectacle/story as a whole. Vālmīki has, moreover, composed this conclusion to the story, in advance of the events it describes, just as his *Rāmāyaṇa* pre dates the living out of the story by its characters, who may even quote his text at various points within the play. We could take this *Rāmāyaṇa* text to be the outermost frame of the (variously re-enacted) story, encompassing it, as a totality, from the start. But in Bhavabhūti's structure, this outermost frame is the most deeply embedded—hence, also, it seems, most deeply real. It is this frame that is quoted back to the principal hero himself, within the drama, and that has generated a conclusion to his story. It is this frame which shines through the play-within-the-play. And it is this same frame that enables the full, though perhaps transient, coalescence of ontic and existential levels, complete with full-hearted recognition of one another by the major *dramatis personae*, in the final act. Sītā walks out of the play to touch Rama with her living hand—this physical touch, *sparśa*, is always essential for Bhavabhūti, the true test of reality—and now, at last, the heroes are, in all senses, reconnected, with themselves, with each other, and with the story that is theirs. The contours of this tragic tale of guilty rejection and separation are, for once, perfectly aligned.

All this, as we are told several times, is the work of the poet, who knows the visionary truth that can be literally embodied—in bodies and in words. Indeed, the two categories seem to be alloforms, each enacting what the poet sees in his inner eye, each moving toward the goal of coalescence. And as it happens—as the frame and its embedded levels become one—the drama melts away, even as time disappears into a timeless present. Rāma—is he still anywhere within the text?—can now bless us, the audience, and all future connoisseurs, and the story that is his own purifying tale. At this final moment, clearly, the drama can, or must, end, since it no longer disposes of a frame; note that at this point, we, too, have merged with the audience internal to Act VII, as Bhavabhūti, the master-poet, seems to have been subsumed within the persona of the first poet, Vālmīki, and as Bhavabhūti's *Uttara-rāma-carita* has merged into Vālmīki's text of the same concluding section of the story. Rāma's blessing is thus, ultimately and fully, a matter of the present, certainly not of any conceivable or theoretical past. The healing memory (*smṛti*) which the characters keep seeking, in the midst of the constant anxiety about forgetting—the memory of a connected and present self in which all levels, all parts of the story, are combined and realigned—is accessible precisely at this moment of far-reaching fusion that abrogates all earlier, painful gaps. It is this state that *karuṇā*, the heart's compassion, the empathic knowing of another from within the self, has initiated, effected, and sustained.

There are earlier moments in this play when such a state of superimposition or coalescence is briefly attained: for example, at the end of Act III, when Vāsantī and Tamasā join, from their separate domains, in singing a verse of blessing that beautifully adumbrates Rāma's final verse. Similarly, the two cousins, Lava and Candraketu, sing, together, three verses on the mystery of love, as if guided by a consciousness alive in a single, unconsciously internalized text. The same process leads to those verses which one character begins and another continues, from across the empty but dynamic gap in the middle. In a system structured like this play, such flashes occur naturally from time to time, and eventually move towards more radical forms of realignment.

Let me restate the main systemic features that are at work: 1) a text, or story, that exists, as an embedded frame, *before* it is lived out or enacted; 2) a subject, who both is and is not himself, poised somewhere near the outer layers of the frame, watching himself within the more deeply embedded layers of this text; 3) internal movements of psyche, or of affective parts of the self, that loosen the calcified or petrified segments of experience, thereby dissolving linear sequence and retrospective time. There is a restless quality inevitable when the external frame is so deeply blended into its own text, to the point of becoming its most internal element: we can see this in the play-within-the-play, when the frame rises up through its encircling outer layers, binding them together rather as the ancient texts say the worlds are impaled—like leaves on a pin—on the single syllable Om.[49] Such a system, by no means limited to the Rāma literature, is nonetheless highly characteristic of it: somewhere Rāma is always watching himself play himself, or overhearing himself overhear his sons speaking of himself, telling him his own story; he is thus partly heteronomous, in that he depends upon yet another, outside listener, if self-knowledge is to occur; but these are patterns not primarily of splitting and displacement, as we might expect, but of far-reaching welding and melting in the mind. It is in this mode that Rāma also knows love, which now encompasses his own cruelty and its forgiveness.

Remember, now, that all this happens in a specific context of performance, the festival of Śiva as Kāla-priyā-nātha. It is within this ritual setting that these radical states of recognition and internal reconfiguration occur. Recall the *sūtradhāra*, in the opening words of the play, as he surveys the empty space before him: "I have become a citizen of Ayodhyā, from *that* time"—words marking entry into the heightened world of the ritual drama, where new identities will arise and grow. I have elsewhere spoken of tautological states, in which an assumed persona or identity—often a divine self—becomes isomorphic with the person enacting a given (ritual or dramatic) role.[50] For a moment, from out of an infinity of potential masks or faces, part-selves and multiple selves, a whole being is created, continuous with his or her inner world, which he or she temporarily subsumes. Such a moment is an achievement, perhaps possible only within the intense ritual modes of heated play, and not meant to last: the ritual itself always and invariably moves the tautological subject back into a more spacious and less focused form of existence, in the everyday, normative domain. Nevertheless, this state of powerful, integrated self-possession in a time that can only be the present may reproduce itself within the drama performed on festival nights: something of great significance thus happens to the god, within the play, and to the audience, as it were "outside" it, but in reality contained—perhaps we should say "cooked"—within the ritual order meant to produce an existential change.

There are more powerful ways to state this thesis, though we cannot begin to work out their implications here. Recognition (*pratyabhijñāna*), memory (*smaraṇa*), tautological self-coincidence (*tād-ātmya*)—all of these are, in a sense, subsidiary parts or stages of a larger dynamic process, though in another sense they constitute the culminating achievements of this process on the level of the individual spectator at the drama or the character within the play. What is really being accomplished through these and other, ritual means is the *creation* of the divine subject—in our case, Rāma and/or Sītā. By creation we mean *not* an *ex nihilo* production of living being but the making manifest of a latent, potential presence, as the flowering tree unfolds from the restless and compacted seed, or as the visible image emerges in contact with the projecting, imagining eye. The ritual maps and controls this process, ensuring its result, just as the Ramayana (in each of its distinct versions) may be said to create Rāma, and as Bhavabhūti's play literally produces the re-composed or reintegrated consciousness of this complex, double entity, at once human and divine. To create this intensity of presence, on various levels, and later to dispel it, is integral both to the entire ritual system and to its aesthetic concomitants and means. Clearly, we need a new theory of poetics and aesthetics that would be capable of addressing such a process, and such a goal, which Bhavabhūti has taken, perhaps, to an ultimate expressive limit—though such a process, informed and contextualized by ritual concerns, is by no means limited, in the field of Sanskrit drama, to his works.

We may ask again, from this new perspective, about the meaning of Rāma's actions, now that the problem of Sītā's banishment has shifted into a different, rather more internal mode. It is all too easy to say that Rāma, in so far as he is committed to his royal dharmic duty, is cruel—or that *dharma* itself, in this public context, belongs to the hardened, surface crust of existence. The conflict that Rāma feels is a real one, not really resolvable at all, as we are reminded by the Ganges in the final play-within-a-play. Yet the guilt that Rāma feels, and that he identifies as truly his, a profound statement of self ("Yes, that is who I am," he says in response to the Earth's words of reproach), seems to go beyond this overt conflict; so overwhelming is this burden that one is almost tempted to wonder if there is not some more hidden aggressive force driving the hero, a force that comes into play at all those neuralgic points in the story when this god-turned-man is revealed as weak, wanting, or even tainted by evil. "There seems to be nothing that Rāma is incapable of doing." Certainly, in the light of everything we have seen in Bhavabhūti's text, we can conclude that Rāma's treatment of Sītā cannot be simply condoned. The *Uttara-rāma-carita* is, among other things, a long, complex, and poignant *J'accuse*. Its subtlety, however, lies in the revelation of a hero who is internally struggling with the blocked, objectified, and petrified pieces of his own consciousness, and who, in the course of watching his own play enacted before his eyes, eventually melts into a more unified existence. This is an inner drama of water at war with stone.

And what of love? We have an extrapolated definition of empathy, *karuṇā*, as the imaginative connection to the implicit story that exists before it is fully lived; as such, *karuṇā* binds the severed levels of existence together and heals the inner wound. Love has something of this same gift, as Rāma tells us in Act VI, in *his* particular definition:

RĀMA: Love and logical causality are, after all, totally at odds.[51]

Some inner reason connects one thing to another.
Loving feelings have no relation to outer forms.
The lotus blossoms each day at sunrise.
The moonstone melts when the moon appears. (6.12)

The world is alive with transformative movement and mysterious interconnections that, however arbitrary they may seem, always reflect an intimate inner tie. And it is this interweaving of seemingly discrete entities, this making of connections on a level of soft, internal, intangible flow, unrelated to externalities but richly enacted within the heart or mind, that our poet identifies with the various forms of love (*prītayaḥ*).

We have come full circle. Rāma's definition in Act VI, in the context of his dawning recognition of his sons, reflects and expands upon his earlier statement in Act I—the classic definition with which we began. *Advaita*, "that state when two become one/ in joy as in sorrow," requires empathy, *karuṇā*, the true energizing force of connection. It also needs to "ripen" over time, cooked deep inside the containing body of the lover; and this cooking, as we now know, removes the intervening veils (*āvaraṇa*) in awareness, allowing for lucid perception of the beloved in the ripening, loving core (*sneha-sāra*). This state encompasses ambivalence: recall that this verse immediately precedes Rāma's cruellest act; and Bhavabhūti shows us over and over how, among the connections that love enables, one often finds those between grief and joy, or insult and delight, or confusion and clarity.[52] There is even a somewhat sinister resonance, throughout this play, between the chiming notes of *karuṇā*—all that is compassionate and empathic—and *dāruṇa*, "harsh, terrible, cruel,"[53] almost as if these domains were intrinsically interwoven in the initial, experienced modes of loving—before the slow, transformative ripening removes the veils. It is, it seems, the poet's business to make this happen by magically fusing the levels of perception in a work of visionary and creative remembering, outside of time: as Lakṣmaṇa cries out to Vālmīki, though without comprehending, as yet, what the drama is actually achieving, *eṣa te kāvyârthaḥ*, "this is the point of poetry!" And, despite the metaphysical tone of these formulations, and the understanding they convey of love as an extraordinary, rare state of almost transcendent connectedness, the process that engages this poet so deeply is expressly defined as ultimately human—indeed as situated at the very heart of the human being, this precarious ability to touch and to weave, "the mysterious knot of feeling, so disturbing, yet common to all who have consciousness, the inner thread of life."[54]

FOUR

# Crying Dogs and Laughing Trees in Rāma's Kingdom: Self-reflexivity in *Ānanda Rāmāyaṇa*

VIDYUT AKLUJKAR

> Rāma's exploits extend over a billion verses.
> O Goddess, I am incapable of elucidating them fully
> even with a hundred million divine years
> and these five mouths of mine.
>
> —Śiva's confession to Pārvatī[1]

Since Śiva Pañcānana, the Great God with five faces, admits his inability to recount the full extent of Rāma's exploits, it goes without saying that mortal poets like Kampaṉ, Tulsīdās, Kṛttibāsa or Eknāth can only hope to succeed in giving expression to a mere portion of it. Yet generations of poets have felt compelled to sing the glories of the most beloved incarnation of God in human form. Many have also felt the need to question earlier accounts of his exploits in order to raise doubts, accuse, explain, justify, and contextualize them. Hence the existence of many Ramayanas.[2]

Among all such questioning Ramayanas, *Ānanda Rāmāyaṇa*[3] (henceforth *Ā.R.*) stands out by its paradoxical stance regarding its authorship. Is *Ā.R.* a work of Vālmīki or is it a later work better than Vālmīki's? The text of *Ā.R.* shows awareness of post-Vālmīki retellings of Rāma story, thus dating itself centuries later than Vālmīki, and at the same time claims to be a work of Vālmīki. In the present paper, I propose to analyse the contradiction. I argue that it results due to a conflict between the authors's loyal devotion to Vālmīki and his loyalty to progressive ideas of justice, equality and compassion. To make sense of the paradox regarding its authorship, I focus on the complexity of *Ā.R.*'s self-reflexive discourse. Since its self-reflexivity is best exemplified by its inclusion of new stories, I go on to analyse a sample of these. The addition of new stories allows the author to question Vālmīki, explain a troublesome issue, offer better alternatives, and re-establish the glory of Rāma. Based on the analysis of *Ā.R.*'s self-reflexive stories, I conclude that the apparent contradiction is 1) a deliberate attempt to hide behind a celebrity to avoid blame and gain popularity for the text, and 2) an attempt to grapple with contemporary concerns such as caste and gender and insert these into a prestigious and popular epic.

*Ā.R.* expresses awareness of the existence of many Ramayanas by using several strategies. It cites extensive lists of actual texts (*Ā.R. Manohara kāṇḍa* 8:62–72),[4] gives catalogues of mythical divisions of the *Rāma-kathā* verses (*Ā.R. Yātrā kāṇḍa* 2),[5] and provides accounts of alternative story-lines.[6] The awareness of other, divergent tellings of the Rāma story is, however, coupled with an interesting expression of self-reflexivity in *Ā.R.* The text shows its composer[7] at once desirous of everlasting fame for the text and yet unwilling to disclose its real historical authorship. The assertion that there are hundreds of Ramayanas, that there is no end to the *Rāma-kathā*, is often juxtaposed in *Ā.R.* with an unabashed claim for its own supremacy. As it says, "O disciple, there are hundreds of Rāmāyaṇas on the face of the earth. However, comparable to this one there has not been, nor will there be" (*Ā.R. Manohara kāṇḍa* 17:115). Such a claim, however, is more complex than a simple boast. Only a careful analysis will help us understand the complexity of *Ā.R.*'s self-reflexivity.

On the one hand, *Ā.R.* declares humbly that the only poet able to capture fully the beauty and the extent of the Rāma myth was Vālmīki. (*Ā.R. Janma kāṇḍa* 2:13–15, *Yātrā kāṇḍa* 2:69–74.) On the other hand, it proclaims that in fact *Ā.R.* itself is the best representation of Vālmīki's creativity, the cream on the top of his full cup (*Ā.R. Manohara kāṇḍa* 8: 69–71). Unlike other Rāmāyaṇas which are authored by individuals like Eknāth, Tulsīdās, or Kampaṉ, *Ā.R.* declares itself composed by the *Adi Kavi,* the original poet, Vālmīki. Such an unambiguous claim occurs several times in the main body of the text. Since *Ā.R.*'s attribution of its authorship to Vālmīki flies in the face of its awareness of other tellings much later than that of Vālmīki,[8] it raises the question of how to account for such obviously contradictory claims. Such a curious blend of fact and fantasy, text-scholarship and poetic licence, desire for anonymity and a claim for unsurpassed fame is a unique feature of *Ā.R.* In order to gauge its gravity fully, let us analyse the narrative techniques *Ā.R.* employs to assert its supremacy, in particular its treatment of new stories and humorous anecdotes.

Besides the obvious goal of increasing the entertainment value of the epic, the addition of new stories in Ramayana serves at least the following two functions, 1) reshaping the mythic characters of Rāma and others, and 2) revitalising the concepts of justice and society in light of contemporary concerns. The addition of new tales to a text composed in Sanskrit, coupled with the claim of its authorship by Vālmīki, further serves the purpose of sanctifying certain elements of these tales even though they did not appear in Vālmīki's text.[9] The study of these shows how, within the tradition of questioning Rāmāyaṇas, the composer of *Ā.R.* assumes a complex stance, at once of an ardent admirer of Vālmīki and still a critic of his characters. In the final analysis, I shall argue that the ultimate purpose, and the one that has gone so far unnoticed, of many of these additional tales is the artistic expression of a complex and sophisticated self-reflexivity.

Since *Ā.R.* is a relatively little known text in the west, let me give some basic information about it.[10] It is a voluminous Sanskrit text of nine cantos and 36 thousand *ślokas,* or verses, depicting in considerable detail the kingship of Rāma (*Rāmarājya). Ā.R.* sums up in the first canto, *Sāra kāṇḍa,* almost the entire story of the *Vālmīki Rāmāyaṇa* (henceforth *V. R.*)[11] up to Rāma's return to Ayodhya after his victory over Rāvaṇa. In its remaining eight cantos, *Ā.R.* elaborates on Rāma's life with his queen Sītā, describing in great detail their day-to-day affairs, feasts and festivities, hunting expeditions, water sports, courtly dealings, justice sessions, pilgrimages and performances of sacrifices. It also includes accounts of the bridegroom choices which King Rāma attends with his sons and stories of weddings of his twins Lava and Kuśa. The life of Rāma and his family is explored with many of his otherwise unknown adventures until the end of their physical presence in this world. The longest canto in two parts, *Rājya kāṇḍa,* focuses mainly on a detailed description of Rāma's reign, Ramraj, one of the central concerns of the text. As we shall see shortly, it is also the place where the questioning, opposing and bettering stance of this text is at its best.

*Ā.R.* has exercised considerable influence on some sects of *Vaiṣṇavas*[12] and also on later versions of the Rāma-story such as those of Sūrdās and Eknāth.[13] There is strong textual support to believe that the composer of the *Ā.R.* was a resident of Maharashtra, although the work became celebrated throughout India. It was translated into Hindi, Marathi, as well as Telugu, and has influenced other creations in northern and southern vernaculars.[14]

*Ā.R.* introduces many new elements in its treatment of the Rāma story. One is an extensive mapping of all major characters from the Rāma story onto the characters from the Kṛṣṇa story.[15] This device serves to contextualize and glorify the seventh incarnation of Viṣṇu. Others are several new accounts of previous births of characters from the Rāma story to explain certain awkward incidents like Kaikeyī's behavior, a humorous depiction and a philosophic resolution of a dispute between a worshipper of Rāma and a worshipper of Kṛṣṇa about the superiority of their favorite deities, and a comparative analysis undertaken by Rāma himself of all the incarnations of Viṣṇu in order to declare the supremacy of the seventh, i.e., the incarnation as Rāma (*Ā.R. Rājya kāṇḍa* 20). In claiming to be the best of all tellings of the *Rāma kathā*, *Ā.R.* makes a point of reminding its readers of these and many other innovations.

One such innovation is in a story which focuses on Rāma's fear of Rāvaṇa, a topic hardly addressed in most other Rāmāyaṇas. A story that ends in a wonderfully self-reflexive defense begins by depicting how Rāma's fear results in a ban on laughter in his kingdom (*Ā.R. Rājya kāṇḍa* 13.1–137). Here I offer a summary closely following the original, rather than a line-by-line translation of the entire *sarga*. Here is what happened.

### RĀMA'S BAN ON LAUGHTER

> Rāma was sitting in his court one day when he heard the hearty laughter of one of his courtiers who was watching a dance of the courtesans. The sound of that laughter reminded Rāma of the laughter of Rāvaṇa's hideous heads as he cut them off long ago, and that filled his mind with a strange fear. He was reminded of those trying times of the famous battle, when as soon as he cut off one of Rāvaṇa's heads, it would roar with laughter while falling near Rāma's feet, and he would throw it back into the sky with his arrows. This he had to

do a hundred and one times before Rāvaṇa was finally vanquished. The heads were laughing at the thought of dying at the hands of Rāma, and falling at his feet to pay respects to him. But the sight of those demonic heads with frightening fangs roaring with laughter and coming down at him from the sky had frightened him then, since he had imagined them coming to devour him. The sound of that unrestrained laughter rekindled that horrid memory in Rāma and hence he decided to ban laughter altogether from the face of this earth. He issued a decree to that effect, and promised punishment to anyone who dared to laugh aloud.

This had a miserable effect on all mankind. People dared not laugh even at home for fear of punishment. All those wonderful activities like dance, music, sports and festivities where laughter would rule came to an abrupt end. Even gods like Brahmā and Indra became worried at the sorry state of affairs on Earth, and decided that something had to be done. Brahmā came down to Rāma's kingdom. He hid himself inside a Pippala tree and started to laugh whenever he saw a passer-by.

This created a snow-ball effect. A wood-carrier was passing by the tree. Suddenly he heard laughter coming out of the tree. Hearing the Pippala tree laugh, he began to laugh as well. The King's messenger heard the wood-carrier laughing his head off on his way to the court and could not restrain himself. He came to Rāma's court laughing merrily, and watching him, all the courtiers began too. There were suddenly ripples of laughter, giving way to giggles and peals. Even Rāma, when he heard everyone laughing around him, suddenly felt the urge to laugh out loud, and actually burst out laughing. The second time he did this, self-reproachfully he checked himself mid-laugh, and began to investigate the cause of this epidemic of laughter. Everyone pointed a finger at everyone else, and finally Rāma heard about the laughing tree.

He sent his army to cut down that offending tree, but as his soldiers went near the tree, they were pelted with rocks by Brahmā from inside the tree, and they could not cut it down. When Rāma heard of their plight, he decided to seek the advice of his priest Vasiṣṭha. Vasiṣṭha was called to the court, but he suggested that they should consult Vālmīki instead. So finally they invited Vālmīki to the court and after worshipping him with all due respect and hospitality, presented him with this new situation to handle.

Vālmīki laughed aloud and said to Rāma, "Rāma, you are the

omniscient one, and still you are asking me? Well, if you want to know, I shall tell you what you already know. You banned laughter, so all these people have given it up due to fear of your punishment. This has created a terrible halt in the life of this entire universe. All festivities, all literary gatherings, all sacrificial performances, and musical concerts have come to a stand-still. Naturally all the gods are concerned with the joyless state of the world, and since Brahmā could not come to talk you out of this state of affairs, he decided to hide in the tree to see if he could make any difference."

When Rāma heard of Brahmā's devious tactics, he decided to go to the laughing tree himself, to control Brahmā, but Vālmīki implored him to reconsider. Vālmīki said,

"Rāma, give up your anger, listen to what I have to say. Consider your own nature. Your form consists of Being (*sat*), Consciousness (*cit*) and Bliss (*ānanda)* (*Ā.R. Rājya kāṇḍa* 13:89). Your life which I described, and taught your twins to sing, is full of bliss. How can people listen to it without feeling the joy, and celebrating it in smiles and laughter? If you ban laughter, that will ruin all my efforts in writing about this joyous life of yours."

Rāma began to think. Vālmīki pressed on his case.

"Consider something else as well, O best of the clan of Raghu. Long ago when I created your life in a billion verses,[16] Vyāsa broke it into pieces and fashioned the eighteen *purāṇas* and several *upa-purāṇas* out of it. Many other sages will fashion many other sciences (*śāstrādīnī*) out of portions of it. However, later on, people will try to focus on only that portion of it which is related in twenty-four thousand verses, and recognize only it as the one composed by Vālmīki. Actually, that portion which relates the evil nature of Kaikeyī, and your exile, and the sorrowful year spent in separation from Sītā, is a portion which captures the sorrow of life. The one grabbed by Vyāsa focuses on wars and strife in life. But the present one focuses mainly on the joy, the bliss in life. The war-centered one is called *Mahābhārata*, the sorrow-centered one is called *Śoka-Rāmāyaṇa*,[17] and the love-centered one is called *Bhāgavata*.

They all have their place. One should recite the war-centered one during morning hours, the sorrow-centered one during afternoon, and the love-centered one during night-time. However, this one, which is *Ānanda Rāmāyaṇa*, should be recited at all times.

Long ago, when Vyāsa broke my work into pieces, and created other texts out of it, I kept quiet, because I realized that later on, in the *Kali yuga,* people of sluggish intellect would be born, and they would also be short-lived, the poor ones. They might not be able to listen to all of my compositions. Hence, I thought, it is good that Vyāsa has divided it into manageable morsels fit for consumption by these weaklings. However, I now implore you, please do not ruin this work of mine, consisting of nine cantos. Do not banish laughter. Do not deform the *Ānanda-Rāma-Caritaṁ,* the blissful life of Rāma which is more attractive. If you ban laughter, then this work will be just like the remaining ones.

Therefore act in such a manner that your wish will be obeyed, while my poem will be preserved as well. Let people laugh but let them not show their teeth. Let them cover their mouth with cloth while they laugh.

Laughter is indicative of Lakṣmī or Prosperity. Laughter bestows happiness. Laughter is auspiscious. There is nothing greater than laughter. That house becomes a temple where a smiling woman resides. Indeed Goddess Lakṣmī resides in such a house, O Joy of the Raghu clan. The sages praise the man whose face bears a smile, and censure the one who has an angry face. However, they also criticise the one who laughs uncontrollably.

Therefore, Rāma, do as I say. Don't worry about Brahmā being too proud. He considers you his father.[18] I will see to it that he comes to you for refuge."

Rāma considered Vālmīki's speech and assured him that he would do as Vālmīki wished. So he removed the ban on laughter. Everyone rejoiced. Even Indra showered the earth with nectar and revived Rāma's wounded soldiers around the laughing tree. Life returned to normal again and laughter regained its rightful place.

The tale has tremendous entertainment value. One can imagine how any *purāṇika* (religious storyteller) reciting this portion of the epic in a temple-hall full of listeners could embellish it to apply to a contemporary political situation.[19] One can also imagine the hearty response of the daily listeners to these delightful "revelations" about their favorite Man-God. The inclusion of this tale in *Ā.R.* with a reference to Rāma, however, achieves much more than simple entertainment.

*Ā.R.* has daringly applied the tale motif of "a king's order with disastrous results" to the *Rāma-kathā* in order to highlight the proper relationship between the ruler and his subjects. The motif of a king's order with disastrous results appears in many folktales and other kinds of stories about famous kings.[20] It is a challenge to take something as idiotic as banning of laughter[21] and apply it to the character of a divinized hero like Rāma, but *Ā.R.* accepts it and succeeds in making it believable by introducing the theme of residual fear.

The tale presents at once a study of psychology of crowds as well as of the workings of the mind of a public authority figure. It capitalizes on the most common experience of fear, and delineates masterfully the cause of fear, elements that trigger that fear by association, the resulting anxiety, attempts to remove the triggering elements by force, and follies of force that frustrate any reasonable solution of the problem. The complex dynamics of fear and force in this tale can be applied to any political situation where people are ruled by force. Rāma's initial fear results in his prohibition of laughter, and its execution by force generates successive fear among his people. The final result caricatures a society where the ruler is totally alienated from his subjects, an exact antithesis of the ideal kingdom of Rāma as it was traditionally understood. The sneaky solution devised by Brahmā, the god who is regarded as Viṣṇu's (and therefore Rāma's) offspring, shows the Creator in the role of a mischievous son who uses guerrilla tactics to hide in a tree to prick the bubble of seriousness resulting from his parent's decree. Besides offering insights into the psychology of fear, the tale also investigates the phenomenon of prohibition, and the uncontrollable nature of laughter. More important, as a valuable comment on society, it depicts how bans can sometimes be traced to deep-set fears of so-called invincible authority figures, how bans and prohibitions usually fail to work, how the forbidden fruit becomes the most unavoidably desirable one, and how the only solution to the problem of fear rests in realizing the ultimate nature of the Self. *Ā.R.*'s focus on the topic of Rāma's fear in this tale is refreshing since it is unheard of elsewhere. However, in showing the human side of a character irretrievably divinized, *Ā.R.* follows the lead of Vālmīki, who had shown Rāma weeping and forgetting his strength at the loss of Sītā.

The final intervention of Vālmīki in this tale seems appropriate from several angles. Intervention of Vālmīki stamps the new tale with a seal of authority. Vālmīki is the traditionally recognized original composer of *Rāma-kathā*. Therefore, theoretically he can solve any new problems that may arise in the story-line. More important, *Ā.R.* uses Vālmīki as the proponent to put forth a revised picture of traditional literature, to delineate differences in the respective approaches of *Mahābhārata, Bhāgavata,* and the two "portions" of the entire Ramayana corpus. Here is an example of how *Ā.R.* self-referentially uses the context of new tales to establish its supremacy over all other tellings, while claiming in the same breath Vālmīki's authorship. Note that in its wide sweep, *Ā.R.* includes as tellings of the glory of Rāma even *Bhāgavata* and *Mahābhārata,* which celebrate Kṛṣṇa's adventures. This goes hand-in-hand with *Ā.R.'s* extensive mapping of all characters of the Rāma story onto the Kṛṣṇa story. It is simply another expression of its view, expressed many times, that Rāma is the ultimate incarnation of Viṣṇu, intrinsically better than all the rest.

Finally, the tale also addresses the main purpose of *Ā.R.*'s creation: to explain the nature of *ānanda,* bliss. The life of Rāma is blissful. The title of the work at hand, *Ānanda Rāmāyaṇam,* reflects this emphasis. Vālmīki's defence of laughter in the above story echoes it. Such an approach to the exposition of *Rāma-kathā* is not only innovative, but it stands in opposition to some other celebrated approaches to the ancient myth. Other earlier Ramayanas focus on the tragic outcome of the tale. Vālmīki was moved by the sorrow of separation of two loving birds, and that sorrow prompted him to engage in the composition of Rāma's life in verse (*V.R. Bāla kāṇḍa* 2:12–17). Hence, Rāma's sorrow of separation from his loving wife forms the central motif of *V.R.* Later poets recognize the tragic element of the Rāma myth as a powerful force and it forms an essential trait of the hero's character in, for example, Bhavabhūti's *Uttara-rāma-caritam.* Bhavabhūti's Rāma even expresses this conviction by saying, "Rāma is born only to experience sorrow."[22]

The author of *Ā.R.* does not agree. He believes that focusing on the calamities and sorrow in Rāma's life presents only a partial view of reality. In a remarkable feat of self-reflexivity, he uses Vālmīki himself to remind Rāma, the hero of *V.R.*, not to spoil the effect of joy in his biography by imposing a ban on laughter! Here the author of *Ā.R.* invokes the author of *V.R.* to tell the hero of *V.R.* to behave himself! To the author of *Ā.R.*, the entire life of Rāma is joyous. Happiness is to recall it, to recount it, to remind others of it. To be immersed in it day and night is to experience the highest bliss. In order to celebrate this bliss the author has included in his work many new details such as joyous journeys Rāma takes, humorous anecdotes in his daily life, his romance and continued loving relationship with

Sītā, as well as his assurances to many other devoted and love-lorn women that they will be rewarded via union with him in his next incarnation, although not in this one. The addition of new tales in order to infuse the text with humour and laughter results in its recurrent claim that *Ā.R.* is the best celebration of Rāma's life. In *Ā.R.*, Rāma is the Supreme God and most characters seem to know this—if not always, then at least at the time of dying, and even Rāma confesses from time to time that he considers this incarnation of his as the most joyous one. [23]

To balance the solitary picture of Rāma's loss of memory of his real self, and his use of unreasonable force to control his subjects in the ban-on-laughter incident, *Ā.R.* uses other accounts which show him as the ideal king whom everyone could approach to demand justice. In fact *Ā.R.*'s chief concern in introducing many of the tales in *Rājya kāṇḍa* seems to be to answer some of the doubts that arise from earlier accounts of Rāma delivering justice. The reign of Rāma, Ramraj, remains proverbial in being just and fair to everyone. The depiction of an ideal kingdom is one of the main themes of *Ā.R.* It devotes an entire canto (*Ā.R. Rājya kāṇḍa* 15) to elucidating the concept of justice as understood and practiced by Rāma. After describing Rāma's practise of *Rāja-dharma* (royal duty), it records in the next canto Rāma's instructions to his princes on ruling according to dharma.[24] More effectively, *Ā.R.* also relates fabulous new tales to make the abstract concepts of justice and equality more accessible to listeners. Here is one about a much maligned animal (*Ā.R. Rājya kāṇḍa* 10: 1–49).

### THE CRYING DOG

One day Rāma heard a dog crying aloud outside his palace. He ordered Lakṣmaṇa to see what was the matter, and if need be, bring the dog to the court. Lakṣmaṇa went, and upon returning reported to Rāma what the dog had said:

"I cannot come to the court, since I am born into a *pāpa-yoni*, a vicious birth of a dog. I am banned from entering auspicious places such as temples, sacrificial halls, kitchens, bedrooms, assembly halls, and kings' courts. So you go and inform the king about me."

Rāma was intrigued by the talking dog and, putting on his wooden sandals, he set out in all his regalia to see the dog. When he saw the dog, Rāma put his staff aside, and standing near the dog, with one leg bent at the knee, asked him with a smile,

"What bothers you? Tell me without fear. No one should ever have any reason to be unhappy in my kingdom."

The dog had a broken leg. But he bowed down to Rāma several times and said with joy,

"O Ocean of Mercy, you had to trouble yourself for my sake in coming here. May you live long. I had not hurt anyone when a monk (*yati*)[25] hurled a stone at me, and broke my leg. That is why I came to you for refuge, Great King."

Then Rāma ordered the *yati* to come there. He came and, when asked by Rāma about the cause of his attack, said,

"I was wandering to collect alms when this wretched dog came and defiled my food by his touch. It was mid-day, and I was hungry, so in a fit of anger, I hurled a rock at him to teach him a lesson, and it broke his leg."

Having heard this confession of the *yati*, Rāma said to him,

"This beast is devoid of knowledge. Having spotted his food, he touched it. It is not his fault. I know that you are the one who has committed an offense against the dog. Therefore you are liable to be punished."

Then Rāma told that descendant of Saramā,[26]

"This *yati* is guilty in your case. I have put him in your hands. You may punish him as you wish."

When he heard Rāma's speech, the dog, descendant of Saramā, said to the Lord,

"May this *yati* be established as the head of a Śiva temple."

Rāma said, "So be it."

He had the *yati* placed in a palanquin, offered him garlands, and sandalwood, and with a great ceremony of musical instruments, songs, and dances carried him to the Śiva temple, and established him as the overlord of the temple. The *yati*, in his ignorance, thought that his luck had smiled upon him.

When Rāma returned to his court his people, who were watching this spectacle with curiosity, asked him,

"Lord, how did the dog come to ask for such a 'punishment'? That *yati* had to wander to find his food earlier, and now he is established in such an eminent position. This must give him great pleasure; this is not punishment!"

Having heard the speech of his townspeople, Rāma said to them, "Ask the dog, and he shall dispel all your doubts."

They went to the dog and asked him. He said to them,

"Listen to what I have to say. Those who misuse the grains grown by farmers in order to honour the wicked, the executives in charge of the *Śivālayas*, the *maṭhas* (monasteries), and the charitable institutions, the ones who steal wealth from orphaned women and children, the abusive speakers, the ones who swindle money offered towards cows, brahmins and Lord Śiva, the ones who cause injustice, the ones who drive away beggars from kings' palaces, the ones who rob others of their wealth and become liable for punishment, the ones who rob the money given to feed brahmins, and the money given to perform sacrifices, and those who amass great wealth at the expense of others, all these obtain a dog's birth in their next life. Believe me, I am speaking the truth. I have been born a dog now thanks to my being an overlord of a *maṭha* earlier. That is why, today, I offered that position to the *yati*. Just to teach him a lesson."

When they heard this speech of the dog, the townspeople were devoid of doubt. They went home, and the dog went his way. The *yati* died, to be born a dog in the next birth on account of his sins, but the former dog obtained salvation since he had already been through the punishment of his sins. Don't think that the *yati* died in Ayodhya, since there is no re-birth for those who die in Ayodhya. No, he had gone for work to some other place, and so he died there.

Where is a *yati* ? Where a dog? Yet a *yati* becomes a dog, and a dog obtains salvation. The great-souled ones understand that the outcome of *karma* is unfathomable.

Where is a *yati*? Where a dog? But there was justice here with Rāma, the Lord of Ramā.[27] There was always Truth here. Since you could see him face to face, there was never any injustice.

The hungry dog stealing food is a common theme in literature but "disregard of its defiling touch by the enlightened" is a culture-specific theme found in several stories about enlightened beings in Maharashtra.[28] A wise dog, who knows the doctrine of *karma-vipāka* (the ripening results of one's own actions) enough to recall his own previous birth and to choose the just "punishment" for the offending *yati*, fits in well with the traditional share of animals, monkeys and bears in the *Rāma-kathā*.

The importance of this tale for the self-reflexive supremacy claimed by *Ā.R.* lies in its placement.[29] In *Rājya kāṇḍa* of *Ā.R.*, in a cluster of tales which describe different instances of Rāma's justice, it comes just before the tale of Śambūka. Both these tales must be analysed side-by-side in order to see their interrelatedness. In *V.R.*, where the Śambūka myth originally occurs, Śambūka is a Shūdra performing penance, and Rāma has to kill him in order to avert the untimely death of a Brahmin boy in his kingdom (*V.R. Uttara kāṇḍa, sargas* 64–7). The connection between the untimely death of a Brahmin and the undeserved performance of penance by a Shudra is made by sage Nārada in *V.R.* After killing Śambūka, Rāma arrives at the hermitage of Agastya, where he receives praise for this deed from the Brahmin sage. However, later poets have felt qualms about the logic of this action of Rāma, and have tried to either criticize it or explain it by adding new detail to the incident. *Ā.R.* has carefully revised the Śambūka incident in the light of bhakti, and *karma-vipāka* (effects of actions), and prefaced it with the tale of a crying dog in order to re-evaluate the controversial elements in that tale.

Unlike in *V.R.*, where only one Brahmin boy dies before his time, *Ā.R.* records seven such instances. A Brahmin boy dies, making his parents desolate. They place the blame of this untimely death on Rāma's shoulders, since the king is literally held responsible for the wellbeing of his subjects. His own observance and maintenance of a proper code of conduct among his subjects serves to ensure the absence of such calamities. Rāma promises to investigate, and Sītā declares that if Rāma cannot revive the dead boy she will give up her own son Lava in place of the dead boy to the grieving parents. While Rāma confers with Nārada, a wailing widow accuses Rāma of having allowed *adharma,* or a breach of proper behavior, among his subjects. While Rāma quickly prepares to leave at Nārada's behest in search of an offending Shudra, five more dead are reported: a Kshatriya from Madhupurī, a Vaishya from Prayāga, an oil-presser from Hastināpura, a blacksmith's daughter-in-law from Haridvāra, and a shoe-maker's daughter from Ujjayinī. The increase in the number of the dead, the inclusion of many castes and of both genders in the count of the untimely dead, and Sītā's compassionate assurance to the grieving parents, all these new details highlight the inclusive sympathies of the author of *Ā.R.*

The action of killing a Shudra occurs rather abruptly in *V.R.*, where there is not much conversation between the Shudra Śambūka and King Rāma. However, in *Ā.R.*, Rāma establishes a rapport with the Shudra ascetic on Mount Vindhya, explains to him compassionately how only the three classes of Brahmin, Kshatriya, and Vaishya are entitled to *tapas*, how Śambūka's actions are out of place, and why Rāma has to kill him in order to revive the seven people suffering the fate of untimely death. Rāma also tells Śambūka that he is pleased with him due to his *tapas*, and that he is entitled to a boon! Śambūka asks that he be famous in future, and that Shudras attain good rewards in the hereafter as well. Rāma declares that they should remember, chant and say the name "Rāma" as many times as they can, and they will thereby attain good regions hereafter. Śambūka asks, "In the *Kali yuga*, Shudras will be born with weaker intellects. They will be busy with their farmwork chores, so where will they find time or inclination to engage in *japa* or regular chanting? How then will they attain good regions?" Rāma responds that when the Shudras greet someone, they should utter the name of Rāma, as "Rām Rām!" and they will thereby obtain the same reward as chanting. Śambūka then asks a further boon composed of two parts: (1) that Rāma, along with Sītā and Lakṣmaṇa, come to reside upon the hill of Mt. Vindhya, so that it will be renowned as a holy place, and (2) that the people who come there first visit Śambūka before they go and take *darśana* of Rāma. Rāma grants him all these boons, and after assuring him that after his death he will go to Vaikuṇṭha, i.e. the heaven attained by Viṣṇu's devotees, Rāma kills the 'well-pleased' (*susantuṣṭam*) Śambūka.

*Ā.R.* changes the tone of the Śambūka myth entirely by introducing elements of Rāma's divinity, and Śambūka's bhakti, and by connecting that tale with the common practice of Shudras in Maharashtra to greet each other by saying "Rām Rām." *Ā.R.* has taken pains to present the Śambūka incident in a more compassionate manner than *V.R.* The purpose of introducing the tale of the crying dog just before the myth of Śambūka in *Ā.R.* seems to play down the inflexibility of Vālmīki's King Rāma in strictly observing the *varṇāśrama-dharma* (duties according to the class and stage of life). In *Ā.R.*, Rāma is sensitive to the misery of even a dog, and capable of bending oppressive regulations about untouchability. However, seven deaths of innocents from all castes and both genders seems to be too expensive a price to pay for one Shudra's desire to do what is not done. Rāma's siding with the dog and delivering punishment to the Brahmin *yati* puts Rāma in a more favorable light, and offers the reader more contexts for witnessing Rāma's execution of justice.

The tale of the crying dog eloquently elucidates the concept of justice which treats everyone fairly, both the high and mighty Brahmins and low-born underdogs. At the same time, note how the author of *Ā.R.* ties the concept of social justice to the traditional concept of *karma-vipāka*, inducing the reader to look beyond immediate reward or punishment. By taking a wide-angle view of the theory of *karma-vipāka*, what seems a punishment (e. g. beheading) may in reality be a reward (placement in heaven), and what appears a reward (e. g. headship of *Śivālaya*) may indeed be punishment leading to rebirth as a dog. The overlord of a *maṭha* is born as a dog due to his *karma*, and a dog attains salvation when he exhausts his *karma*; one's own good or bad actions decide one's birth as a Brahmin, or as a Shudra, or as a dog, and one is free from pleasure or pain only by experiencing the fruits of one's actions. Since the concept of *karma-vipāka* is thus interpreted in the light of the social division into four *varṇas* and four *āśramas,* it allows *Ā.R.* to progress smoothly from the tale of the crying dog to the myth of Śambūka, where the offence is a breach of the given duties of a *varṇa.*

Since the author of *Ā.R.* respects Vālmīki's genius, and has supreme faith in the infallibility of Rāma, he deals with certain problematic old myths by introducing new tales into the corpus. He claims authenticity for these tales by declaring them originally told by Vālmīki, and only retold in *Ā.R.* Invariably, the different narrators of the text declare, "Blessed is Muni Vālmīki, the lord of all poets, who composed the billion-fold Rāmāyaṇa long ago, the extensive, and auspicious Rāmāyaṇa, of which I told you only the essence." (*Ā.R. Pūrṇa kāṇḍa*, 9:63; *Rājya kāṇḍa* 14: 173–4)

The mention of the Śiva temple executives as generally corrupt in the crying-dog story may lead one to take it as a sectarian and bigoted remark, but concluding this would be erroneous. The author of *Ā.R.* takes pains to profess the unity of God, regardless of his names: Śiva, Viṣṇu, Rāma or Kṛṣṇa, just as earlier we saw him proclaiming the unity of *Rāmāyaṇa, Bhāgavata,* and *Mahābhārata* (*Ā.R. Manohara kāṇḍa* 9:75–77). As part of his overall strategy of inclusiveness, we find unambiguous declarations like the following one (*Ā.R. Manohara kāṇḍa* 7: 104–7):

> Rāma himself is to be known as Hara; Śiva himself is the Best of Raghus. There is no difference between the two. The man who conceives of difference goes to hell. The one who imagines Rāma and Śankara to be different has wasted his life like that of the nipple at the neck of a nanny-goat. The heart of Śaṁbhu is Rāma. The heart of Rāma is Śiva. Never should men imagine any difference between the two by advancing invalid inferences.

In a similar vein, *Ā.R.* relates accounts of Rāma making pilgrimages to sacred Śiva shrines to honor Śiva, establishing lingas at certain places, and observing many religious vows to worship Śiva (*Ā.R. Rājya kāṇḍa sargas* 6 to 9). Several praises of Rāma "composed" by Śiva occur in *Ā.R.* It includes several tales to exemplify divine unity from all possible angles while acknowledging the habitual sectarian diversity (*Ā.R. Manohara kāṇḍa* 7: 104–7; 12: 1–50). It even goes to the extent of promising a place in the *Raurava* hell to those who disrespect the unity of God and insult other peoples' gods.[30] Therefore, the reference here to the overlords of a *maṭha* is to be understood in more general terms to apply to all those who embezzle public wealth.[31]

The tale of a crying dog portrays Rāma as an ideal king who is accessible to all, goes to his subjects to seek the cause of their discomfort if they cannot come to him, and wisely detects the real culprit. Nonetheless, Rāma lets the victim deal with the convict and decide his punishment. It reconfirms the more typical portrayal of Rāma as the just king, and the earlier myth of Rāma's ban on laughter seems exceptional among many that conform to the norm. The picture emerges of an ideal society where equality rules, and troublesome injunctions about the defiling touch of certain beings are modified by a wise king by paying more attention to the immediate context. Although the concept behind such an outlook of equality can be found in many other texts, *Ā.R.*'s treatment of it is particularly entertaining and, therefore, memorable. Since *Ā.R.* shows Rāma accusing the *yati* of misinterpreting the well-known religious regulation about purity and pollution of food, the tale functions effectively as lesson. It belongs to a whole treasury of such tales of wisdom scattered throughout well-loved "religious" texts which are heard by people during daily recitations at temples across India, and repeated by temple-going grandmothers to their grandchildren, by travellers to their hosts, and by wandering singers to groups of villagers gathering around them. These tales show them how to be context-sensitive in the application of religious injunctions and how to embrace the spirit of the law rather than its letter. The concept of Ramraj as a utopia is formed among people by listening to such tales.

Besides the strategies which we saw in these two tales, the composer of *Ā.R.* claims supremacy for his composition by indulging in *vyājokti*, or a figure of speech which uses censure to imply praise and *vice versa*. Including *phala śruti,* or citations of merits, that accrue from reading a text is common practice in most religious texts. At the end of every canto, besides giving *phala śruti*, the author of *Ā.R.* relates tales that claim supremacy for his text. Before concluding, I shall recount such an example where he cleverly indicates why his text is not just for everybody.

THE UNEMPLOYMENT OF YAMA

At one time, one of Rāma's messengers left Rāma's service with his permission to perform *tapas*. He went home, read for nine nights the text of *Ā.R.* and then started out of his house. As he was going on the road, a royal elephant came and garlanded him. Then he found himself chosen to be a minister of a nearby kingdom where the king had died, the prince was very young, and the courtiers had decided to choose the future minister by letting the royal elephant garland the lucky person.

When news of the servant's good fortune reached home, many other servants sought permission to leave royal service, and engaged themselves in the recitation and constant chanting of *Ā.R.* Some began to hear it daily, some started to learn it by heart, some began to elucidate it, and some made it their life's mission. Each one of these attained some higher state of life. Some attained wealth, some got good land, some became headmen of townships, some became kings. Some others went to heaven, some to the region of the Sun, others to that of the Moon, or of Varuṇa, or of Kubera. All attained great rewards according to their store of merit by virtue of their different activities connected with *Ā.R.* Soon there were no servants in Rāma's kingdom to do menial tasks, and no soldiers.

Once, neighboring kings came to pay respect to Rāma. No one came forward to report them, no one to receive them. They could not find Rāghava's servants, nor his army. So they came on their own and started to ask Rāma, "Where are all those soldiers? Where are the servants?"

Rāma called his servants, but instead of servants only Lakṣmaṇa appeared. He told Rāma that the servants were nowhere to be found. Rāma was surprised but made his own family be hospitable to these kings, and after they departed he called his teacher to find out what was the matter.

The teacher [Vasiṣṭha] came. Rāma asked, "Where have all my servants and soldiers gone?"

Vasiṣṭha said, "Rāma, Rāma, you know it all, and yet you ask me? Well, I shall tell you. You know how Vālmīki had created earlier the billion-fold verse composition of your life. Out of that *Ā.R.* consists of nine kāṇḍas, which is what these folks have been reading. Each of them has attained a higher state of existence due to its influence. That is why your kingdom is empty. Now I have told you what you asked me about. Henceforth do as you please."

In the meanwhile, having heard about the state of those lucky ones, the entire populace of the earth started reading, chanting, reciting, and rejoicing in *Ā.R.* Soon the entire earth became empty of people, the entire region of Yama became devoid of souls, and all the higher heavens began to overflow with these lucky souls. So Yama found himself suddenly unemployed.

Yama approached Brahmā. They both came to Śiva. He took Durgā along with the other two and they all came down to Ayodhya to see Rāma. They told him about the imbalanced state of affairs, and implored him to do something about it. Rāma heard their concerns and sent Śatrughna to invite Vālmīki.

Vālmīki appeared and when he heard about it, he said with a laugh to Rāghava, "Do something so that my poem is not destroyed and yet everyone is happy."

Rāma said, "So be it." and then he declared,

"From now on, those who have earned their merit by worshiping me for seven births will be the only ones who will develop a taste for *Ā.R.* Not everyone."

Having heard Rāma's speech everyone was happy. The Gods went to their own regions, and the kings went to theirs. From then, only a few people started to know about this *Ā.R.* out of the billion-fold Rāmāyaṇa created by Vālmīki. Not everyone will know about it in the *Dvāpara,* nor in the *Kali yuga.* Only one in thousands who has accumulated merit earned in seven births will be the lucky one who will read it, and understand it. That is the promise of Rāma.

Here *Ā.R.*'s author indulges in hyperbole and humor to glorify the worth of the text. It cleverly combines the usual promise of rewards (*phala śruti*) with the provision of some safety valves to control an overflow of over-zealous merit-mongers by depicting the spectacle of an unemployed Yama not knowing how to spend his leisure. Such an expression of self-reflexive humor rarely occurs in dominant tellings of the Rāma story. *Ā.R.* excels in it. Throughout the work, however, the author affirms that ultimate credit for these tales and the entire beautiful composition must go to Vālmīki.

How does one make sense of the contradictory attitudes of *Ā.R.*, which exhibits its historicity by its knowledge of dated Ramayana tellings, and yet claims authorship by Vālmīki to share in the eternal glory of the most celebrated telling of *Rāma-kathā*? We cannot assume that the author of a text of such sophistication was simply unaware of the contradiction. Although many faithful listeners may actually go on believing the attribution of this text's authorship to Vālmīki, that does not diminish the conscious self-reflexivity exhibited by the text, nor does it cloud the clever and creative one-upmanship practised by its composer.

In a Western context of securing patents for inventions and guarding royalty rights to writings, it may be difficult to imagine a poet first creating a voluminous poetic work in Sanskrit and then surrendering it to the authorship of Vālmīki, not as an orphan at his doorstep but as the more deserving offspring of the genius. Although Indians on the whole are no less possessive about their own creations or, for that matter, their donations, there was and still remains a strong school of donors who believe in secret donations, *gupta-dāna*, as a superior form of donation, and poets and thinkers who believe that it is the thought that counts, not the individual thinker. Coupled with this is the humble attitude held by many devout poets that their own compositions are purified by the stamp of prestigious authorship of a venerable poet like Vālmīki. Such a stamp makes their poems worthy of being circulated among the general populace which is believed to be a form of the supreme God, *janatā-janārdana*. So the process of renouncing one's own authorship to the adoptive authorship of a celebrity then becomes an act of worship of Viṣṇu in the form of society. Several poets have thus donated their own poems to the popular repertoire of a greater, better-known *sant* poet. In the spirit in which a worshiper lights a small clay lamp, places it in a basket on a bed of fragrant flowers, and with great respect towards eternity lets it float on the holy waters of Gangā at Haridwar, the composer of *Ā.R.* has let his work, the fruit of his pride and poetic fancy, float on the holy waters of Vālmīki's *Rāma-kathā*.

By his own admission, his act may be interpreted as his pursuit of immortality. There are seven celebrated immortals in myths: Aśvatthāmā, Bali, Vyāsa, Hanumān, Bibhīṣaṇa, Kṛpa and Paraśurāma (*Ā.R. Manohara kāṇḍa* 8:118–132). The author of *Ā.R.* explains the significance of this belief through the mouth of one of his teacher-narrators, Rāmadāsa.

> Vyāsa is immortal. So how should people recognize who he is on this earth? I shall speak of his form now. Listen carefully.
>
> Those who compose poems in the language of the Gods [Sanskrit], those pundits, those people on the earth are to be known as beings who have a part of Vyāsa in them. Those who in their poems praise Rāmacandra, and Kṛṣṇa and Śiva, and describe their lives, those are to be known as Vyāsa incarnate.
>
> Those who praise kings, prostitutes, and kings's assemblies are not to be known as Vyāsa's forms.
>
> As long as there are praises on this earth of Rāma's exploits, so long will Vyāsa be remembered here and then he will obtain salvation."[32]

The author of *Ā.R.* believes that by composing a Sanskrit text celebrating the exploits of Rāma, he has shared in the immortality of the ancient sage-poet Vyāsa. Therefore, he may not feel the need to disclose his identity.

*Ā.R.* praises the creative genius of Vālmīki at every opportunity (*Ā.R. Janma kāṇḍa* 2:13–15; *Yātrā kāṇḍa* 2:69–70; *Manohara kāṇḍa* 8: 69–70; *Pūrṇa kāṇḍa* 9:63). However, at numerous places, the composer of *Ā.R.* implicitly questions Vālmīki's version of a myth and presents the readers with other, better versions. Wherever he cannot alter the old myths *per se*, he introduces new, parallel ones in order to balance the old ones, in order to create the desired total effect. Sometimes he creates new tales to incorporate his own, contemporary concerns. In several of these tales he invokes Vālmīki at the end, as if to secure his permission for the new incident. Other poets like Kālidāsa and Rājaśekhara have acknowledged the debt of older poets while still retaining authorship over their creations.[33] Therefore, the reader may still wonder why anyone so proud of his creativity would want to remain anonymous.

The author may desire anonymity for many reasons. One could be the stifling social and political conditions of medieval India, where subjects were alienated from rulers. The political atmosphere may seem unencouraging toward straight propagation of an innovative "religious" text, because it happens to be the religion of the populace and not of the ruler. Hiding behind the name of Vālmīki may have protected the composer of *Ā.R.* since the work includes social comments on the nature of justice, false pride, moral virtues, the vices of kings and other executives, and ridicules enemies of public well-being. Thus the message gets delivered to the public with a seal of ancient authority to make it more welcome, and the messenger hides behind a mask. In adopting this mode of creation, the composer of *Ā.R.* may be imitating his Brahmā, who sought to bring about a change in the laughter-less kingdom by hiding inside a tree. As to whether the creator of these words is as successful as the Creator of the worlds—the reader must have the last word.

FIVE

# Rāvaṇa's Kitchen: A Testimony of Desire and the Other[1]

ROBERT P. GOLDMAN

From very ancient times the control of appetite—in the realms of both diet and sexuality—has loomed large in the spiritual consciousness of South Asia. Mastery of hunger and severe dietary restriction both in terms of amount and variety of foods taken are often viewed, along with celibacy, as a *sine qua non* of the religious life, while narratives of dietary and sexual renunciation are, from the ancient Jain and Buddhist texts to the life and practice of Gandhi, almost invariably represented among the principal requirements for moral and spiritual progress.

Although food may not compete with sex for pride of place in the ascetic's catalog of temptations and horrors, in actuality dietary concerns generate a more complex and nuanced set of discourses and practices. Despite recurrent legends and accounts—ancient and contemporary—of men and women so spiritually advanced as to neither require nor consume gross material sustenance,[2] everyone must eat to remain alive. In this way, therefore, eating is differentiated from sex, which is not a biological necessity, at least for the individual. Thus, where the discourse on sexuality concentrates generally on either total abstention, or indulgence primarily for purposes of procreation,[3] discourses of diet must contend with two sets of complex variables, those of frequency and those of type.

Questions of the frequency with which food should be taken, at what times of the day, and in what amounts play a particularly important role in the lives of organized religious communities, although they frequently crop up in connection with the lives of individual renouncers.[4] Far more central and pervasive in South Asia's complex discourse of food are questions of type. For while sexuality, especially as it is envisioned in the religious, literary and technical traditions, presents—aside from the heroic athleticism associated with the *kāmaśāstra*—relatively limited opportunities for variation and virtually none that have differential bio-spiritual consequences, food is, and has at least for many centuries been, virtually infinitely differentiable along a shifting set of registers.

In a wide variety of specific contexts which may vary by religious affiliation, social and ritual standing, time of year, state of consecration, etc., foods may be broadly classified as permissible and forbidden. Such categories are not completely fixed, of course, and may vary, as when—which sometimes happens—a person takes a vow to give up a favorite food for life.[5] Even among those groups of foods that a group or an individual regards as permissible, there may be a complex set of gradations determined by often overlapping sets of criteria, such as for example the popular understanding of the old Sāṃkhyā theory of the three *guṇas*, or qualities, of matter and the spectrum from hot to cool that many people superimpose upon it.

Some people may justify the consumption of foods and beverages, such as meat and spirits, on the grounds that the "rajasic" nature, or quality of inciting passion and energetic action, associated with such fare, is in harmony with their own inherent nature, as for example is sometimes the case with Rajputs.[6] By the same token, those seeking to cultivate the life of the spirit may refrain from such foods or from certain condiments on the grounds that they incite the passions which are widely seen as inimical to spiritual progress.[7] In both these cases an explicit and substantial homology between food and libido is posited.

The mapping of hunger onto the topography of libido is an elaborate and deeply rooted one. Perhaps most cultures know it in some version of the metaphoric ingestion—visual for the most part—of the object of erotized desire. English is not alone in the use of such phrases as "I'll eat you up, I love you so," and in the use of culinary names as terms of endearment. Indic languages, Sanskrit not least among them, often use the same word to indicate the enjoyment of food and of a sexual object, as in the famous *Mahābhārata* story that helps to overdetermine the five Pāṇḍava brothers' polyandrous marriage. According to the passage in question the young men's mother, Kuntī, hearing her sons call out to her to see what they have brought back from their begging rounds (in reality the princess Draupadī) tells them, without looking, "*bhuṅkteti sametya sarve*" ("All of you must enjoy it together").[8]

If, as the example of the Pāṇḍavas suggests, food is indeed strongly homologized with sex[9] and, in a powerfully patriarchal culture like that of South Asia, sex with women, then it would seem likely that the domain of food and diet would be subject to the same kind of powerful bi-polar ambivalence as the latter. In other words these objects would be alternately represented as irresistibly desirable and unbearably repulsive.[10]

In fact the alternate play of desire and revulsion in the case of food and erotized women plays a powerful role in one of South Asia's most widely known and influential cultural artifacts, the *Vālmīki Rāmāyaṇa*. Before, turning to that text, let me begin with a personal reminiscence about how I first became aware of the parallel construction of food and sex in South Asia as sites for the exploration of the binary pairs, indulgence–restraint and attraction–repulsion.

When I first went to India as a graduate student, I had the rare good fortune to be able to study Sanskrit texts at the feet of an extraordinary traditional scholar who is now, alas, no more. He was unusual even by the standards of the many other excellent *paṇḍits* and *śāstrins* with whom I have had the privilege of studying. For he had never been a householder but remained a strict, lifelong *brahmacārin* and was, moreover, more abstemious and restrictive in his diet than virtually anyone I have ever encountered, with the possible exception of some Jain *munis* with whom I have worked. He lived in a small apartment in Pune with a married couple of his caste and region who cooked for him and looked after his few material needs. It was his practice to take no food other than the simple fare they made for him; and I never knew him to take any food or drink whatever outside his home. Indeed, for many years he worked as a Senior Shastri at a research institute a considerable distance from his home, commuting by municipal bus to and from work six days a week. Yet even in the cruel heat of the Deccan summer, I never knew him to take so much as a sip of water during his work day.

Ironically, despite the unusual asceticism he rigorously imposed upon himself, he was—often in striking contrast to his *gṛhastha* colleagues—a man of uncommon warmth, cheerful, and curious about the world outside his own. Nonetheless, despite his extensive reading in *vaidika* and *śāstraic* literature, he was—as a result of his mode of life and his deep concentration on his fields of study—remarkably innocent of the domains of knowledge that lay beyond them. Indeed, he reminded me in some ways of the traditional characterization of the young Ādiśaṇkarācārya, who could defeat the greatest minds of India in all fields of learning save one, that of erotics, where, for lack of experience, he was forced to take recourse to a yogic stratagem.[11]

Despite his otherworldliness and his narrow experience—he could not, for example, point out France on a world map—he had an unbounded and almost childlike curiosity about the ways of the world and of the worldly; and nowhere was this more apparent than in the areas of food and sex. During our many informal conversations before and after our regular sessions of textual study and exegesis, he would often ask me and a colleague animated questions about women he had seen us with and whether we were involved with them romantically and sexually. An equally favorite topic of conversation for him was the veracity of stories he had heard of the—to him—revolting dietary practices of various nationalities. He would excitedly ask, "*Mayā śrutaṃ yat Frāṅkapradeśīyāir maṇḍūkā 'pi khādyante. Satyam asatyam vā*? (I've heard that people in France eat even frogs! Is that true or not?)" or "*Cīnapradeśe janāḥ śvāno 'pi bhuñjantīty āhuḥ. Evaṃ vā*? (They say that in China folks even eat dogs! Is that so?)" When I would answer in the affirmative, he would put his hand to his forehead with a delighted cry of scandalized disapprobation, "*Hā yo, yo, yo*!" There was no question that he regarded these abominations with a peculiar mixture of horror and delight and that he carried this attitude over to his inquiries about what he imagined to be our romantic adventures.

That this kind of ambivalence is deeply rooted in much of Indian culture's complex discourse on the renunciation and the life of the senses is strongly suggested by a close reading of the *Sundarakāṇḍa* of Vālmīki's immortal epic poem, the *Rāmāyaṇa*. This book, the fifth of the epic's seven, is peculiarly well suited to serve as the basis for an exploration of the intertwined realms of revulsion and desire precisely because its action is situated in the realm of the ultimate Other, of ego-alien creatures who represent at once the lure of forbidden pleasures and the horror of a living nightmare. For the setting of the book is Lanka, the legendary island kingdom of the *rākṣasa* monarch Rāvaṇa, and it is part earthly paradise and part living hell. The signification of Vālmīki's *rākṣasas* as ideal representations of Brahminical India's loathed and yet desired Other has been carefully explored by Pollock,[12] who notes the poet's representation of the lives of these creatures as, "a continuous orgy of drink, food, and lovemaking" in order to manipulate "the most illicit fantasies of his audience."[13] Pollock argues, in sum, that the *rākṣasas* represent "all that traditional Indians most desired and most feared. *Rākṣasas* are creatures polluted by violence, blood, and carnivorous filth, who kill and eat those they kill . . . At the same time, in their libidinized forms, they enact the deepest sexual urges—total abandonment to pleasure, as well as absolute autonomy and power in gratifying lust."[14]

The powerful ambivalence towards women as the embodiment of sexuality and thus the site of both revulsion and desire is starkly demonstrated in the *Sundarakāṇḍa's* representation of the two classes of Rāvaṇa's women: the erotically charged beauties of his harem and the grotesquely deformed *rākṣasīs* whom he sets to guard Sītā. Vālmīki minutely describes the two diametrically opposed groups of women as they are seen through the gaze of his monkey hero, Hanumān.

Here, for example, is a condensed portion of the long, lingering and erotically charged description of the women of Rāvaṇa's inner apartments as they lie sleeping after a night of drunken lovemaking:

> And there he saw reclining on the carpet a thousand beautiful women. It was past midnight, and they had all succumbed to the power of drink and sleep. They had ceased their amorous play and now slept soundly in the dead of night . . . . Surrounded by these lovely women, the lord of the *rākṣasas* looked as beautiful as the majestic moon, the lord of the night, surrounded by stars . . . . The women lay there, their consciousness stolen by slumber. Their thick and heavy garlands were disordered, and their fine jewelry lay scattered about them from their bouts of drinking and physical exertions . . . . The pearl necklaces of some had been broken; the garments of others had fallen away. Indeed, with their belt-strings snapped, they resembled young fillies relieved of their heavy loads. Some of them, wearing beautiful earrings, their garlands crushed and torn, resembled flowering creepers crushed by mighty elephants in the great forest. Splendid pearl necklaces—shining with the luster of moonbeams—rested like sleeping *haṃsas*

> [geese] between the breasts of some of the women . . . . With their masses of tiny bells for lotus buds and their large gold ornaments for full-blown lotuses, with their amorous gestures for crocodiles and their radiant beauty for banks, the sleeping women resembled rivers. The lovely marks left on some of them, impressed on their tender limbs and nipples by their ornaments, looked like the ornaments themselves . . . . Their sweet breath, so naturally fragrant, wafted over Rāvaṇa with the added fragrance of sweet wine. Some of Rāvaṇa's women kissed the faces of their rivals under the false impression that their faces were his. Their thoughts thoroughly focused on Rāvaṇa, no longer in control of themselves, those beautiful women gave pleasure to their rivals. Some of those beautiful young women—all adorned with bracelets—lay cushioning their heads on their arms and on their lovely upper garments. One of them lay on another's breast and yet another upon her arm. One lay on another's lap, while yet another lay across the first one's arms. They all lay there mutually intertwined, resting on each other's thighs, sides, buttocks, and backs. In the grip of love and intoxication, they lay there, their bodies all entangled with one another. Those slender-waisted women slept, their arms intertwined, experiencing deep pleasure from the touch of one another's bodies.[15]

By contrast with the evocation of the erotic sentiment, the description of Sītā's grotesque *rākṣasī* wardresses conjures up only the sentiments of revulsion and fear:

> Straining to see Vaidehī [Sītā], Hanumān, son of Māruta the wind god, saw—a short distance away—frightful-looking *rākṣasa* women. One had but a single ear, while another's ears covered her entire upper body. One had no ears at all. Another had pointed ears, while yet another had her nose on her forehead. One had a huge head; another's neck was long and thin. One had hardly any hair, while another was completely bald. Yet another's hair covered her like a woolen blanket. One had pendulous ears and a bulbous forehead; another's breasts and belly hung down. One's lips protruded, while another's lips were on her chin. Yet another's mouth hung open, while still another's knees stuck out. One was very short; another very tall. One was hunchbacked, another was deformed, while yet another was a dwarf. One was snaggletoothed; another had a sunken face. One had yellow eyes, while another's features were distorted. The best of monkeys stared at those *rākṣasa* women, whose appearance caused his fur to

bristle. They were deformed, yellowish, black, wrathful, fond of quarrels, and armed with spears, mallets, and war-hammers of black iron. Some had the faces of boars, deer, tigers, buffalo, goats, or jackals. Some had feet like those of elephants, camels, and horses. Others' heads were sunk into their bodies. Some had only one hand; others one foot. Some had the ears of donkeys, horses, cows, elephants, or monkeys. Some had no noses; others had huge ones. Some had crooked noses or noses without nostrils. Some had noses like elephants' trunks, while others had nostrils in their foreheads. Some had the feet of elephants, some had enormous feet, some had feet like cows' hooves, and some had hairy feet. Some had enormous heads, necks, breasts, and bellies. Some had enormous mouths and eyes, while others had long tongues and nails. Some of those dreadful-looking *rākṣasa* women had the faces of goats, elephants, cows, sows, horses, camels, or donkeys. They held lances and war-hammers; and they were wrathful and fond of quarrels. Those *rākṣasa* women were snaggletoothed. Their hair was like smoke, and their faces were hideous. Addicted to meat and wine, they were constantly guzzling strong drink. Their bodies were smeared with flesh and blood, for such was their food. (*Rām.* 5.15.4–17)

This radically different representation of the bodies of elite women as sites of desire and those of the Other as sources of repugnance is an echo of the well known and fateful *Araṇyakāṇḍa* scene in which Śūrpaṇakhā, the grotesque characterization of uncontrolled female sexuality, is sharply contrasted with the ideal of sexuality bounded by the norms of wifely devotion (*pātivratyam*) and constrained by the conventions of feminine beauty, Sītā (Rām. 3.16. 6–10).[16] Moreover, these dramatic differences in the desirability of the gendered body are closely reflected in the kinds of food associated with these two groups.

The diet of the *rākṣasas*, perhaps more than any other of their features, is a source of fascinated revulsion to the Brahminical sensibility. For above all theirs is a diet of flesh and blood, human as well as animal, taken hot, red, and raw. Typical examples from Vālmīki are his descriptions of the terrifying *rākṣasas* Virādha and Kabandha whom Rāma encounters at different points in the story. In Pollock's vigorous translation they are described as follows:

[Virādha was] a roaring, man-eating monster. Sunken-eyed, huge mouthed, his belly deformed, he was massive, loathsome, deformed

> . . . clad in a tiger skin dripping with grease and spattered with blood, . . . On an iron pike he held impaled three lions, four tigers, two wolves, ten dappled antelopes and the massive head of an elephant, complete with tusks and smeared with gore. (*Rām.* 3.2.4–8)
>
> Ravenously licking his massive lips and massive fangs, [Kabandha] was devouring tremendous apes and lions, elephants and deer . . . he would seize all sorts of animals in his hands—apes, deer, flocks of birds. He pulled in countless animals and pulled them apart limb from limb as he stood there blocking the path . . . (*Rām.* 3.65. 12–20)

But just as Sītā's grotesque and repellent wardresses do not represent the entire picture of *rākṣasa* femininity, neither do these orgies of raw flesh and gore make up the totality of *rākṣasa* cuisine. For just as in the case of sex, so in the matter of food the kingdom of the *rākṣasas* is a realm of excess that is a source of desire as well as of revulsion.

Thus, while the savage *rākṣasas* of the forest are shown as gorging on the most repellent and frightening of foods, the kitchens of their lord's palace produce far different fare for the delectation of Rāvaṇa and his lovers. Consider the detailed attention the poet lavishes on the culinary in its intimate proximity with the erotic as Hanumān continues his search of the *rākṣasa* lord's harem.

> There, in the house of the lord of the *rākṣasas*, the tiger among monkeys gazed upon the great *rākṣasa*'s drinking hall, replete with everything one could desire. In that drinking hall he saw portions of meat set out: venison, buffalo, and boar. And the tiger among monkeys saw half-eaten roosters, peacocks, and jungle fowl on large golden platters. Hanumān saw boars and *vārdhrāṇasaka* birds, prepared with curd and *sauvarcala* salt. And there were also porcupine, deer, and peacocks; as well as various kinds of cocks, *kṛkara* fowl, and half-eaten *cakora* birds; buffalo, *ekaśalya* fish, and goats all properly prepared. And there were soft delicacies, all manner of drink, and every sort of food, along with various kinds of condiments: sour, salty, and pungent. With costly pearl necklaces, anklets, and bracelets scattered about, and with all kinds of fruit strewn among the drinking vessels, the floor, covered with floral offerings, took on an even greater splendor. With its finely wrought beds placed here and there, the drinking hall seemed to be ablaze without fire. And there, along with many different kinds of meats that had been exquisitely prepared by master chefs and set out in the drinking hall, he saw various heavenly

crystal-clear spirits, both natural and fortified. There were rum, mead, and fruit and flower wines, all flavored with various fragrant powders. The floor, strewn with heaped-up garlands and covered with silver jars, crystal vessels, and other vessels of *jāmbūnada* gold, looked beautiful. And there in jars of silver and *jāmbūnada* gold, the monkey saw great quantities of the finest drink. The great monkey saw brimming wine vessels made of gold, jewels, and silver. Some of the beverages that he saw had been half-drunk, some completely consumed, while others had not even been touched. Thus did he wander about seeing here various foods, and there drinks served out in portions, and elsewhere the leftover food. (*Rām.* 5.9.10–24)[17]

This paean to excess in food and strong drink is interpolated into the poet's lingering voyeurism towards the *rākṣasa* women and indeed the eroticism of the passage is only intensified by his culinary digression. The above passage continues:

> And he saw that many of the women's beds were empty and that some of those beautiful women were embracing one another in their sleep. One young woman, overcome by the power of sleep, had taken off another's garment, and embracing her she made love to her in her sleep. The lovely clothes and garlands that they wore stirred slightly from their breathing as if caught in a gentle breeze. A breeze was blowing there, bearing in all directions a varied fragrance of cool sandal paste and sweet-tasting rum, of various garlands and blossoms. Thus a fragrant and overwhelming aroma of sandal for the bath and incense wafted through the Puṣpaka palace. (5.9.26–30)

But the association of the erotic and the gustatory, and for that matter fascination and revulsion, is not simply a matter of juxtaposition for Vālmīki and his audience. Indeed it seems to lie at the heart of his imaginary desire. The space for sensual ambivalence between the enjoyment of women as the object of sexual and gustatory desire, explored so playfully elsewhere, is here in terrifying earnest. For in Lanka we have left the courtly world of the Pāṇḍavas and entered the nightmare realm of flesh-eating monsters.

Rāvaṇa has abducted Sītā to gratify his lust. Indeed, he is mad with passion for her. But he makes it clear that if he fails to bring her to his bed, he is prepared to bring her to his table instead. Approaching Sītā in his *aśoka* grove he woos her with honeyed words, with promises of undying love and all the treasures of the world;

but, when she spurns his advances, he tells her: "I will honor the two-month period that I set as your deadline. But after that, my pretty, you must come to my bed. Once the two months have passed, if you still do not want me for your husband, then they will slaughter you in the kitchen for my breakfast." (*Rām.* 5.20. 8–9)

Perhaps nowhere does this proximity of lust to hunger in the imagination of the epic poet become more starkly apparent than in the exchanges between Sītā and those very embodiments of unregulated desire, her grotesque *rākṣasī* wardresses. Instructed by the frustrated demon-king to wear down Sītā's resistance, the *rākṣasa* women begin to alternately cajole and menace her. Like their master, some of them try first to tempt her with visions of the luxurious life of pleasure she can share with Rāvaṇa, only to then turn on her with threats to devour her. Thus, for example, a *rākṣasī* named Vinatā tells her:

> " You must accept Rāvaṇa, lord of all the *rākṣasas*, as your husband. For he is as valorous and handsome as Indra Vāsava, lord of the gods. You must give up this insignificant human Rāma and take refuge in Rāvaṇa, who is skillful and exceedingly generous and who speaks kindly to all creatures. Covering your body with fragrant ointments and adorning yourself with heavenly ornaments, you must, from this day forward, Vaidehī, become the queen of all the worlds, like the goddess Svāhā, the consort of Agni the god of fire, lovely woman, or Indra's consort, the goddess Śacī. What are you doing, Vaidehī, with this insignificant Rāma, who is, in any case, as good as dead? If you don't do what I have told you, then all of us will eat you up this very moment!" (*Rām.* 5.22.18–22)

Another, Vikaṭā, says:

> "Choose joy and pleasure instead; give up your constant misery. Sītā, you should enjoy yourself to your heart's content with the king of the *rakṣasas*! Timid lady, you should know how transient is the youth of women. You should seize happiness before your own youth passes. Lady of intoxicating eyes, you should roam with the *rakṣasa* king through his lovely gardens and mountain parks. Seven thousand women will be at your command, lovely one. You must accept Ravaṇa, lord of all the *rākṣasas*, as your husband. Or else, Maithilī, if you do not do exactly as I have told you, I shall tear out your heart and eat it!" (*Rām.* 5.22. 28–32)

Other voices join in mingling reference to the fetishized parts of the female anatomy, the conventional stimulants to sexual desire, with the grossest of cannibalistic appetites:

> Then another fierce-looking *rākṣasa* woman named Caṇḍodarī brandishing a huge spear said these words: "The moment I saw this woman that Rāvaṇa has brought here, her eyes darting like a doe's and her breasts trembling with fear, I conceived a tremendous craving. I conceived a desire to eat her liver, spleen, *utpīḍa*,[18] her heart with all its veins and arteries, her intestines and her head." Then a *rākṣasa* woman named Praghasā said, "What are we waiting for? Let's strangle this heartless woman! We will tell the king that the woman is dead, and without a doubt, he will tell us, 'You may eat her!'" Next a *rākṣasa* woman named Ajāmukhī said, "Butcher her; then cut her all up into equal, bite-sized pieces. Then we can all have a share. I hate arguments! So quickly bring lots of things to drink and all kinds of garlands." Then a *rākṣasa* woman named Śūrpaṇakhā said, "I agree with what Ajāmukhī just said. So quickly bring wine, the banisher of every sorrow! Let us eat human flesh and dance before the goddess Nikumbhilā." (*Rām.* 5.22.33–41)

In a culture such as that of traditional South Asia, where social status along the axes traced in Srinivas' concept of "Sanskritization"[19] has been so centrally indexed to restrictions on sexuality and diet, it is clear that these areas are of particularly great importance in the construction of individual and group identity. The homology of the two in psychic as well as symbolic terms, observable in many cultures, appears—I believe the above evidence suggests—to be particularly prominent in Vālmīki's construction of the "Other."

Vālmīki's *Rāmāyaṇa*, both in and of itself and through the vast apparatus of Ramayana versions and representations in all of the languages and regions of South Asia, has had an unusually powerful if not unparalleled influence on discursive formations regarding many central issues in the traditional cultures of the region. Not least among these are questions involving the complex relationship between the life of the body and that of the spirit that concerns the management of desire. This set of questions in turn is played out in the realms of sexuality and diet as critical cultural markers of status and identity. In developing so brilliantly this theme through the opposition of the titanic figures of Rāma, the very personification of self-restraint, and Rāvaṇa, the epitome of license, the epic poet has set the terms for a discussion that has continued in the religious literature of the region, for millennia. It would seem then that a closer examination of the epic's dialectic of indulgence and restraint, most focally in the areas of food and sex, and that of the large corpus of related texts, may shed considerable further light on one of the characteristic concerns of the Indian tradition. This, in turn, will, I hope, give us further insight into one of the most common and yet poorly understood phenomena of human cultures.

# ASSERTIONS OF SOCIAL RANK

SIX

# Dining Out at Lake Pampa: The Shabari Episode in Multiple Ramayanas

PHILIP LUTGENDORF

Tasting one after another, he says, "This one's even sweeter!"
He gazes at them and gushes, "Here, Lakshmana, take one."
The Shabari keeps on handing him *ber* after *ber* after *ber*,
and Raghubir keeps singing out for, "*Ber*, more *ber*!"
— Rasikbihari[1]

## Appetizers (Valmiki and Other Literary Ramayanas)

Near the end of Valmiki's forest book (*Araṇyakāṇḍa*), Rama and Lakshmana, wandering in search of Sita, are directed westward by a celestial being whom they have just liberated from a grotesque demonic form. His name, Kabandha or "belly," described him well, for a sage's curse and a god's wrath had reduced him to an enormous stomach equipped only with a mouth and two huge arms with which he grasped and devoured everything within reach. A vestige of this voracious appetite persists even after his arms have been hewn off by the brothers and his body (by his own instruction) immolated in a pit, permitting him to regain his former *gandharva* shape; for in describing the path ahead, he lingers over its gustatory delights. Noting the many varieties of fruit trees that line the path to Lake Pampa, he urges the brothers, "Climb them or bend them by force to the ground, but you simply must taste their ambrosial fruit before you go." (3.69.4)[2] He follows up this imagined appetizer with a lakeside main course that will consist of tame and easily-snared water fowl ("plump as balls of butter") and equally succulent fish ("choice, fleshy ones, and not too bony") to be charbroiled on skewers (3.69.8–9).

In fact, Rama and Lakshmana will select nothing from Kabandha's menu. Although they observe the "honey-sweet fruit trees densely clustered on the hillsides," they do not pause to taste them, for they are eager for their prophesied meeting with the monkey-lord Sugriva, who will assist them in recovering Sita (3.70.2). When they reach Pampa, the brothers (who are sometimes aggressively non-vegetarian in Valmiki's version), pass up its abundant fish and fowl to dine on evidently vegan "forest food" collected by an aged anchorite identified as Shabari, a servant of the long-departed disciples of sage Matanga (3.70.13). The identity of this woman and the precise nature of the foodstuffs she places before the brothers has been a matter of no small interest to Ramayana tellers and audiences over the last two millennia, and in the popular Hindi parlance of recent times, at least, the expression "the tribal woman's jujubes" (*bhilnī ke ber*) has become a proverbial designation for a humble but loving offering that pleases God, and the verbal signifier of a highly emotional tableau often represented in popular religious art. As with other elements in the epic's "pool of signifiers," as A.K. Ramanujan termed it,[3] the components of the Shabari episode have been rearranged to suit a variety of interpretations that nevertheless cluster, both chronologically and thematically, into patterns. Taken together, they suggest the tension, often noted in Hindu bhakti, between more popular and liberal, and more elite and conservative orientations; between the enthusiastic savoring of the sweet and "juicy" essence of collective devotion, and a more sour perspective that finds such egalitarian impulses unappetizing and indigestible.

Valmiki, the often prolix Sanskrit *ādi-kavi*, is spare in his description of Shabari, who is the last in a series of saintly anchorites whom Rama encounters in the forest book. Although her name implies that she is a female *śabara*—belonging to a non-Aryan hill tribe of the Deccan, whose name, together with such terms as *bhīla* and *kirāta*,

A contemporary 'god poster' image of the Shabari episode

became in time a loose designation for "barbarian" or "outsider"[4]—Valmiki never expands on this association, but simply describes her (in Kabandha's words) as "an ascetic . . . . devoted to dharma" (3.69.19–20), and later, when the princes encounter her, as a "perfected woman" (3.70.6), who offers them a meal she has assembled herself but which we never see them eat. This is followed by a brief tour of the lakeside hermitage and a prophesy regarding Rama's onward journey, and finally by Shabari's self-immolation to rejoin her erstwhile masters in their immortal world. Valmiki's primary focus, here as elsewhere in the *Araṇyakāṇḍa*, seems to be on the wonderful spiritual accomplishments of the forest-dwelling ascetics whom Rama has undertaken to protect—blessings that remain visible in the form of unfading garlands, damp barkcloth garments, and glowing fire-altars, years after the sages themselves have left the earth. Shabari appears as a sort of *chaukidar* or custodian of this empty ashram, and her humble status is suggested by Kabandha's description of her as a "servant" of the sages (3.69.19), by her own admiring account of "those I had been serving" (3.70.10), and by the manner in which she greets the brothers. "At the sight of the princes, the perfected woman sprang up with hands cupped in reverence, and then she bowed to clasp the feet of Rama and of wise Lakshmana." (3.70.6)

This is interesting in that Rama's usual practice, on encountering forest sages, has been to prostrate himself and to clasp *their* feet (e.g. Bharadvaja, Atri, Sharabhanga, Agastya), but again, nothing more is said about this reversal, and it may have been obvious to the Sanskrit poet's audience that in light of Shabari's gender and social situation—notwithstanding her spiritual "perfection"—this was the appropriate etiquette. That Shabari has a special relationship with Rama is implied in the sages' directive to her to await his coming (3.70.11–12), and, in a verse omitted from the Baroda edition, she declares that, by seeing him, her asceticism has borne fruit and her life's purpose has been fulfilled. Another verse found in many manuscripts has Rama declare, just before permitting Shabari to immolate herself, "You have given me great hospitality" (1:666, 3.74.31).[5]

The brevity of this passage as well as its peculiar features suggest that it may be alluding to a story upon which the Sanskrit poet chose not to elaborate, but which he assumed would be known to his listeners, or explained to them by a good singer-expounder. There is also the possibility that this story—which evidently has to do with

A line drawing from the *Bhakta caritrāṅk* of *Kalyāṇ* (1952; plate facing p. 292), showing Rama receiving *ber* from Shabari and offering them to Lakshmana

non-Aryan ascetics—has been suppressed in Valmiki's *Rāmāyaṇa* as we know it, perhaps in the interest of the Brahmanical agenda which would also insert, into the final book of the epic, the sobering tale of King Rama's murder of the Shudra Shambuka for practicing asceticism. Shabari's guru, Matanga, is a shadowy if revered figure in Valmiki, but the same name appears in the *Mahābhārata* identifying a teacher of low-caste origin (13.29.22ff), and, in the *Suttanipāta* of Buddhaghosa, Matanga is called an untouchable *caṇḍāla* who nevertheless "gained the highest fame, and embarked on the path to the gods." (1.7.137ff).[6]

The first major vernacular Ramayana, Kamban's *c.*-twelfth-century Tamil epic *Irāmāvatāram*, is fully as long as Valmiki's version and often expands on its narrative in significant ways (e.g., in the Shurpanakha episode, 3.5), yet its treatment of the meeting with Shabari is shorter still and adds little to the allusive contents of the Sanskrit version. In keeping with the major themes of Kamban's forest book, the emphasis in its brief, final chapter is on *tapasyā* and bhakti—austerity and heartfelt devotion—and Shabari clearly exemplifies both. Identified as an "empress of difficult *tapas*" (stanza 3805), she sheds copious tears when addressing Rama (3803) and looks at him "with true love" (3806). Concerning the meal that she serves the brothers, Kamban merely remarks that "she gave them what they needed" (3803).[7] The Telugu *Raṅganātha Rāmāyaṇa* (*c.* fourteenth century) gives a yet more terse account of the episode, stating only that Shabari offers fruits to Rama, which he accepts.[8]

The influential Sanskrit text, *Adhyātma Rāmāyaṇa* ("esoteric *Rāmāyaṇa*," which most scholars now assign to roughly the fifteenth century) expands slightly on this. A text that is as concerned with ritualistic worship as it is with advaitin metaphysics, it shows Shabari engaged in what is in effect the *pūjā* of Rama, washing his feet and sprinkling the water over her body, and offering him "*arghya* [a libation] and other ceremonial honors" followed by "the choicest nectar-like fruits that she had collected specially for him" (3.10.7–9).[9] A significant elaboration on the earlier texts, however, follows the meal: ceremonial worship normally includes a hymn of praise, and Shabari's takes the form of an elaborate declaration of her own unworthiness to offer one.

> O Thou immeasurable Being! I am an ignorant and low-born woman.
> I have not the qualification [*adhikāra*] to be the servant of Thy servants

> at the hundredth remove. What then to speak of my qualification to serve Thee? . . . . I am not capable of praising Thee with a hymn. What am I to do? (3.10.17–19)[10]

Rama responds with a long lecture on the irrelevance of social status in relation to bhakti, which he then expounds as consisting of nine basic disciplines (*navadhā bhakti*)—association with holy people, hearing of his deeds, repeating his name, etc. (3.10.20–31). After this digression, the conventional narrative resumes with Rama asking Shabari for onward directions, whereupon she seeks his permission to enter the fire. Her reward is described as *mukti* or liberation, and the author adds (in an apparent nod to his primary audience): "Shabari, though low-born, attained *mukti* by Rama's grace. It is then needless to say that a man of high birth, if he be devoted to Rama will certainly attain to *mukti*" (3.10.42–3).[11]

Tulsidas often shows his great debt to the *Adhyātma Rāmāyaṇa* in the Hindi epic *Rāmcaritmānas* (*c.* 1574), and his brief presentation of the Shabari episode includes a discourse on ninefold bhakti that closely follows its own. Rama's comments on the irrelevance of social status to devotion are here pointedly juxtaposed, however, with his stern lecture to Kabandha in the preceding stanza on the evil consequences of disrespect to Brahmins (3.33.8–34.2). As in Kamban and the *Adhyātma Rāmāyaṇa*, Shabari displays intense emotion, falling tearfully at the brothers' feet before seating them reverently in her hut (3.34.9–10). The meal she then serves them receives a memorable *dohā*.

> She brought most delicious fruits and tubers to set before Rama,
> and the Lord ate them lovingly, praising them again and again. (3.34)

Protesting her unworthiness, Shabari describes herself as "lowborn and densely dull," and impure by virtue of both birth and gender (3.35.2–3). The rest of the episode follows the *Adhyātma* version fairly closely, save that Shabari's ultimate destination is described as "the highest state of the Lord, from which there is no returning" (3.36.*ch*.2).

Taken together, the rather consistently terse and allusive accounts of Shabari presented in these major literary Ramayanas that span roughly two millennia surely serve to whet our appetites to know more about this woman of lowly birth and independent lifestyle, and about her special relationship to Rama. Interestingly enough, these literary epics—to which scholars are apt to turn in search of authoritative renderings of the Rama story—are united in their failure to mention what, in the popular imagination today, is undoubtedly the single most memorable feature of the Shabari episode: Rama's consumption of fruits that were previously tasted by the tribal woman, and that have thus been rendered *ucchiṣṭa* or *jūṭhā* ("defiled by saliva"), and subject to one of the strongest of all Hindu food taboos.[12] To savor this delicate matter, we will have to turn to a different menu.

## Entrees
(Priyadas, *Kalyāṇ*, Anjaninandan Sharan)

Diet is one of the principal markers of ritual status in Hindu South Asia and the proscribed and polluting food of the lowly and the outsider is often cited, in Sanskrit literature, among their identifying marks; thus *śvapāka* or "dog-cooker" is virtually synonymous with *caṇḍāla* or *mleccha*, and non-Aryan tribal labels such as *bhīla* and *śabara* evoke both a barbaric lifestyle and meat-centered diet. Even the vegetarian food of such persons carries connotations of wildness, and in this regard it is interesting to note that the *c.* twelfth century *Līlāvatī* of Bhaskaracharya mentions a kind of wild sweet-potato known as *śabara-kanda* ("shabara's root") as well as the jujube fruit, which is referred to as *śabarāhāra*—"the food of shabaras."[13] Jujube (*Ziziphus jujuba*) is a small, wild plum-like fruit with a greenish or yellowish skin; inside, the pulp can vary from tartly sour to moderately sweet. In modern Hindi it is called *ber.* One seldom finds it in bazaar fruit stalls, however, for it is regarded as a wild and second-rate fruit, and it is mostly sold along roadsides in rural areas, usually by elderly women or small children who harvest the fruit that has fallen from trees. As is the case with wild cherries or plums, a bag of *ber* is likely to contain at least some sweet and juicy fruits, but also many others that will prove, to any but the hungriest eater, too sour to bother with. All these qualities—its wildness, its association with poor, rural people and tribals, and its varying quality—help explain the association of *ber* with the Shabari story, and the widely held belief that it was this fruit that the old woman served to Rama and Lakshmana.

I have observed that there may have existed a Shabari story that was omitted from some of the best-known literary Ramayanas, both Sanskrit and vernacular, and yet was alluded to by them and familiar to their audiences. An elaborate version of such a story, of uncertain age, found its way into north Indian Vaishnava hagiographic literature in the seventeenth and eighteenth centuries. The terse *Bhaktamāl* of Nabhadas (*c.* 1624), a highly-condensed "rosary" of some two hundred famous devotees, counts Shabari as eighth among twenty-three *bhaktas* who are termed "beloved of the Lord" (*Hari vallabh*) and who are listed in its ninth stanza. This work appears to have been intended as a kind of mnemonic for Vaishnava storytellers,[14] and its skeletal outline was fleshed out in *c.* 1712 by one Priyadas, who composed an elaborate *ṭīkā* or commentary entitled *Bhaktirasbodhinī* that adds some 630 stanzas. Seven of these stanzas are devoted to Shabari (31–37), and the story they recount has achieved wide circulation and will be summarized here. An early-twentieth-century commentator's introduction tells how the youthful Shabari abandons her own people when they desire to perform her marriage and are preparing to slaughter a large number of animals for the wedding feast. Rebelling against such cruelty, she flees by night to the shores of Lake Pampa where she takes up her abode in the vicinity of Matanga's ashram, subsisting on wild fruits and roots.[15]

> Shabari longs to serve the sadhus and rishis who dwell in the woods, but keeps away from them, conscious of her low birth. At night she sweeps away thorns and pebbles from the paths they will walk to bathe in the lake, and deposits bundles of firewood outside the doors of their huts. In the morning, the holy men wonder "Who has done this?" (31)
>
> Sage Matanga instructs his pupils to stay awake and apprehend the "thief" [who is "stealing" merit, according to the modern commentator], and they capture the terrified Shabari, who falls at Matanga's feet. Seeing her devotion, Matanga sheds tears of love and feels that he has found a treasure. (32)
>
> He tells his disciples that although she is of low birth, her devotion merits the praise of millions of Brahmins, and he instructs her to remain in the ashram and initiates her in the divine name. This angers all the other ascetics, who consider it an affront to their status, but Matanga is unconcerned by their reaction. When he prepares to leave the world, he tells Shabari to remain behind and promises that she will see Lord Rama. (33)
>
> Disconsolate over her separation from her guru, Shabari clings to life in the hope of seeing Rama. One night she is delayed in her sweeping and accidentally touches an ascetic enroute to his morning

> bath. He angrily berates her for polluting him and she flees to her hut. When the sadhu reaches the lake, he finds that its clear water has turned to blood and is swarming with vermin. Failing to understand the real cause of this awful transformation, he blames it on his contact with the "unlucky woman" (*abhāgī*). (34)
>
> Shabari gathers jujube fruits, tastes them, and sets the sweetest ones aside for Rama. Every day, she watches and yearns for his arrival, but when she finally hears that he is coming, she again thinks of her low status and hides in her hut, afraid to face him. Rama comes inquiring of everyone, "Where is Shabari?" (35)
>
> "Where is that fortunate woman (*bhāgavatī*)? My eyes thirst to see her." When he enters the ashram she prostrates before him, but he lifts her up, and seeing him, her sorrow departs and tears stream from her eyes. Bidding him be seated, she serves him fruit and he praises it greatly, declaring that it has relieved his fatigue from the journey. (36)
>
> Meanwhile the rishis are all worrying about the polluted lake, and someone suggests that they ask Rama for a solution. Just then they learn that he has already come, and is seated in Shabari's hut. Their pride is shattered and they fall at his feet. When told about the condition of the lake water, Rama instructs the ascetics to grasp Shabari's feet, and to bring her to the lake; when she touches the water, it becomes pure again. (37)

Priyadas' story shows certain consistencies with the literary Ramayanas examined earlier: Shabari is the disciple of sage Matanga, instructed by him to remain in his ashram after his physical death and to entertain Rama when he wanders that way; she falls at Rama's feet, and serves the Raghu prince wild fruits, which he praises lavishly. At the same time, the story makes several significant elaborations on the epic accounts: it explains in detail the nature of the "service" Shabari renders to Matanga and his disciples, and it depicts her not only gathering wild fruits—identified here as *ber* or jujubes—but also *tasting* them before setting them aside for Rama. Further, it makes one radical departure from the versions I have considered, by placing Shabari's abode not in an eerily deserted ashram still radiant with the presence of departed saints, but in a thriving forest community of flesh-and-blood, but bigoted, ascetics, who fail to recognize Shabari's spiritual attainment because of her lowly birth. This story element, which leads directly to the double transformation of the lake, combines with the motif of the jujubes to make a powerful statement reversing conventional ideas of purity and pollution. Even as Shabari, who is inwardly pure though outwardly polluted, delights the Lord by serving him wild fruits that she has defiled by touching to her lips, the outwardly pure sadhus, inwardly defiled by their arrogance of birth, pollute their own lake by insulting one of the Lord's humblest *bhaktas* and can only remove the defilement by honoring her and placing her feet in the water.

Although it is uncertain whether this story pre-dates Priyadas' time, it is clear that it has achieved wide circulation since. It appears in elaborate retellings in modern devotional works,[16] and its central event—the serving of the tainted jujubes to an enthusiastic Rama—is a common theme in popular religious art, wherein the gaunt and wrinkled Shabari, clad in a white or ochre sari but without a blouse (an indication of age, tribal status, and/or poverty) feeds the beaming Lord; closer examination of such images reveals small and (literally) tell-tale bites missing from each proffered fruit. When the journal *Kalyāṇ*, published by the Gita Press of Gorakhpur and widely circulated among pious *Sanātan Dharmī* Hindus throughout north and central India, produced a "special issue on the lives of saints" in 1952 (*Bhakta caritrāṅk*, one of its annual book-length thematic supplements), it included a lengthy retelling of Priyadas' story in modern Hindi prose, set within a series of accounts of low-caste and tribal devotees (e.g. Bhakta Kirat, Sudama Mali, Bhim Kumhar, Chandali, etc.). Elaborating on the prejudice of the orthodox rishis of Lake Pampa, it describes how they cease eating or even conversing with Matanga after he has initiated Shabari, but he regards them as "deluded" and remains unconcerned.[17] It also develops the theme of Shabari's long wait for Rama's arrival: her daily preparation of her hut to receive him by applying fresh cowdung to the floor, spreading a carpet of flowers, and, of course, gathering wild fruits. In her intense yearning for Rama's *darśan*, Shabari behaves as if mad (*pāgal-sī*), and it is in this state that she accidentally brushes against one of the ascetics as he proceeds to the lake, leading to his angry outburst and the transformation of the water. Also emphasized here is Rama's reciprocal eagerness to see Shabari; his repeated asking of everyone, "Where is my Shabari?" During the climactic meal, much is made of Rama's ecstatic reaction to the fruit; he praises its sweetness again and again, and an inserted couplet declares that, during the rest of his life, no food that he was served anywhere ever pleased him as much. In the final confrontation with the sages, they condemn themselves for their own spiritual blindness: "Fie upon our wisdom, our celibacy, our learning, our lineage, and our skill in performing sacrifices, because we have turned against Lord Hari!"[18]

Modern commentators on the Tulsidas *Rāmcaritmānas* often interpret its version of the Shabari episode in the light of such understandings of the old woman as a love-crazed, intimate devotee. Thus, Anjaninandan Sharan, in the great twelve-volume *ṭīkā* entitled *Mānas-pīyūṣ* ("nectar of the Mānas," 1925–56), interprets the "lovely seat" (*sundar āsan*, 3.34.5) she offers Rama to refer to a bed of flower petals, and goes on to describe her daily *sādhanā* of gathering and arranging the blossoms, since she never knows exactly when he will be coming. Similarly he notes that although Rama has been served forest fruits in numerous sages' ashrams, he has never been said to praise them before (as he now does, repeatedly, in couplet 3.34, cited earlier). Indeed, Sharan rightly observes, "Is it not contrary to etiquette (*niyam*) to praise food in India? But in this case, there is love, and where love holds sway, etiquette cannot endure."[19]

The matter of the defiled jujubes is treated at length by both Sharan and the commentator in *Kalyāṇ*, with revealingly different results. The Gita Press author was probably a Vaishnava Brahmin pandit in the employ of the Marwari editors, and in the midst of his paean to the irrelevance of caste and pollution in matters of bhakti, he inserts a long footnote that argues (a) that Shabari was *not* actually an impure shabara, but a high-born ascetic woman who was merely *named* "Shabari"; and (b) that it is untrue that Rama ate *jūṭhā* fruit served by Shabari; this is impossible because the embodiment of propriety (*maryādā puruṣottam*) would not have done such a thing. References in texts to Shabari "tasting" the fruit, he insists, only imply that she tasted from the various *trees* to determine which ones yielded the sweetest *ber*, and then gathered fruit exclusively from those.[20] Sharan, however, who was a retired civil servant turned Ayodhya-resident sadhu, offers an interpretation of the episode that reveals characteristic Ramanandi liberality even as it pointedly refutes the above arguments. It is worth relishing in full.

> Regarding *jūṭhā* food, the objection may be raised that the embodiment of propriety would not behave in such a way. This statement is reasonable, but at the same time there's the fact that Shabari didn't regard him as a prince, but as God himself. This is clear from all *Rāmāyaṇs*, and God is famished for *love*—what does he

care about pollution and whatnot? Only a devotee can understand this, no one else. Secondly [with regard to the argument that Shabari only sampled fruit in order to select the trees from which to harvest her offerings], how will you answer this question: the hand with which she ate the ber is polluted (*jūṭhā*), and if she then picks more fruit with that defiled hand, won't those be defiled as well? . . . . So, are we to suppose that Shabari carried water with her into the forest to repeatedly wash her hands? Hardly! What will devotees gain from considering such questions? I don't see the point of it at all. Rather, one ought to assert that this path of love is something altogether different. Even today we observe that whereas strict orthodox worshipers place only untasted food before the Lord, loving devotees never offer anything they haven't tasted first, even though according to worldly convention such things would never be considered suitable for divine service. But on the path of love, *adharma* is also counted as dharma.[21]

The fact that the *jūṭhā* fruit is not explicitly mentioned in the *Mānas* does not trouble Sharan, who explains that Tulsidas sought to uphold the dignity of all teachers and sects and to avoid giving offence; however, the commentator asserts that when the great Hindi poet uses the adjective *surasa* ("juicy, sweet") to describe the foodstuffs, "he gives an esoteric allusion to the matter of the *jūṭhā* offering." Further, Sharan quotes a song from Tulsidas' lyric anthology *Gītāvalī* (3.17) which describes Shabari feeding Rama in the manner of his mother, Kausalya, with the maternal sentiment of *vātsalya*. "In this emotional stance," Sharan notes, "there is absolutely no objection to feeding food that has been tasted."[22]

Like Priyadas' story itself, such debates are a reminder of the ongoing tension within popular Hinduism between a sense of order and propriety (dharma, *maryādā*) that erects firm barriers against impurity and institutionalizes a status hierarchy based on birth, and a love-saturated devotionalism that overcomes all proscriptions and barriers. In the metaphors of bhakti poetics, the onrushing and melting force of devotion, transmitted through lyric poetry in the mother tongue, is often likened to the fresh water of lakes, rivers, and streams and is invariably characterized as "sweet"; in contrast, the injunctions of brahmanical orthodoxy, contained in the corpus of Sanskrit literature, are commonly compared to the ocean—vast and profound, but filled with water that is salty, bitter, and unpalatable: the wellsprings of an ideological enterprise of exclusion, containment, and control that Sheldon Pollock has termed "intellectual violence."[23]

## Dessert (Ramanand Sagar)

One of the most prominent and ubiquitous Ramayana "texts" of recent times was the television serialization "Ramayan," produced and directed by Ramanand Sagar, that aired between 1987 and 1989 on India's then single-channel national television network, Doordarshan. Consisting of a main story in seventy-eight episodes and a sequel entitled "Uttar-Ramayan" ("Epilogue to the Ramayan") in twenty-six more, it kept millions of Indians riveted to television screens for a weekly hour on Sunday mornings over a period spanning more than two years. The creation of a self-styled devotee of the Tulsidas *Rāmcaritmānas*, the Hindi-language video epic attempted to promote, to an unprecedented simultaneous audience that eventually swelled to an estimated one hundred million, the theme of "national integration" advocated by Rajiv Gandhi's Congress (I) government. Its meandering and leisurely screenplay—in installments that were sometimes written not far ahead of the shooting schedule—drew on a variety of Sanskrit and regional-language Ramayanas (prominently noted in the credits each week) as well as on oral traditions and the director's own inspirations. Its visual vocabulary derived from a century of mass-produced religious art: god-posters, comic books, and the mythological musicals of the Bombay film industry; but it used the small-screen format and slow pace of a TV serial to give viewers an unprecedented sense of intimate visual communion with epic characters. While urban intellectuals bemoaned the serial's garish sets, slow pace, and melodramatic acting, the majority of viewers greedily devoured its hours of close-up *darśan* of a beaming, cherubic Rama and tearful but brave Sita, along with their entourage of family and friends. Exploiting a new medium that permitted minute exploration of motivation and emotion, the serial advanced a number of striking interpretations that humanized traditional villains or advanced "progressive" messages (e.g. for communal harmony or against dowry).[24] Broadly speaking, the director's endeavor was to deftly utilize word and image to smooth over controversial incidents (such as Rama's and Lakshmana's mutilation of the demoness Shurpanakha, or Rama's unchivalrous slaying of the monkey king Vali) and to produce an unobjectionable "Ramayan" that would resonate with the largest possible audience. By all accounts he succeeded.

Rama's encounter with Shabari occupies the better part of Episode 34, which commences with the slaying of Kabandha. Following the redeemed *gandharva's* ascent to heaven, the camera leaves the brothers to cut to Shabari's idyllic ashram—an earthen hut gaily painted with the sort of designs created by many rural women, and approached by a path that meanders through lawns dotted with flowers. The camera then focuses in on a saffron-clad figure whose white, wispy hair, wizened face, and mouth missing several front teeth perfectly evokes the conventional Shabari of the religious calendars (Sagar boasted of his success in casting actors—often unknowns—who would epitomize the audience's mental image of epic figures): an elderly and maternal rustic brimming with *vātsalya*. As she gazes tearfully and expectantly into the distance, a female voice-over sings of Shabari's life of watching and waiting for Rama's arrival: a series of verses with the refrain, "Gazing at the road, Shabari's whole life has passed." With each verse we see the activity being described: Shabari sweeping the path clear ("lest any thorn prick the Lord," warbles the singer), plucking marigolds and spreading them in a gorgeous carpet over the path, and of course, picking *ber*, and (while the singer declares "Tasting sweet fruits, she daily adorns the platter") we see her sampling each tiny pale-green fruit, discarding some and smilingly setting others on a woven basket-plate.

When the *bhajan* (devotional singing) ends, Shabari is again seen working on her carpet of marigolds, sighing "My Rama! My Rama!" as she sets down each blossom. Shadows fall over her handiwork, and the camera pulls back to show four bearded holy men with Shaiva forehead markings (the north Indian visual code for brahmanical, "vedic" asceticism) about to step onto her pathway. Shabari entreats them not to crush her flowers, and one of the younger men replies in a huff, addressing her as "Crazy woman" (*paglī*), and mocking her, "How many years have you been at this? Has your Rama come yet?" Shabari replies that he will surely come, her guru Matanga has promised this, and when he does, she doesn't want him to think that, "this *bhilnī* doesn't know how to welcome me." One of the older ascetics then remarks that they shouldn't harass her but should use a different path. We see them doing so, and engaging in the following conversation:

YOUNG ASCETIC (annoyed): Sometimes it seems to me that the Bhīl woman has gone mad.

ELDER ASCETIC: Perhaps so, but don't forget that there's little difference between bhakti and madness. From a worldly perspective, a devotee simply appears mad. Shabari is a great ascetic and she has attained mystic powers, but she has no trace of pride in her attainment. This is the mark of a true devotee.

YOUNG ASCETIC (bowing respectfully): Yes, master.

The camera returns to Shabari and a new set of shadows appear; she begins to scold the would-be trespassers only to behold Rama and Lakshmana, who soon identify themselves; she falls to the ground and washes Rama's feet with her tears.

Leading the brothers down the flower-covered path and seating them on the verandah of her hut, Shabari rushes inside to get her tray of fruit: "I'm just bringing it. For years I've been setting aside the sweetest jujubes for you, Lord. Now please eat . . . . They're very sweet, I tasted each one before I kept it." The camera comes in for a closeup of the tiny fruits, each visibly scarred with toothmarks in the whitish flesh. Rama smiles and begins eating; Lakshmana appears shocked and disgusted and has to be repeatedly urged by Rama to try one.

RAMA: Lakshmana, eat. *Vāh!* (with great hesitation, Lakshmana selects a *ber* and slowly brings it to his lips, a look of disgust on his face; Rama continues to eat, beaming)

SHABARI: They're good, right? They're sweet?

RAMA: I have no words adequate to praise them. It's as if, after so many years, my mother Kausalya is feeding me with her own hand. Lakshmana, God himself can't get such sweet fruit in his heavenly world of Vaikuntha!

Lakshmana appears to remain unconvinced throughout, but the visual dialog of love between the old woman and Rama continues for some time, punctuated by his munching of *ber.*

The rest of the episode more or less follows the literary Ramayanas. After describing the way to Sugriva's hideout, Shabari takes the brothers to Matanga's fire altar, above which an unearthly light shines. Here they bow reverently and Shabari entreats Rama, "before I abandon this lowborn body of mine," to bestow on her "the knowledge of bhakti" (*bhakti jñāna*). After the disclaimer that he is only repeating what his gurus have taught him (for Sagar's Rama, like Valmiki's, generally denies direct knowledge of his own divinity), he does so. This is accomplished through a silent tableau of Rama raising his hand in blessing over the kneeling Shabari, while a male voice-over sings the famous passage from Tulsidas describing the ninefold devotional path (*navadhā bhakti; Rāmcaritmānas* 3.35.7–36.5). Shabari then takes her leave, disappearing into a flame that hovers in the air while the brothers bow reverently.

Sagar's portrayal is a pastiche of elements from various sources, and lines of dialog occasionally echo Valmikian *ślokas* or familiar *caupāīs* from the *Mānas*. Moreover, several elements in the episode (Shabari's sweeping the path and decorating it with flowers, her apparently demented behavior, and her charged encounter with the ascetics) indicate the director's familiarity with the Priyadas story or some adaptation thereof—possibly the Gita Press version cited earlier. Having Rama and Lakshmana come upon Shabari hard at work decorating their path, immediately after her encounter with the ascetics, is a clever and original rendering of their first contact (she neither leaps up to meet them, as in Valmiki, nor huddles ashamedly in her hut, as in Priyadas), calculated for maximum emotional effect: the initial case of mistaken identity yields to intense remorse at having failed to recognize the object of her long vigil, mixed with joy and relief at seeing him at last. The *ber* are present, of course, and two different scenes, each accompanied by verbal confirmation of what is happening, leave no room for doubt about Sagar's position on the matter of the tainted food-offering. Like Priyadas, Anjaninandan Sharan, and numerous poster artists, Sagar confronts viewers with fruit that would be unacceptable to almost any Indian, and underscores his message with close-ups of Lakshmana's appalled face (here, as elsewhere, Sagar follows the venerable tradition of allowing Rama's alter-ego to serve as a "straight man" and audience-surrogate, who displays the conventional worldly emotions that Rama's own idealistic actions will pointedly refute).[25]

But on the matter of Shabari's social status, Sagar takes a softer line. There are several references to Shabari, both by herself and others, as a "Bhīl woman," and in the last scene she speaks of wanting to abandon her body "born in a low community" (*nīc kul meṃ utpann*). There is nothing surprising in this, since her very name unambiguously declares her status. But the scene of Shabari's confrontation with the four hermits departs tellingly from the popular Priyadas story of her harassment prior to Rama's arrival. The self-righteous ascetics do not touch Shabari or make any reference to her polluting status; they simply mock her apparent "craziness" in making daily preparation for a visitor who never seems to arrive—and this too is immediately tempered by their recognition of her exemplary devotion. Rather than annoy her, they just take another path, and of course Lake Pampa suffers no pollution. Compared to Priyadas' telling, the sadhus here get off easily, as does nearly everyone guilty of misdeeds that drive the plot—from Kaikeyi and Manthara to Ravana and Kumbhakarna, and indeed to Rama himself—in this maximally non-offensive production. The result, at moments like this, is an unmitigated *sweetness* that some may find cloying.

Especially in the case of Shabari, one may observe that the television director's social and ethical sweet tooth has taken the bite out of her tale as popularized by Priyadas. The honey-like, juicy taste of emotional bhakti remains much in evidence, but what is regrettably missing are other flavors that might enrich the repast, and that the eighteenth century hagiographer skillfully conveyed: the sourness of arrogant, high-born male ascetics, puffed up with pride over their mechanical rites and carefully calculated austerities, and the bitterness of social exclusion based on birth-status (vicariously felt by hearers of the story)—of a life spent cowering in the shadows, in terror of polluting other human beings and even God. Perhaps the video-Valmiki realized that the bad taste of such themes might linger long and produce indigestion in the body politic.

SEVEN

# "Grinding Millet But Singing of Sita:" Power and Domination in Awadhi and Bhojpuri Women's Songs

USHA NILSSON

Beyond the *Rāmcaritmānas* (henceforth *Mānas*) lies a differently imagined world where women unfold the story of Rama and Sita according to their social location and worldview, creating sites of resistance. Furthermore, lower-caste and higher-caste tellings contain both convergences and dissociation. Given the Indian milieu in which I grew up, I assumed that women's Ramayana songs would follow the *pativratā* (faithful wife) dharma and worldview prescribed by Tulsidas. Yet, long before contemporary Indian feminists protested Tulsidas's tirade against women, as illustrated in such verses as "A drum, a rustic, a Shudra and a woman, they are the appropriate vessels for punishment," women singers have resisted and subverted authority in their songs.[1] By doing so they have appropriated additional freedom and played active roles in reshaping their lives.

In this essay, I examine different perspectives upon the story of Rama and Sita in Kayastha, as well as Kahar and Barber, women's songs from the Awadhi and Bhojpuri-speaking areas of North India. I argue that in these songs women not only contradict and resist the dominant male discourse as presented by Tulsidas in his *Mānas*; they also conceal hostility and tensions amongst women of different castes and social status. Women might offer a unitary voice against male domination, but they maintain ambivalent feelings towards each other when they move primarily in their own social spheres. High-caste women support their own system of domination. In my fieldwork I found that all three groups of women consider themselves oppressed by men, but high-caste women in turn dominate and oppress low-caste women whom they employ. High-caste women have a contemptuous saying about "other" women appropriating Sita's story. The phrase *pīsen kōdōn, gāyen Sītā haran*, or "grinding millet but singing of Sita's abduction," extends from the Kanauj area in the West to Eastern Uttar Pradesh.[2] The common Hindi idiom *kōdōn dalnā*, "to be engaged in an inferior activity," foregrounds their scornful attitude and hostility. These high-caste Kayastha women consider it their privilege to sing Ramayana songs; the "other" should not sing Sita's exalted story. Kahar and Barber women know that high-caste women use the phrase "grinding millet but singing of Sita's abduction" as a way to indicate that their inferior station make it inappropriate for them to sing of such an exalted theme. And yet, as a Barber woman named Chandravati told me defiantly, women everywhere, regardless of their caste, sing of Sita Mata (Mother Sita).

## Sources and Context

In searching for songs about Sita and Rama in Hindi, I located a few relevant collections of folksongs and dissertations on Hindi folklore. Since authors had concentrated on collection and genre classification rather than on singers, they did not indicate the subcaste (*jāti*) identity of the singers or the context of the song. Still, the printed material proved crucial to my research, providing multiple tellings of the same song from an area ranging from Kanauj in Uttar Pradesh to Mithila in Bihar. Also, if singers I interviewed had forgotten songs, when I nudged their memory by mentioning a few lines from a written version, they often recalled them. These older academic sources served as prompts for my fieldwork among Kayastha, Kahar, and Barber women.

The Kayastha consider themselves high caste, although they are not explicitly mentioned in the brahmanical classification of the four varnas.[3] Most Kayastha women who sang for me were housewives, ranging in age from their nineties to mid-thirties. Women younger than thirty generally did not know or favor the traditional songs, considering themselves too urbanized and "modern" to bother with them. One informant, 97-year-old Anusuya Devi, received home schooling in Sanskrit and Hindi. After marrying at age thirteen, she learned enough English from her husband to read the newspaper and follow general conversations. She learned the Sita Mangal and Devi songs from her older stepmother. Other singers also learned the songs from their families or picked them up from neighbors, friends or semi-professional singers. Almost all the singers saw themselves as the end of a line, expressing sadness that other women did not value these deshi (local, folk) songs.[4] Among the most knowledgeable singers I met were Anusuya Devi and her cousin, housewives who began their songbooks in 1923. They wrote down both songs they knew and those from every other conceivable source. Recently, she, her sister, and her cousin got together to help recall or find in their songbooks most of the stories and songs they reproduced for me. After much consultation, discussion, and merriment in the process of remembering the past, they reconstructed most of the songs I have included in this article.

Kahar women told me that the traditional caste duties for men were to carry water from wells or bring it from the river to their employers' homes, but they carried palanquins as well.[5] When these services fell into disuse, they found employment as general servants in upper-middle-class households or became vendors. They considered themselves to be on a high rung within the Shudra hierarchy. Most Kahar women, if not at home helping to prepare food that their husbands later sold on the streets, worked part time as maidservants, washing dishes, sweeping and mopping the inner part of the house or taking care of the family's young children. Their ties to their home village were very strong; although they lived in towns and cities, they regarded themselves as village women. None could read or write, so they had no inherited or personal songbooks to consult. They said, just as I found myself, that only very old women from Barber and Kahar castes remembered Sita songs, mostly in bits and pieces. Three Kahar women sang Sita Mangal and the Doe Song translated below. They lived in Talgram, a village in Farrukhabad District owned by Anusuya Devi's father, and came daily to clean grain and perform other household chores. Always veiled, they were of indeterminate ages, but in their childbearing years, as indicated by the toddlers and babies they carried. Instead of regular wages, they received clothes, jewelry, and money at weddings and other such occasions.

Barber women work as part-time domestics in high-caste households, churn butter, and act as masseuses. Some years ago, a few Barber women sang and danced at the head-shaving ceremony of a friend's cherished only son. The high-caste women present at the ceremony considered their performance lewd. Some left frowning, the others laughing but embarrassed. The next day, after much coaxing from me, the eldest singer performed three songs about sexual relationships, including one about Lakshman's sexual desire for Sita. My high-caste friends were quite shocked. Chandravati, a fifty-year-old woman from the Barber jati who worked as a masseus and dishwasher for high-caste women in Lucknow, performed some similar songs for me, including *jansār*, grinding of grain, and *rōpnī*, transplanting of rice seedlings, songs. Another woman in her late forties who wore brightly colored synthetic saris said she knew everything that occurred in her employers' families. I met her at a formal musical wedding event for women, where she served tea and cold drinks to guests. She had learned the songs from her grandmother, who lived in the Azamgarh area, and helped me assemble a group of Kahar women, most of whom were in their late forties and fifties. She told me that traditionally they sang of Sita's abduction and her exile in the forest while they were grinding grain. When they worked as a group in the rice field, they sang more joyous songs, such as ones about Sita's wedding.

## The *Mānas* and Women's Tellings

In the early twentieth century, basic education for high-caste girls in Hindi-speaking areas included learning enough Hindi to read Tulsidas and write letters to family members. Growing up in that milieu, questioning Tulsidas seemed unimaginable to many. Women read, recited, and sang the *Mānas* all their lives, and most practiced its ideals faithfully. The story of Rama in the *Mānas*, along with its inherent patterns of behavior and advocacy of pursuit of right conduct, set out norms to be followed. Tulsidas said a great deal about what he perceived to be women's innate nature, and how men should keep them in line. For centuries, men have looked to Tulsidas for models of appropriate behavior towards wives. Many high-caste women also accepted Tulsi's script, acquiescing to male domination and what they considered superior wisdom.

Most high-caste urban women regularly read the *Mānas* to learn the story and pass it on to their children, imbibing the ideals set in it for social and personal roles. They also studied it to earn merit accrued through each reading and recitation. Public singing and recitation of Tulsidas remains largely a male prerogative; women attend recitations and chanting, but seldom perform the role of a formal reciter.[6] High-caste women often form their own groups, gathering on auspicious days (Tuesday, for example), to recite the entire *Sundara Kāṇḍa* or *Hanumān Cālīsā*. The group meets during the day, when men work in offices and children attend school. Musical instruments such as dholak, cymbals, and khartal accompany the recitation. The group usually moves from house to house weekly, so each member can receive merit for hosting the singing.

The servant women in these houses make a special point to join the event. High-caste women wear their informal saris, but domestic workers dress in their very best clothing and sit at an appropriate distance. Although they listen attentively, they do not participate in the singing. At one session, I asked the main servant's young wife, who had completed her 12th class in school and could easily read Tulsidas, if she would join the singing and chanting. She responded that she did not think she would ever participate. Other servants, such as the washerwoman, were so illiterate that they could not read the numbers on the outside of the house. Yet, these women listened with rapt attention. If they hear Tulsidas often enough, they might memorize bits and pieces but none of them self-consciously tries to memorize the text.

When women of differing economic strata and *jātis* sing the story of Rama together, they follow the traditional story line of the epic. They focus on public events such as Rama's childhood, the plans for his coronation, his forest exile, his killing of demons, and the destruction of Lanka. These incidents are recited in ways very close to the written, but often orally received, text. In this situation, singers fulfill audience expectations by singing of the sacred and familiar.

When women meet in a group of their own, however, and sing about the events close to their life experiences, new forms of the Rama and Sita story emerge. They do not question the divinity of the characters, but they emphasize their human aspects and frailties. They sing songs of marriage, childbirth, domestic tensions, and quarrels, dealing freely with topics such as tensions among Sita's conjugal kin, Rama's insensitivity to Sita's needs and wishes, her pique,

Lakshman's absolute obedience to the king's command despite his misgivings, as well as Kaushalya's cruelty and insensitivity towards subaltern women. Women bring in their own worldview and include social commentary as they sing of Kaushalya's grief as a barren woman or Sita's lamentations upon her banishment to the forest during her advanced pregnancy. Both are accursed: Kaushalya remains childless for a long time and Sita dwells in another man's house. These two situations, childlessness or suspicions of impurity, create great anxiety for a woman in India.

Women's tellings often present a contrary account of a well-established event in Tulsidas. For example, the song translated below ignores Dashrath's performance of a Vedic sacrifice to facilitate the birth of a son as recounted in the *Mānas*, instead legitimizing Kaushalya's contribution to Rama's birth. It begins with a female relative's question to Kaushalya:

[RELATIVE] "Queen! what ritual did you follow
to give birth to Ramaiyaji?"
[KAUSHALYA] "I bathed in the Ganges.
I fell at the Sun's feet.
O, I fasted on Sundays,
That's how I gave birth to Ramaiyaji.
I fed the hungry brahmins.
I gave clothing to the blind.
I lit lamps daily before the Tulsi plant.
That's how I came to have Ramaiyaji."[7]

A similar song, dealing with the power a woman gains by performing rituals, vows, and proper actions, records questions and answers between the King and Kaushalya:

In the royal assembly Raja Dasrath is sitting.
Nearby on the seat is Kosila Rani.
[KING] "Rani, which vrata [vow] did you observe
So Ramji was born to you?"
[QUEEN] "First, I fasted on the eleventh of the fortnight.
Breaking my fast only on the twelfth.
Raja! I worshipped Sunday with the right ritual.
Moreover, I avoided stepping across the space
my mother-in-law cleaned and sanctified.
I didn't even glance at the shadow
of my older brother-in-law.

Raja! when the sister-in-law turned her face away in pique
I pleaded and coaxed her back to good humor.
As a reward Ramji was born to me.
I understood the needs of the hungry.
I clothed the naked.
I fed the hungry, Raja!
I got Rama as the fruit of my penance."[8]

Not only a mother's vows but a wife-to-be's vows are efficacious. In another song, when Sita's friends ask how she obtained Rama as her husband, she answers that it was not Rama who won her by lifting Shiva's bow, but Sita's worship and penance that won her Rama.

In these songs, Kaushalya and Sita empower themselves. They reiterate that one must observe certain rituals they themselves choose, as well as stressing the efficacy of regular vratas (vows), giving of alms, and paying homage to deities in their private domain. Many unmarried girls in Uttar Pradesh observe fasts to get a husband of their choice. Singing songs like these reaffirms women's belief that goals can be obtained as a result of women's rituals, rather than by formal, male-officiated, Vedic rituals.[9]

In the following song, women present an alternate to a key event in Tulsidas: Rama, contrary to the *Mānas*, goes to the forest alone, leaving Sita and Lakshman behind:

[SITA] "O brother Lachhman! My friend in sorrow!
Please go to the forest and bring me news of Rama."
He goes through one forest, he goes through the second.
In the third forest, Madhuban, he finds Rama.
Rama sits under a kadamba tree, he plays on his flute.
[LACHHMAN] "Brother! At home Sital Rani,
is pining for your darshan [sight]."

The hunchback woman throws a tantrum.
[HUNCHBACK] "Why are you going back home?"
Rama cajoles her,
[RAMA] "I'll only stay four months or so."
From her balcony window Sital Rani gazes out.
[SITA] "Here come Rama and my brother-in-law Lachhman."

Rama goes for bathing, Sita holds the datun brush.
Rama speaks to her, Sital doesn't answer.
Rama comes to dine, Sita serves him.

| | |
|---|---|
| | Rama speaks to her, Sital doesn't answer. |
| | Rama rinses his mouth, Sital holds out his toothpick. |
| | Rama speaks to her, Sital doesn't answer. |
| | Rama goes to bed, Sital fans him gently . |
| [RAMA] | Rama grabs her arm, "Let's go to the top terrace." |
| [SITA] | "No, Rama! I won't come to your bed, |
| | Up in the palace tower. |
| | You left me behind. |
| | You can go back to your forest exile." |
| [RAMA] | "A hundred thousand times I swear by father Dasrath, |
| | And my mother Kausalya. |
| | I'll give up the hunchback maid, |
| | But I won't give you up, Sital Rani!"[10] |

This song is neither an isolated one, nor the result of the singer's whimsy or confusion, in spite of how it differs from Tulsi's text. It reveals the full gamut and complexity of Sita's emotions. Although angry, she still pines for Rama, and persuades Lakshman to find him. Once Rama returns, face to face, she lets him see her pique. Meticulously she serves him as a good wife, but refuses his bed, since he has a mistress. By doing so, she affirms her feelings of hurt and pride.

In the next song, with a similar beginning but quite a different ending, the singer has transgressed boundaries set by Tulsidas and the high-caste moral code. While it is a common practice in some social groups for the younger brother-in-law to marry or keep the sister-in-law under his mantle if she has been widowed or abandoned, the tradition-bound higher caste women generally prefer not to take another husband. Folksongs occasionally express sexual tensions, attraction, and relations between the younger brother-in-law and the older sister-in-law:

| | |
|---|---|
| [SITA] | Oh! Lachchman, friend in my troubles! |
| | Go and coax your brother back. |
| | Or else I'll kill myself by taking poison. |

Lakshman seeks Rama but cannnot find him, so Lakshman returns alone. Sita laments:

| | |
|---|---|
| [SITA] | For whom should I make the wedding bed? |
| | and cover it with flower petals? |
| | Whom should I serve, so my grief is gone? |

While she mourns the absence of Rama, sly Lakshman comes with a suggestion:

[LAKSHMAN] Make my bed, scatter flower petals over it.
Serve me, Sister-in-law!
I'll make you forget your grief.

Sita indignantly replies:

[SITA] I have tasted the sweet mango.
I can't eat tamarind.
I've called you Lachhman, the brother-in-law.
How can I call you my man?[11]

In mainstream Tulsidas tradition, this song would be unimaginable: the *Mānas* emphasizes repeatedly the respect that Lakshman has for Sita. He even avoids stepping over Sita's footprints as they walk in the forest. At first the singer, an older Barber woman, refused to sing this song, out of respect for me, whom she considered a high-caste woman. Her concept of acceptable and unacceptable marks the dichotomy between low- and high-caste women's songs. Lakshman does not cast a lustful eye on Sita in high-caste women's world, where the sexuality of a separated or widowed woman is repressed. Thought of any man, let alone Lakshman, replacing Rama would be shocking. In contrast, some lower-caste women's songs deal with such sexual desires.

## Wedding Songs

Women praise Sita at weddings because, as one of the most auspicious deities, she blesses the bride and gives her good fortune. Ordinarily, in traditional weddings, auspicious songs were sung every day, beginning on the day of the *tilak* (which marks the formal engagement) and continuing through the marriage ceremony itself. Between these two events (usually ten days) women of the house, domestic servantwomen, or semi-professional singers played the dholak and sang wedding songs each day. The occasion also demanded hiring of semi-professional singers (*gauhārins* or *gavanhārins*, "ones who sing"). Arriving early and staying late, they sometimes began the first songs if family women were busy, or picked up the slack during the intervals.

Usually the lead singer came from a high caste, but everyone understood that she had fallen into strained economic circumstances, or else a high-caste woman would not earn her livelihood singing in public, even though the audience consisted exclusively of women. The other singers, usually from Kahar or Barber castes, would sing the songs considered risqué or insulting, if the occasion or the audience demanded it. The younger Kahars and Barber women danced to the music and the song's words, but they usually waited till the family women finished singing. These occasions presented the Kahar and Barber women with opportunities to learn the songs sung by their hosts. Unlike the Kayastha women, who depended heavily on their songbooks, the *gauhārins* could sing hundreds of songs from memory. These *gauhārins* remained very much attuned to the mood and the likes of their audience, constantly updating their repertoire.

As the music session began, the bride's mother sang the traditional Sita Mangal and then five Devi songs of praise and prayer.[12] The song translated below came from the notebook of Anusuya Devi, for whom the song was performed at her wedding when she was thirteen. This song, "Sita Mangal," has been sung for four generations at this family's weddings.

> Who ordered the digging of the well?
> Who made the boundary?
> Who is the prince drawing water?
> Who is sitting and bathing?
> Dasrath ordered the digging of the well.
> Lachhman made the boundary.
> Rama, the prince, draws the water.
> Precious Sita sits and bathes.
> Dearest Sita sits and bathes.
> Let's sing Sita Mangal together.[13]

Dashrath has a special well dug, in which Sita can wash, so that she does not have to bathe in the river, as do the common women of Ayodhya.

One song tells of a letter Sita sends to Devi through a demon, who remains unaware of its contents. In it Sita implores all-powerful Devi to kill the demon, because he wants to marry Sita. In response, Devi comes to Sita's help and, assuming her destructive form, annihilates the demon. Most adult women know the story of Sita's abduction and Ravana's pressure on her to marry him. In this song, however, Ravana becomes a generic demon, as often happens in folk traditions. The song also echoes the origin of Devi and her destruction of many demons. Finally, the song emphasizes the nurturing aspect of Devi as Mother and protector. At marriage time, the bride becomes especially vulnerable to the evil eye and other demonic forces, so it makes sense to seek Devi's aid to protect and help the bride, portrayed as Sita. Finally, the song prepares the bride by hinting at the ordeals she might have to undergo in the future, as Sita did.

After the Mangal and the Devi songs, Sita remains the center of the wedding songs. In one song, Devi tells her to ask for anything she wants:

> Sita asks first for the kingdom of Ayodhya
> And River Sarajuji's darshan.
> She'll get whatever she asks for.
> Second, she asks for Kaushalya as her mother-in-law
> And Dasrath for a father-in-law.
> She'll get whatever she asks for.
> Lastly, she asks for the Lord as her bridegroom
> and Lachman for a brother-in-law.[14]

All these requests are granted when Sita marries Rama.

On such joyous occasions, songs that critique social conditions in high-caste communities are often included. For example, this song concerns the ways society judges women as wives:

> The queen sits on her exalted chair
> She is looking at the door.
> [QUEEN] "I see you come, Rama.
> I see your brother Lachchman.
> But I don't see your wife Sita anywhere.
> Where is she?
> Is she lacking in beauty?
> Or is she of lower birth?
> Has she done something wrong?
> Why don't I see her with you, Rama?"
> [RAMA] "Mother! Sita doesn't lack beauty
> Nor is she of low birth.
> I've left her behind and have come alone.
> Her father didn't give enough dowry in her marriage."
> [QUEEN] "Gold lasts for ten days, Son!
> Silver even less.

Silk rips.
O Son, a good wife
fills your life with happiness."[15]

Here, the mother-in-law enumerates the prerequisites for a desirable wife, but money does not appear among them. However, for Rama, the bridegroom, money is all important. Contrary to his epic image, he acts as a greedy and short-sighted male. The song, subtly and cleverly, transfers the blame onto men in asking for the dowry, instead of the women taking responsibility themselves.

## The Suffering of Sita

Sita's plight and her suffering at the unjust treatment by Rama is a point of convergence in the songs of all castes and classes of women. Although Sita is a princess, in the songs by working women she performs household chores like any other woman. She fetches water from the Ganga and Jamuna (the geographic realities are often ignored in favor of the familiar and poetic) and attends to the family cow, collecting cowdung to make the fuel patties. She grinds the grain along with her sister-in-law, Rama's sister, and she goes out to fetch water. In some songs about domestic chores, the blame for Sita's abandonment is shifted from the washerman to a female family member, such as a sister-in-law. In this song, Sita's sister-in-law arouses Rama's jealousy.

The two sisters-in-law went to fetch water together
[S-I-L] "Brother's wife! That Ravana who abducted you,
Won't you draw his picture for me?"
[SITA] "Oh! if your Brother gets to hear of it
he'll turn me out of the house."
[S-I-L] "A hundred thousand times I swear
by the head of my father Dasrath.
I won't breathe it to my brother Rama.
I won't tell brother Lachhman."
[SITA] "Get me a handful of water from Ganga.
A handful of water.
Clean the inner room with cowdung
I'll draw you the image of Ravana."

She creates the arms and the legs
then the heads and eyes.
Suddenly Rama passes through the corridor.
Sita quickly throws her sari end
to cover the image she has drawn.
Ten heads of Ravana couldn't be concealed.
Rama sits to dine, the sister is a wicked messenger.
[S-I-L] "Brother! that Ravana, enemy of yours.
Sister-in-law is drawing his image."

[RAMA] "Oh! Oh! Brother Lachhman!
You stayed with me in all my times of trouble.
I'm going to turn Sita out.
Only then I'd drink a drop of water."
[LAKSHMAN] "My sister-in-law gives food to hungry.
Clothes to the naked.
She is heavily pregnant.
Why do you send her away?"
[RAMA] "O brother Lachchman!
My companion in times of trouble.
I will exile Sita.
She sits and draws images of Ravana."
[LAKSHMAN] "Sister-in-law! Mistress of this great household!
Open your silver box.
Put on your gold-edged sari.
Your father sent an invitation.
At dawn we'll set out."
[SITA] "It is neither my brother's marriage.
Nor the headshaving of my nephew.
My father, Janak the ascetic,
Why has he called me?"
Lakshman seats Sita on decorated chariot.
In the meantime Kaushalya cries out.
[KAUSHALYA] "Daughter-in-law! Where are you going?
Let me come with you."
Rama hurriedly explains to his mother.
[RAMA] "Her father has invited her.
She is going to visit him."

Sita goes through one forest, she goes through another.

[SITA] "Brother Lachhman! I'm very thirsty,
get me a drop of water to drink."

[LAKSHMAN] "Sister-in-law Sital! If you have power of your virtue,
create the water yourself.
If you are pure and full of honor,
bring forth water and drink."
[she makes] a small rippling pond come up,
waterlilies blooming in it.
Sita drinks the water out of her cupped hands.
She feels tired.

There is a small kadamb tree, with a canopy of leaves
Sita falls asleep under it.
Lachchman abandons her there.

[SITA] "Had I known that Lachhman would deceive me
And I would be left
I'd have gazed upon his face to my heart's content.
I would have deeply embraced Kaushalya."

A small kadamb tree with a thick canopy of leaves.
Sita stands under it.
Her eyes streaming with tears.

[SITA] Who'd make a fire for me?
Who'd make the bed for me in the birthing room?
Who'd watch over me the night I give birth?"
The ascetic women emerge from the forest.
They console Sital Rani.

[ASCETIC WOMEN] "We'll light the fire, we'd make the bed.
We'll look after you,
At the time when you give birth."

At the crack of dawn Lava is born.
Kusha is born as the sun is rising.
Sita in the light of woodfire looks at her sons' faces.

[SITA] "Sons! you are born at the time of my sorrow,
When fate is not favorable to me.
Sons! cover yourself with the kusha grass,
Sleep on the kusha.
You'd have to live on wild forest fruits.
Sons! were you born in the city of Ayodhya,
Happy Dasrath would have given away his kingdom.

Kaushalya all her jewels.
Call the Barber from the city.
Tell him to come at once.
Take my message to Ayodhya, Barber.
Put the first auspicious mark of turmeric
On Dasrath's forehead.
Give the second to Queen Kaushalya.
Third to my dear brother-in-law,
but none to Rama.
Don't let even my husband know
About the birth of my sons."
Dasrath gave, as reward, his own horse to the Barber.
Kaushalya her jewels.
Lachchman gave him five formal pieces of clothing.
Happy Barber set out for home.

Rama stands cleaning his teeth at a four-cornered pond.
[RAMA] "Brother! where did you get this auspicious mark?
Your forehead is lit up with a glow.
Who's got a child? Whose heart is full of joy today?"
[LAKSHMAN] "My sister-in-law Sital Rani,
who dwells in Binderaban.
She gave birth.
She sent this mark of celebration to me."

The neem brush slips from Rama's hand,
Falls on the ground.
The water jug rolls, spilling water.
He cries uncontrollably.
His yellow upper cloth is getting drenched with tears.
[RAMA] "O! Call back the Barber, tell him to return at once.
Barber! tell me how Sita is doing.
Bring her back."
[BARBER] "She sleeps on the coarse kusha grass
She covers herself with it too.
She lives on wild fruits of the forest.
Sir! She made a wood fire,
To see the faces of her sons in its flames."
[RAMA] "O Lachman! My brave brother!
Brother, please go to Madhuban once again.
Bring back your sister-in-law."

[LAKSHMAN] [SITA]

Lachman rode out from Ayodhya
And got down in Madhuban.
[LAKSHMAN] "Sister-in-law! Rama has sent for you.
He wants you back."
[SITA] "Lachhman! Go back.
I'm not coming with you.
I'm going to live for my sons
May they live for a long time."[16]

Although details of the song differ in various performances, the song always depicts the hasty, unjust decision of Rama, and Sita's vulnerability when abandoned. Pregnant and alone, she still faces all with courage and fortitude, even though she misses the celebrations that her sons deserved. As in other songs, she is proud, full of dignity and self-respect. When Rama hears of the births, he invites Sita back, perhaps because he needs heirs to his throne, but with two sons, her status is altered in a patrilineal society: she no longer needs her husband's protection.

This song is sung by all women, regardless of caste distinctions. In a male-dominated society, they are aware of their common sufferings, so they find a single unifying voice when they sing of Sita's refusal to aquiesce to Rama's wishes. These songs also emphasize overall betrayal by the conjugal kin: first the betrayal by the sister-in-law and then by Rama and Lakshman. The latter is so faithful to Rama's wishes that he ignores the evidence of Sita's virtue and chastity, even when she creates a pond full of water to quench her thirst. In contrast, the marginalized people support Sita: ascetic women outside the social order, and the lower caste Barber, who follows Sita's instructions to the letter by excluding Rama from the festivities.

## Songs of Resistance

Although women of all classes may join together in offering resistance to a male-dominated society, tensions between mistress and domestic servant appear in many songs. In a traditional social system, women of lower castes perform a variety of services for high-caste patrons. Although high-caste women do not require these services every day, when the need arises occasionally, high-caste women become totally dependent upon such women. Usually a family employs many women in special capacities; only these women will be called to perform the services when a specific occasion arises. For example, a Barber's wife gives a massage to the new mother and her baby, and also carries invitations to homes of *biradārī* women for ceremonies to anoint the bride with oil and turmeric. A Barber's wife also trims the nails of bridegroom and bride, performs the ceremony to ward off the evil eye when the new couple enter their home, and helps decorate the bride and other female guests by putting auspicious red paste on their feet. The Gardener's wife provides flowerbud strands that hang down from the groom's traditional headgear to cover his face when he arrives at the bride's front door. Some families call in a married Washerwoman to offer a pinch of her vermillion to the new bride.[17]

The servers receive a reward or a fee for performing these functions and, occasionally, ritual specialists refuse to perform their duties until their demands are met. A good-natured argument ensues, till the new mother or bride's mother concedes to them. Sometimes the demands are considered excessive, incurring the wrath of the patrons. For example, the *dhagrin* (from the Chamar, or Sweeper, subcaste) who works as a midwife, receives a reward for delivering the child—especially for cutting the umbilical cord, a function not performed by any other caste women. The midwife bargains to obtain a high fee, especially for a boy, since she knows how valued her services are on this occasion. The ambivalence that prevails in the mistress/server relationship results in quarrels about supply and demand. The next song, in which King Dashrath will not satisfy the midwife's demands and sarcastically offers her the baby, illustrates such quarrels:

In a rich city with high brick houses,
Raghupati takes avatar.
Ayodhya is filled with joy.
A call goes to *dhagrin*,
[KING] Come at once and cut the cord
*Dhagrin*! you are the very best,
Cut Ramji's cord.
I'll give you a crescent necklace.
She cuts the cord, she stands up,
She who is the best of her lot.
[MIDWIFE] King! Give me my reward.
The king gives two pieces of women's clothing.
Kosila Rani gives her a silk sari with gold edging.

Sumitra Rani a basket of cosmetics,
for full sixteen ways of decorating oneself.
Yet *dhagrin* quarrels.

[MIDWIFE] This is not enough, this is not enough.

[DASRATH] Okay then, take away this child.

[MIDWIFE] King! your palace shall be empty.
My little hut'll echo my singing with joy.
I'll give away all I have,
to celebrate baby Rama's birth.[18]

The last line tells Dashrath amiably to avoid being a miser and instead give generous gifts at Rama's birth. On a deeper level, it celebrates the child's divinity. The midwife knows that she will attain redemption if the divine child comes to her, since he has taken birth not only to remove evil, but to befriend and redeem the downtrodden, marginalized, and fallen.

Another song demonstrates how the midwife cleverly arranges matters so as to get the better part of the bargain without having to ask the patron to pay her well.

Ramchander is born in the evening
Lakhan in the middle of the night.
"Oh! Oh! I put away my sickle in the evening.
I can't find it now.
Give me your gold sickle,
to cut his cord.
I put away the lamp in the evening.
I can't find the light now.
Let me hold Rama to show you in the glow of diamonds.
I can't find the basin.
Get me that silver basin to bathe Rama."
Ramji is born.[19]

When the midwife uses objects during the birth, afterwards they traditionally belong to her. Other serving women may refuse to carry out their functions until they are satisfied, halting all the auspicious ceremonies, as this song demonstrates:

[KAUSHALYA] "Barber's Pretty Wife!
Don't delay.
Do the welcome ceremony."

[BARBER WOMAN] "I want a pair of bracelets.
For doing this ritual."
Queen Kaushilya gently coaxes her.
[KAUSHALYA] "Barber's wife! First welcome Rama and Siya.
I promise, I'll give you a pair of bracelets."[20]

Here, the Barber's wife refuses to perform the welcome ceremony for the newly married couple until she is promised a pair of bracelets.

Tension between the mistress and her domestic servants is inherent in their relationship. It becomes a struggle for power and domination when the server finds herself in an advantageous position and her mistress resents attempts to subvert high-caste authority:

That *dhagrin*, low-caste whore!
I tell her to cut the cord,
to bathe the child in the bottom half of a broken pitcher.
She says she'd only cut the cord if the sickle is gold,
and bathe the child in silver basin.
She won't cut Ramji's cord,
Unless I give her a winnow full of pearls.[21]

This song depicts the mistress resenting her dependence upon the midwife.

Occasionally a domestic servant becomes aware of a lack in the life of her master and mistress, providing her with an opportunity to view herself as superior to them, despite her lower social rank. In this song, she sees herself as superior because the king and queen are childless:

A bird begins to sing at dawn.
The king opens the window and leans out.
He sees the woman sweeping the courtyard.

[SWEEPER WOMAN] "Alas!" The sweeper wife turns to her husband,
"I glanced at the face of a childless man
First thing in the morning.
The last of his kin.
I hope this day doesn't turn out to be unlucky."
[SWEEPER MAN] "Quiet, Woman! " Her husband scolds.
"You, a low born! You dare to call the king,
who rules the triple kingdoms, barren and unlucky?"

[SWEEPER WOMAN] "You shut up yourself! Scorched-faced, low-born sweeper!
The king has three queens.
All three unable to bear children."

Raja Dasrath covers his face and goes back to bed.
The day passes.
The king lies in bed with heavy heart.
[QUEEN] "O King!" Says Kaushalya,
"Get up and wash.
Eat something.
Or tell me what pains you."
[KING] "O Queen! that low born sweeper woman called me unlucky.
The last of my kin."
[QUEEN] "Don't make yourself unhappy, Raja!
It is our fate.
Whatever is written
Cannot be shunned."[22]

This song reverses the usual power dynamics, as the sweeper woman overcomes her feelings of social inferiority. The sweeper must have given birth, since she considers herself as auspicious, gloating about her luck. Although lowest in the social order, she is not as unlucky as the kingdom's ruler and queens, who suffer from lack of children. More circumspect, her husband worries about the king's power and their dependence on him for their livelihood. The truth in the sweeper woman's words pierces the king's heart. Instead of punishing her for being disrespectful, the king goes back to bed, covering his unlucky face. Even Queen Kaushalya accepts fate's inevitability.

## Convergence and Dissociation

In addition to songs known by both high-caste and low-caste women that question the patriarchy in Tulsidas or explore the suffering of Sita and songs sung by low-caste women that subvert or undermine high caste privilege, I encountered yet a third kind of song from the Ramayana tradition sung in Awadhi or Bhojpuri by women. The Doe Song, which narrates the sad story of a doe whose buck is killed for a feast to celebrate the sixth day celebration after the birth of Rama, exemplifies such a type. Both high-caste and low-caste women sing the song, and it exists in many variants. Note the way the song portrays the anguish of the doe:

| | |
|---|---|
| | In a shady arbor of trees a doe stands, O Rama! |
| [BUCK] | "Doe! Why do you stand so listless?" |
| | The grazing buck asks her. |
| [BUCK] | "Doe! Do you find the grass to be dry? |
| | Are you weary from lack of water?" |
| [DOE] | "Neither is the grass dry, nor the water lacking. |
| | O my beloved! |
| | Today is the sixth day celebration of Rama's birth. |
| | The King's hunters will kill you." |
| | Rani Kaushiliya sits on her high seat, |
| | The doe goes to her and pleads. |
| [DOE] | "Queen! you are cooking the venison from my buck in the kitchen. |
| | I beg you to give me his skin. |
| | I'll hang it on a branch and console myself by gazing at it. |
| | Day after day." |
| [QUEEN] | "Doe! go back home. I won't give you the buckskin |
| | I'll have a drum covered |
| | My Ramji shall play with it." |
| | |
| | Whenever the doe hears the sound of the drum, |
| | she stands under a young dhak tree and mourns for her buck.[23] |

The song's awareness of persecution and the lack of power locates feelings of the subaltern in the character of the doe.

Another version I recorded ends with a particularly wistful last stanza:

The courtyard is empty without a chair.
A temple without a lamp.
"O friend! my Bindaraban is empty without my buck.
Had I been given his skin,
I would have hung it from a branch.
I would have wandered in the forests
Pretending he was waiting for me to return.[24]

Looked at from a different perspective, this is also a song about privilege and the oppression of those less powerful than oneself. The song depicts the Queen cruelly refusing to grant the doe her simple request, the skin of the buck as a remembrance, because the queen wants to make a toy for Rama. Perhaps in response to this seeming cruelty, high-caste women give the Doe Song a slant more favorable to themselves. When they sing about the buck hearing that he'll be killed as a part of the celebration, the buck answers the doe, "If my body is sacrificed in the service of Rama, there is no better use for it. I'll attain liberation from the cycle of births and deaths." To emphasize the merit attained by the singer and the listener, at the end of this song a couplet is added. "Whoever hears or sings this song shall also receive liberation of soul." In these two lines, the high-caste singers try to avoid responsibility and lessen the pathos of the situation by making it a religious act.[25]

As we have seen, in the songs sung by women for themselves or for women in their own community, different dimensions of episodes described in Tulsi's telling emerge. Such songs become more personalized and get infused with different viewpoints. In an unbounded, fluid, and flexible discourse women have reconstructed alternate tellings of the Ramayana. Neither harshly nor stringently, they have refashioned them into statements from women's points of view. Regardless of their social status, they have joined together in contesting dominant patriarchical traditions.

Songs from Kahar and Barber women however, contest as well, the high-caste female hierarchy and domination inherent in the system. In women's songs both Kaushalya and Sita strategize their positions by reversing traditional expectations, but Sita receives more sympathetic treatment than Kaushalya. The songs sung by lower social groups contain subtle sites of resentment against Kaushalya. She is a figure of female authority: as queen, employer, and a high-caste woman, insensitive to the lower-caste women's oppression. In contrast, low-caste women make Sita one of them. Found in a field, of unknown parentage, she suffers injustice at the hand of Rama. Even when she tries to uphold her virtue, she is silenced. In women's songs, she does ordinary household chores like most working women. Truly subaltern, the voices of low-caste women are constrained, metaphoric (as in the doe song), and sometimes inaudible outside their own realm, but the knowledge is there. As such, they sing in ways that both converge and dissociate with dominant groups.

EIGHT

# The Politics of Telugu Ramayanas: Colonialism, Print Culture, and Literary Movements

VELCHERU NARAYANA RAO

When the play *Śambuka Vadha* (Shambuka Murdered) was published in 1920, it caused a considerable stir.[1] The play is based on a story from the Ramayana but was presented in a manner that repelled its readers, who had been used to reading devotional stories of Rama. The author of the play, Tripuraneni Ramasvami Chaudari (1887–1943), whom I will introduce more fully later, depicts the killing of the Dravidian Shambuka as a murder committed by the Aryan Kshatriya king Rama at the behest of his Aryan Brahmin advisers. All traditional readers of the Ramayana in Telugu know that Shambuka is the Shudra who violates the law of hierarchically ordered social classes—Brahmin, Kshatriya, Vaishya, and Shudra—which determines a person's status by birth *(varṇadharma)*. Shambuka performs asceticism, a practice reserved for Brahmins, according to the dharma. As a consequence of this violation, a young Brahmin boy dies, and the father brings the corpse to Rama to seek explanation for this unprecedented happening. It is the king's duty to protect the dharma, and when he performs this duty, no misfortune befalls anyone in his kingdom; no one dies young, and certainly no young Brahmin dies. Rama accepts the blame, and goes out to see if a violation of dharma has occurred within his kingdom.

He finds Shambuka behaving like a Brahmin and kills him as punishment. When dharma is thus restored, the Brahmin boy comes back to life. However, in Ramasvami Chaudari's version, Shambuka is a Dravidian performing religious austerities in his region. Vasishtha and other Aryan/Brahmin ministers of Rama see his austerities as a threat to their superiority and direct Rama to kill him in order to punish what they interpret as the violation of dharma. In order to make it look like a serious offense against gods and cosmic harmony, Vasishtha conspires with the Ashvins, the divine physicians, to cause the temporary death of the young Brahmin boy. Thus Rama is forced to act and kill an innocent Dravidian.

Conventional Ramayana readers were deeply disturbed at this violently unconventional reading of the Ramayana. Bringing to prominence this troubling story from the later part of the Ramayana, which many would rather overlook, proved disconcerting to many Ramayana devotees.[2] Even supposing that such a focus were necessary, plenty of traditionally acceptable options for treating the story were available. For example Kalidasa, in his *Raghuvaṃśa,* gives the incident a flavor of heroic elegance befitting a ruling king. In this version Rama does kill the erring Shudra, but the culprit goes to heaven—far more easily, because the king punished him, than he would have if he had pursued his path of asceticism.[3] Bhavabhuti, the great eighth-century Sanskrit dramatist, presents this story in his *Uttararāmacarita* (The Later Story of Rama). This playwright highlights Rama's compassion and unwillingness to hand down cruel punishment to a Shudra for his violation of dharma. Bhavabhuti depicts the tragic element in the life of a king who must sacrifice his personal feelings of love and compassion in order to perform the harsh duties of kingship. In Bhavabhuti's version the Shudra attains an immortal form, thanks Rama for traveling a long distance to the forest to see him, and becomes a friend of Rama.[4]

According to Chaudari, however, Shambuka was murdered entirely because of a Brahmin conspiracy. Brahmins, who feared a Dravidian rebellion against their Aryan authority, advise Rama to kill the Dravidian sage. In a skillfully developed plot, Chaudari depicts Shambuka as a social activist who organizes Dravidian opinion in favor of fighting for their religious rights of performing asceticism according to Vedic instructions. Rama initially shows reluctance to punish a gentle ascetic, and determines that his guilt or innocence has to be established before he can be punished. Vasishtha, the royal priest, gets impatient at Rama's vacillation and demands that the sinner be instantly beheaded. Rama invites Shambuka to a debate with the Brahmin priests, but Shambuka refuses this debate unless the king assures him that the standard of judgment will be based on the Veda, the revealed texts, and not *smṛti*, the texts written by Brahmin sages. Rama pays a visit to Shambuka and finds conversation with him very convincing and satisfying. He then returns, wishing Shambuka well, but upon his arrival Vasishtha sternly warns him that weak policies will eventually destroy his empire. He cleverly explains to Rama that the mutually supportive relationship between Brahmins and the Kshatriyas has maintained the state from times immemorial. Dravidians will destabilize the Brahmin–Kshatriya bond and eventually ruin both Brahmins and Kshatriyas. For political expediency Rama must kill Shambuka. Rama is convinced, even though he feels unhappy at having to kill an innocent Dravidian. With tragic resolve, admitting that kingly duty allows no room for personal feeling, he reminds himself of the cruel act he has recently committed in banishing innocent Sita to the forest to fulfill his kingly duty. He then solemnly cuts off Shambuka's head. Shambuka ascends to heaven in the form of a flash of light.

Chaudari's presentation of this story ran counter to the basic trust that the Telugu people had built in the Ramayana narrative. Reading Aryan/Dravidian divisions into this story proved repulsive for many Brahmin readers and traditional scholars condemned Chaudari for concocting a false tale. For almost ten years this unconventional presentation faced stiff resistance. The author persisted, arguing in favor of his position in town after town. Gradually Chaudari's reading gained attention, especially with a large educated readership from the Non-Brahmin castes and a modernist cultural movement that questioned Brahmanism and its religious sanctions.

There were serious discussions in town halls, clubs and restaurants, bar-rooms of district courts, the press, and most importantly within literary gatherings. Did Rama really rule with compassion, as depicted in the images of Ramraj, the kingdom of god? Did he act only to preserve the interests of the Brahmins? Why can't Shambuka perform austerities for his own spiritual liberation? Why should such practices be protected as the exclusive right of Brahmins? Was the Ramayana really a sacred text which was meant to liberate all its readers? Might Brahmins have distorted the text to perpetuate their control over the lower castes? Disturbing questions all—about the truth value of the

Ramayana. Educated readers were split into two camps, those that supported the traditional Ramayana interpretations and those that demanded a critical reading.

During the next fifty years Telugu authors rewrote many Ramayana themes, reflecting the new trend of interrogating the conventional Ramayana: they produced plays, poems, essays, books and at least two full-length retellings of the Ramayana. Together these constitute what can be seen as an anti-Ramayana discourse. The general features of this discourse take two directions. Some assume that there was one *Rāmāyaṇa*, the one written by Valmiki and followed by regional language writers, and that has one uniform ideology of supporting the Brahmins. Others assume that there was an original Ramayana written by Valmiki in which the Brahmins interpolated sections in support of their superiority. In either case, the common core of the anti-Ramayana discourse remains its anti-Brahmanism.

In this essay I present a brief study of this anti-Brahmin discourse which contests the Ramayana's claim to truth by questioning the Valmiki text and by rewriting his version to correct his pro-Brahmanic biases. But first I shall outline the historical and social conditions which led to the production of such a discourse.

## The Ramayana Tradition and Valmiki

When we talk of the Ramayana, we begin with the version attributed to Valmiki. Well known to Western Indologists, this version has received academic attention for more than a century. The recent Ramayana translation project, which includes a team of eminent Sanskritists headed by Robert Goldman, has brought the Valmiki text once again to the center. The Ramayana received more compelling attention when Ramanand Sagar's television version made news with its unprecedented mass appeal; the violent destruction of the Babri mosque by Hindu fundamentalists followed soon after. Decades of Western scholarly attention as well as the Indian television event strengthened a homogeneous Ramayana discourse. However, with the burgeoning studies of oral epics and other folk-narrative genres in India, culminating in the publication of *Many Rāmāyaṇas* (1991), scholarly understanding of the Ramayana tradition has been radically diversified. Yet the perception remains that the Ramayana originates with Valmiki. As Sheldon Pollock puts it:

> One may readily concur that the Ramayana can interestingly be viewed not as a fixed text but as a "multivoiced entity, encompassing tellings of Rama story that vary according to historical period, regional literary tradition, religious affiliation, genre, and political context (Richman 1991:16). But these tellings are always *retellings of a text everyone knows* . . . . In short, the foundational version, the version everyone knows in AD 1000–1400 and for the whole millennium preceding this period, is that of Vālmīki and his epigones . . . . (Emphasis in the original)[5]

The position that traces the origin of the Ramayana narrative to Valmiki stands at the very center of the Ramayana problematic. Both traditional Ramayana readers and the leaders of the anti-Ramayana discourse see Valmiki as the author of the *Rāmāyaṇa*. Yet there is a difference: the leaders of the anti-Ramayana discourse state this in a factual mode; they base their arguments on nineteenth-century Western textual scholarship and assume that the Valmiki version is empirically verifiable. For traditional readers and listeners, however, Valmiki's authorship is ideological; they do not base their statement on empirical textual evidence. They believe that Valmiki wrote *the* Ramayana, *any* Ramayana, and *every* Ramayana. Given all this, the question of Valmiki's association with the Ramayana narrative needs to be restated with some conceptual clarity.

For one thing, there is no version of the Ramayana that follows the Valmiki narrative in any significant detail. But then there is rarely a Ramayana author who does not state that he/she is retelling the narrative as Valmiki told it. Valmiki's name and authorship are venerated, even if his narrative is not followed. We can resolve this apparent contradiction when we separate the legendary author from his narrative. Perhaps because we have locked ourselves into a position that claims for every narrative an author who precedes it, we seem unable to dissociate Valmiki from the narrative named after him. And because we believe that every narrative begins as a single original version, to which every other telling can be traced as its retelling, we authorize the Valmiki version as the primary narrative.

We would arrive at a better understanding if we conceive of a situation where a number of Ramayana narratives are composed, based on a story popular in oral tradition, and one specific version becomes linked with the name of Valmiki. Such an association functions to construct an ideological coherence and a status for the narrative. The story of Valmiki and the killing of the *krauñca* birds, included in the Sanskrit text, serves to elevate Valmiki to the position of the first poet, one who has access to Narada, Brahma and other celestial beings. Associating such a venerated poet with a text, in turn, elevates the narrative. I thus see Valmiki as a signifier of the status of the narrative rather than as the producer of a particular text.

This view could also explain why there are several Valmikis. First we have Valmiki the sage who felt compassion towards the *krauñca* bird hunted down by a Nishada hunter, and who uttered the first verse, thus inventing poetry. This is the Valmiki we know in the epic text. Tradition also tells of another Valmiki, the bandit who turned devotee by chanting Rama's name. Brahmins gave him the syllables *rāma* inverted as *marā* because he was ineligible to receive this gift directly; he repeats it as a mantra, and via a process of repetition it turns into the sacred name of Rama. The bandit turns into a sage, around whom an anthill, *valmīka,* grows as he meditates in total devotion; he emerges from this shell when Rama himself comes to see him and asks him to compose his (Rama's) story. Born out of a *valmīka,* he is known as Valmiki. This is the Valmiki of the bhakti Ramayanas.[6] In women's Ramayanas we find Valmiki as the biased biographer of Rama, the author who denied Sita her legitimate place in the epic. During the course of this essay I shall also meet Valmiki, the composer of a smaller, original Ramayana, which was later tampered with by Brahmins, and yet another Valmiki who served the interests of male upper-caste feudal masters to enslave the masses. Finally, there is no *author* called Valmiki: he simply appears, in non-literary Ramayanas, as a character in the narrative. Each Ramayana narrative thus constructed a Valmiki suitable to its needs of authorship—or left him out if no author was needed.

The Ramayana tradition allows for considerable flexibility. Some Ramayanas have earned recognition as superior works of literature, especially those written by great poets such as Kamban or Tulsidas; others, such as those produced by Telugu poets from the thirteenth to nineteenth centuries, have not acquired such acclaim; yet other Ramayanas remain authorless although they are accepted as Ramayanas all the same. This multiplicity suggests that the basic Rama story itself is treated as a kind of a text-field out of which poets, including the authors responsible for the Valmiki version, constructed a Ramayana suitable to the needs of their time and their community of listeners. Elsewhere, I have likened the Ramayana to a language, a language which enables the user to say many very different things.[7]

## The Epic Ramayana and Bhakti Tellings

The Ramayana text named after Valmiki is a literary epic, an *itihāsa*. By an epic I mean a text perceived as history that is ideologically influential, in forming a set of new values, its institutions, and new ideals of good behavior. In the introduction to his translation of *Ayodhyākāṇḍa,* Pollock identifies the new values Valmiki's epic has established for the society of its time. According to Pollock the Ramayana's integral problem is kingship itself and its attendant problems: the acquisition, maintenance, and execution of royal power, the legitimacy of succession, the predicament of transferring hereditary power within a royal dynasty. We are naturally led to wonder why this acquisition should assume such importance for the Indian epic. One explanation may be that the problem of kingship addressed so insistently by the epic texts were new ones and, in their very nature, urgent.[8]

Regional-language Ramayanas are not epics, however—at least not the kind the Valmiki text represents. They differ in the quality of the narration and they function as bhakti texts rather than epics. I use this term bhakti to indicate that their authors composed them in the spirit of devotion to Rama as God.

The central issue of the bhakti Ramayanas is neither kingship nor the maintenance of dynastic power, but a personal relationship of the reader–listener with the deity. Rama reigns as the supreme lord, and the reader–listener enjoys every telling and retelling of his story for the sheer ecstasy of participating in the experience. The intent of the bhakti Ramayanas is not so much to tell a story but to allow the listener to experience Rama one more time in a slightly different way. The listeners already know the story. They have heard it many times, but they want the opportunity to savor their participation in the play of God. Elsewhere I have called this transformation a movement from communication to communion.[9]

However, the transition from communication to communion occurred gradually and unevenly. Many medieval Ramayanas continued to focus on the epic quality of the Ramayana narrative, so they could formulate a new social and political meaning, and a new ideology, through their text. Over the centuries the Rama story has served as a vehicle for many meanings—social, political, theological, familial and personal. Telugu poets of the Ramayana theme, as well as poets in other regional languages, present an infinite variety of modes in speaking about Rama and an endless playfulness in depicting his story. The number of Telugu literary Ramayanas alone is enormous. No theme in Telugu was retold as many times, and in as many ways, as the Ramayana theme.

For over five hundred years, from about the thirteenth to the eighteenth centuries, Telugu poets from Brahmin families composed literary texts which they dedicated to the heads of upwardly mobile peasant-warrior clans, to traders, and to local rulers. Such dedications helped elevate the patrons to the varna status of Kshatriyas. Elevating the patron families to a varna status raised these Brahmin poets in turn to a varna status of what one might call a high-status Brahmin. Thus we find a symbiotic relationship between ordinary Brahmin families and peasant leaders, aspiring together to fill the Sanskritic slots of Brahmin and Kshatriya as approved by the *dharmaśāstras* texts.

A few examples will illustrate this process. Tikkana (thirteenth century) dedicated his *Uttara Rāmāyaṇa* (Later Story of Rama) to Manumasiddhi, a small ruler of Nelluru (Nellore in southern Andhra). Errapregada (fourteenth century) dedicated his Ramayana to Prolaya Vema Reddi of the Reddi dynasty. Hulakki Bhaskara (fourteenth century) dedicated his Ramayana to Sahini Mara, a head of cavalry. Ayyalaraju Ramabhadrudu (mid-sixteenth century) composed the *Rāmābhyudayamu* in the *kāvya* mode, with erotic descriptions of the love between Rama and Sita, and offered it to Gobburi Narasaraju, nephew of the famous Aliya Ramaraya; here the choice of text, and hero, resonates with the name of Ramaraya, the king and founder of the new Aravidu dynasty.

Sometimes rulers from Non-Brahmin families sought to enhance their status by composing a Ramayana themselves. They hoped, by producing a devotional text on Rama, to win respect from their people as good kings. In a way this process bypasses Brahmin intervention to acquire status, though it does not reject Brahmin values. For example, we have the case of a son who composes a Ramayana and dedicates it to his father, whom he describes as a man of great religious merit, a gentle and pious ruler. This text, popularly known as *Raṅganātha Rāmāyaṇamu,* was composed in the non-Sanskritic *dvipada* meter by the non-Brahmin poet, Gona Buddharaju (fourteenth century?). Raghunathanayaka, a Balija who ruled Tanjavur during the early seventeenth century, also wrote a Ramayana. Yet another was composed, again in Tanjavur, by Katta

Varada Raju (circa 1630), another Balija who claims descent from Karikala Chola. The Maharastra king of Tanjavur, Ekoji (late seventeenth century), wrote an *Ekōjī-Rāmāyaṇa* in *dvipada* and, following the custom of the Nayaka kings who preceded him, dedicated it to his father. In fact, the Ramayana seems to be the favorite narrative of ambitious Non-Brahmin kings. However, no evidence exists of any anti-Brahmanic impulse in any Ramayana composition before the nineteenth century.[10]

Thus a huge Ramayana literature in Telugu came into existence in the pre-modern centuries as the creation of Brahmin poets, Non-Brahmin warriors and rulers, and also other devotees—including a famous poetess, Molla (sixteenth century?), from the Potters' caste (Kummari). All of these texts reflect the contexts that generated them and the major patterns of social mobility, from medieval through Nayaka and post-Nayaka times—until the entry of the colonial power into the scene. But the politics and aesthetics of using the Ramayana theme have significantly changed since the later decades of the nineteenth century. I wish to explore the reasons for this dramatic shift; to do so, we need to examine the changing social dynamics of this period.

The most important shift may be traced to the rupture of political ideology at the hands of a foreign power. The British, who controlled political power, in effect took over the Kshatriya position. However, their position was anomalous since they did not need the varna status of a Kshatriya to maintain themselves in power, nor the active role of a Brahmin to legitimize them in that position. This anomaly brutally disturbed the ideological order. Brahmins lost their usual roles as kingmakers, advisers, ministers. Occasionally, they tried to accord the British the status of Kshatriya in the hope of regaining their earlier Brahmin status, but this strategy was not very successful. The British did not need Brahmins to elevate them to a varna status. However, they needed indigenous support in maintaining their administration, and the Brahmins were their best choice. In other words, the British told the Brahmins that they needed them as servants, not as superiors. In this context there were three choices left for Brahmins. Those families that desired to keep the old ways of chanting Vedic texts, learning Sanskrit *śāstras,* and fostering traditional Sanskrit or Telugu poetry, sought the patronage of the remaining small kings, the zamindars—who, while they had no real political power, still needed the trappings of Kshatriyahood and therefore actively patronized the varnahood of Brahmins. A history of late-eighteenth/early-nineteenth-century Andhra would reveal that the zamindars strongly supported Vedic and Sanskrit scholars. On the other hand, people who desired to pursue English education and move away from the lifestyle of the varna Brahmin went to live in modern towns and cities such as Madras. A third choice was to keep working in the old scholarly modes, maintaining traditional values while living in a modern city. Scholars who chose the third option often worked for private publishers, or, if they were enterprising enough, started printing presses. Brahmins of the nineteenth and early twentieth centuries practised all these options in varying degrees. But changes in political ideology, and the consequent change in their condition, have been powerful enough to transform their imagination of their past and mythology.

## Bhakti-ization and Iconization of Rama's Story

The Ramayanas of the nineteenth and twentieth century reflect these changes. I would like to present these practices as representing two modes: Bhakti-ization and Iconization. The Bhakti-ization of Ramayanas is not new to Telugu. We have already observed the transition in the use of Ramayana themes from a complex narrative focusing on the inner world of its characters—as kings and queens, fathers and mothers, husbands and wives—to a song celebrating the experience of a devotee towards God. What is new during this period in Andhra is the intensity of the Bhakti-ization of Ramayanas, which now begin to depict a heightened state of surrender to God. This move requires reducing the complexity of the Ramayana narrative to a relatively straightforward, unproblematic story, where Rama becomes the absolute, flawless, all-powerful God. Even the enemy, Ravana, is depicted in some of these bhakti Ramayanas as Rama's devotee in disguise, too impatient to reach him by the slower route of service; instead, he chose the shorter route of conflict—*vairabhakti*, devotion through enmity. In the larger frame of the Ramayana performance, the performer and the listeners now all become merged into one category, that of *dāsas,* servants.

As an example, I cite a mid-twentieth-century Ramayana, Sripada Krishnamurti Sastri's *Śrī Kṛṣṇa Rāmāyaṇamu*. Perhaps the most bowdlerized of all Telugu bhakti Ramayanas, it was written in full acceptance of Non-Brahmin criticism from reformers like Tripuraneni Ramaswami Chaudari. Sripada told Rama's story in a way that sanitized all the major problematic incidents: Ahalya, in this Ramayana, is a chaste woman; her association with Indra was nothing more than a handshake. Kaikeyi has no idea why she asked to send Rama off to the forest; she does so under the influence of Brahma, who possesses her at that time. Later, she wonders why Rama had to go away and weeps at his departure to the forest. Most striking of all, Rama refuses to abandon Sita in the forest. He does hear from his spies that a certain washerman scandalized the name of Sita. But on inquiry he finds that the washerman is insane and ignores his words. Finally, Shambuka is not killed; he is only asked to refrain from his ascetic practices.[11]

A simplistic reductionist narrative of this kind, devoid of the drama and conflicting motivations of an epic, is bound to be boring. But popular bhakti Ramayana narratives compensate for the loss of complexity of meaning by musical and verbal power. Music of the congregational *bhajan,* as well as the refined musical compositions of composers like Tyagaraja and Ramadasu (Kancarla Gopanna), elevate the fragmented individual consciousness beyond thinking to a realm of oneness, a state of highly satisfying integrity. A popular form of Ramayana performance during this period was the singing, to melodious instrumental music, of a set of songs from the *Adhyātma Rāmāyaṇa*—incidentally the text which informs Tulsi's *Rāmacaritmānas* narrative. Composed by the fine lyricist Munipalle Subrahmanya Kavi (c. 1760–1820), these songs were performed with interspersed prose commentaries by competent performers, engrossing hundreds of people.

A widespread public performance tradition of *harikathā,* invented and popularized by the great singer Ajjada Adibhatla Narayandasu (1864–1945), was another mode through which bhakti Ramayana narratives spread across the Telugu area. Each year almost every town and village in Andhra celebrated the nine-day festival of Ramanavami, culminating on the ninth day of the lunar month of Caitra, which was believed to be Rama's birthday as well as his wedding anniversary. Rama temples and bands singing Rama chants proliferated in the countryside. During this period there was a veritable explosion of devotional expressions for Rama. Songs, rhymes, street plays, chants, and poems, that occupied the public and private space of Telugu life, make a huge inventory. It became a convention for people to write Rama's name first on the page, before writing anything else at all, even a laundry list!

Most noteworthy of all was the tradition of copying Rama's name ten million times, *rāmakoṭi*, as a means of liberation. These performances and practices reinforced Rama's position as the supreme deity and encouraged devotion and surrender. Rama is called the favorite god of the Telugu people (*Telugu-vārī āradhya-daivamu*). So pervasive was this wave of devotionalism for Rama that even a traditionalist poet like the great Viswanatha Satyanarayana sensed its shallowness and parodied it in the following verse:

> Everyone is jumping around like crazy,
> yelling, "Telugu, Telugu!"
> The whole nation is confused. And you
> are part of it, our Telugu god.
> So let me praise you in Telugu,
> until I have let it all out,
> all night long, until darkness ends,
> O Rama, lord of Bhadradri Hill.[12]

To the extent that Brahmins saw their loss of political power as total, their submission to their god became total. Loss of power now becomes a source of power over the God who is imagined as the most powerful of all. In a very paradoxical way, that very God is powerless to disobey the wishes of his devotees, because their devotion to him is greater than he himself. This theme is best illustrated in a newly popular play, *Rāmāñjanēya Yuddham*, "the Battle of Rama and Hanuman," which depicts Hanuman as stronger than Rama—because Hanuman is armed with unfailing devotion to Rama![13]

By the end of the nineteenth century, bhakti Ramayanas occupied the public space in Andhra so completely that they excluded other versions of the story. The change is striking when we compare the use of the Ramayana themes by pre-modern poets with the usage of the new bhakti poets. Pre-modern poets in Telugu used Ramayana themes in nearly all genres of Telugu literature. More importantly, they allowed their texts to breathe. They joked with Rama and even ridiculed him. Here is a verse from Kasula Purushottama Kavi (eighteenth century), referring to Rama's departure for the forest, dressed as an ascetic, renouncing his kingdom:

You gave up the kingdom because your father said so,
but have you ever given up power?
You took off your ornaments because you wanted to,
but you always kept your bow.
You rejected royal robes, of course,
but you have the muscles of a warrior.
We know you denied wealth;
but you never let go of your pride.
All this is a game you played to kill
your enemies. Would anyone believe you were a sage?[14]

Parallel to bhakti-ization of the Ramayana is what I call iconization. Earlier I stated that while Valmiki was revered as a great poet, the Sanskrit version of the Ramayana attributed to Valmiki was not well known. Except for a few scholars who knew Sanskrit, most of whom were Brahmins who possessed a manuscript copy of the text, the Valmiki version was not even widely available. However, by the beginning of the twentieth century Valmiki's text achieved unprecedented prominence. This was due to a complex set of reasons. While the Ramayana became the holiest of all themes, no Telugu literary Ramayana stands out as a sacred text. No author of Telugu Ramayanas was viewed as a saint. There were poets from the past who attained such respect—Potanna, for instance, the author of the *Bhāgavata Purāṇa*—but alas, no one of this class wrote a Ramayana.

To make up for this lack, verbatim translations of Valmiki's text began to appear. In fact, such a project was first completed under the patronage of the Zamindar of Gadvala in the later part of the seventeenth century.[15] The most prominent of such projects was the Ramayana completed by Vavilikolanu Subbarao (1863–1939), appropriately called the Valmiki of Andhra. After his retirement as Telugu pandit at Presidency College, Madras, Subbarao lived the pious life of a devotee, translating Valmiki's text into Telugu, verse by verse. Like the Gadvala version, he thinks of his text as a *yathā-vālmīka-rāmāyaṇamu*—a Ramayana strictly according to Valmiki. In keeping with the belief that Valmiki's text has powerful mantric syllables embedded in it, Subbarao attempted to bring similar syllables into his Telugu text. He supplemented his translation with an elaborate multi-volume commentary. However, this was not quite enough for people who looked up to Valmiki's text as essentially untranslatable.

This view is best illustrated by a late-eighteenth-century text, the *Tattva-saṅgraha-rāmāyaṇa,* which says:

> That idiot
> who rejects the Sanskrit text
> and reads the Rama story in another language
> desires to drink water
> from a mirage.[16]

Religious leaders began to claim that the Sanskrit Ramayana has the powerful syllables of the *gāyatrī* mantra embedded in it; therefore its power does not carry over into a translation. Devotees were encouraged to keep on reciting the Sanskrit Ramayana for the efficacy of the sound, an activity which was called *pārāyaṇa.* The *Sundarakāṇḍa* was identified as especially powerful, and devotees were told to chant it to overcome troubles in life and to achieve success. Publishers released the *Sundarakāṇḍa* in separate volumes with special instructions for chanting. Such books carried specific directions as to what particular section of the *Sundarakāṇḍa* one should chant for such common personal problems as finding a good job, a promotion, a good husband/wife, success in examinations, and so on.[17]

The second reason for the new interest in Valmiki was the popularity of the printing press. If earlier even educated people had depended on a public oral performance of the Ramayana by a pandit performer (*paurāṇika*), now more and more people could buy a copy of their own for private use. In the absence of a highly revered Telugu literary rendering, Valmiki's Sanskrit text became the holy book. It was even available with a verbatim Telugu prose paraphrase printed under each stanza of the original Sanskrit. However, this did not necessarily mean that readers were ready to explore the Sanskrit version to compare the differences between the epic and the bhakti versions. There were two reasons for this. One was the indoctrination of the bhakti Ramayanas, which had generated a general acceptance of Ramayana as a holy text; the very printed book was worshiped as an icon. The second was the role of publishing houses in the production of classical works. Major publishing houses which produced classical Telugu and Sanskrit books were controlled by Brahmin pandits. Vavilla Ramasvami Sastrulu, an enterprising Brahmin scholar, founded what soon grew to be the foremost publishing house of literary and scholarly works in Telugu and Sanskrit. The influence of this publishing house in the production of the Ramayana may be best illustrated by an incident which reportedly happened when the Valmiki text was printed by Vavilla press in Madras in 1856. The Brahmin managers of the press were not willing to have the text typeset by Non-Brahmin compositors—who usually did all the typesetting jobs in the press. (These were the days of the letter press, where lead type was set by hand.) So, they trained Brahmin boys in typesetting specially to typeset the Ramayana. The text was too sacred to be touched by Non-Brahmins even during the printing process!

## Change in the Status of Non-Brahmins

Meanwhile the role of the peasant castes of Andhra had been changing too. In pre-modern Andhra, as stated earlier, the Shudra king acquired Kshatriya status, legitimized by the Brahmin poet. When the British occupied the role of the king, the Non-Brahmin castes were left with no hope of becoming Kshatriyas. In parallel with the ideology of the bhakti Ramayanas, they progressively became the servants of Brahmins.

However, the younger generation of landed castes—Kammas, Reddis, and Kapus—went to western schools, as the Brahmins had done, receiving an education suitable for jobs in the colonial administration. The new jobs these Non-Brahmin young men were seeking placed them in competition with the Brahmins, their erstwhile gurus, and their former collaborators and legitimizers in the pursuit of Kshatriyahood. For the first time in the history of Andhra culture, upwardly mobile Non-Brahmin castes saw Brahmins as their enemies. Among the newly educated Non-Brahmin young men, Tripuraneni Ramasvami Chaudari from the Kamma caste (already mentioned) and Cattamanci Ramalinga Reddi (1880–1951) from the Reddi caste, stand out. Ramasvami Chaudari, trained as a barrister in Ireland, founded a center for his followers in Tenali, a small town in Krishna district, which he called Suta-asramam, after the Non-Brahmin bard of the Mahabharata epic. Ramasvami Chaudari undertook an active campaign of rewriting the Puranas, criticizing the existing texts as Brahmin constructions to enslave Shudras. His most important contribution to the anti-Ramayana discourse, however, is his play, *Śambuka Vadha*, which I mentioned earlier.

At this time the protocols of reading were undergoing a revolutionary change as well. Texts that were orally recited and commented upon in a public performance appeared in print, available for silent reading. Bringing palm-leaf texts into print was not an innocent act of making multiple copies available to readers. Before the advent of the printed text, the manuscript served as the recorded text, from which the performer/interpreter created a new text for his/her audience. This was the received text, which actually lived in the minds of the listeners. Reading the recorded text was a specialist's job and required a certain training in using it. Printing the recorded text, and making it available to readers untrained in using the text, generated new and unprecedented modes of reading. Western education prepared the minds of young scholars to receive the printed text as a univalent artifact, with every page and every word consciously produced by a single putative author.

Assumptions of textual integrity led to complementary propositions such as interpolations and textual corruption. Western textual theories such as Jacobi's claim that the first and last books of the Ramayana were later additions to an original Ramayana became influential among English-educated Telugu intellectuals. Taking advantage of the easy availability of Valmiki's text in verbatim translation, modern scholars began to focus on other deviations from Valmiki in regional-language Ramayana texts. These scholars subjected Valmiki's text to a new type of reading—never practiced before the advent of the printing press. In this new reading, a number of internal inconsistencies and problematic repetitions began to emerge. These were viewed as serious flaws by their author, or irresponsible interpolations by mischievous outsiders.

While the modern Ramayana scholars of this time began to question Valmiki's text, which was now perceived as the authoritative text of the narrative, some of these very same people adopted the freedom available to the Ramayana poets all through the centuries to tell the story in any manner they chose. But they invariably wrote a preface to their literary work questioning the textual authenticity of the Valmiki version as it had been handed down to the present generation. Nearly every writer accepted the textual critical studies of Western scholars. They attempted to find an "ur-Ramayana," written by Valmiki, and to treat all unacceptable and contradictory parts of his text as Brahmanic forgeries, or condemn Valmiki himself for his Brahminic bias.

Ramasvami Chaudari did this with a new confidence by using the race theories of colonial anthropologists who claimed to have identified Aryan and Dravidian races in the Indian subcontinent. For Ramasvami Chaudari, all Brahmins were Aryan intruders; regional landed castes like Kammas and Reddis were Dravidians. In his major work *Sūta Purāṇamu* (1924) Ramasvami Chaudari wrote the Rama story as he wanted it to happen. According to him Ravana is born in the Dravidian tribe of Koyas;[18] when he ascends the throne, he rules as a peace-loving king who prohibits animal sacrifice in his kingdom. He is also a great scholar of the Vedas, a great grammarian, physically handsome, and a noble ruler.

Then the Brahmins of the north come down south and begin their fire rituals which include killing cows, a practice prohibited in Ravana's kingdom. When Brahmin sage Vishvamitra announces a fire sacrifice, Ravana sends Tataka to gently persuade the sage to refrain from killing cows, as it breaks the law of the land. The sage does not listen and Tataka's assistants release the cows from their bonds and put out the fires as a punishment. The Brahmin sage regrets that his attempts to convert the Dravidians have not succeeded. He says:

> I tried my best, but it did not work.
> They just refuse to eat beef,
> nor would they taste liquor.
> That's the cause of all this trouble.[19]

So he goes to the Saketa king Dasharatha and gets his sons Rama and Lakshmana to kill Tataka.

In Chaudari's retelling, Ravana's sister Surpanakha is an old woman; instigated by Brahmin sages, Lakshmana kills her son Jambukumara. Grieving about the loss of her son, she goes to Rama to find out why her son was killed. Angered by his irresponsible reply that her son was an enemy of sages, she attacks Rama with her knife. Rama overreacts, holds the old woman down and orders Lakshmana to cut her nose and ears off. Ravana decides to capture Sita only to teach Rama a lesson; he treats Sita with honor and—most significant of all—entertains no erotic feeling for her.

With his *Sūta Purāṇamu*, Ramasvami Chaudari set the agenda for the anti-Ramayana discourse, and for anti-purana discourse in general. He characterized the Brahmin texts as obscene, immoral, cruel and —of course—Aryan. He had no doubt that all the Sanskrit puranas, and especially the Ramayana, were written to subjugate the independent and highly civilized Dravidians. Sanskrit, Brahmins, and Northern India represented Aryan civilization, and Southern India,

South Indian languages and the Non-Brahmins represented Dravidian civilization. In this scheme of things, Brahmins were perceived as colonizers of the south and all Sanskrit texts, especially the Ramayana, were seen as imperialist. Rama acted as the chief agent of Brahmanic imperialism of Northern India, whereas Ravana reigned as a noble king of the Dravidian south.

All this will sound very familiar to South India scholars. E.V. Ramasami's reading of the Ramayana, analysed in detail by Paula Richman, bears close resemblance to Ramasvami Chaudari's reading.[20] There is, however, an important difference, in addition to the fact that Chaudari's reading appeared several years earlier than E.V. Ramasami's work.[21] Unlike E.V. Ramasami, Chaudari presents a fully worked out Dravidian anthropology. According to him the classification of different castes and their occupations in South India before the Aryan occupation conformed to the following hierarchical order:

1. Land-owning castes like Kammas, Reddi, Velamas: warriors/kings, analogous to the Kshatriyas of Aryan society.
2. Golla, Palli, Kummari and such other castes: priests analogous to Brahmins of Aryan society.
3. Balijas, Komati, Sali and such other castes: trading castes analogous to Vaishyas of Aryan society
4. Kasa, Boya, Cakali and other similar service castes: servants analogous to Shudras of Aryan Society.[22]

This is a sophisticated scheme indeed. In this classification, the Brahmin occupation ranks below that of the Kshatriya. Chaudari's observation that lower castes conduct priestly activities in village-goddess temples in Andhra is accurate. According to Chaudari the Aryan invasion of the south placed Sanskritic Brahmin priests over and above the kings, while simultaneously downgrading castes like Kammas and Reddis, who enjoyed the status of kings, as Shudras.

Chaudari built his anti-Ramayana argument on a larger anti-Aryan argument. For him, the Aryans, wherever they went, suppressed the other races and their civilizations. He extends his anti-Aryan position to the white race of the United States where they suppressed Blacks. Dravidians are faultless, showing love for their family and neighbors. He even suggests that Vibhishana betrayed his brother Ravana not because he was evil, but because Vibhishana's wife Sarama, who is part Aryan (Gandharva), influenced his thinking in favor of Rama.

Their daughter Trijata, who has Aryan blood in her, turns out to be a betrayer, too; she supports Sita and hates Ravana.

As may be seen from the later anti-Ramayana works, Chaudari's general agenda of denouncing the puranas as Brahmanic, obscene, immoral and superstitious found an enthusiastic following, whereas his racial theme—dividing Telugu people into Aryan versus Dravidian—was quietly rejected. Despite general acceptance among university linguistics departments of the existence of the Dravidian family of languages, among which Telugu is included, literary scholars did evince interest in discussing Telugu literature in terms of Dravidian versus Aryan cultures.

While Ramasvami Chaudari was openly anti-Aryan and pro-Dravidian, Ramalinga Reddi was a "modernist," advocating a "progressive" culture in an industrialized, egalitarian, capitalist society. Educated in Cambridge, where he read economics, his main interest was Telugu literature. From the time he returned from England, he devoted his energies to modernizing Telugu literary history and criticism. As regards the Ramayana, Ramalinga Reddi conducted a somewhat subtler form of resistance than Chaudari. As vice-chancellor of Andhra University, he sponsored a critical edition of *Raṅganātha Rāmāyaṇa* (mentioned above). He conducted a well-documented polemic arguing that, contrary to current belief, the Non-Brahmin Buddha Reddi was its real author. He coupled his rejection of the Brahmanic culture with a call for modernism, which soon drew a large number of secularized Brahmin young men into its fold.

## Modernism and its Respondents

Meanwhile, English schools and colleges included in their syllabus powerful new kinds of learning: history and geography, as well as the natural and physical sciences. Students trained in the new schools were asking difficult questions such as: Where was Lanka in relation to the Dandaka forest? How wide was the ocean that Hanuman was supposed to have crossed? How could monkeys have a civilization complex enough to have a society, a kingdom, and a king, and if so, why describe them as animals? In this social and political context Non-Brahmin poets and intellectuals, and later modernist writers including Brahmins, turned against the conventional Ramayanas and began rewriting Rama's story. Invariably these anti-Ramayanas focused on problem areas of the Valmiki narrative, showing that Rama was not as great as he was depicted to be, and that his image was exaggerated to serve Brahmanic, feudal, or patriarchal interests.

Modernism in Andhra expressed itself primarily as a literary movement, which came to be known as Bhava-kavitvam, somewhat similar to the Romantic movement in English poetry. Rejection of the Brahmin past proved easier under the new ideology of modernism and the younger generation of poets and writers undertook the task of questioning the authenticity of the Ramayana narrative as given in the Valmiki telling.

While Ramasvami Chaudari contended with Brahmin scholars, he also used their style and idiom in his endeavors. Although ideologically opposed to them in literary style, he wrote his *Śambuka Vadha,* as well as his other works, in a classical style of Telugu, strictly in accordance with the regulations of prescriptive grammars followed by past Brahmanic poets. He took care to follow Brahmanic literary style, meters, and conventions with considerable skill. Hence, he received the acceptance and praise of his Brahmin contemporaries, who called him the King of Poets *(Kavirāju),* in admiration. In contrast, the modern literary movement of Bhava-kavitvam, which began in opposition to the classical world view, adopted literary conventions that encouraged poets to write in defiance of pandit-made rules. Protest-Ramayana themes adopted by Bhava-kavitvam poets now appeared in a modern literary idiom.

One such play is Muddu Krishna's *Aśokam* (1930), which presents Rama, Sita and Ravana speaking conversational Telugu, looking like your next-door neighbors. Tradition so far had dictated that all mythological characters speak a dialect removed from modern speech, filled with Sanskritic and archaic forms of Telugu. This strategy elevated the characters above the human level and provided them with an aura of distance and divinity. Even demons spoke such a dialect, if they were high-caste characters like Ravana. This convention underwent a radical transformation in the works of Chalam (see below), who made gods speak like ordinary people in his works and whose lead Muddu Krishna followed.

The theme of *Aśokam* is briefly this: Ravana stops by at Sita's house to express his love for her, even before her wedding to Rama. Sita listens to his declaration of love but answers that she has chosen to leave the final decision of marriage to fate and to her father. Then Rama arrives and declares his love to Sita. Sita gives the same answer, but feels attracted to Rama and falls in love with him. Rama meets Ravana and realizes that Ravana too is in love with Sita but, instead of being jealous, he nobly admits that Ravana's love for Sita could be as "pure" as his, so he decides to let Sita choose between them.

Next we meet Sita in the forest. Rama regrets experiencing such hardship in the forest but feels grateful to her for choosing to accompany him there. Then Ravana shows up and invites both of them to his palace in Lanka. He offers to relinquish Lanka for Sita and her husband, and depart to a faraway place. His love for Sita is so great that he offers to sacrifice his empire for her. Next, we meet Sita in the Ashoka grove in Lanka, reprimanding Ravana for being so rash as to bring her there. Ravana admits that he had been wrong, but says he could not resist his love for her; he worships her and could not live without seeing her. Sita tells him how much she understands his feelings for her, but explains that she cannot give herself to him. We finally see Rama telling Sita how deeply Ravana had loved her, and how he spoke of her even at the time of his death. Sita understands, and Rama does too, that Ravana had a pure heart. He was a noble lover. But Sita still goes through the fire ordeal, to satisfy the fears of the people!

Retold in this form, the story may look sentimental and silly. Yet in the atmosphere of the Bhava-kavitvam movement of the 1930s, Telugu literature was raging with poems on platonic love; in keeping with the trend of the times, writers wrote about men who fell in love with women only to sacrifice their lives for women's love, never even thinking of a physical relationship. This play depicts Ravana professing his "pure love," *pavitra prema,* to Sita. The writer makes no effort to depict Rama in a poor light, but then he is not the center of the play either.

Muddu Krishna did not stand out as one of the major writers of the period. Remembered mostly for his anthology of Bhava-kavitvam poems, he is one of the few Non-Brahmin poets of this modern poetry movement. However, the new ideology of modernism seemed to defy the claims of caste hierarchies, at least in poetry, and a number of Brahmin writers themselves wrote anti-Brahmanic poems.

With Gudipati Venkata Chalam (1894–1979), one of those rebel Brahmins, the "Women's reform" anti-Ramayana narratives begin. Chalam believed that women should be freed from the sexual bondage of marriage; he wrote of sexual liberation of women in his novels and short stories. Although they might look mild by present-day standards, such works were revolutionary in Chalam's time. A writer who handled Telugu prose with masterly subtlety and power, he wrote with a sensitive understanding of female sexuality and a passionate desire to affirm female sexual pleasure as the celebration of human life. Sharply critical of Brahmanic moral standards, Chalam relished shocking the conservative minds of his time. In one novel (*Maidānam*), he relentlessly describes the sexual adventures, with two Muslim lovers, of a married Brahmin woman from a conservative family. He wrote a number of plays reinterpreting puranic themes from his rebellious point of view. Among them, the one that concerns us here is *Sīta Agnipravēśam* (Sita Enters Fire, 1935?). Despite his unconventional interest in depicting uninhibited sexuality, Chalam shares the romantic attitudes of love prevalent in the literature of his time.

In his *Agnipravēśam,* Chalam rewrites the well-known Ramayana incident where Sita has to walk through fire to prove her fidelity to Rama. The play begins after the war with Ravana ends, with Sita inviting Rama, with words of great longing and love, to embrace her. But soon she finds out that Rama has doubts about her because she has lived in the enemy's house for an extended time. Ravana had loved her. "Is it my fault?" asks Sita. But realizing that Rama sees her only as an object to be possessed as long as it gives him pride, which he is willing to abandon the moment he sees it might be polluted, she declares:

> Let me speak. Ravana loved me. Even your sharp arrows could not kill his love for me. Your love, it was gone the moment you suspected that another man might have loved me . . . . Did I love him in return? That's what you fear, don't you? If I had loved him, I would have covered his body with mine as a shield against your arrows. Did he molest me? No, he was too noble a person for that. He loved me, even when he knew I would never love him in return . . . . I feel sorry I did not return his love. I shall pay a price for it now. I shall purify my body, which was soiled when I uttered your wretched name, by the flames of fire which touched his blood-stained limbs. You, Rama, rejected me because you fear that my body was defiled by his touch, though you know my heart was pure. This anti-god wanted my heart, even though he knew my body was taken by you. Some day, intelligent people will know who was a nobler lover.[23]

And, even before she finishes her sentence, Sita jumps into Ravana's funeral pyre, performing a sort of suttee for him!

While an influential anti-Brahmanic discourse was spreading through the middle class, especially after the modernist trend beginning with the Bhava-kavitvam movement during the early decades of the twentieth century, a totally unprecedented Ramayana took the literary world by storm: Viswanatha Satyanarayana's *Rāmāyaṇa Kalpavṛkṣamu* (Ramayana, the Giving Tree). As soon as the first volume of this remarkable book was published, the literary world realized its power and beauty.[24] However, there was a problem. Satyanarayana took a vehemently conservative position and spoke unapologetically in support of Brahmins. It was trendy among the educated middle class during those days to be anti-traditional, which also meant being anti-Brahmin. Even Brahmins adopted a vigorous anti-traditional position. The modern English-educated person agreed that Vedas, Puranas and similar old texts kept the country in ignorance; they agreed that caste system, child marriages, proscription of widow remarriage, and all the Hindu practices relating to purity were features of backwardness. India had to change, and nearly everything traditional should be abandoned for a modern, western model. In this context, Satyanārāyaṇa came out in support of traditional customs and values, including the caste system and child marriages. He advocated a society based on the rules of *Mānavadharmaśāstra.*

It would probably have mattered little had Satyanarayana not been a powerful poet; there were plenty of old pandits who argued like him. They were all eventually marginalized as outdated and fossilized minds (*chāndasulu*), with nothing intelligent to say, even if they controlled the knowledge from some old books, for which skill they sometimes needed to be consulted. But Satyanarayana was different. Breathtakingly brilliant, well-educated in English, he was on top of all this, a dazzling poet. When he read his Ramayana verses in public, hundreds of people listened in rapture. Satyanarayana's literary presence and his energetic scholarly and poetic personality made his audience pay renewed attention to the Ramayana. While his Ramayana was admittedly devotional, his depiction of character and his narration of the story were anything but flat. To an audience tired of reading insipid retellings of the Rama story just because Rama was God, Satyanarayana offered a lively and exciting option.

He pre-empted questions about his choice of theme in the opening verses of his six-volume magnum opus:

If you ask, "Why yet another Ramayana?"
my answer is: In this world,

everyone eats the same rice every day,
but the taste of your life is your own.
People make love, over and over, but only you
know how it feels. I write about the same Rama
everyone else has known, but my feelings of love
are mine. Ninety per cent of what makes a poem
is the genius of the poet. Poets in India know
that the way you tell the tale
weighs a thousand times more
than some facile, novel theme.[25]

Such a renewal of the Ramayana with a strong Brahmanic message quickly elicited an equally strong Non-Brahmin reaction. Modernists, secularists and Marxists, all ideologically anti-Brahmin, found Satyanarayana a threat. They felt repelled by Satyanarayana's conservative arguments, which, to them, sounded like a call to turn their backs on a century of progress toward Enlightenment, rational thinking and scientific understanding. Public criticism against Satyanarayana was vehement and relentless. He was attacked as a blind revivalist, a bad writer, a difficult writer to understand. (He used archaic Sanskrit words and compounds testing even the most learned scholar's control of Sanskrit.) Satyanaryana himself took a vehement anti-colonial stand, advocating that the evil of English education had destroyed the dharmic genius of Indian culture and enslaved Indian minds to a foreign ideology. In addition to his *Rāmāyaṇa Kalpavṛkṣamu,* his other publications, too, fueled the anti–Ramayana discourse of the past five decades. Among the leaders of this new anti-Ramayana discourse two writers stand out: Narla Venkateswara Rao (1908–85) and Muppala Ranganayakamma.

Narla Venkateswara Rao, a younger contemporary of the major modernist writers in Telugu, has earned a greater reputation for his leadership role in Telugu journalism than as a writer. But he wrote two Ramayana plays, *Jābāli* (1974) and *Sīta Jōsyam* (Sita's Prophesy, 1979). As the editor of the most widely circulated Telugu daily newspaper, *Andhra Prabha,* he played an influential role in molding public opinion. He stood up for freedom of the press and fearlessly advocated liberal ideas. He wrote his editorials in a vigorous style and they remained the talk of the town day after day. For Venkateswara Rao, Sanskrit and Brahmanic ideas represented a dead past which only blocked the path to progress. He looked to western scholarship for wisdom; ideas of Enlightenment served as his guide to the future. In his *Jābāli,* Venkateswara Rao depicts an atheist character who appears in the *Ayodhyākāṇḍa* of Valmiki's *Rāmāyaṇa.* Jabali, in Venkateswara Rao's play, is a weak character, too scared to face the powerful Vasishtha, the Brahmin minister. After trying in vain to dissuade Rama from going to the forest, by giving him his atheist advice, Jabali sees Vasishtha approaching and escapes with the excuse that he was only testing Rama's resolve. Jabali's conversation with Rama reveals the intrigues, jealousies and pettiness of the Brahmin sages at the court.

The second play, *Sīta Jōsyam,* is more interesting, and also more skillfully written. In a long introduction to this play, Venkateswara Rao says:

> The Ramayana, the Mahabharata, the eighteen puranas—the major aim of all these texts is to protect the caste system; the feudal order. If they continue to be propagated in the way they are now, progress towards a new social order will remain an empty slogan. For about fifteen hundred years, these texts have stood as severe obstacles to our intellectual development and social progress. If we do not remove these obstacles even now, we cannot enter the modern age, nor can we move forward on a progressive path.[26]

In this play Venkateswara Rao depicts the conflict between sages and demons in the Dandaka forest as a conflict between food gatherers and food producers. Rama, depicted as a vain character, kills the demons when the sages flatter him as the greatest warrior of the Raghu clan. Sita, on the other hand, understands that the demons are innocent food gatherers whose livelihood is being destroyed by sages who burn their forests to clear land for their cultivation. The demons fight back. Sita wants Rama to leave them alone. The sages, she advises, are seeking expansion into the south to occupy more and more land, but Rama refuses to listen. He has vowed to protect the Brahmins, whatever the price. The play ends with Sita prophesying that one day he will leave her, to please the Brahmins!

One of the most recent, most complete and also highly controversial of the anti-Ramayanas is Muppala Ranganayakamma's *Rāmāyaṇa Viṣavṛkṣam* (Ramayana, The Poison Tree). By the 1960s the novel had become the major mode of Telugu literature. For about a decade women writers dominated prose fiction and their novels sold in larger quantities than any other works. Serialized in weekly magazines, novels written by women significantly increased magazine circulation. Ranganayakamma is one of the new group of women writers who came into the literary world through her novels. Sometime in the early 1970s Ranganayakamma discovered Marxism, and since then she has stopped writing novels and begun writing Marxist works.

Fiercely polemical in its style, *The Poison Tree* vehemently rejects all Brahmanic as well as Non-Brahmanic interpretations of the Ramayana and proposes that Valmiki's text was written with the sole intention of keeping all low castes and women in feudal bondage. Partly a critical commentary on Valmiki's text and partly a retelling of the story as Ranganayakamma thought it had happened, *The Poison Tree* is a rambling text in a style that spares neither innuendo nor invective against feudalism and Brahmins. Ranganayakamma's belief in Marxism gives her enormous confidence in rejecting Valmiki as an unskilled poet who was writing at a stage in civilization when the art of telling stories and composing books was still in its infancy. Her Marxist knowledge has an answer for everything; there are no uncertainties or questions in her mind about the absolute accuracy of her theory that human civilization progresses in clearly defined stages based on the means of production, and that the Ramayana reflects the feudal stage. She rewrites the story to unmask the mystique which kept the true intention of the narrative hidden from readers. Summarizing her three-volume retelling of the Ramayana, Ranganayakamma declares: "The Ramayana favors men; favors the rich, favors the upper castes, and the ruling class. It supports exploitation; it was never a progressive text, not even at the time it was written."[27]

## Conclusion

What is the impact of these anti-Ramayanas on the Telugu public? None of them achieved recognition as outstanding works of literature, except perhaps *Sīta Jōsyam,* which received the Sahitya Akademi award in 1981. Each one of them remained controversial for a time. Educated readers argued about them. Ranganayakamma's *The Poison Tree* even sold well. It generated violent disagreements; some responded to it as a liberating reading, and others genuinely hated it. Ranganayakamma, a writer not particularly gentle in her responses to criticism, added fire to the acrimonious nature of the debate. The official position of the Marxist parties themselves was somewhat lukewarm: they did not oppose the book but they did not enthusiastically embrace it either. With all the excitement the anti-Ramayana authors generated, they missed out on something that makes a literary text literary. They uniformly failed to understand that literary consciousness of Telugu culture was deeply embedded in myth, a valorized narrative from a rooted past. They failed to create anything even remotely satisfying to sustain a counter-myth. However, author after author wrote a lengthy polemical essay as a preface to their literary work. Their ideas were intellectually provocative, even if their artistic skill was not satisfying. Literary scholars wrote books discussing the value of Ramayana in the light of new knowledge of anthropology, history and science.[28] The essays and books led to serious discussions, charges and counter charges.

As a result of the long and sustained discourse of the anti-Ramayanas, a level of cultural openness was achieved, at least among intellectuals. The religious impact of the bhakti Ramayanas on the public mind was not greatly diminished, but educated middle-class readers became familiar with critical discourse on what is believed to be a sacred text. If in the earlier times, premodern literary Ramayanas and folk Ramayanas kept the multivocality of the Ramayana alive, the modernist anti-Ramayanas have played a major role in keeping the diverse interpretations alive in the face of the homogenization and production of what, one sometimes fears, could become a fascist Ramayana discourse.

NINE

# Thereupon Hangs a Tail: The Deification of Vāli in the Teyyam Worship of Malabar

RICH FREEMAN

Meeting your gods in the flesh is not that unusual in Malabar. People in this northern region of Kerala have been routinely encountering their gods as humanly incarnated, spirit-possessed dancers and priests for the past two millennia.[1] When I first met Bāli in this way, I was relatively uninterested in his particular attributes or origins. I knew him to be the Malabar version of the monkey chieftain Vāli, a comparatively minor character adopted into the region from the pan-Indic mythology of the Ramayana. Accordingly, I also regarded him as one of the most classically Sanskritized beings worshiped through *teyyāṭṭam,* the "dance of the gods," that I had come to Malabar to study. Far more vital to my anthropological interests were the majority of those gods of purely local origin, especially those explicitly deriving from deified human beings. The liturgies used in their teyyāṭṭams recall their lives in Kerala's medieval society, the circumstances of their deaths, and their apotheoses into teyyam deities.[2]

On closer study, however, Bāli has proven to strike deeper roots in the cultural soil of Kerala than I had expected. Many of his teyyam myths and episodes come not out of Vālmīki's *Rāmāyaṇa* at all, but out of regional and folk sources whose themes and concerns remain specific to South Indian and Kerala society. That these are cast in the consciously Sanskritizing frame of the great epic, with its invocation of normative and upper-caste Hindu values, only makes Bāli's linkages to the local context of the lower-caste communities who worship him more contrastively apparent. This dynamic between the Vāli of pan-Indic literary circuits and the Bāli of teyyam myth and ritual also heightens two major interpretive issues surrounding *teyyāṭṭam* itself.

The first and most general issue concerns the way apparently historical persons or types of persons in Malabar are turned into teyyam deities and worshiped in this manner by their communities. Since the most characteristic teyyam gods manifestly celebrate their own origins as former human beings, with social identities clearly anchored in the local culture, the figure of Vāli, a supernatural monkey drawn from the trans-regional literary imagination of the Sanskrit epic, would hardly seem an obvious choice for drafting into *teyyāṭṭam*. This anomaly, however, is only apparent as long as we think of deities as typically transcendent beings, abstracted away from the human condition. By contrast, teyyam worshipers conceive of divinities as powers immanent in their own communities and surroundings, so that deification merely manifests the continuum of powers that flow naturally between human beings and divine ones.[3] Viewed this way, divinizing the mythical and literary character of Vāli in this culture actually works to affirm the force of his essential humanity within the framework of Malabar society.

The second issue raised concerns the way this same social framework shapes human identities in the hierarchy of caste, and the way this system's structural tensions are built into *teyyāṭṭam*. Since teyyams are centrally worshiped among the traditionally lower castes of Kerala, the deities themselves being incarnated by still lower "Untouchable" dancers, we might expect this experience of caste to inform the ethos of teyyam worship. The status conflict inherent in socially disprivileged persons worshiping and even becoming powerfully enhanced deities in fact expresses itself in critiques of the caste order, some overt and some covert, that are woven through teyyam myths and performances. This religiously inspired social resistance that informs much of teyyam worship in turn heightens the unique engagement of Bāli's local mythologies with the Sanskritic values of the epic, and suggests a critique of those values that works from within the context of *teyyāṭṭam* out into the circle of higher-caste, literary culture. Therefore, I view Bāli not primarily as a folk derivative of the Sanskrit Vāli, but rather as the expression of local concerns and values that coalesced into a character creatively harnessing Sanskritic materials to local ends.

In this essay, I examine Bāli's complex nature as a narrative entity in myth and as a ritual entity in society from four angles of consideration. In the opening section, I situate him in his community of worship as a teyyam deity, showing how the ritual matrix of *teyyāṭṭam* and its liturgies tie Bāli's identity, socially and historically, to the communities that worship him. My second concern, over the next three sections, is with showing how various dominant motifs in Bāli's mythology relate to the pervasive tensions inherent in the structure of traditional Kerala society. In the penultimate section, I consider how certain aspects of Bāli's textual representation connect his character in Kerala with wider patterns of transregional scope in India. Finally, I show how certain institutions of Kerala society provided the forum for integrating those thematic and ritual elements of Bāli's character into his promotion and worship as a teyyam deity.

## The Teyyam of Bāli in its Ritual and Community Context

*Teyyāṭṭam* centrally consists of annual festival rites of possession, during which a community's enshrined deities are ritually transferred into the elaborately costumed bodies of specially entitled and trained professional dancers. Through sung invocations, narratives, and the accompanying rituals, a designated artist first becomes possessed by his deity, following which he dances through the shrine compound and amongst the onlookers. At the close of the dance phase, the performer, now the deity incarnate, verbally and ritually interacts with the assembled devotees, dispensing grace and blessings as the god. Finally, there are concluding rituals for returning the god's power from the dancer to the shrine, where it remains until the next rituals of possession call it forth again. There is a whole ritual life to such shrines beyond the annual festivals of *teyyāṭṭam,* however, and there are other personnel who also have regular ritual interaction with and undergo possession by these deities.

Most importantly, the sponsoring community which controls and manages the shrine includes its own possessed priests (called *kōmarams* or *veḷiccappāṭus*), who, unlike the professional dancers, remain dedicated to a single enshrined teyyam of their community for life. These priests are selected by a combination of specific lineage eligibility, divine selection through spontaneous acts of possession, and subsequent ratification by astrological or other kinds of oracular readings. This lineal entitlement often goes back to some founder who had a special relation with the deity, usually initiated through supernatural revelation or through possession. His descendants then continue to both commemorate and re-establish this relation through their own holding of the ecstatic priestly office. The priests dedicated to Bāli are mostly drawn from the Āśāri (Carpenter) caste, who therefore exercise a kind of ritual prominence among the aggregate of Kammāḷar (Artisan) castes who exclusively worship Bāli. Farther down the social scale come the Vaṇṇāns, traditional Washermen of the lower castes, who have exclusive rights to perform the *teyyāṭṭam* of Bāli for the Artisan community.

The Artisan community seems conflicted in the status attributed to their caste identity. Though traditionally classed in Kerala as polluting castes (*avarṇa*), the nature of artisan occupations brought them into closer interaction with higher castes than their low ritual status reflected. In fact, they claimed, along with many other artisan castes of India, the title of Viśvakarma, after the artisan of the gods, which elevates them—in their own reckoning only—to the Vaishya grade of "twice-born" caste-standing.[4] Their desire to claim higher ritual status than Kerala society grants them finds expression in upwardly mobile aspirations in their discourses and practices around Bāli. For example, his worshipers described the teyyam's intricate costume and time-consuming make-up (see illustrations), as being just like *kathakaḷi*, a later "classical" form of staging epic and Purāṇic dramas in Kerala's elite temple theater traditions. Similarly, the ritual vestments of Āśāri shrine priests mimic those of Brahmins in certain respects, and they eschewed the rituals of purification usual among lower-caste priests.[5] As a borderline grade of "polluting" castes, then, the Āśāris perhaps experience more acutely than other castes the tensions of mediating between the ritual purity of Sanskritic Brahmanism and the putative pollution from engaging local religious powers. Bāli may be the perfect deity to express their cultural predicament.

Tension stems from these thwarted claims to higher status, on the one hand, and their vigorous ritual celebration of *teyyāṭṭam* with its attendant rites of possession, blood sacrifice, and liquor offerings, on the other. These basic conflicts of social hierarchy appear in the myths of Bāli that define his discursive existence as a teyyam, conflicts which

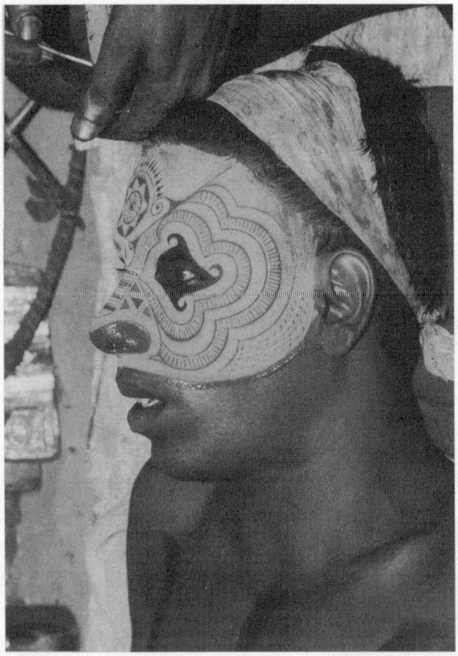

The make-up for the full form of Bāli's teyyam may take as long as two hours to apply.

Bāli's teyyam searches for a foe during a battle sequence in his main dance.

Bāli's teyyam gives advice to a group of devotees.

Bāli gestures in receipt of offerings to a devotee, following his dance sequence.

The song-troupe restrains Bāli during the onset of possession in his preliminary, *veḷḷāṭṭam* form, enacted the night before his full teyyam performance.

have been internalized into the self-perception of the Artisan community from the larger patterns of this society. For example, consider a reason often cited for Artisans' connection with Bāli: they fashioned the arrow which Rāma used to kill Bāli. Thus, the instrument of violence, gore, and death that pollutes the Artisans through their very association with its production, also serves as the instrument which, in killing Bāli, converts him into the deity they worship. Bāli's mortality both establishes his link with humanity and enables him to transcend the human condition by coming back from the dead through possession.

The most revealing cultural dynamic in *teyyāṭṭam* lies in the clearly human origins of many of its gods, including deified ancestors or heroes. In such instances, the individuals who undergo apotheosis have exhibited unusual powers of a martial or magical nature, either during their lifetimes, or through the circumstances of their often violently transformative deaths.[6] Even when no overt memory of the dead as a human individual remains, as with Bāli, the social context of the god's worship is preserved in the liturgies and mapped into the rituals. The founding of the god's worship, its ritual connection to specific communities, and the pertinence of its myths to recurrent social themes are all inscribed into the teyyam liturgies as historical memories with current ritual significance. I therefore want to consider how these liturgies work to tie their social and historical thematics into the context of ongoing worship. Only then can we appreciate how the specifics of Bāli's myths address the tensions of caste society through the performance of his teyyam.

All songs in *teyyāṭṭam* are sung before the onset of possession, and so express the various stages of worship and states of worshipers leading up to the dancer's transformation into the god.[7] The first piece that the performers in a *teyyāṭṭam* sing falls in the genre of *varaviḷi*, "the call to come," addressed to the deity to invoke its presence into the shrine compound. This summons usually includes some cursory description of the god's birth, its original locales, and often descriptions of its appearance, activities, and sometimes human demise and divinization. Bāli's *varaviḷi* begins very simply:

> May you come, O God, Long Tail![8]

This first line addressed to the god in this song, like the last, uses this epithet Long Tail (*Niṭubāliyan*), to focus on the prodigiousness of Bāli's prehensile member. This marks a theme whose significance for

Bāli's character and social identity unfolds in the course of the liturgies.

The piece then moves us immediately into a string of mythical mountains, descending into the various cities known to the Ramayana, and then names the mountains of Coorg (*Koṭumala*) to Kerala's east, where the Kaveri river arises . . .

Where used to reside
Indra, the great king, your father,
Who spied Aruṇa, the mother who bore you.
That day, with Jupiter in the Eighth house, afflicted,
Your own younger brother, with little brother Sugrīva
You battled in a war for your birthright—
And when he took the side of Sugrīva
By the arrow of that blessed Lord Rāma
You were struck and attained the Release of Heroes!

Here is the essence of the teyyam, its span from birth to death, collapsed into this brief compass. The word *tōṟṟam*, the macro designation for teyyam songs, refers both to the origins or appearance of an entity, but also to its reappearance through focused invocation.[9] The word itself thus suggests, somewhat as in the divinities of the Tamil Bow-Song tradition documented by Blackburn, that we may have here a circular cultural logic in which apotheosis after death is explained by attributions of an earlier divine empowerment in life.[10] Furthermore, we often find an unsettling ambivalence at the core of teyyam genesis, a marking of origins as peculiar, mixed, and even mongrel. When the liturgies depict a human birth, the being often turns out to be of mixed caste, or a forest foundling of suspicious origins, sometimes even exhibiting demonic features of appearance or behavior. In Bāli's case, we shall see later how his birth from Indra and Aruṇa, his "mother," cited in the invocation song, fits this pattern. We also encounter further forebodings of conflict in the astrological affliction of "the Eighth (House)," mentioned here, which ordains the fatal battle between brothers. And finally, the arrow of Lord Rāma, which sends Bāli purportedly to the release, or heaven, of heroes (*vīrya-mōkṣam*) connects the Artisans' crafting of the weapon ambivalently with both Bāli's murder and his apotheosis.

But this *mōkṣam*, or release, of Bāli, consists neither of the abstract absorption of high Hinduism, nor even the "heaven" of folk devotionalism. Instead, Bāli descends into the world (perhaps through the underworld) and is established in the fort of the Vaṭuva Rāja,[11] first manifested through possession, and then worshiped by that king as a teyyam. Though the details of this first manifestation are cryptic, the ritual portent is clear, since the verb for Bāli's establishment (*śēṣi-peṭṭu*) signifies both empowerment and possession. The liturgy also specifies in its description of the king's worship of Bāli, that the introductory phase of *teyyāṭṭam,* called *veḷḷāṭṭam* (see photo 2), was performed. But while the festival was in full swing, a guest arrived

> The rites of *veḷḷāṭṭam* and the food offering,
> While receipt of these was going on,
> There came to that place
> The headman of Maṇṇummal,
> The Maṇṇummal Viśvakarma.
> The Maṇṇummal Viśvakarma's
> Dress, and style, his caste marks,
> His restraint and ritual demeanor, seeing these,
> "I don't want to give him up!"
> . . . the God, Long Tail,
> Thus thought to himself.

And so this god, unbeknownst to the Artisan headman, rode back with him in a ritual umbrella to the latter's village of Maṇṇummal, where he again manifested his presence (*śēṣi-peṭṭu*) in the Viśvakarma's ancestral shrine. That the Artisan carries such an umbrella (*veḷḷōla mey-kuṭa*) to the festival shows that he already held priestly office in his own community. From the shrine of Maṇṇummal, Bāli's worship spread in the Artisan community to three other prominent shrines named in the song, and thence, throughout the community at large.

Bāli's devotees accordingly experience their deity as both geographically and socially localized: geographically, in the mountains of Coorg, and socially, in his relation to the community of Artisan worshipers. The oracle-priest of the Āśāris I interviewed cited the lines from the *varaviḷi* that name the four places where Bāli was first established among their community, noting that, "Because these four shrines belong to us, it is we who celebrate this teyyam. Bāli is our community deity (*kula-daivam*)." The priest knew well the locale of the original Maṇṇummal lineage shrine and its village, but did not venture any knowledge about the Vaṭuva Rāja who had originally worshipped Bāli. Since the songs themselves place Bāli's origins from Indra and Aruṇa in the forested Coorgi highlands along Kerala's north-east border, my guess would be that the Maṇṇummal Viśvakarma first went on the fateful pilgrimage there, and that the Vaṭuva Rāja was a tribal chieftain of this area.[12] This interpretation fits a pattern common to many teyyam deities, where they were either originally adopted from tribal communities, or where their transformations chart the absorption of such communities themselves into a settled, lowland agricultural regime, along with their gods.[13]

This short song then ends by verbally transferring Bāli's power from these foundational sites into whatever place of worship the performance is currently taking place. Just as the power of the god's manifestation through possession rites was first channeled into the ancestral shrines, so it flows again into subsequent shrines wherever the rites and liturgies that re-enact these events are repeated.

Previously in the four dawning shrines,
Just as you were empowered,
In this shrine, too, having come
To take up your power,
May you come! O God, Long Tail!

Note how the lines chart the shift from places that were spatially and temporally remote to the present venue of performance, and how the continuity across these contexts comes through the power of the god himself, directly addressed by the reciter in the final imperative and epithet.

The next couple of pieces from Bāli's liturgical texts similarly work to bridge the god's construction as a discursive entity and his performative manifestation in ritual. The stanzas here include direct praise addressed to the god, in the context of performance, but also interweave terse references to Bali's mythical exploits. This terseness presupposes a knowledge of the fuller narratives that occur elsewhere both within Bāli's teyyam corpus, and in the wider regional tradition. Thus, part of the performative effectiveness of such verses lies in their concise invocation of a more extensive narrative background, accessed from within the context of ritually enacted praise. For example, consider this stanza from the second of these pieces, which says merely this:

At the time when Mannaram was lowered in churning the deep,
The gods saw that the beautiful Tāra had come there.
Saying "Praise," they made Tāra a wife for Bāli.
Praised be stainless Long Tail! May you be my support!

This myth exemplifies a number of those whose narrative elements go back not to the prototype of Vālmīki or other such Sanskrit works, but to a shared south Dravidian literary and folk heritage of the Keralas and other Tamils.[14] The story alluded to here establishes Bāli as a great hero, superior to the gods, and finds greater elaboration later in Bāli's teyyam songs.[15] It tells how the gods proved too weak to finish churning the milk-ocean with Mount Mandaram, in their efforts to extract all the delectables of creation. So, the mighty Bāli came to their aid, and seizing the serpent Vāsuki as his rope, he churned the sea by spinning this great mountain. When he did so, a beautiful damsel, Tāra, appeared from the froth, and the gods agreed to give her as wife to Bāli in reward for having completed the task where they failed.

Note that the condensed nature of the mythical allusion in the stanza above allows it to merge in the closing line with the ritual utterance of collective praise, and to articulate with the immediate plea of the worshiper for Bāli's support. This shows that the intertextual density of the myths and their allusions function not only to project a sense of Bāli's larger reality out of the narrative resources, but also to provide junctures where narrative depictions connect with the ritual context. These contextual ties work at different levels, but mutually support each other in contributing to the experience of teyyam's relevance and verity for its worshipers. For instance, in tying the mythical attributes of Bāli's appearance to those of his dancer, the stanza immediately following the one cited above continues:

> Is there any to rival this might of yours, that I could praise more?
> With your splendid stripes and your spotted white tail,
> Wrapping on your pleasing fine silk and donning your Flower Crown
> With kindly grace, stainless Long Tail, be my support!

The presence of the tail in the invocation verbally mirrors its physical presence as a prominent part of the actual costume of the teyyam dancer. Similarly the "silk" in the invocation refers to the red waist-wrap the teyyam actually wears, and the "Flower Crown" is the specifically named type of head-piece donned for Bāli's costume (see illustrations).

In such cases, worshipers visually experience the reality of what is being verbally described. By analogy, this suggests that connections between liturgy and the less tangible levels of social and historical context are equally descriptive of reality. The intimate level of ritual enactment and the larger level of social representations are thus mutually supportive in contextualizing Bāli's myths within Kerala. Ritual histories serve to tie a mythic Bāli into the localized Kerala past, and then connect this localized past into the recurring performative present. For example, note the shift in the following from the historical practices of the founding priest, to the physical image before the contemporary worshiper, to the performative engagement in praise:

> In this world, at that time, in the clan of Viśvakarmas,
> He remained always absorbed in worshipping you as his god;
> Wherever in the world you sport, he kept vows and performed *pūjās*,
> Remaining faithful; And the fine *kaḷiyāṭṭam* and *tiṟakolam* [teyyam rites],
> Because of these, your panther's body is crouched and claws are spread,
> Your gaze like an onslaught, when I see your approach,
> . . . I praise you with this [verse] . . .

Addressed to Bāli, these lines recount the virtues of the originating Artisan (Viśvakarma) priest as the exemplary and archetypical devotee. His foundational rituals of *teyyāṭṭam* in the past are the source of the present deity's form as possessed dancer, which the contemporary worshiper describes in images of bestial and kinetic power. Such verses draft their reciter into acts of praise and ritual, even as they draft a mythical Bāli into his role as the localized object and recipient of that praise and ritual. The invocatory texts we have reviewed show that whatever Bāli's association with the Ramayana, he has been brought into a close conformity with the norms and practices of *teyyāṭṭam*. This is so both in terms of the basic expectations as to how teyyam gods arise, and in terms of how they are socially, historically, and ritually related to the context of worship.

From the perspective of the teyyam tradition, Bāli is only one among hundreds of its deities, most of whom have no direct claims on a Sanskritic heritage. And yet despite Bāli's Sanskritic pedigree, his basic features conform closely to a dominant teyyam-type: a heroic warrior of mighty feats who has been tragically killed, and then comes to be worshiped through oracular signs that eventuate in regularized rites of spirit possession. In the sections that follow, I now want to further indicate how some of Bāli's myths in the teyyam songs thematically strengthen these associations with the social conditions of the culture that produced him.

## Ambivalent Valor in a Beastly Hierarchy

The Kerala society that produced Bāli's teyyam was one of warriors. High-born warriors died noble deaths with lots of fanfare and ritual. Though humbler soldiers usually died meaner deaths, their kin commemorated them as well, and warfare provided a route to status mobility. For instance, a section of the formerly untouchable Tiyya caste was specially elevated under the title *Cēkōr*, because they fought public duels as proxies for their higher lords.[16] As recorded in one famous folk song, the combatants were conducted into the venue with great ritual display, and received lavish gifts and payments from their lords. The rather telling ceremonial prelude to the duel, however, was a cock-fight, a grimly dehumanizing prefigurement of the all-too-human contest that would follow.[17] The ballad literature of North Malabar (*Vaṭakkan Pāṭṭukaḷ*) records how the families of such slain heroes received rich rewards. The stalwarts themselves were immortalized, both in these cycles of songs that still glorify them, and occasionally, in teyyam-like rituals that worship them as godlings.

But nobody likes to die, however glorious the preliminaries, and however enhanced the post-mortem status. Both the medieval folk and high literature of Kerala betray a profound ambivalence over these facts of regular death in battle, which were a recurrent source of productive cultural and artistic tension in this society.[18] These ambivalences and resentments, normal even among the aristocracy, proved even greater among the lower social orders, who also provided the soldiery and henchmen of Kerala's medieval polities. So as in every other aspect of Kerala society, hierarchical tensions of caste, power, status, wealth, and gender inflected the culture of warfare and the vortex of death that it drove. The teyyam of Bāli reveals this association between hierarchy and warfare with marked clarity, and it is these social facts that are paramount, rather than the historical specificity of any particular individual who eventually assumed identification with the epic Vāli.

Accordingly, I see in Bāli's mythology an inherent tension between rising in status through warfare, and the eventuality of a heroic death that marks the ambivalent culmination of that career. In accepting the bitter necessity of this fate, one also accepts the hierarchy of the social structure that can require such an outcome. This submission to death, whether through martial deliberation or a position of servitude, is the culminating act of submission to the social order of life. And yet despite the likelihood of this fate, the style and willingness with which one takes up one's lot can turn a surface conformity into a simultaneously transcendent act of defiant and immortalizing pride in one's identity. It is understandable then how such exemplars of inwardly resistant self-affirmation hold powerful attractions for the whole spectrum of Kerala's traditional underclasses.

Another dimension of contestation in this society concerns the representation of identity itself, and whether such categories of identity are stigmatized, stably configured, or disruptive of the status quo. I have noted above that the beings of *teyyāṭṭam* are often of mixed or dubious parentage. They may be low-born or demonic forest foundlings who are raised in high-caste fosterage, but then later revert to their low natures. Alternatively, they may be socially fostered into higher office than their birth warrants, setting off social tensions that they meet with displays of prowess, but that also bring about their ultimate demise. In such narratives of genesis, parental characters such as gods or sages stand often and transparently for the mythicization of the higher castes, especially Brahmins, who had routinized sexual relations with lower-caste women, but whose children retained the lower-caste status of their mothers. In fact, the warrior caste of Nāyar, counted as Shudra-grade in the Kerala reckoning, were regularly of such parentage.

In keeping with this pattern of dubious origins, the first substantial narrative in Bāli's teyyam recounts his genesis as doubly or triply dubious. For starters, Bāli's mother, Aruṇa, named in the opening song, is a man. This Aruṇa, whose own peculiar origins left him with only half a body, had gone to work as the charioteer of the Sun (though the handicap seems not to have affected his driving). Once on his daily route across the sky, Aruṇa learned that Indra was celebrating a celestial festival in the temple in his heaven, to which only women were allowed. Accordingly, after a hard day at the reins, Aruṇa took the form of a woman by bathing in a magic lake, and that evening attended the festival in this feminine guise. Indra, however, was greatly attracted to "her" and "she" herself felt a responding desire for a child. The fruit of their hurried union was Bāli. Since the child would soon have no mother, though, on Aruṇa's return to normalcy (such as it was), Indra gave the child to Ahalyā and her Brahmin-Ṛṣi husband, Gautama (or Durvāsa), to raise. Aruṇa, in the mean time, had reverted to his usual form and hurried back to the Sun to explain why he was late for work. The Sun asked to see this beautiful feminine form that had so enticed Indra, and on Aruṇa complying, the "arrow of love" (*kāmaśaram*) struck her belly again, this time from solar loins. The result was Sugrīva, and there this song ends. The story picked up elsewhere in the corpus alludes to an incident of Bāli's foster father cursing him and Sugrīva to take the form of apes over some misdemeanor of their and Ahalyā's behavior. Because of this, though Bāli's godly parentage led him to eminence over the simian race, he was forever demoted from higher society and banished to mountain forests.

There are a number of resonances with Kerala's social structure in this myth, of which I will consider only the most salient: the feminization of Aruṇa, the animality of Bāli, and disparities between brothers in parentage and seniority. In terms of the first, I have elsewhere documented how high male gods correspond to the social roles of Brahmins and kings, heaven represents the temple or palace, and goddesses stand in frequently for the lower castes who were brought into relation with these complexes.[19] These lower clean castes who directly attended the Brahmanical order served as the warrior–guardians of society. The price of their admission to the temple, from which the rest of society was excluded, was exacted not only in the hazards of war, but in the stigmatized feminization of their identity. Symbolically, these communities were mythically represented through their goddesses, in a framework where the female signifies inherent impurity and submission, against the male purity and authority of Brahmin gods. This skewed theological mapping of gender onto caste was further literally enacted, since the real-life women of these martial groups were drafted into the sexual service of Brahmins and chiefs as a matter of religious honor. A collective resentment surely shaped the violent natures of these marginally controllable goddesses, who represented the communities of these women and their warrior sons. These sons themselves, the soldiering castes of Kerala, remained only quasi-legitimate, denied the higher birthright of their paternity, and inevitably tainted with the offal of battle and a tinge of the demonic. Bāli fills just such a slot, for he is both a mighty warrior and a socially stigmatized apish hybrid.

This leads us from gender to another way of signaling the asymmetry of hierarchy—the attribution of bestiality. Note that the physical manifestation of Bāli and Sugrīva's ape–natures precipitates in the custody of the Brahmin ascetic couple, Gautama and Ahalyā. In terms of this bestial thematic, many other teyyams similarly recount origins from the planting of human seed in animal wombs, or tell of the ability of lower caste hero–sorcerers to turn themselves into beasts that prowl the forests.

Another tension of this society which obtains in this myth as well is the hierarchy of birth, the issue of seniority and parentage. As elder and younger brothers, Bāli and Sugrīva are also of different paternity, and it is the "quarrel over their birthright," as the *varaviḷi* states, that brings Bāli's death. The struggles over partition of inheritance, well known in even standardly patrilineal South Asian families, could of course be exacerbated where, as in the forced casualness of lower-caste unions, the same woman might bear children by different higher-caste men. Bāli and Sugrīva exemplify just such a situation of different paternal lineages cross-cutting their maternity, as several songs of this teyyam confirm.[20] I think this sibling conflict can be no accident of narrative choice within Kerala, for it inverts the usual Sanskrit epic pattern obtaining with Rāma himself, where conflict arose between the children of different women by the same lordly father. The converse case of Bāli and Sugrīva, however, reflects perfectly the routine situation of all those royal and soldiering lineages of Kerala in their relation to the varied assemblage of Brahmanical "gods on earth" (*bhūsuranmār*) who fathered them.

In terms of the narrative force of these points, then, we should realize that Bāli's teyyam works the theme of his origins just as assiduously as do those teyyams coming from overtly human characters, exhibiting the same array of social concerns with hierarchy. And these concerns are the product not of some generally Indic mythic mind-set, but of the social conditions of medieval Kerala. These social levels are further entangled and energized with psychological dynamics, since the familial cannot be separated from the wider social sphere, given the sexual and reproductive politics that invades the very constitution of "families" and their status in the larger order.

## The Folk-Tail of Bāli

The first and most common epithet for Bāli, throughout his teyyam songs, is Long Tail. The songs themselves emphasize the tail as a prominent feature of Bāli's costume in performance (see photos). At an elemental level, the tail is the sign of the beast in Bāli. In terms of the arguments above, it signifies low status compared with Brahminical models of "civilized" humanity.[21] Consider how the eighteenth–century folk-genre called *tuḷḷal* (street-play) depicts the behavior of these simian brothers with their tails. When Gautama's curse turns the foster brothers into apes, "They grinned and grimaced at passers-by/And showing their antics climbed into tree branches/Where they scampered along shitting and sticking up their tails . . ."[22] This tail of Bāli, however, is also a thing of beauty and the source of his might. When Ahalyā realizes to her horror how unseemly her sons' behavior has become for the family's ascetic lifestyle, she returns the senior child to Indra. Indra, though, is entranced with the ape-child Bāli precisely because of the particular beauty (*baṅgi-viśēṣam*) of his tail (*vāl*).[23] The parallel couplet which bestows on Bāli his name, simultaneously foretells the mighty victories he will experience over all, flagging the clear association between his tail, its beauty, and his martial force.[24]

The polyvocal resonances of Bāli's very name map his awesome might into the image of his tail. In the northern regions of Kerala where teyyam is practiced, *b* and *v* are equivalently interchanged, making for several readings of the name Vāli/Bāli that are deliberately left in play. Although the name Vāli(n) is ostensibly of Sanskrit derivation meaning "one who has" (*-in*) "a tail" (*vāla-*), the meaning for *vāla* itself is not fixed as "tail" in Sanskrit (vacillating with meanings of "hair," etc.). Moreover, *vālin* does not seem to be used in the meaning of "tailed" in Sanskrit as one would expect, but only as the proper name of this ape and of another shadowy demon or two.[25] Such evidence suggests that the name actually comes from *vāl*, the commonly used word for "tail" in the Dravidian languages of South India.[26] As a result, this meaning of *vāli/bāli* as "tailed" is transparent in Malayalam; hence the expanded epithet recurring through our songs, *Niṭu-bāliyan/-vāliyan*, "Long Tail." This initial word-play, however, reflects a greater cultural significance, because the semantic associations call up a play of tropes around Bāli's identity. Through that frequent mutation of metonymy into synecdoche (where a part standing for a whole comes to pervade it as its essential quality), rather than the tail being simply something Bāli, as a monkey, has, it becomes something that makes him what he is—serving as a super-signifier of his super-simian status. We should also keep in mind, however, that he has also been partly *made* to have this status by the curse of his Brahmin "father."

In keeping with this synecdochic quality, we might also expect the tail to be implicated in that other quality which Indra's naming of him brought into direct association with his beautiful bestiality: his ferocious martial might. Here some more lexical play enters the picture. The Dravidian verbal root *val-*, meaning ability, strength, might, etc., is still productive in a number of Malayalam formations.[27] This is also probably the original root for the Sanskrit *bala*, "power," or "force," which has thus been re-cycled from Dravidian, through Sanskrit into common Malayalam usage. Consequently, Bāli's name can be read simultaneously with the various plays off *val/bal* as signifying his physically militant prowess, which is perfectly in keeping with his genetic origins from Indra, the Warlord of the Gods. This kind of play on the name appears routinely in the earliest Malayalam works of the fourteenth through the sixteenth centuries, such as the *Rāmacaritam*, *Kaṇṇaśśa Rāmāyaṇam*, *Adhyātma Rāmāyaṇam*, etc. Our *teyyam* songs contain recurrent word-play reflecting this association with his name: for instance, in "Bāli of great might" (*Bāli mahābalan)*, "the mighty Bāli" (*balamuṭaya Bāli)*, and "the mighty heroics of Bāli" (*Bāli tanre bala-vīryaṅṅaḷ)*. This equation provides the very rationale for his naming at birth, since our teyyam poets say he was "born possessed of might" (*balavānāyi piṟannu)*, and therefore was named Bāli because of his power (*balam periya Bāli ennu pērum iṭṭu*). The paired interpretations of Bāli's named essence as lying both in his possession of a tail, and of great strength, leads to a further symbolic association: paralleling the verbal equation of *val/bal* and *vāl*, his mighty power must lie in the tail itself.

More than mere word-play, the might of Bāli's tail inspires a narrative that is central to his portrayal in the teyyam songs, and reaches still deeper into his South Indian mythology. This episode further serves to heighten Bāli's prowess, since he defeats the arch-demon of the entire Ramayana, Rāvaṇa, thereby making himself the equal and rival of Rāma. This basic episode appears in both the northern and southern recensions of the Vālmīki text, but only in the Uttarakāṇḍa, which is a later addition,[28] and where the episode serves as a kind of retrospective coda to the life of Vāli. Furthermore, the story in Vālmīki's recensions lacks the significant role that other southern Ramayanas grant to Vāli's tail.

The episode tells how Rāvaṇa, having heard of the invincibility of Vāli, sets out to defeat him. He comes upon the ape performing his pious ancestral rites of water-offerings (*tarpaṇam*), which he conducts in regular shifts around the oceans surrounding India. Rāvaṇa sneaks up behind Vāli while he performs his devotions, but Vāli seizes him, tucks him under his armpit, and continues his devotional circuits around India, dunking the helplessly pinioned Rāvaṇa during each of his rites. At the conclusion of this circuit, the exhausted demon is finally released, abjectly begs forgiveness, and the two declare a pact of amity. What the Kerala traditions do is heighten this episode—which is after all a kind of imperial "conquest of the quarters" (*digvijaya*) by Bāli around India—into a narrative episode explicitly named the "Victory of Bāli" (*Bāli Vijayam*). A special song recounts this narrative during the teyyam performance, and references to this episode recur throughout, especially during the recitation that brings on trance in the dancer.

In these teyyam songs, however, in keeping with an earlier South Indian innovation, rather than pinning Rāvaṇa in his armpit, Bāli ensnares and winds him up in his mighty tail. Not only that, but he holds the demon in bondage there for twelve years, beating and bashing him about the countryside, repeatedly dunking him in the ocean, and forcibly putting him under a regime of penance (*tapas*) with neither food, nor drink for the traditional duodecimal cycle of Jupiter.[29] Finally, Bāli brings him back to the simian capital of Kiṣkindha and puts him on display in the court, until the demon's father, the Brahmin sage Pulastyan, comes to beg humbly for his release.[30]

In the initial attack, Rāvaṇa sought first to victimize Bāli by grabbing his tail, the mark of his species and his name, with the demonic surfeit of humanoid arms Rāvaṇa himself possessed.[31] Instead, all twenty of Rāvaṇa's members were instantly encircled and pinioned in Bāli's single, prehensile appendage. In this context, the tail is praised in parallel construction as superior to Rāvaṇa's might, and as a weapon that is like an axe.[32] Commensurably, in a much later episode when Bāli finally lies in his death throes, he beats his tail on the earth, which trembles up to the very heavens.[33] His tail clearly represents both his identity and honor, and as discussed later, he willingly embraces death with glory, in preference to the "stump-tailed" state of defeat. When Sugrīva is deposed by Bāli and flees for his life, this ignominious appellation, "stump-tailed," is applied to him,[34] and contrastively, the epic's noblest simian, Hanumān, displays the plenitude of his tail, in an episode we shall return to later.

In this section of my essay, I have shown how Bāli's tail, as a symbol of his identity, taps into a semiotic of social conflicts that remain unresolved, and hence, productive sources of narrative and ritual tension. The internally contestatory structure of this order, where the social and the mythic are mutually implicated projections of each other, drives the ritual enactment of Bāli's teyyam. Though the bestial may serve as a symbol of social lowness viewed from the upper-caste position, the strength of the tail signals ambivalent recognition of the necessary powers of this stratum. It is this ambiguity, in the *might* of Bāli, that those in this dominated stratum seize upon, not to deny their position, but to try to resignify it as something truly noble and dignified, even in the bitterness of systematically ongoing, and unfairly rigged, assurances of their defeat. Though Bāli serves as the symbol of their victimization, in response to his bestial demotion, the lower castes have him made a god.

## The Human Face of a Social Ape

In support of the thesis that Bāli conforms to the local archetype of a slain, victimized hero, his teyyam liturgies portray the human nature that underlies his mythic simian form. The lines describing his birth, for instance, depict him not as a monkey at all, but as a handsome, human prince:

> Established in the womb of that shining Aruṇa-woman,
> As soon as ten months had passed she gave birth
> To this stainless Rāja-youth (*kumāran*).
> So fine he was when people looked on him,
> His torso, his waist, thighs, his figure, his aquiline nose,
> Without a single defect were the forms of these for this fine fellow.
> Then taking that radiant youth,
> On that day all the necessary rites were respectively done.

Bāli's humanness is further stressed in terms of the necessary life-cycle rites (*karmams*) done for him at birth. In many teyyams, the detailing of these *saṃskāras* (rites of passage) forms a stock narrative sequence, tracing the development of the heroes into maturity, as it establishes them in their social setting and community. Furthermore, the following lines from the earlier cited invocatory song make clear the socio-religious significance of Bāli's human origins for his current worship among the Āśāris:

Originally in human form, in order to aid human kind, were you!
King (lord of *men*)! Stainless Long Tail, be my support!

Finally, let us not forget what teyyam actually entails. Its whole logic replicates through actual demonstration the process by which lower castes, through ritual and discursive practices, can jointly elevate still lower caste performers into tangibly present and living deities for the blessing of the community.

This human nature of Bāli serves not as some abstract contrast to divinity, but rather as a social semiotic in which the bestial nature of Bāli and his victimization by the high-caste Rāma represents the hostility of caste antagonism in this society. A remarkable instance of such hostility is expressed in the *teyyāṭṭam* commemorating an Untouchable of the very low Pulayan caste, a character known ironically as Poṭṭan, "the Dumb." His teyyam records how one day he not only refused to clear the way for a high-caste entourage, but openly and volubly disputed with them on the immorality of untouchability. In some of his most memorable lines, he compares the grandeur in which they live with his own pathetic state:

You gather in great temples, Lord;
We gather only in our clearings.
In temples your offerings are in brazen cauldrons, Lord;
In clearings, ours are in bark buckets.
You go out wrapped in fine foreign silks, Lord;
We go out with our coarse waist-towels.
You go out adorned with sandalpaste, Lord;
We go out daubed with mud . . .
Your domain ranges over several territories, Lord;
Our domain is the irrigation ditch . . .
You will come mounted on elephants' backs, Lord;
We will come mounted on buffaloes' backs . . .
Why, O Lord, do you rant over caste?
If you are stabbed will blood not flow?
If we are stabbed will blood not flow? . . .
We will all one day gather in the temple of the Great One,
There you and we shall be together.
Then why, O Lord, do you rant over caste?[35]

One of the favorite topics of Ramayana criticism among Hindu apologists and Western commentators is the attempt to justify Rāma's shooting of Bāli from in hiding, while the latter was battling Sugrīva.[36] Usually commentators treat this issue in the abstract as a largely theological problem of justifying god's ways to man (or monkey). In keeping with what we have noted, though, I think the rootedness of the mythic to the human interests of worshipers is highlighted in teyyam.

I am particularly struck by the similar parallelisms we just noted from Poṭṭan, and the following censure of Rāma by the stricken Bāli, shaming him in his slaying of a poor monkey:

You reign over territories,
We reign over forests.
You are heroes of humankind,
We are members of the monkey race.
You have fine cash and gold and jewels,
We have shoots, and leaves and fruits.
Your wives are singularly fine,
Ours are not at all nice.
Even if you take Sugrīva's side,
This act was unworthy, O King!

Revealingly, Rāma's retort does not address the substance of Bāli's claims, but rather his being out of place in the social order, his violating the hierarchy:

Listen Monkey-Lord! Between us
Are you saying there is nothing at all to quarrel over?
Is this land not touched with calamity,
Is the community in this land not called Kiṣkindha?[37]
And Tāra, on the day long ago when the ocean was churned,
Did you not steal her away as a thief?
Curses! Did you not long ago, towards Sage Mataṇga,
Put a blight on him? You Ape!
Now you whose fate it is to eat raw fruits,
Are you not lying around, replete with gold?

The stylistic parallels of Bāli's charges to those of Poṭṭan, above, make the parallel substance of their purport clear. More revealing, however, is Rāma's rant on the nature of Bāli's "crimes" and the ramifying implications at the level of general and political well-being. Bāli, of low birth and race (*jāti*), has committed three capital offenses. First, he has transgressed the sexual perquisite of the high-born to monopolize the desirable women of lower caste. The anthropological and historical literature has long testified to the institutionalization of these sexual relations in medieval Kerala. Though Bāli's complaint that monkey-wives lack appeal is clearly disingenuous in his own case, Rāma's attribution of this marriage as "theft" rings factually false, and reveals his own offended sense of propriety in an ape enjoying such a jewel of womanhood. The second offense refers to an episode in which Bāli slew a demon, and its gore splattered the hermitage of a Brahmin sage, Mataṅga. This incident involves that nexus of ritual pollution, particularly severe in Kerala, where fouling a Brahmin with offal, and a Brahmin religious adept at that, was an especially heinous infraction. Then finally, Rāma objects in general to Bāli's transgressing the material norms of sustenance and livelihood. In Kerala's sumptuary structure, it was literally a punishable crime for lower castes to own, use, or display many material items of clothing, consumption, and dwelling. This general accusation that the low-born Bāli has flouted the norms of this birth, his "fate" (*vidhi*), ties back into the opening charge that he has dared to take on the rule of a kingdom, which, against Rāma's representation of "calamity" (*anartham*), here, is elsewhere throughout these songs described as magnificent, prosperous and happy. For these crimes, in Rāma's "dharmic" exposition, Bāli deserves to die.

And yet rather than simply succumb to his fate, the Bāli of our *teyyāṭṭam* willingly embraces death in a fashion attended with glory. Rather than opting for continued life on earth after having been wronged and worsted in this way, he chooses to die. In an innovation apparently unique to this teyyam, Rāma clearly offers Bāli the boon of restoration to life in this world, for he says,

> Your manliness has all been as it was ordained.
> Now tell me which you want:
> Do you want the earth, or the heaven of heroes?

Bāli's answer is unambiguously and heroically built around his reputation as a warrior:

> I want no more the earth, Best of Men!
> Called "Bāli" and called "Stump-tailed,"
> With two such names, I will not rule.

Here we find a clear play on words between the Bāli of "power," in those semantics we reviewed earlier, and the word *vaṭu-bāli,* where *vaṭu* means both "stained" or "wounded" and "stunted" or "dwarfed." *Vaṭuvāli* is an idiomatic expression meaning to have lost one's power. Recalling that *vāli* literally means "having a tail," that the Bāli teyyam's dominant epithet is Long Tail, and the especial might of this tail in the vanquishing of Rāvaṇa, I have literalized this idiom as "stunted" or "stump-tailed" to bring out the word-play. For Bāli, in any case, the preservation of his name that his divine father Indra gave him and that he subsequently earned through life, is clearly worth dying for.

The glorious nature of these heroic deaths are nonetheless sorrowful, and we should not miss the sense of pathos, which is palpable throughout the teyyam.[38] Indeed this teyyam includes three pieces that dwell on this pathos, two on the lament of Sīta for Rāma, while separated by her captivity in Laṅka, and one on the lament of Tāra for her husband, our slain hero. Though the separation of Sīta proves temporary, she does not know this, and indeed wonders whether Rāma is himself dead. In the case of Tāra, this shorter piece recapitulates the main events of Bāli's life that brought him to death. Emotionally, these pieces thus embrace the sorrowful side of teyyam, as not only commemorating heroes and their eternally divine powers, but further mourning the loss of loved ones that each such death also signifies, a loss which teyyam itself attempts to overcome by bringing them back to life in rites of communal celebration.

Though the pieces expressing the sorrows of these two women would seem to parallel each other in general theme and title (Sīta's Sorrow and Tāra's Sorrow), the social polarity that orients their husbands' antagonism characterizes their own relations to each other as well. Just as we have found clear expression in the dialogue between Rāma and Bāli that a status hierarchy lay at the root of the latter's murder, so Tāra's lament reiterates the similar theme that also runs through Bāli's songs: that he is victimized through being haplessly caught up in the affairs of higher-ups. Tāra not only remarks on Bāli's tragic embroilment with the "hero" and "heroine" (*nāyakan* and *nāyaki*), Rāma and Sīta, but further specifically levels the charge point-blank at Sīta:

> "Sīta is the cause of Bāli's destruction,
> Bāli who is righteous": thus Tāra weeps.

These mythic characters enter into social scenarios expressive of the historical experiences of the groups who sponsor and perform the *teyyāṭṭam*. Tāra's lament ends by eliding the grief and indignation over the narrative Bāli's fate, into the actual motivation for performing this teyyam. What happened was "declared wrong by various people" (or "castes," *jāti*), she complains, and this is why a perpetual lamp (*nantārv-viḷakku*), the items of worship, and teyyam were established for her "golden-crowned Bāli."

## Tell-tail Traces in the Textual Life of Bāli

Having reviewed something of the way Bāli's figurement ties both into the specific context of his *teyyāṭṭam* and into the general ethos of medieval Kerala's lower-caste and martial life-world, I want to turn now to the briefest consideration of the kinds of textual circuits through which the Bāli materials moved inside and outside of Kerala. Because I lack the space for any detailed textual comparison and analysis of Bāli's teyyam songs here, I will instead take up just a few major motifs that give a sense of the textual complexities, but also demonstrate how these processes of adaptation and interpretation grew out of the social hierarchy of the culture of Kerala.

The corpus of the songs for Bāli's teyyam are among the longest in the genre, and form a patchwork that is often narratively repetitive, but that also shows deviations and inconsistencies between and amongst the texts themselves. They were undoubtedly composed at different times, probably by different castes with different footings in Sanskritic and local knowledges. We can demonstrate this to be the case with other teyyams, where the upward rise of a deity and its worship by higher castes led to the composition of new songs for it by more Sanskritized elites, and where the opposite movement led to more localized associations. Bāli's teyyam songs similarly betray composition in divergent linguistic styles with significant variations in the narrative content. For instance, we have two complete tellings of the killing of Bāli within his teyyam corpus. One, more Sanskritic in style and narratively closer in its fidelity to Vālmīki, contradicts its more rustic counterpart in a number of key details. It is in fact called, "The New *Tōṟṟam* Recitation," presumably in recognition of its later addition to the corpus.

To begin with Bāli's own beginnings, the teyyam myth of Bāli and Sugrīva's origins does appear in wider Sanskrit tellings of the Rāma story, but with some significant changes in detail. This tradition comes not from Vālmīki's *Rāmāyaṇa*, as scholars have reconstructed it through the critical edition, but rather in a lengthy and recurring interpolation. Significantly this interpolation occurs mostly in North Indian manuscripts that belong to the Southern recension of Vālmīki, and in a later devotional text of fourteenth-century Northern India, *Adhyātma Rāmāyaṇa*.[39] In this Sanskrit version of Vāli and Sugrīva's birth, the father-mother of our monkey duo is not Aruṇa, but is himself already an ape, born miraculously of Brahmā. Like Aruṇa, he takes the form of a woman through a dunk in a lake, though here by inadvertence rather than through any intention to visit Indra's world. "She" is also "impregnated" by Indra and the Sun, respectively, but Indra spills his seed in her *hair*, while the sun does so on her neck, from which the two lordly monkeys are produced. It is thus because of his birth from her "hair" (*vāla*) that Vāli receives his name, reflecting the uncertainty in the Sanskrit semantics of *vāla*, and contrasting with the transparency of vāl as "tail" in South Indian languages with its thematic associations. This difference suggests an originally southern narrative of Bāli's origins that was borrowed into the north, in a linguistic environment where these word associations did not exist, and hence underwent secondary elaboration. This hypothesis gains further support because the interpolation resurfaces in *Adhyātma Rāmāyaṇa*, which had apparent sectarian connections to South India, in its origins, and a definite later connection with Kerala.[40]

Within Kerala itself, we find evidence for the Bāli origin myth dating back at least to the fourteenth century, and continuing through a variety of performance genres into the present. The Cākyār community, the caste that staged Sanskrit dramas of *kūṭiyāṭṭam* in the tradition of Kerala's temple theater, has preserved acting manuals that record Malayalam commentaries on mythical themes that they recited before their audiences. One of these, on the Rāma play *Abhiṣekanāṭaka*, gives the myth of Bāli and Sugrīva's origins virtually as it occurs in Bāli's teyyam today.[41] The most conservative guess on the age of this prose would place it around the fourteenth century, though the *kūṭiyāṭṭam* tradition in Sanskrit must go back several centuries earlier, to the time of the Cēra courts. This tradition yielded to the more famous and popular tradition of vernacular, but still highly Sanskritized, staging in *kathakaḷi* and allied forms in the seventeenth and eighteenth centuries, and then to the non-theatrical street recitations known as *tuḷḷal* in the eighteenth century. We have a complete "Origin of Bāli" by Kuñcan Nambyār in this last form,[42] showing that this narrative of Bāli and Sugrīva's origins from Aruṇa had a continuously popular life in Kerala from at least the fourteenth century down to our present teyyam recitations.

Reaching wider in the region and deeper into the past, we find that our teyyam's version with the charioteer, Aruṇa, as our hero's "mother" was represented in the tradition of the Tamil Purāṇas, as well.[43] Possibly still farther back in the Kerala–Tamil tradition, myths feeding into Kampaṉ's *Rāmāyaṇa*, of the twelfth century, likely included a version of Bāli and Sugrīva's origins similar to the interpolated Vālmīki passage and Sanskrit *Adhyātma Rāmāyaṇa*.[44] Though Kampaṉ provides the earliest written documentation in Tamil that attests to the perdurance of these themes, there is no reason to privilege this inscription as the origin of these Dravidian myths. I read Kampaṉ as the literate recording of myths that must have had a longer circulation in South India. Kampaṉ himself is often cursorily cryptic in his mythical allusions, which seem to presuppose a much larger body of localized narratives that reach farther back than his composition. For example, in what is probably the ninth-century Sanskrit drama of Śaktibhadran, a Cēra court poet of Kerala who begins his play by apologizing for being a southerner, he includes a verse that mocks Rāvaṇa as one who still bears the scars around him from being bound in the tail of Vāli.[45] This reference, antedating Kampaṉ by perhaps three centuries, thus attests that the *Bāli Vijayam* episode had already found its way into Sanskrit in Kerala.

Another famous incident in the life of Bāli, his churning of the milk sea, alluded to in the most archaic of his teyyam pieces, gets expanded elsewhere in the songs. While absent in Vālmīki's text or the later *Adhyātma Rāmāyaṇa*, early documentation of this myth occurs in Kerala in the original text of the *Abhiṣekanāṭaka* itself, and reaches back again to Kampaṉ, whose Tamil *Rāmāyaṇa* contains several clear references to the episode.[46] In Kerala, the myth appears again in the great *Rāmāyaṇa Campu* of the fifteenth century, a number of *kathakaḷi* plays, and is especially relished in both of the eighteenth century Bāli street-plays (*tuḷḷals*) of Kuñcan Nambyār.[47] Thematically, this motif reiterates the social tensions I have highlighted, in that a miscegenated ape accomplishes in some fashion what the gods cannot, and generates for himself a celestial mate, Tāra, in the process. Bāli indeed mocks the gods in the *Abhiṣekanāṭaka*,[48] and we have seen how his marriage to Tāra is particularly irksome to the Rāma of our teyyam songs, who partly justifies Bāli's murder as a dharmic execution.

In a narrative flourish considered a hallmark of Kampa<u>n</u>'s Tamil text, Vāli reads the name of Rāma inscribed on the arrow that has shot him down.[49] The *Abhiṣekanāṭaka,* as a classical Sanskrit play, contains the same narrative element, showing that this motif had crossed the cultural divide between these languages. This same motif is variously present or absent through later Kerala works, vacillating perhaps because the southern innovation and the Vālmīki scene are in this case mutually contradictory. Bāli's teyyam includes *both* versions in different songs. In the more archaic *tō<u>r</u><u>r</u>am,* Bāli reads the name of Rāma on the arrow, as in Kampan, while in the piece called the New *Tō<u>r</u><u>r</u>am* Recitation, he falls to the ground, wondering who struck him, and then looks up to see Rāma approaching, as in Vālmīki.

Instead of multiplying these examples of evidence for how particular narrative and thematic coherencies situate the Bāli of teyyam and tie him into a South Indian complex, I close this brief but suggestive overview by returning to the prominent symbolism of the tail. We saw that the "Victory of Bāli" (*Bāli Vijayam*) episode in *teyyāṭṭam* centers on his ensnaring Rāvaṇa in his mighty tail and carrying him as a trophy around the quadrants. The narrative role for Bāli's tail in this myth is pervasive in South Indian tellings of this myth, going back to Kampa<u>n</u>, and beyond in the Kerala tradition.[50] We also saw, however, that the northern texts have Rāvaṇa carried around only in Bāli's armpit, a difference which parallels the northern "interpolated" origin myth in missing the whole association of Vāli with the tail as both originary index and synecdoche of his beastly might. It is very telling in this context that while the commentarial and Kerala renderings of Kampa<u>n</u> follow the Sanskrit narrative of how Bāli's monkey–mother became a woman, they reinstall the southern semantics of Vāli's name to the scenario of his actual birth. Indra is accordingly attracted to and ejaculates on the ape-woman's tail to explain the necessary derivation of Vāli's naming from the word *vāl.*[51] Thematically, when we pair this insemination of her "tail" with that of her throat for Sugrīva, we seem to encounter an added dimension to the low birth of these monkeys through their generation in acts of "unnatural" sex. Whatever the psycho-sexual connotations we might explore, I read this as a commentary on the potential immorality and perversity of the inter-*jāti* relations that were a routinized, but ambivalent, practice in the historical situation of South India, and especially of Kerala. In any case, though, the textual issue of this regionally southern commitment to the tail as an essential focus of Bāli's identity is undeniable.

One of the few episodes in this teyyam that does not pertain to Bāli, himself, concerns that other mighty ape, Hanumān, and also features attention to his tail as an index of his might. This episode deals with Hanumān's visit to Rāma's wife, Sītā, during her captivity in Laṅka, and Hanumān himself being captured by Rāvaṇa. Since Hanumān comes as a messenger whose life should be spared, Rāvaṇa decides that in lieu of killing him, since a monkey's valor lies in its tail, Hanumān's should be lit afire and burned. But then, a remarkable thing happens: as the soldiers wrap his tail in oil-soaked rags to burn it, it begins to grow, so that they cannot reach its end. Finally, they threaten to bring the cloth of Sītā to wrap it (thus disrobing and shaming her), at which point the monkey's tail returns to normal size and he submits to the punishment.[52] (He later breaks free, using his burning tail to set Laṅka on fire, nearly destroying it.) Eḻuttacchan, whose sixteenth-century Malayalam adaptation of *Adhyātma Rāmāyaṇa* is the most famous devotional text of Kerala, has exactly the same reasoning expressed by Rāvaṇa. In preparing to similarly punish Hanumān's defiance, Rāvaṇa there explains, "The basis of prowess is neither in word, nor hand, nor foot. For monkeys, their prowess rests on their tail."[53] While the song in Bāli's teyyam that recounts this same episode lacks any such explicit explanation for why Hanumān's tail should be targeted, the way Rāvaṇa's henchmen stop the tail's growth in that song is equally suggestive: instead of threatening to bring Sītā's garment to bind his tail, they bring a soiled menstrual cloth to wrap it with, whereupon, "he immediately shrunk it back as before, and it was contained." Hanumān recoils from this threat to his prodigious "manhood" just as Bāli chooses death to becoming the figurative "stump-tail" (*vaṭubāli*) that he would, had he chosen to live after his felling by Rāma's arrow. In semiotic terms, the opposite of man is *both* beast *and* woman; the recurrent imbrications of monkey–men with men–women express the mythic registry of a society put together from a hierarchy of discrepant and contestatory orders. The tail of the beast, as in *teyyāṭṭam,* hangs on actual men, men of low status whose ancestors followed women goddesses into death to be worshiped themselves as gods.

## Institutional Mediations

The Ramayana tradition goes back farther than anything we have considered here, and the Tamil bhakti movement, that included Kerala, had brought in North Indian and Sanskritic gods through a complex assimilation with the earlier traditions of worship around ancestral hero-stones and possession rites.[54] In keeping with the stratified nature of this society, processes of assimilation developed unevenly, distributed across multiple layers of the social formation, with the upper strata moving farthest from earlier practices, and lower strata tending to retain them. In Kerala, the performative arts were the media of this complex religious articulation, with the temple-theater a key institution in the bloc of higher castes, and festival forms such as *teyyāṭṭam* working similarly through the middle and lower levels of society.

The earliest evidence we have of a very early corpus of Vāli myths in Kerala, such as Kampaṉ drew upon in Tamil Nadu, comes from the Sanskrit Rāma plays like the *Abhiṣekanāṭaka*.[55] In this Kerala tradition of staging Sanskrit drama, called *kūṭiyāṭṭam*, the Cākyār community provided commentaries in Malayalam for that probable majority of the audience who did not know Sanskrit. Their drummers, the Nambyārs, included an even more accessible prose form of Malayalam recitation, and from the fourteenth century, at the latest, a corpus of Bāli myths circulated that had much in common with the themes of Kampaṉ, a couple of centuries earlier, and with our later teyyam myths. While much of the content of the commentary tied local myth and story into the themes of the play, the effect was often overtly parodic of the Sanskrit material, with the Cākyārs playing the role of the *vidūṣaka*, a Brahmin clown. If we recall that these performers, though often sired by Brahmins, were Non-Brahmin temple servants, addressing an audience that reached down to the Shudra-grade soldiery of the Nāyars, we can perhaps appreciate the appeal of antinomian characters and commentary, which we know engaged the audience fairly directly.

While this *kūṭiyāṭṭam* tradition lingered on into the modern period, it was largely supplanted by *kathakaḷi* in the seventeenth century (growing through some courtly intermediate forms), which we can regard from a high-caste perspective as at once the vernacularization and infusion of Nāyar or Shudra influence into temple theater. The actors themselves now came from the Shudra-grade castes, and while

Sanskrit verses lingered on in certain slots, they yielded their prominence to a largely Malayalam medium. Simultaneously, many of the folk-Purāṇic stories once consigned to unofficial commentary, were upgraded into constituent narratives of the play itself. Correspondingly, antinomian characters like Bāli, and even demons, like Rāvaṇa, come out of the woodwork and are promoted to full-fledged "heroes" (*nāyakar*) of their own polished works. Pieces like the "Origins of Rāvaṇa," the "Victory of Rāvaṇa," the "Killing of Bāli," and the now familiar "Victory of Bāli" appear as elaborately staged and highly popular *kathakaḷi* plays, featuring these protagonists as valiant or tragic heroes.[56]

How were such plays around Bāli designed to engage the life situations of their Kerala audience? Let us consider the *kathakaḷi* work, the "Victory of Bāli," where we find a revealing plot innovation that precipitates Rāvaṇa's entanglement with Bāli and his tail. The plot construes this entire encounter as a politically orchestrated instance of filial vengeance in which Bāli captures Rāvaṇa to repay a similar indignity visited on his father, Indra, by Rāvaṇa's own son. This contrivance establishes a context that would be recognized in the local idiom as a "family-" or "lineage-feud" (*kuṭi-paka*), an institution endemic to medieval Kerala, that in many instances drove the engine of polity. The entangling of familial and chiefly politics recurs throughout our teyyam, most notably in stressing how Bāli's murder by Rāma is merely the price of buying the support of the fratricidal (and regicidal) Sugrīva for Rāma's own project of killing Rāvaṇa in retaliation for Sītā's abduction. It is the unfairness of his own hapless entanglement in this social networking of alliance and enmity that Bāli decries in his death throes as so grossly capricious and undeserved. On the basis of the parallel ballad literature, we will see below that such "mythic" scenarios of intra-and inter-familial feud and alliance bore an acute relation to the socio-political realities that audiences of those times regularly experienced.[57]

The last juncture in the movement downward from the Sanskritized and literary circles of the temple, and outward into the wider society, comes through *tuḷḷal*. This performative tradition of the eighteenth century ostensibly began when a disgruntled Nambyār temple-theater drummer, Kuñcan Nambyār, took his art out of the sacred precincts and adapted it for the street audiences of lower caste whom high castes denied temple-entry. *Tuḷḷal* indeed takes all of the themes of Purāṇic temple-arts and turns them into a lively genre of narrative song and drumming, modeled explicitly on the performance modes of lower-caste religious festivals. Those mythic themes particular to Bāli's teyyam appear in most developed form in those pieces Kuñcan Nambyār specifically composed on the origins and the victory of Bāli.

While *teyyāṭṭam* dominated worship for those castes who, like the Āśāris and the many polluting castes below them, could not enter Brahmanical temples, Shudra-grade castes such as the Nāyar, Cākyār, and Nambyār participated in both religious realms. Like Āśāris, they might worship local gods in their own teyyam shrines, along with their domestic war-goddesses, and simultaneously worship Brahmanical gods in the temples of their high-caste fathers. Just as these middling castes functioned to mediate socio-religiously and biologically between the Brahmins and blocs of polluting castes, the temple art forms they developed similarly mediated the world of Sanskrit epic mythology into Malayalam, and into more local religious forums. Given their experiences of warfare and sexual coercion under Brahmanism, some among these castes must certainly have identified with those below them in society. What else might it mean to elevate down-trodden and victimized figures like Bāli, and even overt demons, to the status of heroes?

But though this section has tended to chart the historical movement of mythic material from Sanskrit "downward" through the religious-performative institutions, the mediation worked both ways. Not only was the downward movement of Sanskrit myth into the Artisan community at once a sign of their own upward aspirations, but, as we have seen, much of the actual Sanskrit content, locally and regionally, seems to come from the promotion of indigenous themes into higher-status ritual and linguistic idioms. If the Bāli of *kathakaḷi* was reaching down into society, then the Bāli of *teyyāṭṭam* was also reaching up. Little wonder that his character and characteristics have taken on such hybrid and polyvalent significations.

The kind of identification and relevance that Bāli's model might hold for his worshipers can be glimpsed in the medieval ballad of a hero of the untouchable toddy-tapper caste, elevated to soldiery so he could kill or die as a proxy for his Nāyar lord. As he sets out with his lord for his fatal duel, he sees many evil portents that signal his demise:[58]

> Just let me say one thing, O Lord.
> I am twenty-two years old now.

Saturn is in his affliction,
And Jupiter has come into the Eighth.
When that Jupiter went bad on that day for Bāli,
That very day, Bāli was killed.
Bāli died from that arrow in ambush.
Let that divine fate be accepted.
Let us set out and proceed, O Lord.

And so, he went forth, and so the Bāli-paradigm replicated itself with his gloriously tragic and immortalizing death.

The legacy of Bāli's adoption into *teyyāṭṭam* registers the contradiction of several historical and differently positioned voices laminated together. Thus, cheek-by-jowl we have one Bāli, who prefers death to living with the injustices and indignities he has suffered through the acts of an "Āryan-born" lord and his "Āryan wife," and another Bāli, who seems converted by the lecture he gets in his death-agony on the karmic orchestration of all life's stupidities and on the godhead of his murderer. This latter Bāli, however, belongs to the "New *Tōṟṟam*." The Bāli of the older mournful piece which brings on the actual possession in the Washerman-priest, utters only his accusations against Rāma, and then his resolve to die. These final words indeed announce receipt of "the gracious boon of dying" which ends Bāli's narrative life, but simultaneously brings on his birth as a god who dances among his worshipers and speaks to them as a living presence.

# MODALITIES OF SAYING

TEN

# The Voice of Sītā in Vālmīki's *Sundarakāṇḍa*

SALLY J. SUTHERLAND GOLDMAN

In the fifth book (*Sundarakāṇḍa*) of his epic poem, the *Rāmāyaṇa*, Vālmīki has opened a door through which we can, perhaps, hear the muffled voice of a traditional upper-class woman of the "Epic age." For with her words, *"dhig astu paravaśyatām*, how wretched to be under the power of another," and the ones that follow, Sītā, the epic's heroine, voices her disaffection with her world. The voice is doubly mediated through the poet's and that of his character Hanumān. Nevertheless, her voice can be heard. To the outside world, she capably defends herself, her lord, and the patriarchy for which he stands. But to herself, stripped of the support of that patriarchy, her words express uncertainty and doubt, and, if ever so briefly, portray a woman at odds with and defiant of the patriarchy that controls her life.

In many ways the *Sundarakāṇḍa* of the *Vālmīki Rāmāyaṇa* emerges as the Book of Sītā. Up until this point in the epic, Vālmīki's rendering of the heroine's character is somewhat sketchy, with few opportunities to develop it in full. We learn of Sītā's determination and moral fortitude when, in the *Ayodhyākāṇḍa*, she insists that Rāma allow her to accompany him to the forest. Despite her aggressive verbal tactics,[1] Sītā's ability to convince her lord that he should grant her permission to go into exile with him primarily serves to enhance the audience's notion of Sītā as a *pativratā*, the perfect wife,[2] but does little to lend further complexity to her character. Sītā re-emerges briefly at the end of the *Ayodhyākāṇḍa* when she meets with Anasūyā, the wife of Atri.[3] In the *Araṇyakāṇḍa* she appears as a voice of reason when she warns Rāma not to take up weapons against any creature who has done no harm.[4] Later in that same book she becomes the focal point of Śūrpaṇakhā's jealousy and, eventually, the object of Rāvaṇa's revenge and desire.

Given the restrictions on conduct articulated for upper-class women in the classical literature, situations that allow development of the heroine's character are limited. *Śāstraic* injunctions admit only a limited number of types of *nāyikās* (heroines) and *nāyakas* (heroes).[5] Moreover, the concerns of Vālmīki's epic prove primarily masculine, leaving little opportunity for expression by women of feminine concerns.[6] The few instances where such expression appears are always mediated through at least the voice of Vālmīki, if not through the words of another, most commonly male, character in the epic.

Only in carefully constructed conditions—conditions which maintain the moral integrity of a woman and yet place her in a situation wherein she must respond to unexpected and alien circumstances—can one find the scope to circumvent traditional restrictions and provide an arena for the articulation of the complex emotional and ethical concerns and realities of female characters.[7] In the *Sundarakāṇḍa* Vālmīki has crafted such a situation where, outside the confines of the *antaḥpuram*, "inner apartments," of Ayodhyā and without the protection of her lord, we are finally allowed to "see and hear" Princess Sītā, cut off from the traditional supports that have framed her world. Isolated, she must now take on the uncomfortable and culturally dystonic position of defending her own integrity and deciding her own course of action, guided only by ethical and moral parameters, which are themselves unable to account for her situation.

In the setting of Rāvaṇa's *aśoka* grove, Vālmīki is free to not only invoke the sympathy or sadism[8] of his audience towards the forlorn, helpless heroine, but he is able to create a situation wherein the heroine's voice might be heard outside its culturally apposite environment. Granted it is heard only through Vālmīki's own voice and that for the most part it echoes the patriarchal standards of her world; nevertheless, it is still heard. Sītā's situation forces her to act in ways that are most often associated with the realm of empowered males in patriarchal discourse—decision-making, interaction with males outside the family, and even the mere fact of being heard.

Sītā's situation is precarious; and she and the epic audience remain well aware of it. Vālmīki has constructed the character of Sītā to represent a perfect wife, a *pativratā,* early in the epic. But, because of that same *pātivratyam*, "devotion to her husband," she has been removed from the protective confines of Ayodhyā; and, seemingly through no fault of her own,[9] abducted by the king of the *rākṣasas*, Rāvaṇa. Traditional attitudes toward women, attitudes articulated by Manu, for example, on the *svabhāva,* "inherent nature," of women,[10] will eventually force Rāma to cast suspicion upon her virtue. Even though throughout the period of Sītā's confinement within the garden of Rāvaṇa's *antaḥpuram* Vālmīki, through the voice of Hanumān, takes special pains to assure the epic's characters and audience of her chastity, this very chastity is continually called into question. Vālmīki has created a situation from which the heroine cannot, and does not, escape without social censure.

That Sītā does not fall prey to her imputed *svabhāva* is a fundamental assumption of the text of Vālmīki. Epic audiences and traditional interpreters explain her ability to maintain her virtue in such adverse circumstances at various levels of interpretation—religious, ethical, narrative. A crisis of character arises from the clash between the culturally normative attitudes about and expectations of women and from Sītā's abduction and actions necessitated by her need to defend herself from Rāvaṇa's advances and preserve her chastity.

## The Patriarchy Defended

The epic narrative has placed Sītā in a desperate and vulnerable position, taking her out of the control of and away from the protection of her husband, locating her in the garden of the *antaḥpuram*, "inner apartments," of another male.[11] The emotional intensity of the situation is still further heightened when Rāvaṇa comes to the *aśoka* grove in an attempt to seduce her.[12] Sītā must now interact with a male, with whom social codes of proper behavior prohibit interaction, a figure from whom she would normally be scrupulously guarded.[13] Throughout Sītā's verbal encounter with Rāvaṇa, Vālmīki takes great pains to reassure the audience that she remains chaste in thought and deed. This encounter between Rāvaṇa and Sītā establishes a parameter that allows both figures to interact while still providing the necessary assurance concerning the sexual integrity of the heroine. In doing so, it reveals to us a multifaceted view of the heroine and antagonist both of whom—although the former more so than the latter—Vālmīki has heretofore painted in largely monovalent and culturally normative strokes.

Rāvaṇa, as Hanumān views him in the confines of his own palace here in the *Sundarakāṇḍa*, is a somewhat more complicated figure than one might suppose from his monolithic and maniacal characterization earlier in the epic. Hanumān gazes on the sleeping demon:

> With his red eyes, great arms, garments shot with gold, and his precious dazzling earrings, he resembled a great storm cloud. His body smeared with fragrant red sandalpaste, he truly resembled a cloud laced with streaks of lightning and reddened in the sky at twilight. He was handsome and could take on any form at will. Surrounded by heavenly ornaments, he looked like Mount Mandara slumbering with its trees, forests, and thickets.(5.8.5–7)

As is typical with many epic passages, the descriptions focus on the physical; for the physical sphere is the locus of the manifestation of internal qualities. In addition the physical description is used as a site of desire to further highlight Sītā's resistance and dilemma. The similes attune us to not only his outward beauty, but remind us of his power and strength. But later, we are also reminded that he possesses great virtues, making him a fit opponent for Rāma:

> Oh what beauty! What steadfastness! What strength! What splendor! Truly, the king of the *rākṣasas* is endowed with every virtue!
>
> If this mighty *rākṣasa* lord were not so unrighteous, he could be the guardian of the world of the gods, Indra included. (5.47.17–18).

In the *Sundarakāṇḍa*, Vālmīki rarely lets us forget the *rākṣasa* king's sexual nature. In the opening *sargas* of the book, the detailed descriptions of Rāvaṇa's *antaḥpuram*, "inner apartments," and of his thousands of wives construct for the audience a world of excess and hedonism beyond the imagination of ordinary men.[14] Rāvaṇa, however, is not merely an agent of desire, but the object of feminine desire as well. His handsome and awe-inspiring figure[15] is one greatly desired by women so much so that the women of his harem are all completely devoted to him. Moreover we learn that these women, unlike Sītā, have come to the lord of the *rākṣasas* willingly.

For those women were the daughters of royal seers, the *pitṛs*, the *daityas*, *gandharvas*, and *rākṣasas*. And they were all passionately in love with him.

That immensely powerful warrior had, however, not taken a single one of the women there by force; rather, they had been won over by his virtues. With the sole exception of Janaka's daughter, who was deserving of only the best, not one of them desired another man or had previously belonged to one. (5.7.65–66.)[16]

Rāvaṇa's abduction of Sītā takes on new dimensions with this revelation. Only through this action has Rāvaṇa committed a transgression important enough to earn him the wrath of Rāma. The *Sundarakāṇḍa* develops Rāvaṇa's character in a manner that is perhaps not radically different in this respect than that of other important male characters of the epic such as Daśaratha or Sugrīva.[17] Thus, like so many other masculine heroes of Vālmīki's epic, Rāvaṇa's primary flaw is his uncontrolled sexuality, a sexuality that Vālmīki rarely lets us forget. And his downfall, like those of Daśaratha and Vālin, will stem from his insufficient containment of his desire. The poet thus describes the *rākṣasa* as he hastens to see Sītā: "But as for Rāvaṇa, in his urgent desire to see that fair-hipped woman with her black hair, her full breasts crowding one another, and her dark, darting eyes, he advanced towards her." (5.16.28) As Rāvaṇa addresses Sītā, it becomes clear that he is not merely a tyrant seeking to destroy an enemy through the seduction of his wife. Now he speaks as a suitor, completely infatuated with Sītā and willing to promise her anything in return for her affection. Within his palace walls, Rāvaṇa is given a voice with which he can articulate his inner eroticized emotions. Here, Vālmīki has allowed his antagonist, the consummate demonic figure, the very antithesis of the human, to express feelings and emotions associated with the human world. He tells Sītā, "I long for you, wide-eyed lady . . . . please look upon me with favor."[18] Clearly Rāvaṇa is not used to having his will thwarted. His words are "honeyed" and yet "fraught with meaning" (18.1). He tells her that his abduction and seduction of her is "perfectly appropriate behavior" for a *rākṣasa* (18.5).[19] At the same time, he is the love-sick suitor, for he swears: "I will never touch you, Maithilī, unless you desire it, though Kāma the god of love, may rage through my body to his heart's content." (5.18.6) Thus Rāvaṇa, for whatever motivation,[20] must, it seems, have his love reciprocated. The other women of his inner apartments are completely devoted to him; so it seems must Sītā be. Like Daśaratha, he is willing to cede control of all his possessions to fulfill his desire.

> You must trust me, dear lady. You need have no fear on this account. Give me your true love . . . .
>
> Since you have won me, lovely lady, how could you be undeserving of such things.
>
> You must be my wife, Maithilī! Abandon this folly! You shall be the chief queen over all my many magnificent women.
>
> All the choice things I have taken by force from all the worlds shall be yours, timid lady, as will my kingdom and myself. (5.18.7,11cd, 16–17)

Rāvaṇa's heart-felt confession of love, his willingness to give Sītā all, and his promise of sexual restraint present the audience with a different, more human, view of Rāvaṇa's character, and one clearly at odds with our earlier vision of the unrestrained, unrelenting tyrant. Vālmīki through his "humanizing" of Rāvaṇa, i.e., by giving him a "voice," has also provided a means through which the epic can maintain the character of the heroine. Rāvaṇa has been partially removed from the world of the "other;" and at the same time has exposed his own Achilles' heel.

Sītā, on the other hand, ironically the object of great sexual desire, remains symbolically represented throughout the *kāṇḍa* as an asexual figure. Her unsurpassed beauty is of course never at issue; however, in traditional literature, inherent beauty is commonly associated with and judged by accouterments that adorn it, for true beauty alone is worthy of them. Thus Rāvaṇa tells Sītā, "You must put dazzling jewels upon your limbs and let me behold your natural beauty, fully and appropriately adorned" (5.18.21cf). But Sītā has abandoned her ornaments, or at least most of them, earlier in the epic, secreting only her precious *cūḍāmaṇi* ornament, a wedding gift, in the folds of her garment. But dressed in the garments of an ascetic woman, covered with dirt, her hair twisted into a single unornamented braid, called *ekaveṇī*,[21] that falls down her back, devoid of any ornamentation, lost in devotion to her lord/husband Rāma, partaking of no food, Sītā's appearance and demeanor constantly reminds the epic audience that, in the absence of her husband, Sītā has—quite appropriately in the cultural context—withdrawn her sexuality.

Classical Sanskrit texts tend to idealize the silent and subdued heroine, the patriarchal ideal.[22] Yet, Sītā must respond to Rāvaṇa's advances. Despite the carefully crafted scene, her verbal encounter with her monstrous suitor remains fraught with uneasiness over its impropriety from the perspective of the poet and his audience. Prior to speaking a word to Rāvaṇa, Sītā—not for the first time[23]—places a piece of straw between Rāvaṇa and herself. This gesture is given a variety of interpretations, but in this context, the most compelling reading is that the straw represents a screen, putting in place a symbolic purdah, which provides token protection of Sītā's chastity.[24]

Even as she begins to speak, Vālmīki calls our attention to Sītā's condition[25] and again reminds us of her devotion to Rāma:

> Weeping, trembling, and afflicted with sorrow, poor, lovely Sītā, lady of the sweet smile, mourning for her husband and, utterly devoted to him, placed a blade of grass between and replied, "Turn your thoughts away from me and fix them on your own wives." (5.19.2–3)

At this point, Sītā, despite her pitiful condition, finds the strength to respond to Rāvaṇa and embarks on an emotionally charged chastisement of the *rākṣasa* overlord, marking a dramatic change in her demeanor. No longer "drawing her thighs up over her stomach and covering her breasts with her arms (*ūrubhyām udaraṃ chādya bāhubhyāṃ ca payodharau*)" or "swaying from side to side (*veṣṭamānām* [*athāviṣṭām*] . . . . ,)[26] she, now—as if gaining energy from her own words—condemns him and his behavior, telling him to enjoy his own wives, and that: "other men's wives bring ruin upon a man—promiscuous, evil-minded, his senses unrestrained—unsatisfied with his own."(5.19.8) Sītā's words throughout her response to Rāvaṇa refer repeatedly to the power of Rāma and her devotion to him. She reinforces them with threats of Rāvaṇa's imminent downfall at her lord's hands as well as reminders of the *rākṣasa's* own despicable behavior. Her passionate soliloquy reminds us of her brutal treatment at the hands of the *rākṣasa* and recaptures for us our image of the monomaniacal monarch of the *Araṇyakāṇḍa*; in addition it presents to us a picture of a strong, devoted wife—even at this time of utmost adversity—ever trusting that her husband will come to her rescue. Sītā eloquently speaks out for her lord and the patriarchy for which he stands.

Rāvaṇa resents such a response articulated in a woman's voice. Although he represents the "Other," he clearly also participates in a patriarchal social structure that functions under similar standards to that of the *āryan* world of his enemy. When spurned and rebuked in this fashion, Rāvaṇa abandons his cajoling, lover-like behavior and resorts to the discourse of male dominance and physical violence In his rage he threatens her:

> Whenever a man treats a women gently, he ends up being humiliated. The more I speak sweetly to you, the more I am rejected.
>
> Nonetheless, the desire for you that has arisen in me reins in my anger, as a skilled charioteer reins in his speeding horses on the road.
>
> That is only reason I do not kill you, my pretty one, despite the fact that you deserve death and dishonor and remain devoted to that false ascetic.
>
> A gruesome death would be fitting for you, Maithilī, for each of the harsh things you have said to me.
>
> I will honor the two-month period that I set as your deadline. But after that, my pretty, you must come to my bed.
>
> Once the two months have passed, if you still do not want me for your husband, then they will slaughter you in the kitchen for my breakfast. (5.20.2–3,5–6, 8–9)

In his attempt to gain Sītā's affections, Rāvaṇa has momentarily empowered Sītā.[27] This empowerment is concomitant with Rāvaṇa's own willingness to give up his power, under the sway of sexual desire. But his advances spurned, Rāvaṇa reasserts his dominance and Sītā loses hers.

Immediately following upon this highly charged interaction, Sītā, in a little noted passage, receives encouragement from the women of Rāvaṇa's harem who have accompanied him there. The women are deprived of an actual voice, and must communicate through gestures

> Now when those wide-eyed daughters of the gods and *gandharvas* saw Jānakī being threatened by the lord of the *rākṣasas*, they became distressed.
>
> They tried to encourage Sītā, who was menaced by that *rākṣasa*, some with movements of their lips, others with gestures of their eyes and faces.(5.20.10,11)

The interjection of the *ślokas*, whatever their intent, here serves as a confirmation that disempowerment is equated with a loss of voice.[28]

Sītā, taking their message to heart, reasserts herself once again, continuing to revile her captor in an intensified manner. Her words are belittling and she taunts Rāvaṇa, calling into question his strength, power, virility, and moral conduct.

> You are not ashamed to insult the lord of the Ikṣvākus just so long as you keep out of his sight.
>
> And why is it, ignoble wretch, that these cruel and hideous eyes of yours—all yellow and black—do not fall to the ground as you ogle me?
>
> And how is it, villain, that your tongue does not shrivel as you speak to me, the wife of a righteous man and the daughter-in-law of Daśaratha? (5.20.17–19)
>
> It is only because I have not been so ordered by Rāma and because I wish to preserve intact the power of my austerities that I do not reduce you to ashes with my own blazing power, for that is what you deserve. (5.20.20)

These words provide the first indication that Sītā possesses the power to rescue herself and destroy the *rākṣasa* lord. The passage does not make specific the source of her ascetic power, but, clearly it derives in large part from her *pātivratyam*.[29] It could also be argued that the source of her power stems from her close association with a mother goddess figure in the epic.[30] The claim of feminine empowerment, let alone the reality of it, threatens Rāvaṇa's masculinity. But Sītā's failure to take advantage of her ability to destroy the *rākṣasa* is a reflection of the fear of emasculating her own husband. Rāma's power as a husband, lord, king, and even god, would be diminished, if not destroyed, if he did not have complete control of her and serve as the only source of her salvation. This view is echoed later in the *kāṇḍa* when Sītā refuses to accept Hanumān's offer to rescue her.[31] Sītā, in keeping with the mores of her tradition, could well possess great power, perhaps even a power greater than her husband. However, in Vālmīki's text, she must not use it, even to save her life, without the permission of Rāma.

The encounter can be understood as a sexual power struggle between Sītā and Rāvaṇa. Confronted with the threat of the Other,

Sītā, empowered through her *pātivratyam*, her belief in and devotion to her lord, defends her chastity. Her empowerment gains sanction only in the service of the patriarchy.

## The Rhetoric of Resistance

Vālmīki depicts Rāvaṇa's rage at Sītā's assault on his character and appearance as even more intense than that expressed earlier in the encounter. He orders his hideous and deformed *rākṣasī* guards to taunt Sītā. Intent on her destruction at that moment, he is lured away by the charms of one of the harem women who have accompanied him. Once again the lovely women of the harem, identifying perhaps in some way with the heroine, have their silent "voices" heard and come to the rescue of Sītā.

Left in the *aśoka* grove and guarded by the grotesque and terrifying *rākṣasīs*, Sītā now must bear their taunts and threats. The menace of these *rākṣasīs* is ever-present; but the immediate threat to her chastity, posed by Rāvaṇa's presence, has for the moment passed. Sītā, giving way to distress, loses her composure and breaks down in tears. Under a *śiṃśapā* tree in the center of the garden, she begins to brood. Her situation is desperate. The time limit set by Rāvaṇa is nearly at an end. She faces certain death or dishonor. Rāma has not, and apparently will not, come for her. She must decide on her own course of action and turns her struggle inward.

Sītā's soliloquy at this narrative juncture articulates the very real social, ethical, and moral problems that confront her in her hour of desperation. It also affords an opportunity for Vālmīki to give voice to her despair, providing a space in the narrative for Sītā to reflect upon her own situation. This reflection leads to a momentary breakdown of some traditional boundaries and allows a narrative space for a rhetoric of resistance.[32] Sītā repeatedly claims, like many heroines and heroes of the epic and *kāvya* literature, that separated from her husband she will surely die. Although she has been taken from her lord and is a prisoner in the *aśoka* grove of Rāvaṇa, she continues to live albeit wasted from fasting.[33] How is it possible, she wonders, for her to survive for even a moment in such circumstances? She immediately turns to self-chastisement: she must, she concludes, have little merit or she must have committed some grave offense in a previous life to deserve such a fate in this one.

Afflicted, overcome by grief, her mind overwhelmed with sorrow, Maithilī sighed, shed tears, and lamented.

Overcome by grief, the lovely woman cried out, "Oh Rāma!" and then again, "Oh Lakṣmaṇa!" "Oh Kausalyā, my mother-in-law!" "Oh Sumitrā!"

"Since I have been able to survive even for a moment misery such as this—separated from Rāma and harassed by these cruel *rākṣasa* women—the popular maxim that the *paṇḍits* quote must be true indeed, 'It is impossible for a man or a woman to die before the appointed time.'"

"Like a woman without a protector, this wretched woman, whose merit must be small, must surely perish, like a laden vessel struck by strong winds in the midst of the ocean.

"Unable to see my husband and fallen into the clutches of the *rākṣasa* women, I am collapsing under my grief, like a riverbank undercut by water.

"How fortunate are those who are able to see my lord—his eyes like the inner petals of a lotus—who walks with the valorous gait of a lion and yet is so capable and soft-spoken.

"Separated from celebrated Rāma, there is no way that I can survive any more than if I had consumed virulent poison.

"What kind of crime did I commit in a previous life that has made me experience such cruel and terrible suffering?

"Engulfed by this great sorrow, I wish to end my life. Guarded by these *rākṣasa* women, I will never see Rāma again. (5.23.10–19)

Initially, Sītā's reaction is to blame herself, as do many victims.[34] Overwhelmed by the hopelessness of her situation, Sītā longs for death, but knows she cannot kill herself: "How pathetic is this human state! How wretched to be under the power of another! Although I wish to, I cannot end my life."[35] The commentators try to elucidate what Sītā means here by her being "under the power of another," her *paravaśyatā*. The term is ambiguous, since the word *"para"* could refer equally to Rāma, Rāvaṇa, or to the *rākṣasī* guards. The sixteenth-century commentator Govindarāja, quite plausibly, thinks that she refers to the fact that as a wife she belongs to her husband, and therefore is not free to kill herself.[36] In this case, the word *para* would refer to Rāma. The *śloka* thus appears to articulate Sītā's unwillingness or inability to act, even to commit suicide, without permission of her lord.

Even though some might see Sītā as a victim of her husband's thoughtless action, when he makes Śūrpaṇakhā the object of his jests,[37] Sītā reminds herself (and the audience as well) that her husband could do no wrong: he is filled with excellent qualities. Given the circumstances, it must be she who is at fault. She can only place the blame for her circumstances on herself and Rāvaṇa. While Rāvaṇa clearly deserves blame, she never suggests the culpability of Rāma, or even Lakṣmaṇa,[38] nor does she mention the joke played on Śūrpaṇakhā. Sītā continues to have faith in her lord.

> Rāghava is renowned, wise, capable, and compassionate. Therefore I think that it must be the exhaustion of my good fortune that has made this virtuous man so pitiless. (5.24.12)

> Is it that I am completely devoid of good qualities, or is it just the exhaustion of my good fortune, that I, Sītā, a young woman, should be bereft of Rāma, who is deserving of only the finest things? (5.24.42)

But nevertheless doubt torments Sītā:

> For why has he who single-handedly annihilated fourteen thousand *rākṣasas* in Janasthāna not come for me?
>
> This *rākṣasa* Rāvaṇa, who holds me captive, has very little strength. Surely my husband is capable of killing him in battle.
>
> Why then has Rāma, who slew in battle that bull among *rākṣasas* Virādha in the Daṇḍaka forest, not come for me?
>
> Granted, it is difficult to assault Laṅkā, which is situated in the middle of the ocean. Still, there is nothing in the world that can stop the flight of Rāghava's arrows.
>
> Why has Rāma, so firm in his valor, not come to rescue his beloved wife, who has been carried off by a *rākṣasa*? (5.24.13–17)

Surely there must be some reason that Rāma has not come. Sītā rationalizes:

> I think that the older brother of Lakṣmaṇa must not know that I am here. For if that mighty man knew it, would he then endure this outrage?
>
> For the king of the vultures, who knew that I had been abducted and might have so informed Rāghava, was slain in battle by Rāvaṇa.
>
> If Rāghava knew that I were here, then in his wrath, he would this very day rid the world of *rākṣasas*.(5.24.18–19,21)

Or barring that, she thinks that, perhaps, Rāma does not know that she is still alive.

> Lakṣmaṇa's elder brother, Rāma, must not know that I am alive. For if they knew, it is impossible that the two of them would not scour the earth for me.(5.24.37)

Or, she wonders whether he no longer has any need for her or, perhaps, has just forgotten her:

> The wise royal seer Rāma, who is desirous only of righteousness, is, in reality, the supreme soul. Perhaps he has no use for me as a wife.
>
> Generally people have affection only for those who are actually present. There is no love for those who are far away. But then again, it is only ingrates who diminish their affection in this way. Rāma would never do so.
>
> Or perhaps the two brothers, the foremost of men, have lain down their weapons and are wandering in the forest as forest-dwellers, subsisting on fruits and roots.
>
> Or perhaps Rāvaṇa . . . has slain the heroic brothers Rāma and Lakṣmaṇa by means of some trick.(5.24. 40–41,44–45).

Filled with despair Sītā repeats her longing for death:

> At such a time as this, I can wish only to die, but even in such suffering, death is not permitted for me. (5.24.46)

As the *sarga* closes, Sītā has sunk into the depths of depression. Giving up all hope of rescue, she finally reacts against the constraints of her social ethos. Realizing that her situation lacks any hope, she resolves to take her own life.

> Abandoned by my beloved, celebrated Rāma, and fallen into the clutches of the wicked Rāvaṇa, I shall end my life. (5.24.49) [39]

The passage allows a heretofore unafforded opportunity to see the heroine in her most needy moment. We, the audience, hear, in her "own voice," or at least her voice as it has been created for her by Vālmīki, a reconstruction of her situation. Sītā's pitiful words express an emotional truth to which many women would assent. De Beauvoir speaks of this trauma of abandonment, "A break can leave its mark on a man; but . . . he has his man's life to live. The abandoned woman no longer has anything."[40] Sītā, stripped of her defenses, vocalizes her overriding fear: that abandoned by her husband, her life is meaningless.

As *sarga* 26 opens, Vālmīki intensifies the feeling of abandonment by linking it with death.[41] Here Sītā is compared to "a little girl abandoned in the midst of a desolate wilderness," a phrase understood by the commentators to refer to the practice of exposure as a means of female infanticide.[42] Vālmīki has equated abandonment with death for females.[43] But for Sītā who is so completely a product of her patriarchal world, no escape exists, even in death. Through Sītā's voice, Vālmīki now elaborates on the ethics of suicide:

> Virtuous folk in the world have a popular saying that there is no such thing as untimely death. Alas it must be true if I, who lack all merit, have managed to survive even for a moment under such abuse.
>
> Surely suicide could not be reckoned as a crime in my case, since this creature—so hateful to my sight—is going to kill me anyway. (5.26.3,5ab)

With no hope of rescue, and facing certain death at the hands of the *rākṣasas*, suicide, which would preserve her chastity and be preferable to such a death could not, she concludes, be condemned.

Sītā now continues her lament, resolved to abandon her own life, giving voice once more to her wretched condition. She decides that, because of her, Rāma must be dead, "Those vigorous sons of the lord of men must have been killed on my account through the strength of that creature in the form of a deer,[44] just as a pair of bulls or lions might be killed by a bolt of lightning" (5.26.9)—or, perhaps even worse, uncaring or treacherous: "Once you have carried out your father's orders to the letter and have returned from the forest with your vow accomplished, you will, I think, make love with wide-eyed women, carefree, your purpose accomplished." (5.26.14) This passage represents the lowest emotional ebb of the epic; the culmination of the downward spiraling fate of the epic couple. We find the conflicted heroine, abandoned, yet dutiful. When she initially appears in the *kāṇḍa* and gives voice to her emotions, we find her identifying with and, to a large extent, defending the patriarchy that rules her world. She is so enmeshed in that world that she is incapable of taking her own life. For she is unable to make decisions on her own as she is under the power of another (*paravaśyatā*), her husband. In the course of her soliloquy, she makes a transition to the point where she gives up her faith in her own power as a *pativratā,* the culture's normative ideal Woman, and is willing, despite social strictures, to commit suicide, which she has rationalized to be the least dishonorable of a series of horrible choices. While her virtue is never jeopardized, her faith in her husband wavers, if ever so briefly.

> My taking you for my sole divinity, my long suffering, my sleeping on the ground, and my rigorous adherence to righteousness—all this—my utter devotion to my husband, has been in vain, like the favors men do for ingrates.
>
> All my righteous conduct has been in vain and my exclusive devotion to my husband useless. For, pale and emaciated, I cannot see you; I am cut off from you without hope for our reunion. (5.26.12–13)

In order to reach this point, the heroine must convince herself that Rāma has completely abandoned her. At the opening of her soliloquy she articulates her doubts but rationalizes them, but by the end she can find no reason for Rāma's failure to come to her rescue after such a long period of time (ten months). Sītā resolves to kill herself, but in her captivity has little access to the means for doing so. She says:

> But as for hapless me, Rāma, after having loved you so long, given you all my heart—to my own undoing—and practiced my vows and penances in vain, I shall abandon my accursed life.
>
> I would quickly take my life with poison or some sharp weapon, but there is no one in the *rākṣasa*'s household to give me either."
>
> Burning with grief and brooding on all these things, Sītā gathered her woven braid in her hand and said, "I shall hang myself by my woven braid and enter the presence of Yama, god of death."(5.26.15–17)

At this very moment, good omens presaging Hanumān's arrival in the *aśoka* grove appear, foretelling the reversal of the epic couple's fortunes.

Vālmīki has fashioned his expression of resistance as an articulation of the ultimate self-denial, suicide. Furthermore, Vālmīki has constructed this resistance through the feminine voice which expresses and then reinforces the dominant culture's attitudes toward gender. As the cultural ideal of Woman, Sītā, in her soliloquy, gives voice to her doubt, her feelings of abandonment, and her lack of faith in the patriarchy. This, reinforced by her resolution to commit suicide, is all distinctly inscribed as feminine. This inscription, in turn, reinforces the cultural construct of Woman so carefully established throughout the narrative frame of the *Sundarakāṇḍa*.[45] Thus, at least at one level, the resistance detected in Sītā's words serves the larger narrative as a valorization of the masculine world and its patriarchal code. However, keeping in mind this inscription and resistance in the service of the patriarchy, we can also detect in Sītā's words, if ever so faintly, the voice of a woman. For, in her desperation, Sītā has had to confront her own seemingly irremediable dependence on her husband.

ELEVEN

# Two Poems on Sita

BINA AGARWAL

## SITA SPEAK

Sita speak your side of the story.
We know the other too well . . .

Your father married you to a prince;
told you: be pliable as a bow
in your husband's hand.
Didn't you note
Ram *broke* the magic bow?
They say you, ideal daughter,
bowed your head in obedience
as you were sent away.

With your husband you chose exile:
suffered privation, abduction,
then the rejection —
the chastity test on scorching flames,
the victim twice victimized.
Could those flames turn to flowers
without searing the soul?
They say you, devoted wife,
questioned him not
and let him have his way.

Your brother-in-law, so quick to anger
on his brother's behalf, left you,
mother-to-be,
alone in the dark forest,
exiled again.
His brother's command!
Some citizen's demand!
Was injustice to you
not worthy of his anger?
You, loving sister-in-law,
bore this too in silence
and let him go away.

The sons you nurtured with such love
amidst nature and the wild woods,
sons with the prowess to challenge
their father's army,
were disarmed with a word.
Unhesitant they joined him,
heirs of his land. Their lineage accepted
yet your purity still doubted!
You, fond mother, stopped them not.
Bowing to the test, palms folded in farewell,
you bid the earth beneath to give way.

The poets who wrote your story,
with such sympathy for those
who questioned your fidelity,
proclaimed: women, like beasts and shudras,
deserve a sound beating.
How could such verses bring you glory?
Yet they recited them as holy, and
unchallenged got away.

Sita speak!
You who could lift the divine bow in play
with one hand,
who could command the earth with a word,
how did they silence you?

## BEYOND CAPTIVITY

New leaves on the Ashoka,
translucent;
filtering the morning light
as do the blue veins of an infant's wrist.

Innocence.
Pristine freshness of spring leaves
everywhere. Yes also in that grove where
Sita, nature's source,
thought herself a prisoner —
also in that Ashoka Vatika.

Sita, our legacy!
Why did you need
to prove your innocence?
Did the flames cool on touch —as they say?
For your sisters the fires come ablaze.
Before the fullness of their summers
they perish. Innocent. Can they prove it?
Can you prove them so?

You belonged to the earth, they say,
were of the earth.
This earth that greens with each monsoon.
The Ashoka bloomed too in Ravana's garden,
unpossessed, unpossessable.
Those light-filled leaves,
could they ever be fettered?

Sita, Shree, stree.
Captive of a name? A religion? Love?
Was that love that bound you? Or those
nuptial knots before the fire —
the omnipresent fire.
Love perished with your test.

Beyond captivity. Pristine freshness
of new shoots in the spring.
Blossom again Sita,
in these translucent leaves;
yes, even in Ravana's garden.
With the sap that flows from hand to hand
you, we, can regain this earth.

TWELVE

# Kṛttibāsa's Apophatic Critique of Rāma's Kingship

TONY K. STEWART AND EDWARD C. DIMOCK

Of all India's heroes and heroines, Rāma is acknowledged to be most nearly perfect, and his rule, the fabled Ramraj stands as the idyllic golden age of dharmic propriety. It might seem to underscore this general attitude that the Bengali *Rāmāyaṇa* of Kṛttibāsa is said by literary historians to be the most popular single book in all of premodern Bengal; and the contemporary editions of that text—any shopper can choose from as many as a half dozen editions at any given moment in the Calcutta book markets—confirm that it has retained its popularity. The text that circulates today in these inexpensive formats—the only way it is available, incidentally—and which is read in the universities for examinations, as well as for devotional or home entertainment, is often profusely illustrated with color plates, conveniently placed to enhance the narrative that is, judging from the total dearth of interpretive notes, assumed to be accessible by any literate Bengali. It is a popular story for popular consumption. Variations among these editions are virtually nil—only the occasional misprinted *akṣara* (letter), or the insertion of a homonymous lexical equivalent seem to distinquish them[1] —while the language itself has settled into a gentle and predictable idiom that is to medieval Bengali the equivalent of what J.A.B. van Buitenen used to describe as the "kitchen Sanskrit" of the *Mahābhārata*.[2]

A cursory reading of this popular text, however, produces two immediate impressions that lead us to question what Bengalis think of Rāma, for the text, like a number of other regional Ramayanas, insists on including the *uttara kāṇḍa*. In this final book, Rāma's reign is brought to an untimely end, and with a twist that differs from other well-known conclusions, for Rāma and his three brothers are slain and revived before their final departure to heaven. Coupling that with a curious recurring imbedded commentary—negative regarding Rāma's character and motives, and often placed diegetically in the mouths of characters who are interacting directly with the protagonist—the image of Rāma that lingers is less than complimentary. That the text is ambivalent in its telling of Rāma's shortcomings, softening direct criticism by an immediate negation that usually deflects the agency for questionable actions onto the impersonal workings of fate, suggests that the challenge was important for its author or authors. The form of this rhetorical strategy, a double negation (Rāma is not good; no, Rāma is not really to blame), either subverts the concept of dharma, for Rāma is supposed to be the epitome of righteousness, or simply produces a discredited image of Rāma that holds him culpable for his moral failures, an image that flies in the face of his impeccable character and kingship so taken for granted throughout much of the rest of India. His culpability is given explicit narrative form when, toward the end of the *uttara kāṇḍa*, his twin sons rid the earth of Rāma and his brothers, and the *(a)dharma* they embody; thus the earth can be cleansed and his sons can repair the damage and institute a new, proper dharma.

## Playing Politics with Texts

The expectation that Rāma is good has been reinforced by scholars who have approached the text with their own expectations about the story, especially its relation to the designated standard, the Sanskrit of Vālmīki. The very same scholars who speak with pride of Kṛttibāsa's popularity, in the same breath lament the fact that today's printed texts seem to coincide very little with older manuscripts.[3] A survey of the MSS that are available in the repositories of the contemporary Indian state of West Bengal and the country of Bangladesh suggest that there are but few complete MSS of this popular *Rāmāyaṇa* from any period.[4] Like its counterparts in other regions and languages of the Indian subcontinent and Southeast Asia, the text is long (500 printed pages, more or less, in double columns), and that reduces the prospect of a complete text. But other nearly equally long texts, such as the *Dharma Maṅgala* of Ghanarāma Cakravartī[5] or the *Caitanya Bhāgavata* of Vṛndāvana Dāsa,[6] or the considerably longer *Mahābhārata* of Kavi Sañjaya,[7] have survived in multiple complete MSS, so what is it that makes this text different? For one thing, the text lends itself to episodic treatment, fitting for public performance and consumption in detachable segments, on the order of the *Mahābhārata*. While many *kāṇḍa*s are copied *in toto*, many individual episodes within those *kāṇḍa*s have been loosely strung together in an overarching framework; the units within the framework tend to be discrete and able to be independently presented and manipulated without varying the overall narrative structure of the text. For those with a devotional bent, the individual episodes serve a variety of religious functions, from simple parables to often biting social commentary. William Smith notes that, in the nineteenth century, copying the text as single or small sets of episodes was an act of piety suitable for small as well as better financed patrons.[8] These episodes clearly have a life that is significant as part of the Kṛttibāsa *Rāmāyaṇa*, but also semi-independent of it.[9] A comparison of manuscript material with printed editions from the ninteenth and twentieth centuries confirms that the text continues to be transformed, mainly through the accretion and deletion of discrete episodes; yet the *uttara kāṇḍa*, a peculiar repository of many of these idiosyncratic tales, does take a definitive shape by the late-eighteenth or early-nineteenth century.[10]

The concept of the Ur-text, which historically has driven so much of the traditional scholarship as it has sought to reconstruct the original sources, seems to give way here to a more malleable construction of living, perhaps applied, literature. The most used text, the preferred text, is the most inclusive, the biggest; and in Bengali, the Ramayana has for several centuries included the *uttara kāṇḍa*. Yet, the stories of the *uttara kāṇḍa* are frequently labeled apocrypha;[11] this is an unfortunate designation that has served more than anything to discount them. To be apocrypha they must lie outside some widely accepted normative standard, and Smith has made the case that that standard in Bengal is Vālmīki's frame.[12] Vālmīki was certainly a significant factor in the way the story has appeared in its Bengali retellings. But Bengali Ramayanas, including Kṛttibāsa's, have been in effect approached by scholars seeking standardization as recensions of the Ur-text: little scholarly attention has been paid to these stories because they are aberrant from Vālmīki.[13] But as Gerard Genette has somewhat irreverently noted in another context, "What is oldest does not necessarily tell the truth about what is most recent, and the recovery of origins must not end up assigning any kind of hermeneutic privilege to what is earliest," lest we produce an "archaizing cult of the literary Ur-Suppe."[14] The devaluation of the later text can only be the result of holding the texts to a previously conceived standard—a choice based on the arbitrary assumption that original is better—that, when one simply appraises the MSS and printed material of this *Rāmāyaṇa,* does not seem to be of particular concern to its author or authors. So we might best begin by assuming that these tales of the *uttara kāṇḍa* are not recensions of Vālmīki at all, but stories that share something in common, yet have the integrity to make their own points that are locally relevant, else they would undoubtedly fail to be reiterated. Whether or not Kṛttibāsa held the opinions expressed in the *uttara kāṇḍa* is insignificant for this project, because the text that goes by his name is what Bengalis most often promote as their *Rāmāyaṇa.*

Texts, we would suggest, are changed by the people who use them in order to make them personally and culturally relevant; and what is most important in a text is what will be revalorized in each generation, so that the parts that endure are the ones that are preferred by its readers.[15] The *uttara kāṇḍa* of Kṛttibāsa's *Rāmāyaṇa* endures. We would further propose that what constitutes relevance will occur in works under the names of authors who have transcended their historical specificity and who have assumed a symbolic function as purveyor of important cultural attitudes; in Bengali literature this "author-function" is filled by the likes of Caṇḍīdāsa, Kṛttibāsa, and Rabindranath.[16] When an author is transformed through popularity into a culturally consumable author-function, where the name becomes a tradeable commodity whose mere presence sanctions, the priority that is automatically extended to an author's personal choices (i.e. here, the "real" Kṛttibāsa) is supplemented or even displaced by the use of that author's name to promote other causes (i.e. the popularly circulated Kṛttibāsa). Sometimes these emendations are consistent with the original author's perspective and at other times they are blatant appropriations for radically different ends. But the symbolic capital of the author's name, as Pierre Bourdieu would propose, is pressed into the service of any of a variety of issues.

Consequently, whether Kṛttibāsa is personally responsible for the contents of his *Rāmāyaṇa*, especially the questioned *uttara kāṇḍa*, or whether it has been cobbled together by others using his name, makes no difference to its currency, and therefore its validity and relevance as representative of its readers; this is so with today's text, which probably assumed its current form in the late-eighteenth or early-nineteenth centuries.

Daśarathi Rāya, a prolific and erudite poet of the folk theatre in the mid-nineteenth century, suggests that some of the episodes of the *uttara kāṇḍa* may belong to a different textual tradition altogether. Daśarathi wrote a large number of *pāñcālīs* (narrative poems, often sung, sometimes devotional but in Daśarathi's hands and those of other poets of the *kabiwalla* tradition, more witty and clever than heartfelt) on the Rāma theme, elaborating on Kṛttibāsa or adding detail and episodes not familiar from that text. At one point, in the course of the poem describing how Lava and Kuśa, twin sons of Rāma and Sītā, overcame Rāma on the battlefield—part of the narrative we will examine below—Daśarathi remarks, "This is not the story of Vālmīki, how Raghunātha fell in battle; these words are according to Jaimini."[17] This Jaimini, certainly not the famous Mīmāṃsaka of the name, was perhaps the author of a text called the *Jaimini-bhārata*, of which, says Vettam Mani, "only the *Aśvamedha Parva* exists."[18] The *Jaimini-bhārata* is also mentioned in passing, by Kṛttibāsa himself at the beginning of the section of the *uttara kāṇḍa*, called "The singing of the *Rāmāyaṇa* by Lava and Kuśa." While it would be tempting to assume—as many have—that the material in the *uttara kāṇḍa*, not found in Vālmīki's Sanskrit would contain the most divergent material, perhaps in the sense of a redactor proffering a proper reading of the preceding text by adding, as Daśarathi has suggested, extraneous material from other sources, the text of Kṛttibāsa's *Rāmāyaṇa* does not reveal the kind of narrative break or inconsistency that would erupt from the mixing of narratives with radically different etiologies. While this *uttara kāṇḍa* does contain very telling, sometimes unexpected, perspectives, they are frequently confirmed by readings in other *kāṇḍa*s, and do not appear to be altogether gratuitous; the key stories are generally consistent with, if not integral to, the narrative, so that no matter its source, the narrative retains a unity that renders moot many of the challenges to its "authenticity." That the *uttara kāṇḍa* is so widespread among the Kṛttibāsa *Rāmāyaṇa*s in Bengal, and that the dates of these MSS are consistent with much of the rest of the text, are both empirical facts that bear out this contention of integrity.

Perhaps the two most telling sets of stories in the *uttara kāṇḍa* are those that negatively critique the relevance of Rāma's kingship for a Bengal that is anything but traditional in its social organization and governance. Rāma's irresponsibility is stressed by the portrayal of his attitude toward and the banishment of a very pregnant Sītā for reasons rather ambiguous, and the need to exterminate what the *uttara kāṇḍa* sees as his adharmic rule is borne out in the later encounter of Rāma and his half-brothers with Rāma's own sons Lava and Kuśa, a classic parricide through ignorance begat by the formers' willful misconduct. These apparently subversive themes are, however, not isolated or idiosyncratic in the history of Bengali letters, especially in the nineteenth and twentieth centuries. As has been suggested, it is hard to imagine that a Bengali book could remain popular and continue to sell year after year, were it not congenial to a basic Bengali sensibility; the *uttara kāṇḍa* reveals much about what might be characterized as a basic lack of confidence in traditional structures of governance and proper conduct. If the opinions of Kṛttibāsa and Daśarathi can be considered in any way archetypal, perhaps Bengal never did develop a "proper" way of thinking about kingship in general and the Ramraj in particular, or about *sannyāsīs* (in the Bengali spelling) and other traditional institutions of a classical Hindu polity. This story from the *uttara kāṇḍa*, of the debate between the *sannyāsī* and the dog, would certainly suggest it.

### THE SANNYĀSĪ AND THE DOG [from *uttara kāṇḍa*]

When he heard this [praise of Rāma], Lakṣmaṇa Ṭhākura was delighted, and just at that time a dog appeared. The dog's eye was bloody and his body white; he was emaciated and exhausted from fasting, and was withered and thin. He walked on three legs, as the fourth had been cut off, and his body was all covered with bloody welts from the blows of a stick. As he had only three legs he had to limp along very slowly. And as he made a bow to Lakṣmaṇa he was awash in the tears that flowed from his eyes. So Lakṣmaṇa Ṭhākura asked the dog,

"Tell me, why have you come to this place?"

And the dog said, "Listen, Lakṣmaṇa Ṭhākura. I will tell you of my sorrow in the presence of Śrī Rāma. If Rāma gives me permission, and does not have contempt for me, then I shall tell you of my misfortunes in the midst of the court assembly."

So Lakṣmaṇa went into the presence of Rāma, and told him of his conversation with the dog: "The dog came a little way into the door, and he asked for your permission to come before the court." So Rāma told them to bring the dog immediately, and they brought him there. The dog, filled with devotion, touched his head to the ground and said, with his paws pressed together, these righteous words:, "You are Brahmā, you are Viṣṇu, you are Maheśvara; you are Kubera, Varuṇa, and Yāma; you are the sun and the moon, and the gods who guard the directions; everything is your creation, and you are what comes after life; you are the *avatāra* of Viṣṇu, the saviour of the fallen; though I am a dog, my being has been fulfilled by the sight of you.

And Rāma said, "How you do go on, speaking such praises over and over again. Tell me instead why you have come here."

And weeping, drenched with the water of his tears, the dog said, "A *sannyāsī* beat me for no reason; I had done him no wrong. And I am in great distress because of the blows of his stick. After three fasts I came here into your presence. I pray that you ask that *sannyāsī*, here before the assembly, why he beat me with that stick."

And Rāma said, "The assembly will hear his answer. Quickly have that *sannyāsī* brought here. Everyone together will decide what is right and what is wrong, and why a *sannyāsī* brought harm to a living creature."

So at the order of Rāma a messenger went immediately and brought the *sannyāsī*. In his hand was a clay water-pot, and on his shoulder a deer-skin. The messenger greeted him respectfully, and brought him to Lakṣmaṇa, and Lakṣmaṇa brought him into the presence of Rāma. Raghunātha then asked the *sannyāsī*:

"Why did you leave aside your *svadharma* and harm a living creature? If you act contrary to dharma you will live in hell. What kind of a *sannyāsī* is it who has anger in his body? Abuse and harm of others is the worst kind of crime. And if a *sannyāsī* especially becomes one who mistreats others he falls into the worst kind of hell. A *sannyāsī* who puts away from him avarice and drunkenness and lust is respected by all the world. You are a *sannyāsī*, and yet have a temper—what is his fault, that you have beaten this dog with a stick?

With his palms pressed together the Brahmin *sannyāsī* said: "Listen, O Nārāyaṇa, and then tell me whether I have done a misdeed or no. All day, until the evening, I say my beads on the bank of the Gaṅgā, and in the evening, in hope of alms, I go to the city. One evening, my body was burning with the fires of hunger, as I went about begging, and there, right across my path, there was this dog lying. I shouted 'Get out of my way!' in a loud voice, but the wretched thing remained there on the path, and did not get out of the way for me. One of his eyes was closed, and he was looking at me out of the other one, and I burst out in anger and hit him on the head with my stick. What more can I say to this assembly? If you have to, then punish me."

And Rāma said to the assembly, "Now you decide. Whom should I punish for whose offence?"

And with their palms together the assembly said, "It seems to us that a proper judgment would go like this: a King's Highway is not only for the passage of kings and nobles, but everyone in the world, both high and low, can walk upon it. If there is need, then one moves to the side. The *sannyāsī* is the offender here, and his offence is that of egotism."

Then Śrī Rāma said, "Accordingly, I shall punish the *sannyāsī* following the *dharma-śāstras*. The proper punishment for *sannyāsīs* is that they be forbidden to bathe in the Gaṇgā."

And the dog got up and appealed to the assembly: "Do not punish this *sannyāsī* so; instead, you should reward him according to what I am about to say. You should give this *sannyāsī* the burden of the government of Kaliñjara."[19]

At the words of the dog everybody laughed, and agreed to make the *sannyāsī* the king of Kaliñjara. And as soon as he was appointed, the *sannyāsī* mounted onto the back of a rut elephant, and taking the royal staff in his hand he displayed his majesty to everyone, and when they saw his costume everyone laughed, for he wore a loincloth, while over his head was the royal umbrella.

And when Rāma was asked why he had endowed this *sannyāsī* with the royal symbols, Rāma said, "Because of the request of the dog. The dog knows well the facts of the matter."

And so the dog politely said to the assembly, "In a former birth I was the king of Kaliñjara, and I constantly worshiped Sadāśiva. There was a temple there, and inside it was a blue-colored Śiva liṅgam, and apart from the king no one was to worship it. Śaṅkara had to be worshiped in special kinds of ways, and every day the king had to eat *prasāda*. Yet such was the curse of Śiva that when that king died he would be reduced to doghood. In the country of Kaliñjara, Śiva is very tough. So I was a king, and now I am a dog. Being in the body of a dog is a very difficult way to go, but now, because of the sight of you, I am delivered."

And everybody said, "There is no doubt at all now about the [justice of] the matter. The king of Kaliñjara becomes a dog." And when the dog had finished speaking he made his salutations to Rāma and slowly made his way toward Vārāṇasī. Fasting, he abandoned his life there, and because of the sight of Rāma, he dwelt in heaven afterwards . . . .

## The Issues of Rāma's Propriety and Decency

While offering such ambivalent, if not perspicacious, appraisals of the impossibility of good kingship, Bengali literature, through and including Rabindranath, has at the same time tended to champion the causes of women in the face of a traditional cultural frame that often suggested that to do so was not standard, or even appropriate. And in the case of the Bengali *Rāmāyaṇa*, these two (critique of standard political constructions and gender constructions) are not unrelated. The learned Daśarathi Rāya mentioned above, whose obvious interest in the Ramayana generated a number of his rather acerbic appraisals of the foibles of traditional society, includes among his *pāñcālī* a poem about the "hatred" (or malice and antipathy [*dveśa*]) of Rāma toward Sītā.[20]

As the hatred of the *deva*s (gods) for *asura*s (demons),
as the hatred of Yavanas for Hindus,
as the hatred of Rāvaṇa for Hanūmān,
as the hatred of ascetics for the sacrifice of animals,
as the hatred of a bad son for his father's younger brother,
as the hatred of Ṣaṣṭhī for a barren woman,[21]
as the hatred of a spiteful person for another's fortune,
as the hatred of the Beauty of the Tripuras for the *tulasī*,[22]
as the hatred of a madman for water,
as the hatred of Śukamuni for women,[23]
as the hatred of Dakṣa for Sadānanda,[24]
as the hatred of Manasā[25] for the smoke of incense,
as the hatred of the orthodox for Bhagavatī,[26]

as the hatred of Śiva for the lover of Rati,[27]
as the hatred of Bhīma for the family of the Kurus,
as the hatred of the serpent for the arrow,
as the hatred of the thief for good advice,
such was the hatred of Rāma for Janakī.

The hyperbole suggests that only such strong feelings of contempt and indifference could possibly account for Rāma's handling of Sītā when he banished her to the forest, for according to Kṛttibāsa, he did not even have the courage to face her. This is a common note in Bengali tellings of the tale; he relegated the task to Lakṣmaṇa, who was forced to dissemble when she began to read the ill omens while they were on their ostensible trip to visit relatives. In biting phrases, Sītā disparages Rāma for his cowardice and Lakṣmaṇa for being his accomplice, when she reveals her pregnancy: "Were I to kill myself now I would kill Rāma's son. My shame, my lord, would then accrue to the entire population. Were it not for that compounding offence, I would take my own life. In birth after birth may this Rāma be my lord . . ."

The deflection of Rāma's guilt in the last phrase characteristically marks the recurring strategy of double negation, the popular way of criticizing without actually seeming to do so. But this disparagement could be attributed to the heat of the moment, except that it hardly stands alone, perhaps most strongly resonating with the much earlier and foreboding episode of Bāli's reproach for Rāma's unconscionable act of fighting him for no apparent reason.

After Rāma's celestial fire-breathing arrow has struck Bāli, reigning king of monkeys, in the chest, a bewildered Bāli excoriated the approaching Rāma as follows:

BĀLI REPROACHES RĀMA [from *kiṣkindhyā kāṇḍa*]

"You have been born to the royal estate and know the Law. By what regulatory code could you fell me, Rāma? The hare, the rhinoceros, the tortoise, the iguana, the porcupine—only these five among the clawed or horned animals of the wild are deemed suitable for eating. Listen mighty scion of Raghu, no one has ever heard of my flesh being numbered among those, for it is proscribed. Nor may anyone sit on my hide, for I am not a deer. What practical use, then, is the monkey species? I am a monkey and faultless, for what reason do you attack me? There can be no such authority in all the kingdom to justify this. What country have I ransacked? On whom did I inflict misery? What egregious fault has precipitated the premature end of my life? You have not taken birth in some ordinary clan, but in the lineage of Raghu. Everyone commends you, saying you abide by the Law. I do not know the Law that sanctions your actions—how you could slay me when I have committed no offence? People say that Rāmacandra is the very shelter of mercy, but what kind of mercy have you shown me? Under the guise of an ascetic Rāma roams the forests; who could ever be slaughtered by one who respects all life? Everyone agrees that Rāma is the Law-incarnate, the *dharma-avatāra*. How does this treatment reflect that goodness, Rāma? Show me the humor in fighting your cousin-brother; what pleasure could you possibly gain from smiting me, Rāma? Nowhere have I seen, nowhere have I heard of such a thing; only a murderer would take someone's side in a war not his own. If in direct armed confrontation such a missile were to smite me, it would have no more taken my life's breath than a hard palm-slap to the chest. Knowing we were squaring off for battle, I would have calculated the risks, but in this situation, Rāma, you struck me with the stealth of a common thief. Would I have been so brave had I been aware? How unperturbed would you have been going into full proper battle with me? Sugrīva is my enemy, and I strive for his destruction, but I have no quarrel with you, so how could this untoward event have come about? How will you show your face to the society of good and honest men? 'By the subterfuge of shameless deceit did I slay king Bāli.' King Daśaratha is the true incarnation of the Law, the *dharma-avatāra*; though you have been born his son, you are a disgrace to the family heritage. Daśaratha Rāja's mind was ever fixed on the Law, while for you his son this can never be said. Utterly bereft of propriety, you honor your father's glory by a sincere desire to join ranks with the good-for-nothing Sugrīva. When the sinful join forces with the wicked, the only counsel is evil intrigue, otherwise, why would I be so put upon? You clearly have undertaken this action to effect my release from the [status of] of monkey, otherwise how could I have been made to undergo such trials? . . ."

Characteristically, this indictment of Rāma was again sidestepped by shifting blame to an impersonal force of dharma; and time and again it was not Rāma, but his father who was held to be the embodiment of dharma. Kṛttibāsa made clear that neither he nor his characters accepted Rāma's acquittal when he records the curse of Tārā, Bāli's wife, moments later on the battlefield. By levying her curse with the same argument and force of righteousness, Tārā censured Rāma for his unconscionable immediate action: ". . . Just as assuredly as I am the ideal faithful wife in the country of Bhārata, you will be made to suffer long days weeping for your Sītā. This curse I have laid on you can never be undone. For the sake of Sītā, Rāma, shall your body burn in agony; for the sake of Sītā you will be made to give up your life, and the whole point of this birth will be to suffer your days in abject misery." Yet in her wrath to guarantee punishment for his offence, she provided him and the commentators with an easy deflection for his eventual banishment of a perfectly undeserving Sītā once again deflecting his culpability to the inexorable workings of fate.

And so Tārā's curse came true as Rāma, seemingly bewildered at the turn of events, despatched Sītā to her exile in the company of Lakṣmaṇa, who abandoned her to the sage Vālmīki, in whose *āśrāma* she bore and raised the twins Lava and Kuśa. These twins, never knowing anyone other than Vālmīki as their father, were raised in an exemplary fashion, and by virtue of their exalted heritage, they were gifted, and they eagerly and efficiently learned the traditional arts from Vālmīki. These twins would become the tool of his redemption, for they would cleanse the earth of Rāma's confounded dharma. But to do so, they must act innocently, which is only possible if they are unaware of their royal origin. Kṛttibāsa goes to pains to make clear that the two not only never knew Rāma, they never even knew his name. The righting of Rāma's many wrongs would begin with the fateful decision to undertake the *aśvamedha* kingship ritual, the justification for which had arisen somewhat indirectly because of a general uneasiness that had begun to grip the kingdom. Many stories in the *uttara kāṇḍa* attest that the kingdom was decaying from within. Rāma had heard the rumors and gradually came to realize that his people were unhappy. But it took the brave courtier Bhadra to make it explicit, repeating to Rāma that even though his subjects generally prospered, they did not prosper nearly as well as they did under his father's rule.

Many people gossiped of his undue attachment to Sītā, who, they argued, could not possibly be stain-free after being held captive by the *rākṣasa* Rāvaṇa. But the text makes unequivocal Sītā's blamelessness; her innocence was assured and had already been proved in the first ordeal. The problem, opines Kṛttibāsa, lies elsewhere. That the country does not prosper ultimately can only lie with the actions of its ruler, Rāma himself. Hinted sporadically throughout the text to this point, Rāma's responsibility dominates the remainder of the narrative. It was Rāma's unmeasured response to these rumors that eventually caused him to banish Sītā and guarantees his future disgrace. After Bhadra broke the news, a number of illustrative tales confirmed the general malaise which had overtaken Rāma's rule. For all their pointedness, these tales too soften their impact by the characteristic double-speak, pointing to Rāma's liability, only to deflect the increasing complications as somehow "not his fault." An impersonal disruption of dharma-*sans*-agency is usually to blame; but in spite of the numerous deflections and general indirection, Kṛttibāsa ensures that the karmic responsibility always works its way back to Rāma. A good example is the story of the young couple who wondered why, even though they lived in the righteous kingdom of Rāma, and they themselves were dharmic, their five-year-old son had died inexplicably. For them, it was an unmistakable omen of evil, and so they complained directly to Rāma: "We have lived lives in accord with dharma, we have committed no sins . . . Only in a lawless kingdom does famine and pestilence reign. Through a failure of proper conduct does the king eat the fruits of hell. Our son died in the kingdom of Rāma even though it was not his proper time . . ." Rāma searched far and wide for the cause and discovered a Shudra who was performing a series of sacrifices inappropriate to his station, and so he slew him:[28] dharma required it, he claimed. But even though dharma was blamed, Kṛttibāsa makes Rāma atone for slaying this man, to wash away the stain, and to try once again to reinstitute a proper dharma, which has clearly been disrupted, but by whom is not quite clear. Ultimately, it was this attempt that persuaded Rāma to perform the *rājasuya* sacrifice. Bharata and Lakṣmaṇa, however, were alarmed and tried to dissuade him, claiming that throughout history that sacrifice had proved fatal to perform; better that he undertake the *aśvamedha*, a suggestion with which he agreed. The ever-vigilant fates were not to be so easily sidestepped, for Rāma and his brothers would be slain before the end of the sacrifice, and it would be his slayers—his own sons, Lava and Kuśa—who would emerge as the ultimate winners of the *aśvamedha*, and who would reconstitute dharma as it was meant to be in the tradition of Rāma's father, not Rāma.

The *aśvamedha* was carried out according to the presciptions that were common to the Veda; the horse symbolically represented the king, and was released to roam "freely," but conveniently accompanied by an army. After one year, the horse was slated to return to its point of origin to be sacrificed, the land it had covered considered to be coterminous with the kingdom—and the logic is straightforward, for anyone who captured or killed the horse would have done so in the face of its army and, if victorious, would rightfully rule; if not, they too would be conquered. After all were assembled and the visiting kings, sages, ascetics, heavenly courtiers, and myriads of gods were all properly seated and honored, Rāma released the horse in the charge of his youngest half-brother. The horse was released and in quick succession it traipsed victoriously through the eastern, northern, and western quarters, with Śatrughna valorously keeping pace. But trouble awaited in the southern country, the land where Vālmīki's hermitage nestled deep in the forest, where Lava and Kuśa stood guard in his absence, their innocence in direct contrast to Rāma, as they played wargames in the forests.

### LAVA AND KUŚA DETAIN THE HORSE

> . . . they saw the royal decree of challenge written on its forehead: "Rājā Daśaratha took birth in the Solar Dynasty. He ruled with virtue and truth and has now gone to his place in heaven, but his son Raghunātha still lives on the earth. The four brothers—the revered Rāma, Lakṣmaṇa, Bharata, and Śatrughna—rule the kingdom of Ayodhyā. Śrī Rāma has initiated the *aśvamedha* sacrifice to assert royal sovereignty. The horse for this *aśvamedha* sacrifice is under the protection of Śatrughna, with his throngs of soldiers numbering two full *akṣauhiṇī*[29] armies." When the twins read the text of the edict they were offended and seethed with rage sufficient to incite them to capture the horse and tether it to the tree. The twins bound that horse so thoroughly that the two *akṣauhiṇī* divisions would never be able to free it. After securing the horse the two brothers returned to their mother, who lovingly fed them sweetmeats . . . .

Neither Śatrughna, nor any other, had imagined that anyone would seriously threaten the horse, much less successfully capture it. When the news was reported to Śatrughna, he was instantly wary, for the situation was not only unexpected, its portents were less than favorable. He found himself facing mere children, and his boasting of Rāma's and his brothers' might meet but taunts.

. . . This talk only infuriated Lava and Kuśa, who roared back with a furious challenge. "You are four brothers, we are but two. We would like to see you try to take the horse now. Have you come to us just to die stupidly? When you try to retrieve the horse, great peril will befall you." So did the sons of his brother heap their scorn and abuse, none of them realizing their relationship.

And so with much mutual invective and rebuke did the three wade in to a great pitched battle. The two brothers let fly with such a flurry of weapons from all directions that Śatrughna was soon hard pressed and tired and could not effectively engage . . . .

Gradually Śatrughna's armies rallied to hem them in. But just as quickly and with the confidence of those who know themselves in the right, the boys proceeded to destroy Śatrughna's armies. Suspecting, but not knowing who they were, Śatrughna hesitated, fearing they may be gods. After a fierce struggle, with insult and invective as thick as the weapons they hurled at one another, the boys prevailed, rejecting Śatrughna's plea for truce. After they slew him, they collected trophies from his person, then headed home to their mother, Sītā.

Seven soldiers survived to report back to Rāma in Ayodhyā; their news portended only the worst. Rāma listened to the miraculous tale of the routing of his armies, secretly recognizing that what was about to transpire could not avoided. He contemplated:

RĀMA DESPATCHES BHARATA AND LAKṢMAṆA TO DIE IN BATTLE

"Disaster has surely struck and there is no averting the fates. Of all the many great kings to have been born in Solar Dynasty, none has ever suffered the humiliation of falling in battle. Rāvaṇa killed Anaraṇya Mahārāja and then I slew him and his clan in battle. The unbeateable Lavaṇa was Rāvaṇa's nephew, and he made *deva*s and *daitya*s and all manner of other celestials and humans quake in fear. It was from Rāvaṇa himself that Lavaṇa derived so much of his strength and greatness, yet my brother Śatrughna killed him."

Bharata and Lakṣmaṇa moved to console Rāma. "To die in battle is the dharma of the Kshatriya. Lay aside this unseemly lament, O Lord, do not suffer this melancholy. No one is to blame when the fates engender disaster. When you cast out your perfect wife, the *pativratā* Sītā, we all knew then that an uncalled for breach of the Vedic injunctions had occurred. The gods know that Sītā is fully without sin or stain, yet you make Sitā's heart burn with sorrow even though she is free of fault. If you command it, Śrī Rāma, we will go today and capture those two young brothers."

And so as Bharata and Lakṣmaṇa had suggested, the revered Rāma gave them the order to go.

Kṛttibāsa's indictment of Rāma, placed in the mouths of Bharata and Lakṣmaṇa, lays bare his guilt, but without malice and whose consequences are now out of their hands. When they reached that place, the battlefield was being ravaged by dogs and jackals, ripping up the dead bodies. They found Śatrughna and lamented. First Śatrughna, then Bharata, and finally Lakṣmaṇa—in ominous succession did they succumb to the unassailable innocence of the boys. In each battle, the heroes saw the twins as "two Rāmas" approaching and knew their doom. Then it was Rāma's turn, and his was but a repetition of his brothers', albeit harder and longer with amplified invective and proportionately greater disaster. Arrogant and boastful in the manner of all triumphant Kshatriyas, Lava and Kuśa added humilation to physical defeat.

### LAVA AND KUŚA HUMILIATE RĀMA

. . . As Rāma contemplated his position, he grew indifferent; but Lava and Kuśa called out to renew their taunts. "Everyone in the world says that you are the epitome of dharma, Rāma, yet you have personally destroyed untold numbers by methods deemed untoward. Should three men direct their anger toward two, they destroy dharma and perish through their own faults. You had elephants and horses and infantry without number in your armies, but we are only the sons of a virtuous woman, a *satī*, and for that we have been protected."

Rāma felt deeply his shame and spoke briefly, "What you say has some truth, but I have done nothing inappropriate. I am the king of kings on this orb, the earth. I did not realize that my armies came for their own destruction. Who is there in the three worlds to overcome me? Save a son, there is none other to triumph. My defeat can only come about through the agency of my son, for the *śāstras* say that only a son is able to defeat his father. The two of you boys appear to be my very spit. If you are my sons, I will not fight. Tell me your ancestry, if you are my sons, you two young boys who go by the names of Lava and Kuśa. The valiant and invincible Rāvaṇa ruled the country of Laṅkā, but battle with me means the end of one's lineage."

The two boys scoffed as they listened to Rāma's boasting. When he was done, they jeered Rāma with disdain. "Listen to the drivel you are spewing, Śrī Rāma. Why are you so afraid to engage in battle? You whine 'My sons, my sons,' and inquire of our parentage. Will knowing such things allay your fears of fighting? You have heard the stories of fathers fighting their sons and you call us 'sons' because down deep you are worried. You are master of battle, a self-anointed king, yet you shamelessly refer to us over and again as your sons. How many times have you boasted how you destroyed Rāvaṇa, you know fully well that he fell at the hands of the brave warrior. How much more talk is there to be, Rāma?

They traded invectives, which quickly escalated to battle. But the going was tough for both sides and Rāma began to realize that he had met his match.

In the ensuing lament, when Rāma fully realizes that he is finished, Kṛttibāsa invites him to shoulder direct responsibility and just as quickly allows him to shed it onto the fates. It is perhaps a real indication of Rāma's blindness that he does not recall his own ignominious murder of Bālī and the curse levied by Tārā; but in the heat of battle he does remember a curse from a Brahmin who foretold his death by his own sons. Rāma now knew he was to die and chose to do so in battle, befitting a Kshatriya, but shamefully in conflict with children, his own abandoned offspring, a strategy that rescues him from the embarrassment of losing to any other lineage, for Raghu's lineage was always triumphant. As the moment approached,

RĀMACANDRA'S DEFEAT AND FALL IN BATTLE

. . . both brothers took aim and shot: Śri Rāma staggered to the earth, no longer conscious. The curse of a Brahmin long ago had ordained that he would be slain in battle at the hands of his own sons. Lava encircled him with a weapon named "The Missle of Parts," then twisted his bow round his neck. Kuśa released his weapon by the name of "Conquerer of the Imperishable" and shot him through the chest, pinning Rāma to the ground. Rāma twitched as the last little life eked out of him.

Quickly the two brothers advanced toward Rāma. Rāma could move no more, for the weapons had left him inert. Lava and Kuśa snatched the ornaments from his body, taking the earrings from his lobes, and lifting the headdress from his skull. They stripped the armbands from his biceps and slipped the rings from his hands. The two boys looted his body armor, and took his bow and mighty weapons, leaving nothing behind.

Hanūmān and Jāmbuvān—those two being immortal, a hundred *manvantaras* could not slay them. But they were powerless to rise because the weapons had knocked them unconcious—and so it was that Lava and Kuśa crossed them on the way home. Seeing the monkey and the bear along the path they were following, the two were amazed to look at their faces. So they bound them and slung them over their shoulders, and the two young brothers, victors in battle, happily went their way.

## Iterations of Irreverence or "Enough is Enough"

William Smith has noted that the "*Uttara kāṇḍa* puts Rāma in a bad light, perhaps that is why it is often omitted."[30] But based on passages such as those above, and many others, we would argue that that is precisely why it is much more frequently included, and why it survives in every printed edition of the text that circulates today. These stories of the *uttara kāṇḍa* reflect two closely related attitudes that recur in the perspective of a people who have never been fully integrated into the mainstream attitudes of the traditional Bhārata, the *madhya deśa*. If old saws are to be believed, Bengalis have always been slightly out of step with the rest of India and South Asia generally (half a step ahead, according to the aphorism sometimes attributed to Netaji, "What Bengal thinks today, India thinks tomorrow"). Rāma has had his highly respected share of devotees, but it seems that there has always been, since the time of Kṛttibāsa and probably before, a slight edge given to the noble losers, not only Sītā, but the *rakṣāṣa* king, Rāma's foe Rāvaṇa. Much like Milton's view of Lucifer ("the Carrier of Light," an epithet and characterization to which Michael was not insensible), Michael Madhusudana Datta's view of Rāvaṇa was that "he was a grand fellow . . . the idea of Ravan elevates and kindles my imagination."[31] And indeed, Michael's poem *Meghanādhvadha kāvya* ("The Epic of the Slaying of Meghanādha), is an extraordinary version of an episode from the Ramayana story in which the admirable son of Rāvaṇa is treacherously, one must confess, slain.[32] While giving Rāma and Lakṣmaṇa and the others their deserved share of high-sounding epithets, it is clear where Michael's sympathies lie: they do not lie with "Ram and his rabble."[33] In spite of Nirad Chaudhuri's suggestion to the contrary,[34] Michael is not being idiosyncratic or deliberately obtuse in favoring the usually demonized opposition; and the wholesale elevation of *rākṣasas* is one of the abiding complaints of literary historians who see this as an overly Vaiṣṇavizing effect.[35] And Michael's near contemporary Daśarathi Rāya does not disguise his attitude, as we have seen, which must have reflected the attitude of a number of people who flocked to hear him. According to Daśarathi, Lava and Kuśa killed their father and, in a manner even more disrespectful of Rāma than Kṛttibāsa had intimated, "in a state of well-being, surveyed the field of slaughter," and saw "the wishing-stone upon his throat, its blue jewel flashing, and the diadem of diamonds and pearls upon his head, and they were delighted" and stripped them from his body. Then they tied up the invincible Hanūmān, who had been knocked unconscious, and Lava, standing over him, said laughing, "Hey, brother Kuśa! In all my time in the forest I've never seen a beast like this one. Can you imagine, a flea-bitten forest monkey going into battle with human beings? Anyway, how are we going to get him home? He must weight 100 or 150 maunds,[36] too much for the two of us. He's not made of cork, either. You know, monkeys are only bodies, and they have no sense at all . . ."[37] This is not the type of reverence for the great warrior, Rāma's closest ally, that one would expect to find in other parts of India.

One of the curious things about the *uttara kāṇḍa* is that the whole Ramayana is replayed, meaning, among other things, that Sītā has to undergo another ordeal, which does not sit well with some of Kṛttibāsa's actors, to say nothing of audience, as we shall see in a moment. And it is this deliberate replay that provides the opportunity to correct any perceived social injustice. This is the way it works out:

After killing their father Rāma and all his brothers, and his armies, the twins Lava and Kuśa go happily home to tell their mother Sītā of their feat. She is understandably grief-stricken at their action, and the boys try to make amends, leading her to the battlefield, where she sees "all around, fallen elephants and horses in unimaginable numbers," and lying among his brothers her husband Rāma. Grieving and holding Rāma's feet, she tells the boys that he was their father, and they too, "their hands to their heads," wept. They said, "Forgive us, mother. Do not weep any more. The three of us together will wipe away this stain. We are consumed with grief because the fault and crime are ours: we are guilty of parricide, and burn with the pain of this. We cannot bear to live. There is no forgiveness for a sin as great as this; we will burn ourselves in the fire today, and become ashes." Sītā says, "I'll go first; you do what you want to do." So the three of them went to the Yamunā's bank and made a pyre and lit it; they bathed and put on clean clothes, and circumambulated the flames.

In the meantime, Vālmīki was sitting in meditation on Mount Citrakuṭa, and when he saw the smoke of the fire in his mind's eye, he just as quickly reappeared at the hermitage. At Vālmīki's request, Sītā explained how it had all come about, not forgetting to remind Vālmīki that it was he who taught the boys the skill in archery that had brought about her widowhood. Vālmīki assured her that everything would be well, and he instructed one of his students who was nearby to go to the hermitage and bring back the water of life from a well there. And, while muttering a mantra, Vālmīki sprinkled the water over the battlefield, ". . . the corpses of the soldiers rose up in numbers, their bodies renewed. And when the water of life touched them, Rāma and Lakṣmaṇa and the others rose up . . ." Sītā and her twins, much relieved, saluted Vālmīki for his poetic prowess—for his story is much happier now—and went home to the *āśrama*.

Rāma, granted this new lease on life, finished the horse sacrifice that he had begun some time before, and Vālmīki came, with four hundred of his students, among them the twins Lava and Kuśa. Vālmīki instructed the twins, "You have been taught by me not only warlike skills, but knowledge of music. Tomorrow, you two will sing the *Rāmāyaṇa* [at the request of] Rāma; you two will declaim my poetry, and the whole world will have cause to recite it. If Sarasvatī is gracious, I shall become a star poet . . . When you sing the *Rāmāyaṇa*, and come to the part about the renunciation of Sītā, do not say anything bad about Rāma. Rāma is the Lord of the World, most highly honored, and it would not be right to say bad things about him."

So the twins, dressed as ascetics in bark clothing, appear in the assembly and retell the story from beginning to end, whitewashing Rāma's role as instructed. After a month, the singing of the *Rāmāyaṇa* was finished, and Rāma was pleased, and asked the boys about their lineage, for he had not recognized them, apparently suffering from amnesia after his earlier death and revival. They lied, upon instruction of Vālmīki, who knew he had a good story to finish, saying that they were sons of a woman named Sītā, they were students of Vālmīki but did not know who their father was. Rāma embraced the boys, weeping, and said: "I have no wife anymore, and no sons. Through some fault of my own I banished Sītā, while she was pregnant."

Since everybody is going through the whole Ramayana again, Sītā must also go through a second ordeal. The women especially were not happy about this, and they said to one another: "he doesn't know what is in Sītā's heart. Why is he sending her to live in the forest? Why does he insist on this trial? What is this complete madness?" And in particular, three royal ladies, wives of the king, took exception. But after being excoriated for his failure to understand Sītā, Rāma presses ahead. Vālmīki likewise protests to Rāma, but Rāma persists in his course.

Sītā however is no pushover this time. She speaks softly and acquiesces, but her words are a reproof: "You brought me to this country, and then astonished me by banishing me to the forest. I became an ascetic there, and lived at the hermitage of the *muni*, and ate roots and berries, and was chaste. I had no more place in my father's family, nor yet in my husband's. Then you disgraced me, making me endure a trial by fire . . . . I shall disappear, my lord. I'll cause this misfortune to be wiped away. I have met with no success in this world; I shall go to hell. From today your shame will be dissolved; you will see no more the face of Janakī. You have insulted me, examining me in the court. I shall be born again and again, and in every birth you will be, my lord, my husband. [But I pray that] in no other birth will you make my life so difficult."

And Sītā spoke to the Earth: "O Earth, as you are a mother, do as a mother should. The shame of this your daughter is also your shame. Much sorrow, O mother, weighs upon my heart. Let me always be at your feet to serve you. Take me into your womb—Sītā begs this small boon at your feet." There was a door from the seventh underworld, and suddenly there rose up from that door a golden throne "which lit in all the ten directions this mortal world." Earth appeared in human form, and calling out, "Daughter!" in a deep and booming voice, she lifted Sītā onto her lap on that lion throne and said, "If Rāma wants to make the people happy by putting you to an ordeal, let him come here [to do it]. We two will dwell in the underworld as mother and daughter." But as Sītā was about to disappear, Rāma grabbed her by the hair and would not let her enter the underworld. Instead, "in her own form," i.e. as Lakṣmī, she went to heaven, and "the gods were very happy."

Finally, it would seem, Rāma may have done Sītā a good turn. But in Kṛttibāsa's telling, and that of some others, Rāma's actions are as problematic as his rule is suspect, and that seems to be a commentary on the nature of rule itself. Bengal has historically been a difficult place to assert political authority, as Buddhists, Hindus, and Muslims learned before the historical Kṛttibāsa, and the Britsh "Company" and Crown, the Congress Party, and now the CPI(M) have subsequently. Perhaps in Bengal, a land coveted by many, resistance to rule has become ingrained as kings come and go, and cynicism about the possibility of truly beneficent rule, a mantle of survival. The narrative structure of Kṛttibāsa's *Rāmāyaṇa* seems to offer a sometimes indirect critique, giving voice to the inexpressible. The technique comes in many guises, strategies to figuratively misdirect the expected line of the plot, literally "break the meter" (*chandobandha*) of a tale, by deliberately obfuscating intention (*chandabandha*), so that the reader or auditor can choose a preferred meaning,[38] and at the same time take advantage of the observation that, as in any rhythmical or expected structure, it is the off-beat that gets your attention. Rāma is not alone as the subject of these witty gibes, which are part of an old and great tradition. As if to acknowledge this, a famous ditty has been attributed to one of Bengal's best loved post-Independence governors, who perhaps was reminded of Rāma and his famous dog:

> Of the Fates, suffer I worst of all,
> damned to be governor of West Bengal.
>
> —B. C. Roy

THIRTEEN

# The Ramayana and its Muslim Interpreters

VASUDHA NARAYANAN

Although in North India Hindu nationalists destroyed the Babri Masjid, believing it to be built as an act of Muslim suzerainty on the site of the exact birthplace of Lord Rama, we find different patterns of relationship between the story of Rama and Muslims elsewhere in India. The Tamil-speaking region of India has sustained for many decades a long tradition of Muslim scholarship on the major Tamil version of the Ramayana, written by Kamban. Called *Irāmāvatāram*, "the Descent of Rama," Kamban's Ramayana narrates the story with poetic elegance that has won it the attention of literary connoisseurs for centuries. Muslim poets and scholars of Tamil Nadu have studied Kamban's Tamil Ramayana with diligence and enthusiasm. This paper focuses on two noteworthy instances where there has been an intense engagement by a Tamil–speaking Muslim with Kamban's Ramayana. In the seventeenth century, the author of the Tamil biography of the Prophet, Umaru Pulavar, was strongly influenced by Kamban's Ramayana. In the latter part of the twentieth century, M.M. Ismail has established himself as a scholar of the Tamil Ramayana. This paper looks at the ways in which two Muslim writers have responded to *Irāmāvatāram* and how one has utilized it as a literary model when writing a Tamil biography of the Prophet Muhammad.

## Kamban's Tamil Ramayana and Umaru Pulavar

While mention of Rama does occur in early Tamil poems (first to fifth century CE), he does not seem to have played a significant role in this early literature.[1] It is quite remarkable, therefore, that knowledge of the story of the Ramayana, as well devotion to Rama, became as widespread as it did by the time of the poet-saints known as the alvars (*circa* seventh to ninth centuries CE). The alvars seem to have known the narrative as presented by Valmiki's *Rāmāyaṇa,* and allude to several incidents from it in passing; but they also relate other incidents not present in the Sanskrit version,[2] suggesting that a strong oral tradition may have also existed before the time of Kamban.

Although scholars do not agree upon when exactly Kamban lived, the dates for the author range from the ninth century CE to the twelfth. Justice M.M. Ismail, the noted Tamil Ramayana scholar, has tended to accept the earlier date, quoting a laudatory verse which says that the first recital of Kamban's *Irāmāvatāram* took place in Saka 807, which corresponds to 885 CE.[3] Although very little is known about Kamban, it is generally held that he was born in Terazhundur, a small village in the Thanjavur district, fairly close to the Kaveri river. This river is described in some detail in his version of the Ramayana. Tirumankai Alvar (*circa* ninth-tenth century CE), one of the twelve South Indian Vaishnava poet saints, who may have been a contemporary of Kamban, sang about the Vishnu temple at Terazhundur in his *Periya Tirumoḻi.* The Sri Vaishnava community of South India holds that Kamban was a devotee of the ninth-century poet-saint Nammalvar and wrote a poem called *Caṭakōpaṉ antāti* in praise of him. Oral tradition maintains that Kamban first inaugurated his *Irāmāvatāram* in a special pavilion at the great Vishnu temple in Srirangam.

Although the poems of the alvars had been incorporated into Vaishnavaite liturgy, *Irāmāvatāram*—despite being considered a literary classic—did not become a part of regular devotional exercises in the temple or home. A few passages function as prayers in manuals, and some of the songs from Kamban's Ramayana (especially Sita's wondering who Rama is when she first sees him) have found their way into the daily Tamil idiom and become part of the singing repertoire of people who perform classic music and dance.

Muslims in some areas of Tamil Nadu have the last name

"Marakkayar." This word, they claim, derives from the Tamil *marakkalam* or "ship;" *marakkayar* means "shipmen." Although the Tamil lexicon indicates that the origin of the word may possibly go back to the Arabic *markab* ("mount" or "means of transportation," by extension, meaning a horse),[4] the name "Marakkayar" or "shipmen," say the Tamil Muslims, attests to their belief that their ancestors were seafaring. Many Marakkayars believe that their ancestors either came directly from Arabia or were Tamil people who accepted Islam after direct contact with Muslim traders from the Middle East, within a few years of the Prophet's death (and by some accounts during the lifetime of the Prophet himself). They believe that they descend from early Tamil converts or from Arab traders who settled down in the Tamil-speaking areas around the seventh-eighth centuries CE. That is, they do not see themselves as descendants of converts who embraced Islam through coercion after the Muslim conquest. They view Tamil literature and language as their heritage; Tamil is their native language and the literature is theirs.

Over the centuries, Muslims in Tamil Nadu have studied both secular works and Hindu religious poetry in Tamil and utilized many traditional Tamil literary conventions with great skill in their religious writings. Some of the greatest scholars of Kamban's Ramayana have been Muslims. For at least three hundred years, Kamban's *Irāmāvatāram* has been studied and enjoyed by generations of Muslim scholars in Tamil Nadu. One of the earliest serious scholars of Kamban and one whose own writing owes a great deal to Kamban's Ramayana is Umaru Pulavar "Omar the Poet," (*c.* 1665–1773).[5]

Umaru Pulavar composed the Tamil epic poem, *Cīṟā Purāṇam* ("The Purana of the Life of the Prophet"). *Cīṟā* is the Tamil transliteration of the Arabic *sirah*, a word used for hagiography, specifically the biography of the prophet. Puranas, a genre in Hindu literature in Sanskrit or Tamil, include pious accounts of the salvific deeds of a divine being, sometimes seen as an incarnation of the supreme deity, and contain long poetic accounts of this person's wondrous qualities. Puranas have been written about Hindu Gods Vishnu and Shiva, as well as to Goddess Durga and other Goddesses. The purana about Vishnu celebrates his various incarnations to save human beings. Tamil puranas generally deal with deities, hagiographies, or the sanctity of a sacred place.

In Umaru's account of the life of the Prophet, he carefully follows many of the literary conventions found in Kamban's Ramayana. To say that is not to detract from Umaru's greatness; in Tamil literature, as in Indian literature in general, we frequently see performing artists and poets borrowing from a particular source and then expanding or embellishing it. In a culture that values respectful study and paying homage to one's elders and superiors, borrowing from their music or literature indicates reverence. Rather than total appropriation, followers borrow phrases, descriptions, similes, ideas and sometimes the arrangements of certain chapters. In this context, when one seeks to place oneself in a literary or religious tradition, one would never assert that one writes in a completely original way or that one's ideas have never been enunciated before. For example, members of the "orthodox" schools of Hindu philosophy always dutifully described their teachings as mere explanation of what was already said in the Vedas and other earlier literature. Musicians, dancers, and artists usually credit their talent to the training received from their teachers. To borrow and to improve on it or to embellish an idea does not constitute plagiarism, but marks one's humility and deference to the weight of tradition.

Many of Kamban's ideas can be traced to other earlier poets; however, he leaves his own distinctive mark on his Ramayana. Umaru too, shows abundant knowledge of other literature, yet his work too is strikingly original. Like Kamban, he begins his epic narration of the Prophet's life with a chapter describing the country, followed by one wherein he describes the main city. Both poets use typical Tamil literary conventions to talk about the wealth and prosperity of the land.

As did the Tamil epic poet Kamban, Umaru Pulavar gives extensive descriptions of the country and the city where the prophet is to "descend" (*avatāra*). This is followed by a list of the ancestors of Muhammad. Umaru apparently never travelled to Arabia, and his description of the country turns out to describe Tamil Nadu. In the utilization of this method too, he follows Kamban. Kamban transposes the Tamil landscape to Ayodhya in northern India. Descriptions of the river Kaveri are transferred to the river Sarayu. Umaru Pulavar projects the Tamil landscape on Arabia. Kamban talks of the heavy rolling clouds that drench the Kosala kingdom with rain; Umaru describes the torrential rain in Arabia which makes the fields of rice and sugarcane rich and fertile.

Tamil classical (*caṅkam*) poetry, especially the *puṟam* ("outer," poems typically dealing with chivalry, praise of kings, and war) verses, usually includes description of the beauty of a king's land. In the Tamil verses of classical poetry, we find roaring cascades (the presence of water indicated prosperity in South India, where drought was all too common), well-irrigated and fertile lands, lush fields of paddy and sugarcane, blossoming lotuses, and bees sucking nectar from flowers redolent with honey. The waterfalls and rivers carry precious gems which have fallen from the jewelry worn by people who come to bathe there; such details reveal that the king's land abounds with riches. Classical poets also describe the cities in considerable detail: prosperous seaports, terraces looming like mountains, tall palaces rising to the sky. They are centers of culture where bards and courtesans flourish because there are wealthy and generous patrons; their presence, therefore, is indicative of a country's wealth.

The wealth of a nation rests on its ability to produce food, which depends on rainfall. Poets praise the prosperity of a land by describing the abundant rain over the land. Umaru Pulavar talks of the white clouds drinking up the sea water, becoming dark, and heading for land (Arabia). The clouds cover the mountains[6] and storms rage. The storms abate but the heavy rains continue, flooding the land (v.4), and it becomes chilly. Elephants, lions, and other animals feel the cold and, forgetting the enmity between them, gather in one place (v.4). Elephants, deer, squirrels, tigers, bisons, giant lizards, monkeys, lions, spotted deer, anteaters, lemurs, bears, wild dogs, buffalos, porcupines, humped bulls and other animals, huddle in the cold, shivering (v.5). Because of the high winds, trees on the mountains fall (v.6). Flocks of birds fly, frightened, and floods of water come down the emerald slopes of the mountains on to the plains (v.7). The flooding streams approach the houses of the wide-eyed gypsy women with red lips who live on the foothills. The streams drop as water falls over the emerald mountains, knocking down the banana trees and woodapple trees. The rains fall from the mountains like waterfalls, and swiftly flow through the land, carrying with them aromatic wood and jewelry which floats away from the rich women who bathe in the waters.

Kamban describes how by bearing these riches, the torrents resemble merchants carrying precious goods:

> Carrying the pearls, gold, peacock feathers,
> beautiful white ivory from an elephant, aromatic *akil* wood,
> sandalwood, matchless in fragrance,
> the floods looked like the merchants [bearing precious goods].[7]

Umaru uses the same simile in *Cīṟā Purāṇam* to describe the Arabian landscape:

> Carrying the fallen sandalwood,
> branches from the dark *akil* tree,
> pearls from the broken elephant's horn, white ivory,
> more precious than these, red rubies, radiant in three ways,
> carrying these all towards the sea,
> the stream, laden with rich bamboo, looked like a merchant [bearing precious goods].[8]

Here too the floods sweep away gems from the mountains (v. 9).

Kamban, in his Ramayana, also uses the analogy of the courtesan embracing a king and taking away his jewelry:

> Like a courtesan embracing her lover
> his head, his body, his feet, as if in desire
> all for a minute [and fleeing with his ornaments]
> the floods embrace the peak, the slopes, the foothills
> and sweep away everything.[9]

Umaru Pulavar, too, employs the same simile to describe the rush of the waters through the Arabian countryside:

> Like a courtesan embracing the king
> majestic like the mountain,
> giving him pleasure,
> and then sweeping away gold which gives us prosperity,
> precious gems, pearls, and all splendid things,
> and flees the frontiers,
> the floods swiftly flow
> carrying with them all riches.[10]

As Umaru continues his description of the countryside, he incorporates particular settings into his poetry. The river flows through the mountainous (*kuriñci*) land (presumably of Arabia), springs through the desert (a recognized category in the landscapes of Tamil poems), and flows into the forests (v. 12–13). Reaching cultivated land (*marutam*) it fills the lakes, ponds and tanks (v. 15). The streams break through the lakes and approach farming lands. They sweep through the sugarcane plantations and slush up the ponds where the lotus flowers, beautiful and fragrant, bloom (v. 18). The water is then contained and used for irrigation (v. 17). Umaru compares this body of water held in many tanks, ponds, lakes, and areas where the lotus flower blossoms to life (*uyir*) which appears in hundreds of forms. This idea reminds one of the Advaitin notion that a single soul (*ātman*) appears in many forms and bodies and seems to be many. While Umaru does not elaborate on his analogy, he seems at home with these Vedantic ideas.

Where did Umaru get his poetic ideas from? The earliest Tamil literature recognizes five landscapes. The *caṅkam* poems (also known as the poems of the classical age dealing with romantic or heroic themes) refer to five basic situations. These situations correspond in poetry to five landscape settings (*tiṇai*), birds, flowers, times of day, gods, etc. The five basic psychological situations for *akam* or "inner" poems are love-making, waiting anxiously for a beloved, separation, patient waiting of a wife, and anger at a lover's real or imagined infidelity. These correspond to the mountainous (*kuriñci*), sea-side (*neytal*), arid (*pālai*), pastoral (*mullai*), and agricultural (*marutam*) landscapes respectively.[11]

Both Kamban and Umaru describe these landscapes skillfully, believing them to be the lands Kosala and Arabia. As we saw, Umaru's descriptions closely resemble the descriptions of Kamban in the first two chapters of his *Irāmāvatāram*. Even though the details are exquisitely similar in spirit and in concept, both poets have their own inimitable style in literature; their individuality also shines out. Reading both descriptions is similar to listening to the same *rāga* played by two maestros.

Kamban and Umaru also share poetic language when each describes the wedding that plays such a central role in each epic. The long chapter on Fatima's wedding contains a beautiful description of Ali's procession through the city of Medina; it parallels Rama's procession through Mithila in Kamban's Ramayana. Let us consider Kamban's description of how the women in Mithila rush to get a glimpse of Rama:

Like a herd of deer closing in
Like a flock of peacocks wandering
Like a shower of brilliant meteors[12]
Like flashes of lightning coming close
With bees that flutter around their garlands
  humming in tune
With bands of anklets and rings tinkling

Women, their hair adorned
with flowers soaked [with honey]
swiftly thronged around.

Not caring that their hair had loosened
  and come cascading down
Not heeding their waist belts that broke loose
Not pulling up the flower-soft clothes that slip away
Not pausing to rest their tired waists
they encircled him [Rama].
Coming close they cried, "Make way, make way."
Women who lend splendor to the city
swarmed around him like bees tasting honey.[13]

Umaru follows Kamban's description in talking of the women in Medina who rush to see Ali:

Anklets swirled on their feet,
the golden belts around their hips tinkled.
The ornaments on their radiant breasts—
  breasts as sharp as the tusks
  of a lusty elephant
flashed.
Their hair, adorned by flowers
fragrant and fresh, dripping honey,
spilled out from their constraints.
Like many moons flowering on the ocean,
young maidens thronged around.[14]

The women in Medina, watching Ali's procession, are seen to be wearing jewels (anklets and waist belts) like Tamil women. Conventionalized descriptions of their breasts, pointed and sharp, follow. Their hair, which should be demurely gathered together in swirls of fragrant flowers filled with honey, loosens in their mood of abandon. The words suggest an erotic mood, appropriate for the wedding. They are filled with longing at the sight of Ali. According to Tamil literary conventions, a woman's body becomes pale when she is parted from her lover or husband. The young women of Medina bear this pallor that signifies this special lovesickness. Women in Medina overflow from the balconies trying to catch a glimpse of this handsome bridegroom. When they see him, they wonder: Is all this charm and beauty to be monopolized by just one woman?

The women swarm around like an ocean, says Umaru, and then he uses metaphors connected with the sea to describe them. In doing so, he moves beyond his following of Kamban, and strikes out on his own:

> Eyes like darting fish,
> necks, exulting like conches;
> teeth like white pearls, smile
> through parted lips,
> which flash like corals.
> With golden skin growing pale with longing
> flowers loosened like shining foam,
> A sea of women, swarm thick
> without any gap between them.[15]

Using the sea as the primary metaphor, Umaru speaks of the women splashing forth like the ocean. The poet comes from and lives on the seashore; he is lavish in his use of metaphors from the sea. Fish, conches, corals, pearls, and sea foam all appear as elements of comparison in describing these women. A poet's skill was frequently seen in the use of metaphor and similes, and descriptions of the human body—both for men and women—were particularly relished by the audience. Umaru certainly excels according to all Tamil standards in these areas.

Umaru Pulavar availed himself of the riches of the Tamil language in Kamban's Ramayana and he in turn enriched Tamil literature through his *Cīṟā Purāṇam*. Umaru Pulavar was not an isolated example of a Muslim scholar at home with the Tamil Ramayana. When we peruse the annual programs on the "Festival of Kamban" held every August in Madras, we regularly encounter names of Muslim scholars who have studied the Tamil Ramayana. Perhaps the best known among the Muslim scholars committed to the scholarship of the Tamil Ramayana is Justice M.M. Ismail, former chief justice of the Madras High Court.

## Justice M.M. Ismail's Interpretation of Kamban's Ramayanam

Justice M.M. Ismail has led a high-profile life as a high court judge and as a scholar of Kamban's *Irāmāvatāram*.[16] He was born on February

8, 1921 in Nagore, a town just a little north of Nagapattinam, on the eastern coast of the state of Tamil Nadu. Nagore, an area with a high Muslim concentration, is not a large city, yet Ismail sees it as cosmopolitan in nature due to two factors. First, Hindu and Muslim pilgrims from all over India and Sri Lanka come regularly to visit its *dargah* (burial shrine) of Shahul Hamid (*c.* 1513–79). Second, many of the men in Nagore travelled on business to Southeast Asia, and stayed there for several months at a time.

Most of the Muslim men and women in Nagore apparently did not study beyond an elementary school education—they were businessmen who travelled extensively in Singapore, Thailand, and Malaysia. Many of them, Ismail recalls, learned to write only so they could communicate with letters to their families back home. Most of the children (boys and girls) attended a *madrasa* to learn the Koran; after three or four years the boys went to an elementary school and the girls continued their studies at home. Although the recitation of the Arabic Koran was taught, pupils did not learn its meaning in Tamil, the mother-tongue of all the pupils. After about three years in a *madrasa*, Justice M. M. Ismail joined the Nagore Municipal Muhammadan Boys Higher Elementary School. Because he had gone to a *madrasa* and then joined elementary school, he was older than most boys in his class. He wanted to do well so that he would catch up with his peer group, and because of his hard work and intelligence, he was allowed to skip several grades.

Ismail recalls that all his teachers in elementary school—except the Urdu teacher—were Hindu Brahmins (p. 184). His teachers took pride in his academic ability; Justice Ismail remembers their confidence in him with affection. He recalls one incident with poignancy. When the British governor of the Madras Presidency drove by their elementary school, the teachers took the students out to watch him. As the motorcade passed them, Krishnamurthi Aiyar, one of his teachers said, "Our Ismail will one day become a governor like this and become famous." Years later he became the Chief Justice of Madras High Court and was Acting Governor for a brief time. During this tenure, Ismail says that as he drove by his old school, he remembered his teacher's words and divine grace which made all this possible, with gratitude and humility (p. 187).

Later, due to the affectionate mentoring of all his teachers at the Nagai (Nagapattinam) National High School he became interested in Tamil literature, specifically Kamban's *Irāmāvatāram*. He recalls that one of his teachers, N. Aravamudan, went out of his way to encourage the success of non-Hindu students: Sri Aravamudan urged him to do well in his examination, confessing that this was his first position as a teacher. He feared that if Non-Brahmins did not do well, people will say "the Principal is an *ayyaṅkar* [Brahmin Srivaishnava]; this teacher Aravamudan is also an *ayyaṅkar* [i.e. from the same caste and community]—and so though he has no experience or ability, he was appointed as teacher. You must get the highest grade in the school and be sure there is no talk like that." When Ismail stood first in his school, he travelled forty kilometers to Kumbakonam to convey the news to his teacher, who lived in the Brahmin quarters right outside the temple. On hearing the news, the teacher, who lived in the orthodox section of Kumbakonam and who normally would not touch non-family members, joyfully embraced the student.

Ismail also notes that in his youth there were no tensions between the Hindus and Muslims and that he was the favorite student of all his teachers (pp. 202–3), many of whom were Hindu Vaishnavaites. For example, Sri Santhanam Ayyangar, a student of the renowned Tamil scholar and savant Dr. U. V. Swaminatha Aiyar, taught him in the last years of high school. Blessed with a powerful singing voice, he recited and sang Tamil songs and poetry with eclat, thrilling students. Ismail says that such teachers lavished care upon the students; he attributes his interest in Tamil literature to them: "These were the teachers who imparted to me my enjoyment of Tamil literature" (p. 204). Ismail's description of his teachers conveys his feeling that students and teachers shared a desire to learn. Their appreciation of the beauty of Tamil literature transcended traditional rules of caste purity and pollution.

Outside school, Pa. Pavanna Dawoodsha Sahib mentored Ismail, encouraging his elocution skills. This gentleman was called the "Ramayana Sahib" due to his extensive knowledge of the Kamban Ramayana (p. 209). Ismail concludes, "It is because of my relationship with these good people that I learned to enjoy [Tamil] literature in general and obtained a taste for the Kamba Ramayana in particular" (p. 207).

In contrast to many of the people in his hometown who were members of the Muslim League, Ismail joined the Indian National Congress and participated in India's struggle for Independence. Justice Ismail majored in Mathematics for his undergraduate education in the Presidency College of the Madras University and later attended the Madras Law College. He received his degree in law in 1945 and then became an advocate attached to the Madras High Court. In 1967 he was appointed as a justice of the Delhi High Court; later that year he moved to the Madras High Court, where he eventually became the Chief Justice in 1979. He was the interim Governor of the Tamil Nadu state in 1980.

Justice Ismail has given hundreds of speeches and talks on the Ramayana throughout Tamil Nadu and to many Tamil speaking communities all over the world. He spoke regularly on the text during All India Radio broadcasts. Many of his books contain chapters based on these discourses. In addition to many essays on Kamban, he has also written several books that carry out sustained studies on a particular theme or a specific character. Thus *Mūṉṟu viṉākkaḷ* ("Three Questions") examines the episode of Rama killing Vali and *Vaḷḷaliṉ vaḷḷal* ("Most Generous among the Generous Ones") analyzes the character Guha in Valmiki, Tulsidas, and Kamban.[17]

Justice Ismail, a great admirer of Kamban, considers him to be not merely a great poet, but a *jñāni*, a wise person, commenting: "There is no doubt that Kamban's ability is super-normal (*acātāraṇam*> Skt. *a-sādhāraṇa*) and trans-human (*apaurṣēyam*)."[18] Intimately familiar with almost all of classical Tamil literature, Ismail is also well-acquainted with the Sanskrit *Rāmāyaṇa* of Valmiki and the *Rāmcaritmānas* of Tulsi, through translation. Ismail places his studies of the Tamil Ramayana in two perspectives: comparing it and distinguishing it from earlier Tamil secular and devotional literature on the one hand, and the Sanskrit and Hindi Ramayanas on the other hand.

Ismail has written penetrating studies of the characters, including the "second-order" cast from Kamban's Ramayana. He has commented on Tara (the wife of Vali and Sugriva)[19] and on Trijata, the daughter of Vibhishana and the only woman who befriends Sita in Lanka.[20] Shatrughna, a half-brother of Rama and a shadowy character who is best known for his devotion to Bharata, has also received Ismail's scrutiny.[21] Ismail has written on Shabari as well, comparing Kamban's portrayal of her character with that of Valmiki and Tulsidas.[22] One of the longer articles in such character studies focuses on Shurpanakha, the demon sister of Ravana.[23] Called "She who has five speeches," the article analyzes five situations where Shurpanakha has major lines: Shurpanakha's encounter with Rama and Lakshmana; her report on Sita to the demon Khara; her lament over Khara's death; her description of Sita to Ravana in the court of Lanka; and finally her taunting of Ravana when he imagines that Sita has come to him with love. Justice Ismail's most complete personality study of a minor character—with the exception of Vali—is on Guha, the boatman who ferries Rama across the river in the beginning of the exile.

Justice Ismail also analyzes Kamban's poetry in the context of earlier Tamil literature, with which he is intimately familiar. Thus when he discusses the concept of romantic love in Kamban's Ramayana, he also examines this notion of love in earlier Tamil literature such as *Kuṟuntōkai* and later works such as *Periya Purāṇam*.[24] He quotes profusely from the Jain work, *Cīvaka Cintāmaṇi*, as well as the Shaiva and Vaishnava saints, engaging one in scholarly rigorous but aesthetically enjoyable discussion on Kamban.

Justice Ismail has included his studies on *Cīṟā Puṛaṇam* in his discussion of other Tamil literature, thus introducing many people to the beauty of these Tamil Islamic works. He has also pointed out the similarities between Kamban and Umaru Pulavar in some of his short articles. Tamil works on Islam have been relatively unknown outside of a college curriculum to Hindu students. A Tamil-speaking Hindu may not pick up a whole book on Tamil Islam, but when the discussion on *Cīṟā Puṛaṇam* occurs as part of a broader essay on Tamil literature or Kamban's *Irāmāvatāram* in particular, it reaches a larger audience. It introduces one to and raises one's awareness of Islamic works in Tamil.

Throughout his life, Justice Ismail has been recognized and decorated for his scholarship by many Hindu groups. In South Asia, scholars recognized for their erudition receive gifts of titles, medals, symbolic shawls, and prizes. Justice Ismail has received dozens of prizes and awards for his oratory talents, writings, and knowledge of Tamil literature. When he was just nine years old, he stunned his village with his oratorical skills during the Milad un Nabi (the Prophet's birthday) celebrations. His forte in speaking was—and continues to be—the Kamba Ramayana. In 1978 *Kampaṉ Kaḻakam* (The Kamban Society) of Palayamkottah and Tirunelveli invited the well-known Tamil scholar P. Sri to confer upon Ismail the title of "The Beacon Light of the Kamba Ramayana." In 1979, he was awarded an honorary doctorate by Annamalai University. The Rotary Club of Madurai honored him with the Paul Harris Fellowship in 1989, citing his scholarship, especially on Kamban's

Ramayana, and his efforts to disseminate that scholarship and knowledge of Indian culture in general. In 1991, Narada Gana Sabha, an elite cultural organization in Madras, honored him with the title "Rama Ratnam" (the Gem of Rama). In September 1997, the Azhwar Aiyvu Maiyam (Centre for Alvar Research) gave the Ramanujar Award, named after the famous 11th century Vedanta theologian Ramanuja, to Ismail.

An honor that Ismail cherishes particularly is the esteem shown to him by the "Shankaracharya"[25] of Kanchi Kamakoti Pitham. This Shankaracharya (known as Chandrasekhara Saraswati) formerly served as the Hindu pontifical head of a *smārta* (a sectarian Brahmin community) monastery and had a large following, numbering in the hundreds of thousands, all over India. The Shankaracharya and Justice Ismail have met several times for friendly and scholarly discussions and conversations over the last thirty years.[26] Justice Ismail recalls that after he published one of his books, the Shankaracharya was so pleased with the 410-page work that he sent for the author. The book *Mūṉṟu Viṉākkaḷ* ("Three questions"), focuses on a particular incident in the Ramayana which some Hindus find hard to accept and justify. It involves Rama's killing the monkey king named Vali and giving the throne to Vali's brother, Sugriva. Ismail explores three questions in the whole book:

1. "Did Vali have to die and be killed by Rama?"
2. "Was the manner in which Rama killed Vali correct?"
3. "Did Rama's fame diminish by the way in which he killed Vali?"

Ismail analyzes Valmiki's and Kamban's account of the episode where Vali is killed in light of these three questions. His lengthy deliberations consider many arguments, utilize many methods and ultimately justify Rama's actions, at least in the Ramayana according to Kamban. Ismail takes Vali as an emanation of Indra and Sugriva as the emanation of Surya. Vali was to have helped Rama overcome adharma, and instead "defected," losing sight of his mission. Although a divine being, his understanding of dharma remains incomplete; he does not proceed on the path to help Rama, and is eventually eliminated.[27]

In justifying Rama's action, Ismail also analyzes a special incident recounted by Kamban that does not appear in Valmiki's telling of the Ramayana. In it, Vali receives a favor from Shiva: if he battles face to face with a person, he can appropriate to himself this opponent's strength and victory. Although this boon would not have worked in the case of

Rama—he is the supreme being—Rama still risks a blot on his name and dharma rather than make it seem that Shiva's boon is ineffective.

Finally, Ismail analyzes the context of the episode, and Vali's discussion on ethics just before he dies. Vali talks to Rama at length, and in his final words he entrusts his son to Rama. Remember, Rama had just shot Vali; but instead of ranting against his killer, Vali puts his son in Rama's care. Based on these lines and other issues, Ismail demonstrates how Rama's character remains flawless in Kamban's version of the story. The Shankaracharya's words approving Justice Ismail's treatment of the episode were simple: "You are the Chief Justice. You have rendered justice to Rama."[28]

Not only Hindus within Tamil Nadu, but Hindu communities in the diaspora as well have honored Ismail. In 1993, Hindus from the Cleveland area and the Canadian Council of Hindus celebrated Justice Ismail's scholarship on the Ramayana. The Hindus of the Greater Cleveland area annually celebrate the festival of Tyagaraja, an eighteenth-century musician, composer, and ardent devotee of Rama. In almost every classical Carnatic music concert, as well as in special music fests dedicated to him, musicians perform his compositions and celebrate his devotion. Because Rama, the object of Tyagaraja's devotion and the subject of Kamban's epic, has been the focus of Ismail's scholarship and erudition for decades, the Cleveland association and the Canadian Council of Hindus honored his decades of scholarship and achievements.

In Tamil Nadu, and in the diaspora, Hindus have tended to take it for granted that Ismail and other Muslims have become experts on Kamban's Ramayana. Only after the Babri Masjid demolition did Hindus in the diaspora become self-conscious about the irony of the South Indian situation, where some of the great scholars of Kamban's *Irāmāvatāram* are Muslims.

## Concluding Remarks

Ismail has remarked with justifiable pride that in every generation there is at least one Muslim who is an authority on Kamban's *Irāmāvatāram*.[29] Umaru Pulavar, in the seventeenth century, is the first celebrated example that we know about. Tamil literature encompasses both secular poems of love and war and later on, moving devotional hymns to Vishnu, Shiva, Murugan and other deities, as well as Jain and Buddhist works. It is within this pluralistic context that we should place Kamban's Ramayana. Although Tamil Vaishnava poetry composed by the alvars became part of domestic and Vishnu temple liturgies, and Shaiva poems were used in Shiva temples and Shaivaite homes, the Tamil Ramayana was never pressed into devotional use. Neither has it been part of domestic piety, nor did it attain the popularity of the seventeenth–century *Rāmcaritmānas* of Tulsidas in Hindi. The Tamil Ramayana was not considered to be "revealed" or inspired in a manner analogous to the poems of the alvars, although Ismail and other Tamil scholars consider Kamban's ability (Tamil *tiṟamai*) to be *apauruṣēya* or trans-human.

Although a detailed study of the reasons why Kamban's Ramayana never attained ritual status lies beyond the scope of the focus of this paper, as noted, Rama seems to have been a relative newcomer to the south and his limited popularity developed comparatively late; archaeologists have noted that images of Rama and temples to him are not among the earlier artifacts found in Tamil Nadu. Lack of high-caste and royal/political patronage, as well as lack of sponsorship by prominent Vaishnava leaders in the Chola and post-Chola periods may have been other possible reasons which would have to be explored to see why the Tamil Ramayana was not enacted, sung, and used in devotional exercises like the poems of the alvars. Kamban's work has been counted as a literary, if not devotional masterpiece, and it may be that the very lack of appropriation on the ritual level made the work a "safe" text to be intimately studied by people from other religious communities.

Tamil-speaking Muslims have produced some of the best scholarship on Kamban's Ramayana. This scholarship has prevailed through the centuries—even during times when there have been heightened tensions between Hindus and Muslims in northern India. There is strong participation by Muslims in the *Kampaṉ Viḻa* or "Festival of Kamban," an annual celebration devoted to the scholarship on this poet. Justice Ismail's immersion in Tamil literature and Kamban's Ramayana took place in the years just before partition and Independence in 1947. In general, while Tamil-speaking Muslims have studied Arabic and Persian forms of literature and adapted them to Tamil genres, as well as showing reverence to Muslim saints from other parts of India and the Middle East, they have on the whole maintained a linguistic and cultural identity distinct from Urdu–speaking Muslims in Hyderabad and northern India, or Bengali–speaking

Muslims. Tamil-speaking Muslims value both the antiquity of their Arabic origins and the linguistic importance of Tamil. This Islamic link with the Tamil language was particularly evident in the successful campaign mounted by the Tamil Muslims in the 1930s to ensure that Hindi would *not* be made a compulsory second language in the academic curriculum. While the Urdu-speaking Muslims from Tamil Nadu supported this measure, the Tamil-speaking Muslims agitated against it along with the Tamil-speaking (Non-Brahmin) Hindus. Here the hold of linguistic identity proved stronger than the pull to align themselves with people who followed the same religion, but who spoke a different language.[30] The trauma of the partition had less effect in the deep south and the Tamil Muslims were—as were most other South Indians—relatively insulated from the north.

In contrast, the aggressive stance of some Hindu nationalists since the 1980s seems to have prompted a sense of insecurity among the Tamil Muslims which is revealed in their new songs and writings.[31] Because the figure of Rama and the Ayodhya issue have become contentious, it is not clear whether the tradition of Muslim scholarship on the Tamil Ramayana will continue with the same vigor after the Babri Masjid event. Since thousands of readers and members of the Tamil-speaking public have been introduced to the wonders of Kamban through the speeches and writings of Justice Ismail, this will be a loss for all interested in Ramayana studies and Tamil literature.

# APPLIED RAMAYANAS

FOURTEEN

# Yes to Sita, No to Ram: The Continuing Hold of Sita on Popular Imagination in India

MADHU KISHWAR

There is no escaping the fact that the Sita of popular imagination has been deeply influenced by the Sita of *Rāmcaritmānas* by Tulsidas.[1] In many other versions of the Ramayana, such as the one by Valmiki, the couple's close companionship and joyful togetherness stand out as prominent features of the Ram–Sita relationship, rather than the self-effacing devotion and loyalty which have become hallmarks of the modern-day stereotype of Sita. The medieval telling of Tulsidas marks the transition from presenting Ram and Sita as an ideal couple to projecting each of them as an ideal man and woman respectively. As the epitome of propriety, *maryādā puruṣottam,* Ram's conjugal life has to be sacrificed at the altar of "higher" duties. Sita, too, gains importance insofar as she sets a high standard as an ideal wife who acts as the moral anchor in a marriage, and stays unswerving in loyalty and righteousness, no matter how ill-matched her husband's response. The power of the ideal wife syndrome in Tulsi's *Rāmcaritmānas* somehow overshadows the happy conjugal life of the couple prior to Sita's rejection. This medieval Sita also lacks the versatility of the Sitas of Valmiki and other earlier Ramayanas, especially those prevalent in various regional languages. Nevertheless, the Sita of Tulsidas has played a vital role in molding the psyche of too many Indian women, especially in North India. This paper begins a preliminary exploration into why the Sita symbol continues to exercise such a powerful hold on popular imagination, especially among women.

## In Their Own Words

Young girls tend to name public figures like Rani Lakshmi of Jhansi, Indira Gandhi, and Mother Teresa as their ideals, but those already married or on the threshold of marriage very frequently mention Sita as their ideal, except the few who consciously identify themselves as feminist. At this point of their life, the distinction between an ideal woman and an ideal wife seems to often get blurred in their minds—and this includes not just women of my mother and grandmother's generations but even young college-going girls in small towns and villages as well as in metropolitan cities like Delhi. If you ask people to name a symbol of the ideal wife, they frequently name Sita as their first choice.

This Sita image indeed lends itself to diverse appeals, which is perhaps why it has continued to hold its sway over the minds of many people in India over the centuries. When I ask women if they find this ideal still relevant, many respond that the example Sita sets will always remain relevant, even though they themselves may not be able to completely live up to it. This failure they attribute to living in kaliyuga, and to the fact that in today's debased world it is difficult to measure up to such high norms. However, most women add that they do try to live up to the Sita ideal to the best of their ability while making some adjustments in light of present-day circumstances.

Even though I have selected the interviews from which I quote, they are fairly representative of the variety of answers I got on the subject. All the women I quote extensively as representative examples are employed outside the home. They come from different cultural backgrounds and income levels: an upper-middle-class Punjabi woman employed as a college teacher; a Muslim woman from a middle-class family, also teaching in a college; a woman employed as an office clerk from an eastern Uttar Pradesh family; a Bihari Brahmin woman from a poor peasant family (wife of a rickshaw puller) who works as a domestic servant in Delhi. All names have been changed to protect their identity. Most of the interviews were conducted in Hindi and translated by me.

Abha, a woman in her late twenties, comes from a Brahmin family from eastern Uttar Pradesh. Her parents are fairly conservative and deeply religious, but they have not discouraged Abha and her sister from taking up jobs and earning an independent income. However, Abha would not mind giving up her job after her marriage if marital obligations require that she become a full time housewife. She feels sure she can adjust under any circumstances to virtually any family into which her parents marry her. She has a strong sense of self-respect but never asserts her rights in an aggressive manner. Abha's family worships Ram as their *iṣṭa dev* (chosen deity) and her father, she says, is a total Ram devotee. Yet she is very strong in her condemnation of Ram.

She says about Sita: "Sita is undoubtedly an ideal wife according to the norms of our society, but I feel that she should have rebelled more. She should have refused even the first *agniparīksha*. How dare Ram doubt her integrity in the first place! I don't think it was in deference to social opinion that he subjected her to such a humiliation, because even before anyone else said anything, he insulted her for having been a captive of Ravan—as if she chose it. It is because he had these unworthy doubts in his mind that the second time round he got swayed by the comment of a mere dhobi (washerman). The condition in which he abandoned her [she was pregnant then], and the way he did it can by no means be called dharma. It was cruel and foolish. I fail to understand why they call Ram *maryādā puruṣottam*. He certainly failed in his *maryādā* as a husband.

"Tulsidas deliberately underplayed this injustice done to Sita by making it appear that Ram banished only the shadow Sita and kept the real Sita by his side. Tulsi wanted to make Ram appear as a god rather than the ideal, though imperfect, human being that he is in Valmiki's *Rāmāyaṇa*. Tulsidas tried to cover up the negative traits of Ram which bring down his stature in people's eyes. In the process he might have uplifted his *Rāmcaritmānas* into a great devotional text, but ended up doing great injustice to Sita by covering up for Ram's actions. In contrast, Valmiki shows Ram for what he was, because Sita had sought shelter in his ashram and Valmiki had witnessed Sita's pain and humiliation at her rejection. Ram is lucky that despite such shameful acts, he was elevated so high by society, though now we all understand that he did wrong. Sita should have protested more strongly. My idea of an ideal husband is naturally Bhagwan Shiv because he really could not think of life without Sati. For instance, even though Sati goes to the ceremony being held at her father's house despite his advice, when she jumps into the fire, he feels such grief that his dance of destruction threatens the entire universe. He rests only after he brings her back to life. He is so utterly devoted to her that in her next birth Parvati has to do severe asceticism to convince him that she is his own Sati. Up to that point he would not even look at her, so engrossed was he in his devotion to Sati. In fact, the two make an ideal couple. Both Shiv and Parvati listen to each other. An ideal wife cannot by herself make an ideal household. It takes both to make one."

Neerja teaches Sanskrit in a college and is married to a very successful business executive. Theirs is an upwardly mobile middle-class family which doesn't exactly worship Ram as their *iṣṭa dev,* but believes in the power of Ram-Nam. For her an ideal woman is one who stays within her *maryādā* and is a loyal companion to her husband without losing her dignity or self-respect. The first example that comes to her mind of an ideal woman is Sita. But in her view Ram is far from being an ideal husband: "So enamoured was he with the idea of being considered an ideal king that he did not even treat his wife with elementary consideration—a wife who was completely devoted to him, had surrendered herself so totally to him, and who was altogether flawless. Tulsi tries to be too smart in attempting to exonerate Ram by depicting him as casting away only a shadow Sita—not the real one. I personally even object to the first *agniparīksha.*

"He should have trusted his wife and taken her word. That is how an ideal husband should behave. A good husband is one who assumes equal responsibility for the running of the household. After all, a family cannot be a one-person show. He should provide not just economic, but also moral and emotional, support to his wife. Most women have a fine sense of their responsibility, their *maryādā,* but men also need to realize their responsibilities.

"Lord Shiv comes closest to being an ideal husband, but I begin to doubt him as well. Lord Ram was Shiv's God to be worshipped according to Tulsi's Ramayana. How can he worship someone like Ram if Shiv is to be considered the model of an ideal husband? However, the popular and more accepted image of Shiv is that of a devoted husband. It is believed that devotees have to appeal to Parvati to get his blessings or boons. Hence the prayer *Om Namo Shivāyai* (I bow before Parvati) because she mediates between him and the world." Commonly, many Hindus perceive Shiv as the easiest to please among the various gods, requiring no mediation, even though Parvati carries a lot of influence with him. Nonetheless, Neerja bestows on Parvati the power to control people's access to Shiv. She also asserts firmly that Sita is still a valid ideal for today's world: "If you cannot enter marriage with a Sita-like commitment you may as well not get married." However, in the same breath she adds, "Even though every woman enters marriage in the same spirit, very few find themselves in conducive circumstances. So you have to do a bit of tit for tat, to fight for your rights in today's world. Sita lives up to the ideal of a wife fully. However, her appealing to Mother Earth to take her back into her bosom should not be interpreted as suicide. It is a statement of protest, that things had gone beyond her endurance limit. It amounted to saying: 'No more of this shit.' I don't think a woman should commit suicide if her husband deserts her. You can't destroy yourself for a man."

When I ask her what she would do in Sita's predicament, her reply shows characteristic ambivalence: "I might just have a breakdown. However, I would first try to persuade him that he is wrong. But if that doesn't work, I will go my own way." Does that mean she will remarry and build a new life? "No, I will never go for remarriage. A second marriage is even more risky. Where is the guarantee that the next fellow will be any better? Go my own way means I will go ahead and fulfill my responsibility toward the family, my children. I will not abandon my duty mid-stream."

She admits to having a rather unreasonable husband who, she says, "acts like a boss even at home," whereas she feels that at home men should act as husbands and fathers, leaving their egos and bossiness outside. She doesn't consider her own marriage a happy one, but she says it gives her satisfaction and pride that other people think hers is a very good marriage. "When people comment that we are an ideal couple, on the one hand it hurts a lot but at the same time I feel happy that I have been able to maintain such a good façade. After all, social respect is very important for one's survival."

She feels strongly that women must fight for their rights in marriage; however, she is also very clear that she will never fight back with her husband's weapons: "Sometimes he uses foul and abusive language. That is when I don't take it any more, I just stop talking to him. I am very clear on this point. I will not stoop down to his level, not retaliate in the same demeaning way—no tit for tat."

Devyani, a Brahmin from eastern Bihar, works as a domestic servant and masseuse. Her husband used to beat her frequently and brutally. Over the years she has worked hard to tilt the scales in her favour by finding ways to earn more than he does; he earns little and contributes even less to the family budget. She takes primary responsibility—financial and otherwise—for her three children. Her only daughter recently got married out of Devyani's savings without any monetary help from her husband. She has had extra-marital affairs—including a longstanding one with one of her brothers-in-law. A very attractive woman, she enjoys using her charm on men. For years she had such a bad marriage that she would have happily left her husband, had she found someone really responsible. She feels marrying a second time is okay, but "one has to put a full-stop there and settle down whether the second husband is good or bad, because a woman can't be forever changing husbands." Thus, she is not enamoured with the notion of strict monogamy.

Yet even in her view, an ideal wife is one who acts like Sita, though she is quite harsh in her view of Ram as a husband: "He cruelly drove out even such a *Mahā Satī*. She was able to retain social respect because she was a *Satī-Sāvitrī*. But if a woman's own husband is to start stigmatising her—where is she to go? Sita was lucky that old *Bābā* [Valmiki] in the forest gave her shelter. But will a woman find anyone to shelter her in today's world? Even if the whole of society is bad, a woman can live a good life as long as she has a good husband. But if her husband turns out to be bad, there is no place left for a woman. This fellow Ram, he really broke his wife's heart!"

She too feels that "a good housewife requires a husband like Bhole Shankar [Shiv] who never caused pain to his wife and always listened to her in everything. Ramji went around trying to be a great man in society while he treated his own wife with such cruelty. There are lots of men like that, who ruin their own wife in trying to act very pious outside. If I got a husband like Shiv I would really worship him, as one does even now for his devotion to Parvati. He never once betrayed her."

Interestingly, Sita's appeal transcends religious barriers. Several of my Muslim students and colleagues also mentioned Sita as an example of the perfect wife.

Razia, a woman in her mid-forties, is respected by most of those who know her because she is very quiet, dignified, and easy to get along with. She was widowed after eight years of what was a very happy marriage to a medical doctor. He not only earned well but treated her with love and affection and took great delight in providing her with all possible comforts, even luxuries. His sudden death from a heart attack came as a big blow, shattering her emotional life. She has raised two small children alone, depending only on her own income and strength. Her in-laws virtually turned her out of her marital home and she had to fight hard to secure even a portion of her husband's own property, since her in-laws wanted to grab it all. Razia's husband was virtually the only earning member in his family and he had supported not only his parents but also his sister and two brothers, including one older than him.

When asked about her notion of an ideal wife, she responded: "I can't mention an example from real life because you can't really tell from outside what is the actual situation in a family. But among historical/religious figures, Sita undoubtedly comes to mind first of all. She made it her aim to live for Ram and his children. She sacrificed her all for him. That is why she rose above ordinary human beings. I have done exactly the same in my own life. My husband was such an ideal husband—one could not ask for better. That is why I kept his name connected to mine even after his death. Had I remarried, I would be known as someone else's wife. Whatever tasks he left incomplete, I have tried to fulfill. However, even if I had not been lucky enough to marry such a good man, I still would have done the same. After children come, your target in life is their well-being and future—not just your own fulfillment. Unless you are willing to sacrifice your own self-interest, you will never be held up as an example for others." Does her family hold her up as an example? "Yes, they certainly do, and respect me a lot for having performed my responsibility so well despite such odds."

What is her notion of an ideal husband? "One who understands his wife and respects her wishes." Who would she hold up as an example? She too rejects Ram and says: "I don't know other examples in the Hindu tradition, but in our Muslim tradition we hold up the Prophet as an example of an ideal husband." What about his having several wives? "He did not do it for himself but for the welfare of those women. But he kept all of them happy." I ask her, would she accept being one of many wives? What if her husband had married three other wives? "I couldn't have tolerated it. Actually, in real life it is impossible for a woman to be happy in the presence of co-wives. Leave alone keeping four of them happy, it is quite an achievement if you make even one wife happy. Very few men succeed in that. So four is out of the question."

Thus, while Razia feels the Sita ideal is still valid and something she has tried to live up to fairly successfully in her own lifetime, she rules out the acceptability of a Prophet-like husband in today's world because she feels the Prophet's example can only be followed in a distorted way.

## Men's Responses

There is virtually no gender divide in India as regards views of Sita. It is not just women who hold Sita as an ideal; men, too, bow before her in reverence. However, while for most women Sita represents an ideal wife, men mostly think of her as Sita Mata (*jagajananī*). She is not just the daughter of Earth but Mother Earth herself, who inspires awe and reverence rather than evokes images of a desirable spouse. As a 23-year-old young man from my neighborhood put it: "Sita is like a mother to whom you go for blessings. You can't think of her as a wife because you never feel anywhere near equal to her." She is an object of worship rather than an object of desire. Her blessings prove as precious as her curse could be deadly because it would be born out of deep anguish, not mere anger. She seems too formidable a match in her role as a wife, but when put on the motherly pedestal she becomes nurturing and compassionate.

Indian men, on the whole, no less emphatically condemn Ram as an unfair husband who treated the most virtuous of wives shabbily and cruelly. Men relate to her as a much wronged, but awe-inspiring, mother whose hurt they have to ameliorate much in the way that Lakshman and Lav-Kush will battle on her behalf with Lord Ram himself. Ghanshyam, who works as a peon in an office in Delhi, sums up Ram's fatal flaw appropriately in a way that denies him any special privileges on account of his obsession with being a good king. "He can't be anyone's idea of a good husband because he was suspicious, unreasonable, and easily misled by rumors."

Hindi writer Pandit Buddhinath Mishra describes Sita Marhi, the birthplace of Sita, as the most important *tīrtha* (pilgrimage site) on this earth because *Ādyashakti* (The Primordial [Female] Power) appeared in this land as the daughter of earth and went back to Mother Earth after disdainfully rejecting all the riches of Raja Ram.[2]

India's leading socialist thinker, Ram Manohar Lohia, went the farthest in rejecting Ram as a husband. I quote: "Of all the three or four faults I see in Ram, his treatment of Sita is the worst of all. Sometimes in argument young men try to present Ram as a devotee of democracy [who listened to his citizens] and, therefore, foresook Sita at the saying of a dhobi . . . Even if one were to grant this, how do we justify the first *agniparīksha*? What was the compulsion then? Is it democracy that one man's opinion becomes so supreme? The question is, even if we grant that he was a great devotee of democracy, did he have no other options? Could he not give up his throne and accompany Sita to the forest? The whole episode stinks . . . It often causes much surprise for me. How can any woman in India have affection for Ram considering the way he behaved with Sita?"[3]

Then referring to some North Indian women's folk songs in which Ram is roundly abused for his misdemeanor, Lohia goes on to say: "In India there have been lakhs and crores of women who have called Ram a sinner on behalf of Sita at the time of childbirth, marriage and such occasions . . . The people who write books are polite and well mannered but the laboring women who work in the fields . . . their heart's bruises sometimes speak . . . the word sinner is strong indeed. Only those women who labor in other people's farms, who are used to earning their living from hard labor, can dare speak such words. The others perhaps won't dare."[4]

However, as we have seen in the interviews quoted above, upper-class women and men do not hesitate either to use fairly tough words against Ram when he is pitched against Sita. After all, even his own doting brother Lakshman, who treated his word as sacred, turned against Ram over Sita. The arch devotee Hanuman's sympathy also lay with Sita, not to mention Sita's most ardent champions against Ram—her sons Luv and Kush. Valmiki too is on Sita's side. On this one question Ram is declared guilty by one and all.

Ram may have forsaken Sita, but the power of popular sentiment has kept them united. Her name precedes Ram's in the popular greeting in North India: *Jai Sīya Rām,* as also in several *bhajans* and chants. People see him as incomplete without her. The injustice done to Sita seems to weigh very heavily on the collective conscience of men in India. The few who try to find justification for Ram's cruel behavior toward Sita take pains to explain it in one of the following ways: a) Ram did not doubt Sita personally but he had to respond to the demands of his dharma as a king; he knew she was innocent but he had to show his citizens that, unlike his father, he was not a slave to a woman, and that he was a just king willing to make personal sacrifices for them; b) he suffered no less since it was an act of sacrifice for him as well and he lived an ascetic life afterwards; c) he banished only the shadow of Sita, while keeping the real Sita by his side all the time.

The interpretation of Shastri Pandurang V. Athavale, foremost socioreligious reformer and founder of the Swadhaya movement, typifies the far-fetched apologia offered by those who wish to exonerate Ram. They even drag in the modern-day sacrosanct notion of nationalism in an attempt to explain away his conduct: "What we have to remember is that it was not Ram who abandoned Sita; in reality it was the king who abandoned the queen, in the performance of his duty." He had to "choose between a family and a nation. Ram sacrificed his personal happiness for the national interest and Sita extended her full co-operation to Ram. To perform his duty as a king, Ram had sacrificed his queen, not his wife . . . . At the time of performing the *ashvamedha yajña* [horse sacrifice proclaiming royal sovereignty], many requested Ram to marry another woman [which could be done according to the command of holy scriptures]. Ram firmly replied to them: 'In the heart of Ram there is a place for only one woman and that one is Sita.'" Athavale is at pains to point out that Ram's abandonment of Sita was a symbol of the highest self-sacrifice. "Sita was dearer to Ram than his own life. He had never doubted the chastity of Sita . . . For had it been so, he would not have kept by his side the golden image of Sita during the sacrificial rites."[5]

However, even a passionate devotee of Ram like Athavale finds it hard to justify all of Ram's actions. "Once Ram appeared callous, even cruel. Upon the death of Ravana, after the battle of Lanka, an extremely happy Sita appears before Ram. Sternly Ram says to her, 'I do not want you who has been looked at and touched by another person. You may go wherever you want to. You may go either to Bharata, Laxmana, Shatrughna, or Vibhishana and stay with any of them.' We do not know for what purpose he was so harsh, or what he intended to convey to Sita by these words, but it is equally certain that they were terrible words . . . Even the people who heard Ram saying such bitter words wept. Everyone felt the bitterness of those words, the injustice that was done, but none dared to protest or plead."[6]

I have never heard any man unconditionally endorse Ram's behavior toward Sita. He has not been forgiven this one injustice through all these centuries, despite his other great virtues. The film *Sampoorna Ramayan,* made by Bollywood director Wadia, goes so far as to declare that Ramrajya is worthless if it fails to give justice to women. Encouraged and trained by the sage Valmiki himself, Luv and Kush take upon themselves to vindicate Sita's honor before Ayodhya's people and win over their hearts by singing the challenging song summarized below:

> Till such time as the miseries of the Sitas of Bharat are ameliorated, O Ram, your Ramayan will never be complete. [*He Rām tumhārī Rāmāyaṇ tab tak hogi Sampūrṇa nahin*] . . . As long as the maker of Ramrajya listens to a dhobi and deceitfully abandons the mother of Bharat's future in a forest, till then poet Valmiki is not capable of finishing his Ramayan. When state policy becomes evil (*nīti* becomes *anīti*) and injures the pure life of a woman; when Jagdamba (Mother of Creatures) herself is made to burn in fire, that is the sure sign of decline of a civilisation.

Harsh words these! They question the claims of Ramraj on account of injustice done to one woman! But that one woman has come to represent the entire *nārī jāti* (womankind).

## Sita as Mithila's Daughter

The most powerful indictment, however, comes from the people of Mithila, the region which is the parental homeland of Sita, through numerous folk songs of the region. An account of what the injustice done to Sita means to the people of Mithila comes through poignantly in several of the accounts by leading Hindi writers published in the form of a travelogue. Organised by the doyen of Hindi literature, Sachidanand Vatsyayan, in the early 1980's, the project called for a large group of Hindi writers to travel through the region connected with Sita's name. They started at her birthplace, Sitamarhi, went on to Janakpur, came to Ayodhya, and ended their journey in Chitrakoot. Various writers explain the purpose of this project as an exploration of why and how the Ramayana, the story of Ram and Janaki, and the locales associated with their names, have become part of people's consciousness and have influenced the value system of the educated, as well as the illiterate, and thereby defined their cultural identity.[7]

They say that Sita belongs to the very consciousness of Mithila—present in the land, in the water, and in the air. "Her pain sits heavy on the hearts of Mithila's people."[8] Sita is not just the daughter of Janaka in this region but a daughter of all of Mithila because, as the folk songs of this region testify, popular sentiment says that had Raja Janaka, by some chance, not gone to plough the fields that particular day, someone else from any *jāti* might have gone and found her. In that case she would have become that person's daughter. Therefore, Sita is treated as everyone's daughter in Mithila. Just as in Mithila the entire village is considered as one's *naihar* (parental home)—not just one's actual father's abode—various folk songs show the entire people of Mithila grieving over Sita's fate.[9] Some songs depict women of different strata pleading with their respective husbands to go and fetch her after Ram sends her away. However, Sita in her pride and dignity refuses to return and brings up her two sons all on her own.

Various writers of this anthology describe the dignity with which Sita suffered privations after Ram's painful rejection, and how it has remained alive in people's consciousness as if their own daughter experienced this injustice. Even today, the people of Mithila avoid marrying off their daughters in Marg-Shish because Sita got married during that month. Even today, the people of Mithila do not want to marry their daughters into families living in Avadh—in fact anywhere west of Mithila. They repeatedly recite Sita's name in marriage songs but Ram's name is omitted. At the end of the song there is usually one line which says "such a Sita was married into Raghukul" (the family name of Ram).[10] A beautiful folk song of Mithila, quoted by Usha Kiran Khan, depicts a daughter telling her father what kind of a groom he should find for her. After describing various qualities she is looking for, the daughter advises her father: "Go search in the north, go south, or get me a groom from the east. But don't go westward, O Father, get me a groom from the north."[11]

This daughter of Mithila has a status higher than that of Ram in her own region. Various polemical songs depict Ram as inferior to Sita.[12] The people of Mithila never tire of advising one to remember that Ram had to prove himself worthy of Sita before her father offered his daughter to him. This is how one of the folk songs of this region describes it: "Every day Sita used to clean and smear cowdung in the temple courtyard. One day her father Janaka saw her lift the heavy Shiv bow with her left hand while smearing with her right hand the floor where the bow was kept. At that very moment he vowed that he would marry his daughter only to such a man who had the valor to break that bow into nine pieces. Hence, the condition of *swayaṃvara* that Sita would be given in marriage to a man who could break the bow and thereby demonstrate exceptional strength. People of Mithila still believe that though Ram passed the initial test of winning her, he failed to prove a worthy husband."[13]

Another writer, Shankar Dayal Singh, commented on how he sensed the pervasive sentiment of anguish and pain in the collective consciousness of this region's people at the injustice done to Sita. He goes on to say: "This region has taken a strange revenge in a silent way. From Pauranic times, everywhere, in every village and small town (*qasba*) are found Shri Janaki mandirs, where Ram and Lakshmana are also present along with Janaki. But the temples are named after Sita as evidence that somewhere the pain of Sita is still hurting the people's collective consciousness, as though to say: Ram, you made our Sita walk barefoot in the forests. Ravana challenged your manhood and forcibly carried away (abducted) Sita. Though this mother of the universe (*Jagajananī*) went through the fire ordeal to prove her innocence, you abandoned her. Our daughter, our sister, was treated thus by Ayodhya. But we are careful of our *maryādā* [honor, propriety]. That is why, O Ram, we will keep your idol in the temple. We will even worship it, but the temple will be known in Sita's name. That is why the whole area is littered with Shri Janaki mandirs. There are Sita legends attached to every spot, even trees and ponds."[14]

Vatsyayan comments on how in Chitrakoot people offered them leaves from a tree believed to be the one from which the abandoned Sita used to eat in order to still her hunger. What is the proof offered? The leaves taste sour but if you drink water after chewing some, the water tastes sweet. So the lore has it that Sita used to drink water after filling her stomach with these leaves and that sweet aftertaste helped sustain her. Thus, her memory is kept alive in the natural, and not just the cultural, landscape of Mithila.[15] As writer Lakshmi Kant Varma sums it up: "Sita's *sahanshīltā* [the quality of dignified tolerance] is written on every leaf of Balmiki Nagar"—the ashram where she spent her years of banishment.[16]

## Mahatma Gandhi's Sita

The Sita symbol has been used by a whole range of reformers to convey radical messages. For instance, Sita was also Mahatma Gandhi's favorite symbol in his attempt to reach women with a message of self-respect, autonomy, and faith in their own strength. Gandhi, more than any other leader, exhorted women to break the shackles imposed upon them by society, overthrow repressive traditions, leave narrow domesticity and claim their rightful place in the social and political life of the country, rather than live a life of hapless dependence. He encouraged many women to stay unmarried so that they could devote themselves to social causes. And yet Sita proved his favorite heroine, not to be dismissed as a mere legendary figure. It was Sita's higher type of valor which he wanted Indian women to cultivate: "A woman in our country was brought up to think that her place was with her husband or on the funeral pyre." He would "far rather see India's women trained to wield arms than that they should feel helpless."[17]

However, a Sita would not need arms to protect her—those were the weapons of the weak, in Gandhi's view. The real strength of a woman was her "purity" and "fearlessness." This "dazzling purity" could disarm even the most beastly of men. "It is my firm conviction that a fearless woman who knows that her purity is her best shield can never be dishonoured."[18] Gandhi argues that even the great physical might of Ravana dwindled when pitched against Sita's moral courage; he dared not touch her against her will even while she was held captive by him in his own palace. To Gandhi, "Sita was no slave of Rama."[19] Long before feminists articulated the notion of marital rape, thereby implying that husbands could not demand sex from an unwilling wife as a marital obligation, Mahatma Gandhi took an unequivocal stand advocating a woman's autonomy over her own body. Once again Sita was used to drive this message home: "Woman must cease to consider herself the object of man's lust . . . I cannot imagine Sita even wasting a single moment on pleasing Rama by physical charms."[20] A woman could say "no" even to her husband if he approached her carnally against her will. "I want woman to learn the primary right of resistance. She thinks now that she has not got it."[21] He insisted that a woman had the right to her own body which she does not surrender for a lifetime with marriage.

Gandhi's Sita is no doubt made to exemplify many characteristics that many dominant Ramayanas do not portray as characteristics of Sita. For example, in his version she becomes a symbol of swadeshi. Gandhi could not imagine Sita "wearing foreign finery! Sita was the soul of *Ramrajya*."[22] "In the days of Sita every household had its *charkha* just as they had a hearth in every home. Sita also spun her own *charkha* which might have been bedecked with jewels and probably ornamented with gold, but all the same it was still a *charkha*."[23] He popularized khadi by telling women: "as a first step towards attaining bodily purity you must wear pure, homespun khadi just as Sita did in days of old."[24] Mahatma Gandhi expected modern-day Sitas not to just sit at home serving their men endlessly but to come out of the house and show leadership in working for women's rights. But they were also to become leaders of men. Modern Sitas should "teach the art of peace to the warring world thirsting for that nectar."[25] For Gandhi, like Sita, "woman is the embodiment of sacrifice and therefore, nonviolence." Nonetheless, one should not mistake woman's spirit of self sacrifice for passivity and slavery to her husband; Gandhi encouraged contemporary Sitas to practice *satyāgraha* against their husbands. He asked women not to co-operate with their menfolk, to refuse to cook for them, and even starve themselves in protest so long as men "do not wash their hands of dirty communal squabbles."[26] He was convinced that "in this war against war, women of the world will and should lead. It is their special vocation and privilege."[27]

Though Gandhi adds many new meanings to the Sita symbol, the active pacifist role that he has in mind for her is not altogether alien to even Valmiki's Sita. The *Araṇya Kāṇḍa* of Valmiki's *Rāmāyaṇa* records an interesting interaction between Ram and Sita where she actually admonishes him for becoming too prone to violence: "Three evils are born of desire: speaking untruth . . . coveting another's wife and harming those against whom one has no quarrel . . . And this third great evil, thirst for blood where there is no enmity, to which the ignorant are prone, seems to be alarmingly near you."[28] Gandhi repeatedly emphasized that an important reason for his choosing nonviolent *satyāgraha* as the method and philosophy of his struggle was so that women could play a leading role in the freedom movement, as well as in public life. He discouraged them from channeling all their energies into domesticity and wifely duties. Instead he wanted modern-day Sitas to become the leaders of men in rebuilding India as a just, self governing, and exploitation-free society.

## Freeing Sitas from Bondage

In recent years, Sharad Joshi of Shetkari Sangathana has developed an equally creative use of the Sita symbol. I witnessed the power of Sita's story to move men's hearts in large areas of Maharashtra when I was working with Shetkari Sangathana on the Lakshmi Mukti programme, part of the Sangathana's campaign to empower women with economic rights. (Sita is believed to be an incarnation of Lakshmi.) The Lakshmi Mukti campaign tried to communicate the idea that the peasantry could not get a fair deal or prosper, as long as the curse of Sita Mata stayed on them, as long as they kept their *gṛhalakshmīs* (household goddesses of prosperity) enslaved by keeping them economically dependent and powerless in the family. Sharad Joshi, the Sangathana leader, emphasized that the followers of the Sangathana should not wait for government laws to be framed to enforce the economic rights of women. Instead, farmers should do it voluntarily as a long overdue gesture of gratitude towards their own Lakshmis.

The Sangathana announced in 1989 that any village in which a hundred or more families voluntarily transferred a piece of land to the wife's name would be honored as a Lakshmi Mukti gaon (a village which had liberated its hitherto enslaved Lakshmis) through a public function in which Sharad Joshi would personally distribute certificates of honor to each such family. During the campaign tours to persuade the peasant followers of Shetkari Sangathana to voluntarily transfer a portion of the family land to the wife's name, Sharad Joshi's speeches revolved around the Sita story, which seems to have played a big role in evoking a positive response from the men. Joshi would explain the Lakshmi Mukti campaign by first pointing out how a farmer's wife toils for her family selflessly and how crucial her labor and care prove for the well-being of the family. Then he would go on to ask his audience: "But then, how do we men treat our Lakshmis? Often no better than Ram treated Sita, one of the best wives anyone could have." He would then go on to recount the kind of sacrifices Sita made for Ram and talk of her devotion and loyalty:

> When Ram was banished to 14 years of forest exile, Kaikeyi had not demanded that Sita go with him. She could well have remained in the palace, but Sita insisted that wherever Ram goes, there goes Sita. She said, my place is by your side. She suffered numerous privations

> for him joyfully. Finally Ravana abducts Sita for no fault of hers, but to teach Ram a lesson for his misbehavior with Ravana's sister. Though Ravana respected Sita's chastity and did not violate Sita against her will, her own husband subjected her to the cruel humiliation of *agnipariksha* to prove her chastity. Even fire could not touch her, but on their return to his kingdom, at the mere hint of a slanderous remark by a dhobi, Ram asks Lakshmana to take Sita away and leave her in a forest. He does not ever personally explain anything to her.

And then step by step Joshi expatiated on the cruelty of Ram, arguing that even if his dharma as a king demanded the sacrifice of his marriage, he could have behaved more humanely towards her.

> In that entire capital of Ayodhya, this queen could not call any place her own for mere shelter. Could Ram not have told his queen that though they could not continue living together as husband and wife because of the opinions of Ayodhya's citizens, she could live apart in another palace? Or offered her a small house? Or at least a small room or dungeon where she could live quietly with her children? But no, Maharani Sita became a *bhikārinī* [beggar] overnight simply because her husband turned against her and pushed her out. It did not occur to him that if his subjects were not willing to accept her, that he too could have followed her example. He could go along with her after saying to his subjects "If Sita is not good enough to be your queen, then my place is by her side. I cannot stay here either."

Joshi emphasized the cruelty of a king who lived in a palace after making his wife and children beg for food.

Joshi would then go on to narrate the legend associated with the Sita Mandir at Raveri village in Yeotmal district, whose existence was brought to our notice by Sangathana workers from that area. There are few Ram Mandirs without Sita, but there is at least this one Sita Mandir without Ram. The region's lore maintains that after being banished by Ram, Sita roamed from village to village as a destitute woman. When she came to Raveri village, she was in an advanced stage of pregnancy. She begged for food but the villagers, for some reason, did not oblige. She cursed the village, vowing that no grain would ever grow in their fields. The villagers say that until the advent of hybrid wheat, for centuries no grain grew in their village, though plenty grew in neighboring villages. The villagers all believe in Sita Mai's curse. Her two sons were both said to have been born on the outskirts of the village, where a temple was built commemorating Sita Mata's years of abandoment.

After narrating the Sita Mandir story, Joshi would go on to warn his audience of the curses of their Sitas. Hence their poverty, their inability to obtain their due from society and the consequent economic and social slavery. He told his followers that redressing the wrongs done to their own Sitas was a precondition for the peasantry's success in their fight for justice, and effective resistance of their own exploitation. He would conclude by saying that the Lakshmi Mukti programme aimed to ensure that no modern day Sita would ever have to suffer the fate of Ram's Sita because she had nothing to call her own. By transferring land to their wives, they were paying off "a long overdue debt" to Sita Mata. He would then explain at great length the privations their own Sitas suffered, the hard work they put in, and the sacrifices they made in order to keep the family going.

In village after village I would see men reduced to tears listening to the story of Sita. Hundreds of villages have already carried out the Lakshmi Mukti programme of land transfer to wives. Most of the villages that carried out Lakshmi Mukti celebrated it as though a big festival. The entire village would be cleaned up and decorated, with men dancing to the beat of drums. We would be received with much fanfare by women performing *ārtī* and singing songs. Men seemed even more elated than women and much of the initiative for preparing villages for Lakshmi Mukti came from young male cadres of the Sangathana. Some of the men I interviewed described the whole campaign as a *mahāyajña* (great sacrificial ritual). Within a couple of years hundreds of villages had already been honored as Lakshmi Mukti gaons; hundreds more had volunteered to follow suit. The occasion would attract many people from neighboring villages. After each public meeting, men from the surrounding villages would volunteer to effect similar transfers of land in their own village, provided Joshi joined them likewise for the celebration.

In addition to the charisma and credibility of Sharad Joshi, I attribute the appeal of the movement also to the power of the Sita story. Men were told they were atoning for the wrongdoing of Ram and they felt good about being called upon to do this. Sharad Joshi himself admits that the Sita story moves him so profoundly that he himself has been reduced to tears whenever he reads those sections of the Ramayana which describe Ram's banishment of Sita. In his view, Valmiki introduces the injustice to Sita not to hold up Sita's dignified suffering as an example for women but to turn people against Ram-like behavior. "Why otherwise would he show him behaving so crudely in those episodes, even though Ram never loses his dignity elsewhere, no matter how difficult the circumstances? He could have easily made Ram into as perfect a husband as he was a son. Instead, by saddling him with such a flaw, such crudity of behavior in contrast to Sita's dignity, Valmiki wants to show how difficult it is for even supposedly perfect men to behave justly towards their wives."

## The Importance of being Sita

Hindus talk of Ram, Sita, Shiv, Parvati, and sundry other gods in very human ways and feel no hesitation in passing moral judgment on them. In other words, gods and goddesses are expected to live up to the expectations of fair play demanded by their present-day devotees, who are ordinary mortals. Their praiseworthy actions are neatly sifted from those where the gods fail to uphold dharmic conduct. Such criticism and condemnation do not imply people are irreligious or irreverent; instead they acknowledge that even gods are neither perfect nor infallible. This provides a far greater sense of freedom and volition to individuals within the Hindu faith than in religions where god's commandments must be obeyed unconditionally and the god is upheld as a symbol of infallibility.

The continuing hold of Sita on popular imagination is part of a larger belief system. It is a common sentiment among Indian women (and men) that ideals set in bygone ages are still valid and worth emulating, though they admit few people manage to follow them in today's world.[29] Many women actually try to shape themselves in the Sita mould. For instance, in a study carried out in Uttar Pradesh, 500 boys and 360 girls between the ages of 9 and 22 years were asked to select the ideal woman from a list of 24 names of gods, goddesses, heroes, and heroines of history. Sita was seen as the ideal woman by an overwhelming proportion of the respondents; there were no age or sex differences.[30] That was a 1957 survey. However, Sita continues to command similar reverence today even among modern educated people in India. Ram and Sita are not seen as remote figures out of a distant past to be dismissed lightly just because we are living in a different age and have evolved different lifestyles.

They are living role models, seen as having set standards so superior that they are hard to emulate for those living in more corrupt ages, the products of kaliyuga.

Despite such positive associations in the popular mind, Sita is not a favorite with some feminists. Certain feminists dismiss her outright and many, in fact, condemn her as a harmful, negative role model. Some of those who disapprove of Sita-like behavior tend to present Draupadi as an alternative role model. One example is Meenakshi Mukherjee's article, where she regrets that the Sita ideal, which represents the "dead weight of tradition," is far more popular today than previously. In her view, Sita is a woman who "subordinates her individual will to the wishes of her husband." Draupadi by contrast "clenched her fists and cursed, she burned with anger that her husbands were incapable of avenging the insults she had suffered."[31] However, Draupadi has failed to become a comparably popular symbol. One reason could be that the idea of being wedded to five husbands does not seem attractive to most women, when some wives find it hard enough to cope with one. But there are other reasons too.

Indian women are not endorsing female slavery when they mention Sita as their ideal. They do not perceive Sita as a mindless creature who meekly suffers maltreatment at the hands of her husband without complaining. Nor does accepting Sita as an ideal mean endorsing a husband's right to behave unreasonably and a wife's duty to bear insults graciously. Instead, she is seen as a person whose sense of dharma is superior to and more awe-inspiring than that of Ram—someone who puts even *maryādā puruṣottam* Ram—the most perfect of men—to shame. Most women (and even men) I have spoken to on the subject refer to her as a "flawless" person, overlooking even those episodes where she acts unreasonably (e.g., her humiliating Lakshman with crude allegations about his intentions towards her), whereas they see Ram as possessing a major flaw in his otherwise respectworthy character because of the way he behaves towards his wife and children.

Thus, not just modern-day Sitas but even many traditional women and men reject Ram as an appropriate husband. Hindu women's favorite husband has forever been Bhole Shiv Shankar—the innocent, the trusting, the all-devoted spouse who allowed his wife to guide his life and his decisions. Unmarried women keep fasts on Monday, the day assigned for Lord Shiv, and pray that they may be blessed with Parvati's good fortune. Shiv and Parvati are the most celebrated and happy couple in Hindu mythology, representing perfect joy in togetherness, including in their sexual union. Their mutual devotion, companionship and respect for each other are legendary. Most important of all, the modern domesticated Shiv is not seen as a bossy husband demanding unconditional obedience but as one who respected his wife's wishes, even her trivial whims.

Pauranic descriptions of Shiv show him as the least domesticated and the most rebellious of all the gods, one whose appearance and adventures border on the weird. He is so unlike a normal husband that Sati's father never forgives her for marrying Shiv. Yet, Hindu women have selectively domesticated him for their purpose, emphasizing his devotion to Sati/Parvati as well as the fact that he allowed his spouse an important role in influencing his decisions. At the same time these women conveniently overlook the many very prominent and contradictory aspects of his life and deeds. Interestingly, Parvati is not just seen as *gṛhalakshmī,* as someone whose reign is confined to the domestic sphere. She also controls and guides Shiv's dealings with the outside world, constantly goading him to be more generous, compassionate and sensitive to the needs of his devotees. While there has been a lot of discussion and analysis of the demands put on women in the Hindu tradition and the sacrifices expected of ideal wives, we have failed to evaluate the demands put on an ideal husband. The Hindu tradition might valorize wives who put up with tyrannical husbands gracefully, but it does not valorize unreasonable husbands. On the contrary, it places heavy demands on them and expects high levels of sexual and emotional loyalty from them if they are to qualify as "good husbands." Shiv, for instance, is perceived as someone who cannot live without Parvati.

There are also several practical reasons why Sita-like behavior makes sense to many Indian women. The outcome of marriage in India depends not just on the attitude of a husband, but as much on the kind of relationship a woman has with her marital family and extended kinship group. If, like Sita, she commands respect and affection from the latter, she can frequently count on them to intervene on her behalf and keep her husband from straying, from behaving unreasonably. Similarly, once her children grow up, they can often play an effective role in protecting her from being needlessly bullied by her husband, and bring about a real change in the power equation in the family, because in India children, especially sons, frequently continue living with their parents even after they grow up. A woman can hope to get her marital relatives and her children to act in her favor only if she is seen as being more or less above reproach.

Most women realize the difficulties of making men assume their domestic responsibilities. Social and familial controls must encourage men to keep their commitment to providing a stable home and prevent them from extra-marital affairs which can seriously jeopardize the stability of a marriage. Thus, many women avoid taking on the ways of men. To respond to a husband's irresponsibility by seeking a divorce or having an affair herself would only allow a man further excuses to legitimize his irresponsible behavior. Thus, behaving like Sita can function as a strategy to domesticate men, to minimize the risk of marriage breakdown, and to avoid the status of being a single parent, with its consequent effect on children. A man breaking off with a Sita-like wife is likely to invite widespread disapproval in his social circle and is, therefore, more likely to be kept under a measure of restraint, even if he has a tendency to stray.

Even the gods revere Sita, a woman who refuses to accept her husband's tyranny yet remains steadfast in her love for him and loyalty to him to the very end. Many people perceive Sita's steadfastness as a sign of emotional strength and not slavery, because she refuses to forsake her dharma, even though Ram forsook his dharma as a husband. That various gods themselves come down to earth to defend her without her soliciting their help—unlike Draupadi, who appeals to Krishna to intervene—and express disapproval of what Ram does to her, shows that she is more revered than he is.

Sita's offer of *agniparīksha* and her coming out of it unscathed does not signify an act of slavish surrender to the whims of an unreasonable husband; instead, it is an act of defiance that challenges her husband's aspersions, a means of showing him to be so flawed in his judgment that the gods have to come to show up Ram for his foolishness. She emerges as a woman that even *Agni* (the fire god)—who has the power to destroy everything he touches—dare not touch or harm. Thus, in popular perception Sita's *agniparīksha* does not belong in the same category as the mandatory virginity tests that Diana had to go through in order to prove herself a suitable bride for Prince Charles, but rather is seen as an act of supreme defiance on her part which shows her husband to be unjust and foolish in doubting a woman like her. It only underscores the point that Ram is emotionally unreliable and that he behaved like a petty minded, stupidly mistrustful, jealous husband and showed himself to be a slave to social opinion.

The refusal of Sita to perform a second *agniparīksha*—which Ram demands in addition to the first one that she had offered in defiance—sticks in the popular imagination not as an act of self-annihilation but as a momentous but dignified rejection of Ram as a husband. Note that Sita is considered the foremost of the *Mahāsatīs* even though she rejected Ram's tyrannical demand of that final fire ordeal so resolutely and refused to come back and live with him. Humbled, he is left grieving for her; even his own sons reject him. Ram may not have rejected her as a wife but only as a queen in deference to social opinion, but Sita rejects him as a husband. In Kalidasa's *Raghuvaṃśa,* after her banishment by Ram, Sita does not address Ram as *Aryaputra* (a term for husband that literally translates as son of my father-in-law) but refers to him as "king" instead. For instance, when Lakshman comes to her with Ram's message, she conveys her rejection of him as her husband in the following words: "Tell the king on my behalf that even after finding me pure after the fire ordeal held in your presence, now you have chosen to leave me because of public slander. Do you think it is befitting the noble family into which you were born?"[32]

The final rejection of Ram by Sita has come to acquire a much larger meaning in popular imagination than one woman's individual protest against the injustice done to her. It is a whole culture's rejection of Ram as a husband. For instance, people will say approvingly: "He is a Ram-like son, a Ram-like brother, or a Ram-like king." But they will never say as a mark of approval, "He is a Ram-like husband." To quote Sharad Joshi of Shetkari Sangathana, "If Ram had not been smart enough to win Sita for a wife by his skill in stringing Shiv's bow, if instead Janaka had decided to match their horoscope and it had predicted that Sita would abandon him, I doubt that Ram would have ever found a wife. No father would have consented to give his daughter to a man like Ram—his claims to godlike perfection notwithstanding." Most people I talked to echoed this sentiment: "*Rām honge baḍe ādmī par Sītā ne kyā sukh pāyā?*" (Ram may have been a great man, but what good did it do Sita?)

I have never heard even one person, man or woman, suggest that Sita should have gone through the second fire ordeal quietly and obediently and accepted life with her husband once again, although

I often hear people say that Ram had no business to reject her in the first place. Ram's rejection of Sita is almost universally condemned, while her rejection of him is held up as an example of supreme dignity. By that act she emerges supremely triumphant, simultaneously leaving a permanent stigma on Ram's name.

FIFTEEN

# The Ramlila Migrates to Southall

PAULA RICHMAN

On October 19, 1979, Southall Black Sisters (henceforth SBS),[1] a feminist group of South Asian and African Caribbean women from Southall, Greater London, ended their Ramlila, as usual, by burning an effigy of Ravana. Both their Ramlila and their representation of Ravana, however, proved unique in many ways. SBS framed and periodically interrupted their rendition of the Ramlila with humorous commentary that gave a topical slant to incidents, relating them to socio-economic conditions, domestic and national politics, and sexism. Ravana wore a huge mask, on which each of his ten heads had been drawn to represent an aspect of the racism that non-white groups in Britain encountered, including faces of Enoch Powell, Maggie Thatcher, and other political candidates, the insignia of the riot police, and an image standing for restrictive immigration laws.

This Ramayana performance presents some fresh and articulate voices telling Rama's story; it also discloses a great deal about how a religious text can migrate from South Asia to Britain, retain its formal contours, and express diverse aspects of the diaspora experience. The first section of this paper explores how the SBS Ramlila relates to the particular circumstances of migration that shaped the Southall community. Next I examine who produced this Ramayana telling and why they told the story as they did. The penultimate section considers the aspects of the SBS Ramlila that had the greatest impact on participants. Finally, I analyze how the SBS Ramlila relates to wider patterns within the performance traditions of Rama's story.

The account of the SBS Ramlila reconstructed here tells of an ephemeral performance that grew out of a specific set of circumstances and occurred at a precise moment in the history of South Asian immigration to the United Kingdom. Yet the lessons revealed in the play, and memories of it, yield more lasting insights about the diversity of the Ramayana tradition. Analysis of the SBS Ramlila, along with John Kelly's discussion of Rama's story in Fiji (the following essay), reveals the multivocality of symbols of evil and the ways in which migration shapes the meanings of Rama's story.

## South Asian Immigration to Southall

The SBS Ramlila responded to events that occurred in Southall, involved women who worked/lived in Southall, and took place in a building used historically for many activist endeavors in Southall. To reconstruct the history and meaning of this performance, therefore, we need to consider why Southall became a center for certain kinds of anti-racist activism in the 1970s, as the second major group of immigrants from South Asia joined forces with the earlier group who arrived in Greater London in the 1950s, as a consequence of the Partition of India in 1947.[2]

Primarily Sikhs or Hindus and mainly Punjabi speakers, many of those who arrived in the first cohort came from the peasant proprietor class and had lost land, savings, and security through the dislocation that accompanied Partition. A large number of them could find jobs only at factories in or near Southall at low pay, with long hours and few benefits. Many South Asian men worked on assembly lines and custodial crews in industries and at Heathrow Airport, while South Asian women were employed in large numbers in laundries and bakeries. Since the majority of early immigrants were not fluent in English, factory owners sought them as cheap labor unlikely to receive protection from the nearly all-white British unions.

Over the next decade, many men who planned a short stay in the U.K. to save money and return home ended up staying on, at least partially because minimal wages and high housing costs made it difficult to accrue savings. Gradually, some sponsored family members to join them in Southall. Elder males within the community who spoke fluent English helped new arrivals get settled, providing advice and temporary financial support. Some formed labor organizations to combat the racism of white unions and work towards promotion out of minimal-wage, low-status, physically demanding work in which they felt trapped.[3]

As the South Asian community in Southall grew, its members experienced increasing hostility from white residents. When South Asians attempted to purchase homes or gain admission to Council Housing near their workplace, they encountered major obstacles. As a result, in the 1960s Southall's housing problem became the worst in the borough, forcing immigrants to remain in crowded and substandard dwellings. South Asians also had to fight attempts to direct all immigrant children into the lowest academic tracks. Anxiety grew among white residents of Southall, who expressed fears of a "Black invasion" of housing and schools. As Tories called for a fifteen-year residence requirement to get onto Council Housing waiting lists, local government agencies began bussing immigrant children to schools far from Southall, so that they would not "overwhelm" the Southall schools.[4]

In the late 1960s and early 1970s a new group of South Asians, with a distinct migration history, joined the now-settled earlier immigrants of Southall. During the colonial period, the British Government had encouraged Indian traders and merchants to settle in its African colonies and function as economic middlemen between colonizers and their indigenous colonial subjects. Soon after independence, South Asians were ordered, at short notice, to relinquish their assets and leave Kenya (1967) and Uganda (1972). In response to this major dislocation among fairly prosperous South Asian immigrant communities in Africa, many of them—as British passport holders—came to England.

These new arrivals brought middle-class urban experience, as well as their skills as owners of small businesses.[5] As earlier and later immigrant groups merged talents and numbers, the South Asian community in Southall achieved a strength that made it unique in the United Kingdom, as a contemporary observer noted:

> [N]owhere else in Britain does an Asian community now have what Southall provides—its own cinemas (two show only Indian films), travel agents, marriage bureaux, banks, grocers, insurance agents, cafes and clothing and jewellery stores . . . Asians from all over Britain,

> and even from Europe, look to Southall for their household, social and cultural needs. Asians feel at home there; it is their town in a very real sense.[6]

Yet the highly publicized arrival of the new immigrants also brought increasing attacks on them.

Major attempts were mounted to prevent more immigrant arrivals and the National Front (henceforth NF), a party that presented itself as protecting the "racial purity" of England, stepped up the intensity of its attacks on immigration. The NF had begun as a marginal political entity, but gained increasing visibility by playing upon the notion that Britain was becoming "swamped" by outsiders.[7] In addition, incidents of racist-inspired maiming and killing of lone Black people by large bands of white youths encouraged many young South Asians to band together and take precautions to ensure self-defense. South Asians shared concern for their physical safety with African Caribbeans in the area, both of whom found themselves targeted not only by white youths but also by police brutality.

Alarm, therefore, met an announcement that the NF would hold an election meeting on April 23, 1979 in the Southall Town Hall, because the NF party was fielding a candidate within the borough. Area residents planned a peaceful demonstration to protest the NF meeting in the heart of their community: women and children would sit outside the Town Hall and, by their sheer numbers, prevent entrance to the meeting. Those in progressive movements throughout the country were asked to participate. On the meeting day, people active in liberal, radical, anti-fascist, and labor groups arrived in Southall, including many Asian and African Caribbean members of local and more distant communities.

As later accounts have revealed, the NF was playing the "race card" with consistency right before the elections. NF speeches regularly led to outbreaks of violence afterwards.[8] NF members took them as evidence of the threat that Blacks posed to "the English." The extent of police deployment in Southall on the day of the NF meeting was ominous. The Special Patrol Group (SPG), a corps of riot troops, arrived in Southall early on the day of the planned meeting. Both foot police and equestrian officers, as well as police dogs and a helicopter hovering above the area, signaled that the police expected a major conflict.

Police officers began by cordoning off the area within a mile of the Town Hall, pre-empting any effort to stage a protest at its entrance. Some protesters went to a restaurant opposite Town Hall, set up a sound system on its roof, and loudly played reggae music interspersed with anti-racist slogans, in order to drown out the sound of the speeches. Others gathered at the edge of the cordon. Tension on both sides increased. Inevitably, conflict broke out between police and demonstrators. Southall residents and visitors then found themselves battling police armed with truncheons and other riot gear. Hundreds of people in the crowd sustained injuries, a school teacher from New Zealand died as a result of a blow to his head by an SPG truncheon, and ambulances were unable to break the cordon to help the wounded; 700 people were arrested, 342 of them charged with breaking the law.

Two radically different accounts of the April 23 events began circulating. "Mainstream" English-language newspapers reported a set of unlawful acts of mob violence against representatives of the state, the police. For example, the front-page headline of *The Daily Telegraph* on April 24, 1979 read "Asian Fury at Election Meeting," with a sub-headline "40 Police hurt in protest over National Front," and an interview with Enoch Powell, former Conservative minister, who emphasized that the Southall events confirmed his prediction made eleven years earlier that Britain was headed for a civil war. Quite a different view emerged from accounts within Southall, which viewed the NF meeting and the coming of riot police as a racist attack. For example, the May 1 issue of a local Southall newspaper, *Punjab Times,* proclaimed "Monday's police terrorism has convinced people that Southall has been reduced to the status of a British Imperial Colony."[9]

Many people injured in the conflict assumed that, once the truth was known, policemen responsible for the brutality would be disciplined and charges against Southall residents would be dropped. Confidential reports (released to the public only much later) show that police brutality was widespread, as Southall residents perceived. Yet, in what many impartial observers regard as a flagrant miscarriage of justice, not a single policeman was penalized after the Police Department's inquiry, while legal cases against Southall residents dragged on, accruing large legal costs and crippling ongoing Southall community life.

A statement from the *Report of the Unofficial Committee of Enquiry* provides evidence of how deeply the events of April 23, 1979 alienated the Southall South Asian community as a whole: "Many have testified to us of their belief that what occurred was a deliberate assault on the whole small community."[10] The events seem to have been a turning point for those Southall residents who had until then tried to ignore or resign themselves to the racism they encountered on a regular basis. The report noted: "members of that community were already well aware of the racialist strains in British society as a whole; but, even with that knowledge, what happened in their town on April 23 came as a severe psychological shock. Many have observed to us that they had never conceived that the British police could behave as they had seen them behave on that day."[11] Police action on April 23 was taken by Blacks in Southall as evidence that the state had no compunctions about willfully endangering their lives.

The events in Southall strengthened already existing bonds between many South Asians, especially younger ones, and African Caribbeans, against the rhetoric of the NF and its right-wing sympathizers. The NF targeted all non-white people, as well as Jews, whatever their racial origins. The events in Southall led many South Asians and African Caribbeans to see themselves as joined in a larger Black identity, because of their shared history of colonialism and the racist assumptions upon which it rested. In the 1970s the term "Black" was (and, in some British circles, still is) used as a political term to indicate unity among various non-white minority groups fighting racism.[12]

## The Context of the SBS Ramlila

In 1978 a group of women in Southall who called themselves the Southall Black Sisters (henceforth SBS) began meeting regularly to discuss shared concerns. The group contained women of South Asian descent born in Britain, women with South Asian parents who had grown up in East Africa, and women of African Caribbean descent born in Britain or the Caribbean. The Asian community in Southall was larger than the African Caribbean one at that time and each group had different pre-immigration histories. Yet women in SBS found that their roots in colonized countries and their experience of racism and sexism in Britain had given them many shared feelings, issues, and hopes.

The founding members of SBS ranged from teenage schoolgirls

to young postgraduates and working women. Some initial impetus for the formation of a women's group came from two women engaged in academic research on South Asian communities in Southall. Another member commuted to college elsewhere in the London area but spent her summers doing community projects in Southall, where she grew up. With both Asian and African Caribbean women in the group, SBS represented the diversity of the Southall population more fully than the exclusively South Asian labor groups mentioned above.

SBS undertook a series of community projects to improve the lives of girls and women in Southall and co-operated with other groups organized to combat racism in Greater London. They also staffed an advice center on Saturdays at the Southall Rights Building, volunteering their time to give information about legal rights and to provide support to women experiencing difficulties in their families or relationships. Heretofore, male elders and community leaders had dealt with domestic violence and related issues within the South Asian community by encouraging women to avoid conflict in the family. SBS felt that women needed advice from other women, especially those who did not have a vested interest in maintaining the status quo within families.

Some male members of the Southall community greeted the formation of SBS with suspicion. A few saw SBS as troublemakers who threatened the stability of the family structure, especially because they gave help to women who fled their homes on account of domestic violence. Other men felt that the South Asian community should speak as a single group, and SBS would undermine that. In addition, some worried this new group might later siphon funds away from established social-service organizations or draw support away from such groups as the Southall Youth Movement, founded in 1976 to combat racist attacks.[13] Nonetheless, SBS-initiated projects, such as picketing the "Miss Southall" beauty contest, won them support in the larger community. Feminist goals in this case and in the SBS Ramlila paralleled those of some male-dominated groups which had earlier been suspicious of SBS.

Four factors shaped the SBS decision to perform a Ramlila in response to the incidents of April 23, 1979. First, as an anti-racist group, they sought some form of symbolic action that would make visible their outrage at police brutality against the Black population of Southall. An appropriate gesture seemed to be a benefit performance whose proceeds would be donated to the Southall Legal

Defense Fund, an organization helping to defray the legal costs of those charged in the April 23 conflict. Although SBS realized that the performance might not raise a large amount of money, they viewed the benefit as a material contribution and an expression of solidarity.

Second, they wanted to undertake a project that would publicly demonstrate their connection to the cultural traditions of their community, as understood by their elders. Such an event would show that criticisms of SBS as being divisive for the community were unwarranted. SBS chose a Ramlila because of its link with Diwali, a major South Asian festival of lights long popular in North India, in which Hindus lit lamps to welcome Ram home after his destruction of the demon Ravana.[14] Before communalism in India became as pronounced as it did, lighting lamps and sharing sweets with one's (Hindu and non-Hindu) neighbors were common at Diwali. SBS chose a Ramlila at Diwali because of its traditional connections with unity, celebration, and good fortune.

Third, the story of Ravana's destruction resonated strongly with recent events. Ramlila celebrates the victory of good over evil, dramatizing an account of an oppressive rule destroyed by the perseverance of those committed to virtue. At a symbolic level, it presents a parallel to Southall resistance to police brutality, and might give comfort to those still recovering from the physical and psychological wounds of April 23.

Finally, the shared feminist convictions of members of SBS challenged them to find a special way to depict the story of Rama and Sita. The portrayal of Sita in most well-known tellings of the story could be seen as reinforcing patriarchal views of gender.[15] SBS members did not want to stage a play that could be seen as contradicting the feminist tenets of SBS. On the other hand, if they found an appropriate way to incorporate their critical views into the play, it could provide them with an opportunity to share some of their political convictions with their community. At that time they were the only inside group that could mount a critique of sexist attitudes within their community to improve it, rather than attack it from the outside to disparage South Asian culture, as some racist groups had done. Therefore, members of SBS chose to stage a unique Ramlila that would combine cultural appreciation with cultural critique. Many South Asian members of SBS had participated in Ramlilas during their school years. SBS decided to produce a Ramlila similar to such plays in general, but differing in ideological goals. This drama would question patriarchal attitudes in the community, but do so in a spirit of affection and celebration.

Immediately, complex issues surfaced. Several Marxist members of SBS felt that supporting the project would affirm religious ideals (according to classical Marxist thought, religion is the opiate of the masses, as well as being epiphenomenal). Second, as one member asked, "What's the contribution of this play to the African Caribbean community?" The Ramayana was linked primarily with South Asian Hindu culture, so why should African Caribbeans, or indeed, other South Asian religious groups such as Sikhs and Muslims, see it as a meaningful drama for them?[16] In response, the group decided to create a Ramlila that would strengthen and celebrate the entire Southall Black community, while simultaneously contesting patriarchal ideologies. But this, pointed out another member of the group, might offend orthodox members of the community who would come expecting to hear a pious interpretation of the story. Would such a performance defeat the goal of bringing the community together? SBS wanted to create a thought-provoking Ramlila that would take into account these multiple concerns.

Financial and temporal limitations contributed to the improvisational nature of the production. SBS had almost no funding, and exactly three weeks for preparing the drama, which was to be staged on October 19, 1979. SBS received help from many people. Because the event would contribute to the Southall Defense Fund, the Indian Workers Association loaned their meeting room as a venue.[17] An Indian classical music teacher volunteered to provide musical accompaniment to enhance the mood of the scenes. An Indian restaurant in Southall provided free sweets for distribution to members of the audience. Samosas (fried dumplings stuffed with a spicy potato filling) were donated for sale at the performance as a fund-raiser. Several women donated old saris to be sewn into a stage curtain, while others lent jewelry and other props. Many women outside of SBS helped set up the stage, put out chairs, distribute sweets, and sell tickets. The performance was publicized in local shops and by community groups, as well as some nationally based anti-racist groups.

The collaborative manner in which SBS wrote the script, in keeping with its principle of coalitional practices, led to a play whose emphases had been intensely debated, critiqued, and revised before the performance. Perminder Dhillon, to whom primary responsibility fell for synthesizing the many ideas for the script, recounted in an interview with me the intensity and excitement of putting the play together. She recalls that one night after rehearsal, the entire cast went to her family's home to continue discussing the play. As it became late, one by one people eventually dropped off to sleep in the sitting room. Awakening the next morning in dismay, they had to call angry parents and convince them that they had intended to return home the night before. Several others recalled this night well, and saw it as one of the strongest bonding experiences of the group. The collaborative manner in which the play developed also meant that the SBS Ramlila represented the views of the group in a way that no performance put together by a single director could.

## The Structure of the SBS Ramlila

SBS told Rama's story in ways that would encourage members of the audience to question some widely accepted cultural assumptions about women, but would still contain elements that made the drama clearly recognizable as a Ramlila. The play included the familiar events in the story: Rama's birth, the exile to the forest, the abduction of Sita, and Rama's victory over Ravana. Although the narrative remained fairly standard, certain decisions about casting and framing devices introduced multiple perspectives into the drama.

In contrast to some Indian dramatic traditions, where men play female and male roles (because acting is considered a disreputable activity for women), in the SBS Ramlila women played all the parts.[18] In addition, casting choices deliberately thwarted traditional expectations. For example, Sita was played by a tall Asian woman, while Rama was played by a short African Caribbean woman. This casting undercut notions that the story "belongs" to a single ethnic group. It also subverted a widely held belief that a "proper" wife must be shorter than her husband.

In a manner crucial to its critical edge, the production included a storyteller and two jesters, who mediated between the events depicted and the audience:[19] the storyteller would come onstage, give background for the upcoming scene, and begin to comment on its significance. As she did so, the two jesters would interrupt her, drawing the audience's attention to traditional sayings, pointing out topical parallels, or interrogating certain assumptions about women reflected in the scene. One jester, a South Asian woman fluent in both English and Punjabi, included well-known Punjabi expressions in her speeches. The other jester, an African Caribbean woman, found ways to translate those Punjabi phrases in her comments, mediating for audience members who did not know Punjabi. Both functioned to disrupt the familiar, easy flow of the Ramayana narrative and question stereotypical gender roles in the play.

For an example of how this structure worked, consider how the Ramlila deals with the birth of Rama and his brothers. After many childless years, Dasaratha performed a special sacrificial rite, as a result of which his three wives conceived and gave birth to male children. What a great celebration the king sponsored! At this moment the first jester said,

> Yes, it was like that when my brother was born—a great celebration and my family passed out laddhus [a round sweet made of brown sugar and butter]. But when I was born, they didn't celebrate. My mother said "*Hi Veh Raba, soota mundiyan dha thaba*."

Immediately following the first jester's comments, the second one responded by paraphrasing the Punjabi comment in English, and adding her own economic analysis of the situation:

> She said to God "Why don't you just throw me a bunch of boys?" Why such jubilation when the son is born, but not the daughter? She must have been worrying about the dowry to be paid for the marriage of a daughter.

The interchange between jesters directs the listeners' attention to the socio-economic forces that immediately begin to shape parents' attitudes toward their children: it was not a daughter per se that was disagreeable; instead it was the custom of giving dowry for a bride, and thus commodifying her, that allowed such fears about and responses to the birth of daughters to continue.

One performer recalled that her mother brought to the play a grandmother and some elderly aunts who spoke Punjabi and knew little English. They were used to sitting through community meetings conducted in English without understanding them, in order to meet friends and feel part of their community. Until the first jester's comment, they had viewed the drama primarily as a pious reiteration of Lord Rama's greatness, enjoying the event in their own terms, as a religious holiday and a chance to socialize. Their perception of the Ramlila received confirmation as they entered the theater and received special Diwali sweets. They received the first jester's idiomatically Punjabi comments with laughs of recognition; the play was calling attention to the greater value placed on male babies than female babies, a fact of life with which they were all too familiar. The fact that women outnumbered men in the audience meant that a number of them had personal experience of these differing ways in which the birth of a girl or boy was greeted.

The majority of those of South Asian descent who attended the SBS Ramlila spoke English. For example, one member of the cast recalled that her mother brought along not only pious older womenfolk but younger sisters, brothers, and cousins, who were fluent in English as a result of their schooling. Thus the second jester's translation of the Punjabi phrase and the dialogue between the two jesters enhanced the process of questioning certain gender assumptions that might otherwise have been received without further reflection.

The jesters included pointedly topical comparisons to show that the relationships in the story were not only ones enacted in some mythic past, but echoed events in the daily life of the audience. In one scene, for example, Sita begged her husband to take her along on his forest exile, but he refused, claiming that her life would be too harsh for her: her tender lotus-feet might get cut by thorns and bruised by rocks. Sita hit him on the shoulder with a thump and said, "I'm good enough to wear myself out doing all the housework in our home, but not good enough to go to the forest with you?" Submissively, Ram replied, "Whatever you say, my dear." His response parodied the way a "proper" *wife* is "supposed" to answer her husband's commands.

At another point, when the narrator enumerated the heavy duties that fall to a wife, a jester interrupted, saying, "yeh, it's a bit like how hard the women at T'walls Factory work, isn't it?" Many South Asian women worked long hours at T'walls, a local factory, and then returned home to cook and clean house. The jester inquired why women have to work a shift outside the home, and a shift inside the home as well. The scene also undermined the gender construct of wife as a weak creature.

The Ramlila presented these topical comments humorously in a non-threatening way, linking them to daily life by referring to familiar places. Among the actors and audience members whom I interviewed, it is this topical humor that has remained most sharply etched in people's memories of the Ramlila. Almost everyone remembered the funny asides of the jesters, a few repeating the Punjabi line quoted above. Several others recited word for word, as a high point of the performance, the line about Sita's tender lotus-feet and its irony; here were women who had to deal regularly with multiple pressures and dangerous work environments in factories, laundries, their homes, and their journeys to and from work. They never had time to worry about their tender lotus-feet.

Members of the cast raised questions about notions of masculinity as well. In a scene set in the forest, for example, Rama's brother Lakshmana heard the sounds of wild animals and cowered in fear and then ran to hide behind Sita, who reassured him, "Don't worry, I'm here." This line would be particularly comic for regular Ramlila-goers because Lakshmana is usually portrayed as the fearless warrior, ready to attack anyone who poses the slightest threat to Rama, Sita, or their kingly lineage.

The objects of critique shift from gender relations to the current electoral situation in Southall toward the end of the Ramlila, as Rama battles Ravana. The interpretation of Ravana as Evil Incarnate guided the appearance of the character playing Ravana, who wore a huge round mask with depictions of ten different visual images. Several of the heads were enlarged photographs of specific people, including Enoch Powell, major figures in the NF, a local member of the Ealing council who was leader of the opposition at the time, and even Prime Minister Margaret Thatcher. Other heads represented oppression in more abstract form. For example, the hat worn by SPG police was drawn onto one head to stand for police brutality. A black bobby's hat over a drawing of a pig symbolized the everyday policing to which the community was subject. Another drawing represented the increasingly restrictive immigration laws which threatened to tear apart families and penalize those whose parents were not born in Britain. The symbolism of Ravana, therefore, encompassed crucial concerns not just of South Asian immigrant communities, but of African Caribbean ones as well.

The practice of culminating the Ramlila by burning Ravana in effigy, accompanied by celebratory fireworks, is an ancient and venerable one, symbolizing the conquest of good over evil. In the SBS production, after Rama defeated Ravana, the storyteller said to the audience, "I'll see you in the carpark, where we'll finish Ravana off." There SBS set off fireworks, much to the delight of the spectators. In this Ramlila, the destruction of Ravana's effigy symbolized the desire to end racism in Britain. This final message brought together the concerns of the varied members of the audience: Punjabi and English speakers, South Asians and African Caribbeans, people from Southall and anti-Nazi activists that came from afar. The fireworks gestured to a celebratory moment when all people in Southall could live without fear, humiliation, or deprivation of their rights.

## The SBS Ramlila Reconsidered

Despite the time, thought, and effort that went into staging the SBS Ramlila, few tangible artifacts remain to testify to its impact. Yet oral interviews reveal that many participants viewed the performance as crucially formative in the development of their thought and behavior. Several identified the Ramlila as occurring at a transformative moment in the history of the South Asian community in Britain.

In the 1970s, major London papers and magazines did not list information about cultural events in the South Asian community in the United Kingdom. Most London journalists did not take into account events in Southall, located beyond the last stop on the metro tube line. The only public artifact of the Ramlila found in the Ealing borough library archives is a small notice in the local *Southall Gazette* of Friday, October 19, 1979:

> SOUTHALL "Black Sisters" are presenting an updated version of Ram Leela, the Hindhu religious festival at 7:15 pm in the Dominion Hall on Friday night. Songs, music and dances will be followed by a bonfire in the Dominion car park and a firework display.[20]

Note that the reporter put "Black Sisters" in quotes, as if the phrase might be unfamiliar to readers. The write-up mentions neither the play's political context nor Ravana's burning, instead presenting the event as a Hindu musical entertainment. No items or reviews appear in subsequent editions.

No formal script is extant. Few people recalled exactly which Ramayana incidents appeared in the Ramlila beyond the usual birth of the royal heirs, circumstances that led to exile, abduction of Sita, and defeat of Ravana. One of the organizers of the production did find me a one-page program from the performance. Another dug up two old photos of the Ramlila: one shows a curtain created from old saris and the other depicts the homemade mask of the ten-headed Ravana with the ten different politically-inspired faces. Everyone I interviewed recalled the role and antics of the jesters quite vividly.

Initially the only remnant of the performance I found was an essay by Avtar Brah in *Charting the Journey,* a set of writings by Black women in England. In the essay, Brah assesses challenges Asian and African Caribbean women faced in forming a united front against racism. She notes that, "We had to make connections between our oppression in Britain and that of women in the Third World." Within that context, Brah analyzes her role in the SBS Ramlila, which she describes as "our own feminist version of Ram Leela." She contrasts it with "the classic Hindu epic which depicts Sita, the central female character, as a subservient and devoted wife." Describing the SBS interpretation of Ravana as a "symbol of evil," she recounts how her group "burnt an effigy with each head representing a specific evil (for example the racist immigration laws) which our communities are made to suffer in Britain."[21] These lines led me to find and interview participants in the SBS Ramlila nearly twenty years later.

Perminder Dhillon, who assumed primary reponsibility for the Ramlila script and now works as a filmmaker in London, spoke with enthusiasm about the challenge of shaping the play to take into account issues raised in SBS discussions about religion, feminism, and racism. Dhillon interpreted the SBS Ramlila as an example of a coalitional political practice that provided a united front of Asian and African Caribbean women to combat racism and sexism. She linked the play with the power of culture, noting that the Ramlila joined stories from the ancient past with the contemporary situation of Black people in Britain.

Another SBS member, Parita Mukta, recalled the play in light of feminist resistance to dominant cultural norms. Mukta published a book that examines current perceptions of Mirabai, the sixteenth-century Rajasthani female saint who refused to consummate her arranged marriage with her royal husband because of her intense love for God Krishna.[22] Both the SBS Ramlila project and Mukta's study of Mirabai point to spaces within Hindu tradition where women have voiced resistance to patriarchal norms. Mukta's memories of the SBS Ramlila focus on its opportunities to oppose racism and sexism within a framework of Gandhian non-violence and socialist humanism. She emphasized that these ideals must be linked to issues of immigration, colonialism, and Indian women in order to practice feminism in Britain without becoming divorced from South Asian culture.

Several other members of the original SBS recalled the performance as a formative opportunity for personal growth. The play developed out of a fluid and improvisational process so it enabled members who had never staged a drama to have a role in shaping it. Several noted that the SBS Ramlila was the first piece of theater they saw that related to the stuff of daily Southall life, such as the names of local factories and familiar Punjabi phrases used by grandmothers. One woman, now an articulate lawyer in a flourishing legal practice in Ealing, recalled being terribly shy as a teenager; her part in the play provided her first sustained experience of public speaking.

The multiple registers of the play enabled participants to move across and between the usual boundaries that they negotiated in everyday life. For example, the casting decisions offered unusual opportunities: women took on the roles of men, short people acted as fierce and intimidating warriors, an African Caribbean woman played the role of an Indian deity who takes human form on earth as a righteous king, women expected to be modestly quiet played humorous jesters. One cast member recalls how much more she enjoyed acting in this drama than in school plays: she enjoyed the freedom to speak in a familiar way, rather than in the elevated accents of Shakespeare or the BBC. Her speeches in the play encompassed multiple registers of English and Punjabi.[23]

Several of the original SBS members, speaking in the 1990s, look back on the 1979 Ramlila as a moment of singular unity. Some of the other South Asians in Britain that I interviewed who had not been involved in activist groups in the 1970s and 1980s saw the "Black unity" movement of that period as a stance of community activists, rather than entire communities, and viewed "Black unity" as a temporary achievement. In the mean time, some rifts have developed between many Hindus, Muslims, and Sikhs, as well as between African Caribbeans and South Asians, that make it difficult to recapture the sense of a "pan-minority" unity signified by the term "Black" at the time.[24] Some sociological research suggests that increasing competition for Council funding and housing, as well as the tensions caused by the financial constraints of the Thatcher and Major years, have tended to pit one community against another.[25] But today the concept of coalitional politics among subjugated groups in society has again gained prominence; coalitions among groups that share goals across religious and historical differences can be extremely effective. Thus for cultural, historical, and practical reasons, this Ramlila performance deserves our consideration.

## The SBS Ramlila and Ramayana Tradition

In the last decade, scholars of the Ramayana tradition have analyzed its diversity in increasingly nuanced ways. As attention has moved away from treating Valmiki's *Rāmāyaṇa* as the Ur-text and other tellings as mere divergences from it, greater attention has been paid to the many tellings of Rama's story in their broader social context.[26] If one views the SBS Ramlila within this wider perspective of Ramayana scholarship, it becomes apparent that the SBS created a religious performance that resonates with certain strands within the Ramayana tradition.

Recent ethnographic work has documented the presence of women's tellings of the story that include particular emphases not found in men's renditions. For example, Narayana Rao has collected songs from a group of Telugu-speaking Brahmin women that concentrate on everyday events in the lives of women, rather than kingly policies and war.[27] The SBS Ramlila also emphasizes events that affect women in the story: childbirth, Sita's decision to accompany her husband into exile, her bravery in the forest, her abduction, and the destruction of her abductor. Furthermore, jesters emphasized incidents that relate to constructions of gender, mocking ideas about women's limitations in order to critique them. The SBS Ramlila continues a tradition of women's tellings of the story that selects incidents relevant to women as worthy of interpretation and exegesis.

Ramayana scholars have also demonstrated the extent to which tellings of Rama's story take on local specificity, both by domesticating the characters and incorporating topical references into performances.[28] Research on Ramlilas in North India has shown how certain performances become closely associated with particular places. For example, performance conventions of the Ramlila of Ramnagar

(Benaras) are linked with the geography and use of leisure in the city. Even specific neighborhoods in Benaras have their own Ramlila productions, produced by pooling local contributions and re-enacted in specific ways that link them to previous performances in the same neighborhoods.[29] Like such tellings of the Rama story wedded to particular locales, the creation, production, and reception of the SBS Ramlila is grounded in Southall. The jesters' comments in particular, reflect everyday struggles of Southall residents to attain financial security, avoid racist attacks, and maintain dignity.

Finally, folklorists and performance scholars have shown many differing ways in which Ramlilas, puppet plays, and dance dramas incorporate improvisation and humor into Rama's story.[30] Romila Thapar identifies this topical content of Ramlilas as one of its most precious features.[31] Perhaps the SBS Ramlila's satirical references developed in response to the same kind of impulses that have led folk artists in India to incorporate topical comments into their performances—the impulse to make a traditional story relate to people's everyday lives in ways that cultural performances patronized by wealthy elites cannot.

The Southall Ramlila provides scholars of the Ramayana tradition with a striking example of its tremendous scope for symbolising evil. In different tellings, authors and performers have conceptualized Ravana in diverse ways. Portrayals range from Ravanas driven by lust, greed, and hedonism to tragic or even heroic, but unfairly maligned, Ravanas. In particular periods of time, storytellers have identified Ravana with Muslims, British rule in India, and others perceived as outsiders.[32] The SBS Ramlila identifies Ravana as a symbol of the British state, and in particular as a symbol of the threat the state poses to its citizens through police brutality. A key moment in North Indian Ramlilas has been the burning of Ravana's effigy.[33] The SBS ended its Ramlila with the burning of Ravana to dramatize their desire to end the racism that had plagued their lives and well being in Britain. Their way of depicting Ravana's ten heads shows how Rama's story can encompass forms of evil directly related to immigrant life in Britain.

Finally, the SBS Ramlila raises intriguing questions about the nature of representation in the context of South Asian immigration. For example, one might ask the question—whose "culture" does the SBS Ramlila represent? It cannot be equated purely with Hindu identity, since key members of the production were African Caribbeans and/

or Marxists. Even among South Asians, both Sikhs and Hindus were involved. Nor could it be said to be an exact reflection of the entire Southall South Asian community, since the audience was made up primarily of women. Furthermore, it is possible that some orthodox Hindus might even find the performance "inauthentic" because the play did not linger on auspicious scenes for *darshan* of Lord Rama, as most pious productions do. Finally, one could not label it a pristine transportation of a particular Indian regional performance to Britain, since its performers used an eclectic style of script-development and borrowed from a number of dramatic forms.

Rather than arguing that the SBS performance was not a "real" one, one must question the notion of a homogeneous Indian tradition transplanted to England. The Ramayana tradition has long encompassed both authoritative and oppositional tellings. Although authoritative tellings tend to reaffirm the power of the king, the priest, and patriarchy, SBS self-consciously sought to avoid reaffirming such patriarchal norms. The oppositional telling of the SBS suggested ways of overcoming sexism within their own community and racism within the wider British community. The diversity of their Ramlila represented the diversity of the non-white population in Southall. Its combination of cultural appreciation and cultural critique may mirror the ambiguities and contradictions of other South Asian diaspora communities as well.[34]

My analysis of the SBS Ramlila suggests the necessity of viewing the Ramayana tradition through the conceptual categories of race, class, gender, and colonialism. Some of the topical humor of the SBS Ramlila makes sense only in terms of the socio-economic background of South Asians in the subcontinent and East Africa and then their class background later in Britain, with their many hours of low paid, non-unionized work in factories and laundries. The reversals in casting and the quips of Sita in response to voiced concerns about her tender lotus-feet make sense only in terms of the realities of gender constructs among this South Asian community, where many women put in a full day of factory labor and then return to continue working within the home. The specific identities of Ravana's ten heads demonstrate how gender and class issues must be seen within the context of racialized immigration policies and threatening electoral rhetoric. That the burning of Ravana won applause from various groups within its audience suggests that the SBS Ramlila succeeded, at least temporarily, in bringing together people with different histories and political stances. Some would argue that the events in Southall in April 1979 created a unique moment in the history of the Black community in Britain. If so, by the same logic, the performance of the SBS Ramlila also created a unique moment, a celebratory one but also a salutary one in that the links between racism, class, and gender became visible in a drama about Rama and Sita.

SIXTEEN

# Fiji's Fifth Veda: Exile, Sanatan Dharm, and Countercolonial Initiatives in Diaspora

JOHN KELLY

Study of the Ramayana in the history of South Asian diaspora can lead us to understand the transformation or attenuation of Indic culture in distant, obscure sites. But it might also teach us surprising things about the history of political uses of Ramayana narratives more generally. In the indenture colonies especially, Ramayana imagery informed anticolonial political debates and movements. Themes of exile and quest for Ramraj gained concrete, local political references. Diasporic sites such as Fiji are commonly described as distant leaves of a vast Indian cultural banyan tree. If we must have arboreal metaphors for diaspora, the indenture colonies were not merely leaves. They are also among the roots, for political phenomena as disparate as Gandhi's satyagraha and the destruction in Ayodhya. This essay will explore the history of many kinds of uses of Ramayanas in Fiji, and especially the capacity of Ramayana narratives there to inform a new kind of self-consciousness, a Hinduism imagining itself in exile, longing for return.

In 1948, Gyani Das of Nasinu, Fiji, published a Hindi-language pamphlet in Delhi, "India's Colony Fiji."[1] As he wrote it, the history of indentured labor emigration to Fiji unfolded in a devotionally-constituted universe:

> Those Indians who came to Fiji during the Indenture period were made to suffer unrestrained oppression and outrage. Those who passed through this ordeal and are still living tell us that the British people in their oppression of the Indians during the Indenture period surpassed even Ravana and his demon army. They had to perform the hardest work and those who slackened were slapped, kicked, punched and abused . . . .
>
> It is also heard that in the days of Indenture, one woman was required to serve three men, but, in fact, this was not so. It may be that the British had this end in view when they sent Indian women out, but these women stuck to their principles and did not accept two or three husbands. Those women who were forced to submit to this practice saved their chastity by killing themselves. It was, of course, a different matter with prostitutes. Some prostitutes (for there are prostitutes in practically all countries) did get enlisted and come to Fiji and were given to debauchery, but because of their misconduct it is wrong to say that all women who came from India during the Indenture days were equally blameworthy. Indian men finding themselves unable to see their women prostituting themselves with white planters and overseers, resorted to openly murdering them. The result was that these prostitutes became scared and corrected themselves. One hangs one's head in shame and shivers to write the stories of sexual indulgence and misbehavior of the white planters and overseers in those days which are significant. It is difficult to understand how cruel, shameless and low those British planters and overseers were who unashamedly committed such wicked deeds and revealed them afterwards. But they could not live in peace for long. In order to avenge themselves for the dishonor, brave Indians put them to death whenever and wherever they found them. This display of bravery by Indians had far-reaching effects. Even today other races fear Indians and would not dare touch their girls. When the pains of oppression caused by human demons could no longer be tolerated, they supplicated God for deliverance. Their cries penetrating all barriers reached their Motherland and made not only Indians but even a Britisher like Mr C.F. Andrews, shudder. In face of a forceful agitation by Indians, iniquity had to give way and in 1917 the Indenture system came to an end.

Although it is largely implicit, a comparison with the suffering of Sita in the Ramayana runs throughout this narration of the oppression of migrant Indian women by the "human demons" of indenture period in Fiji.[2] Fiji's British "surpassed even Ravana," and the destruction of their indenture system was an inevitable result of the intervention of possibly divine forces raised by supplication for deliverance.

In this and other ways, many Indo-Fijian Hindus have found their history in the Ramayana, and have put themselves, via the Ramayana, into the world. Taking as established Paula Richman's point that there are many Ramayanas, I seek to contribute to the documentation of diversity in its realizations, and to further the critical exploration of what Sheldon Pollock has called its "unique imaginative instruments."[3] In his persuasive review of vast political redeployment of the Ramayana narrative in South Asia from the eleventh to the fourteenth century, Sheldon Pollock shows how an elite used the epic in new ways to connect themselves to a mythic theocratic past, divinizing the favored kings and demonizing invading Central Asians. Divinization and demonization, the linked imaginative instruments emphasized by Pollock, are both at work in the political imagination of Gyani Das. The literal demonization of British planters and overseers carried Das to the point that he considered revenge murders justified and effective. But what provided deliverance, what broke down all barriers, transformed hearts and led those with power to actually destroy the evil system, was anguished supplication of divinity. In colonial Fiji, apparently far more than in middle-period South Asia, the same narrative logic was acutely focussed on the sexuality of women, inscribing not so much gender as two classes of femininity, bifurcating women between virtue and evil, between principled suffering and debauchery, Sita and prostitutes.

Much can be learned by tracing Gyani Das's narrative and other similar ones as distant leaves of the Indic tree. This perspective and method, seeking Indic continuities and local transformations, has dominated diaspora studies. I hope, in what follows, to do something more—to begin to reintegrate the vicissitudes of the Ramayana in Fiji (and by implication, its career in the indenture colonies and labor-migrant groups more generally) into our grasp of the narrative's past, present and future as a whole. Thus I shall note not only local transformations on Indic themes, but also translocal connections, toward a history of transformations in which indenture colonies might have had some impact on culture and politics in India. In addition to seeking a history of Ramayana-framed divinization and demonization in Fiji, I want to open for attention other imaginative instruments within the Ramayana narrative, use of which perhaps began, and was certainly especially visible in indentured labor colonies: the present as exile, as a time of unmerited suffering, and as a time of struggle; also, especially from Tulsidas, the special virtue of steadfast suffering, and its destiny, divine intercession and triumph over evil. Pollock, like many Ramayana scholars, seeks an effective way of addressing contemporary violent Hindu nationalist uses of the Ramayana before and after the destruction of the mosque in Ayodhya. But his essay has more to say about the eleventh to fourteenth centuries than it does about the colonial period. For colonial India, Pollock describes mainly an absence of Ramayana-oriented politics. Apart from minor instances, he supposes the Ramayana political imaginary to be "repressed or displaced." Displaced I think it is, but not in this Freudian sense. No doubt Pollock could have done more with Gandhi's frequent invocations of Ramraj and the devotional logic of satyagraha.[4] But he is surely correct that in large part, and increasingly after the fall of the Raj, Indian nationalism was "a nontheocratic movement led by a westernized elite",[5] not seeking its present or future within its epic past. And this makes more important the astonishing prevalence of Ramayana invocation in the cultural politics of indenture colonies.

In sum, then, I claim to be describing not a distant branch of the tree but a missing link in the chain of Ramayana politics. Certainly for Fiji and, I strongly suspect, generally across the indenture colonies and elsewhere in situations of state-organized labor migration the imaginative instruments of the Ramayana became crucial tools for the moral reinscription of selves and world in terms not only more dignifying than those intrinsic to the plantation capitalist machinery, but also virtually, and sometimes actually, empowering of countercolonial initiatives. For its tropes of exile and struggle, as well as for its powers to divinize self-interest and demonize enemies, the Ramayana narrative came to have great value in the emergent societies of indenture colonies, made up largely of unlettered young adults cut off from caste, family, friends and elders. And I suspect that we will better understand contemporary Hindutva Ramayanas, and their politics, if we get these Ramayanas and their countercolonial dynamics into the genealogy. Even Gandhi's own Ramraj politics, so different both from the Hindu nationalists even of his day, and from his more secularist Congress allies, seem less the product of idiosyncratic genius, when one remembers that unique among Indian nationalist leaders, he found his political feet fighting the cause of laborers in an indenture colony, South Africa.

After an overview of diaspora, we will begin with the reception of the Ramayana in Fiji as a "holy book." Then we will turn to the establishment of the *Rāmcaritmānas* of Tulsidas as a sufficient, circumstantially necessary, social and moral inheritance for many Fiji Hindus: the Ramayana as the epitome of Hindu virtue, and a portable core for culture in exile.

## Diaspora, Part One

When did the Indian diaspora begin? There is no consensus about what "diaspora" means. If it means no more than migration, and if "Indian" refers to no more than the terrain that is now India, then we can assign no beginning. There has been a highly self-conscious middle-class migration from India, especially into Anglo North America in recent decades. There was also, predating this, a vast indentured migration of agricultural workers from South Asia to Assam, Ceylon, and many sites in Southeast Asia, the Caribbean and elsewhere. This labor migration started at least as early as the first decades of the nineteenth century, first to Mauritius and the slave colonies of the Caribbean, and finally to Fiji as the last new destination starting in 1879.

But while this is the beginning of organized South Asian migration to Fiji, it is not the whole story of diaspora from South Asia. Concurrent with this indentured migration to Fiji and elsewhere came a much smaller stream of free emigrants, especially Gujaratis seeking mercantile opportunities, and Punjabis seeking farm land and/or government service jobs. This Gujarati emigration (in some ways) connects to a Gujarati commercial migration history that was intrinsic to the Indian Ocean and Southeast Asian maritime commercial capitalism of the very long run, the market network that awed Marco Polo, and thrived for centuries before the Portuguese succeeded in finding a maritime route into it.

Dating can be more precise for the later, British government-managed indenture system, that great engine for global distribution (and though the British were not all conscious of it, the manufacture) of so-called "coolies." But it too has more complex antecedents than is generally recognized. The regions of North India from which the most people emigrated under indenture (e.g. Shahabad in Bihar and what are now the eastern districts of U.P.) were sites of out-migration for centuries before. Large numbers of men from these regions traveled far in order to enter into armed service (*naukarī*) for merchants and rulers in Central Asia, for the Moghuls, and for others. We can overturn oversimplified twentieth-century stories of the British forcing mobility, change, cash employment and emigration onto peasants theretofore tied by centuries to their soil. Yet indenture was a dirty trick, as became infamous in folkloric memory. The rise of "coolie" emigration followed in the wake of the absolute decline of the military labor market, a market done in by the Raj itself. Even before the Mutiny, the East India Company simultaneously suppressed military employment by any except itself, yet shifted in its taste in soldiers away from those domiciled in these restless, conquered regions. In short, then, in regions where it was an old story for boys to travel off into military service, and come back men of personal and financial substance, the infamous dirty trick of indenture was neither migration nor servitude but rather the racism and other injustices specific to the British system and intrinsic to the idea of "coolies" itself.[6]

And when, in all of this, is there a diaspora? If diaspora entails at least consciousness of connections, of movement from a homeland, then surely both the Indian Ocean networks of Gujarati merchants and the trans-Central Asian circuits of military service were always, already diasporic (and not entirely disconnected from each other, either). In fact, these two migration patterns would probably qualify as diasporic whether we tighten the definition of diaspora toward ongoing social and cultural circulation with the homeland, even intentions and sometime realities of return to it, or if we tighten it toward the establishment of permanent and significant presence in the sites of new residence. Even if diaspora, as a very specific subset of migration patterns, requires all these things—scattering departure from a homeland, memory of that homeland and consciousness of the scattering departure, ongoing cultural and human circulation to and from the homeland, and permanent establishment in the sites of new residence—diaspora from South Asia are not a specifically twentieth century phenomena, nor in most senses a specifically "modern," versus "traditional," phenomenon, nor a product of European or colonial impetus. We proceed in hope, then, that inquiry into uses of the Ramayana narrative in diaspora, here especially in

Fiji, can carry us not only to some insights into the history of this diasporic consciousness but also toward a better perspective on its effects on South Asian history.

## Holy Books

> I admit that the present oath does not appear to be binding. I am advised that Hindoos wd. swear on either the Qita or Ramain as they may elect, Mohammadans on the Koran.

So wrote R.M. Booth, Fiji's Inspector-General of Immigration and highest ranking authority on Indians, on March 19, 1916. He wrote on the cover sheets to a Fiji Colonial Secretary's Office minute paper, amidst a brief bureaucratic controversy. "Qita" was amended by a later hand, into "Gita."[7]

We are entering colonial Fiji in the indenture period, by way of its court rooms, and the choice is not arbitrary. More than 60,000 indentured laborers came to Fiji from 1879 to 1916, three quarters from across North India, via the depot in Calcutta, the final quarter from the depot in Madras. Each one visited a court room on the way out of India, wherein a magistrate ascertained that he or she (40 women per 100 men, almost all twenty-six years old or younger) had agreed to an indenture of five years of labor in exchange for passage to Fiji. By one account, recruits were advised by recruiters before their brief moment in court, "that when the magistrate asked us any question, we should just say 'yes.' If we didn't do this then we would be charged and thrown into jail."[8] Once in Fiji, further appearances in court were common. In fact, the indenture system overwhelmed nascent colonial Fiji's court system, engendering more than 80 per cent of its cases, both civil and criminal. While the violence of the indenture lines requires its own explanations, the reason for the civil overload is simple: unlike slavery, indentured labor was a contract with the laborer, and relied upon penal sanctions at least as much as on direct violence for enforcement of masters' rights. Indentured laborers came to court charged with absence, insolence, or simply failure to complete tasks, for which they could have pay withheld, be fined, and also have their indenture extended, sometimes all three. In the most extreme year there were 1.6 times as many civil prosecutions for violations of labor law as there were indentured laborers in Fiji. A very high percentage of the indentured laborers, thus, found themselves in civil court as a defendant at some time during their five years of indenture, this leaving aside criminal cases, visits as witnesses and more rarely, as a plaintiff.

There, starting in late 1916, Indian witnesses in court were, like Christian witnesses, given the option of swearing their oath to tell the truth on a holy book, and given the choice between a Ramayana (alas, whose Ramayana entirely unspecified) and a Koran. (Before this, they had merely been asked to verbally swear by God, Parmeshwar, the Ganges or the Koran.) The Colonial Secretary's circular of December 6, 1916 to all District Commissioners and the Chief Police Magistrate reflected some uncertainty on the matter:

> I am directed by the Governor to inform you that it has been represented to the Government that, instead of the existing method of administering oaths to Indians in the law courts of the Colony, it is probable that oaths would be considered by Indians to be more binding were they administered, in the case of Hindus on the "Ramayan," and in the case of Mahomedans on the "Koran."
>
> 2. A copy of each of these books has therefore been sent to you under separate cover, and I am to request that they be used in future in the administration of oaths to members of the Indian Community *in cases where it is found that the taking of an oath on one or other of the Books referred to is binding upon their consciences.*

The portion I have italicized was added to the final draft of the circular by the Colonial Secretary. From whom did the "Government" receive almost entirely satisfying representations concerning what was probable about Indian witness psychology? From whom, following Booth's first reference, did they learn their spelling, and the advice that led them to choose between the Gita and the Ramayana? From their Indian clerks and interpreters, whose usually invisible translations and transcriptions produced most of the tangible evidence of these courts. The most authoritative in these files, J. Chowdhury and Salim Buksh, each submitted memoranda advocating use of the Ramayana and Koran. The latter's views were also invoked on technical points by Fiji's Attorney General.

Curiosities abound in this fuddled bureaucratization which will detain us but only briefly. Booth, by June 1916, had determined that the Ramayana, but not the Koran, was available for purchase in Fiji, costing six shillings, and that both were attainable cheaply in India. A letter requesting multiple copies of both was sent to the Government Freight Agent in Calcutta. The District Commissioner, Ba District (hereafter, Ba D.C.), remained extremely skeptical of the government's plan. After receiving the December 6 circular, he wrote on January 24, 1917 that he had asked every Hindu witness what oath he considered binding; "In no case has a witness declared that an oath on the Ramayan was the highest oath recognized by his conscience."[9] To evaluate this bit of data, we might try to imagine the scene of these interviews, witnesses standing in courtrooms, speaking through the Ba D.C.'s interpreter, present in a dangerously white-controlled space for some other very concrete and consequential business. It is also important to know that the Ba D.C.'s view was already determined before this bit of *inter alia* research. He had written back to the Colonial Secretary immediately upon receipt of the December 6 circular:

> May I ask if it is possible that "Ramayan" is a mistake for Vedas or Shasters? The most generally accessible work of reference to my hand is Chambers' Twentieth Century Dictionary. It's description of the Ramayan is—"one of the two great epic poems of ancient India". The Vedas & Shasters on the other hand are definitely religious books, the holy writ and the holy commentaries. There would seem to be small religious sanction in an attestation on the Ramayan. I am afraid lest it's use in local courts might, to the one Indian in a hundred in this country to whom the word Ramayan carries any meaning at all, appear as comic a business as would appear to us the swearing on the Iliad of a Greek fruitseller in Chicago.[10]

Chowdhury's memorandum, written earlier, had presented diametrically different views: "many a time, persons coming to lay information have suggested that if the defendants would swear on a 'Ramayan' (a sacred book for the *Hindus* and held in great veneration) or 'Koran' (for the Mohmedans) they would be perfectly satisfied and forego their claims." The Attorney General solicited Buksh's views on the Ba D.C.'s claims. Buksh affirmed, citing "famous writer R.C. Dutt," that the Ramayan and the Mahabharath [*sic*] "together comprise the whole of the Epic literature of the ancient Hindus," providing unparalleled insight into ancient society, culture, religion and thought. "The Vedas or Shastxx [unreadable]" on the other hand, were

> obsolete owing to the difficulty of understanding the high Sanscrit in which they are written + I can assure you Sir, that there are none in Fiji who can claim to have read the Vedas or to have understood the meaning thereof. Even in India it is rather hard to come across Vedantists (those versed in Veda). I am sure most of the Hindus in Fiji haven't either known or seen the Vedas. The Ramayana has become the household book of very Hindu, and can be easily understood by one and all. The Ramayana is held in the same veneration by the majority of Hindus throughout India as the Holy Bible or the Koran by the Christians + Mahomedans respectively. I am quite sure that 75% of the Hindus in Fiji have true faith in the Ramayan.

The government took Buksh at his word, and wrote back to the Ba D.C. that "His Excellency [i.e. the Governor] is satisfied that the 'Ramayan' and 'Koran' are held in the same veneration by Hindus and Mahommedans respectively in Fiji as is the Holy Bible by Christians."[11] Should we be?

We can be certain, from other sources, that the Ramayana narrative was remembered, reproduced and disseminated in Fiji by the 1910s both via Ramlilas and in public readings. Sanadhya reports that they were, by 1914, performed annually in Labasa, Navua, Lautoka and other areas. On the one hand, as Ali's 1979 interviews with surviving indentured laborers make clear, religious practices varied in both content and intensity from plantation to plantation, just as the sexual rules and levels of violence varied. As one remembered it, on his plantation, there was no one to read the Koran or the Ramayana.[12] But if this information suggests some randomness, there was also a clear symbolic momentum in the public performances, not only of Ramlila, but also of the most popular ritual festivals of indenture days, the Moharram "Tazia" processions and riots of Holi, both of which were avidly celebrated by "Hindus" and "Muslims" alike. All three reconstituted participants in connection with divinity outside of and in antagonism with their ordinary social relationships, expressed variously in the bombardments of Holi, the aggressive mourning for the Moharram martyrs, and for both Moharram and for the indenture period Ramlilas, the creation, parading and destruction of enormous edifices. And it was the Ramlilas that were perhaps the clearest symbolically. As then performed, they climaxed with the immolation of twenty or thirty-foot tall Ravanas, in a virtual destruction of evil.[13] The Ramayana narrative, uniquely, provided the imagery of exile or banishment. As literary critic Vijay Misra summarized, Fiji "easily became the forest of Dandak in the Ramayana, a temporary state from which Rama and Sita would some day return. It was a perfect structure and Indians in Fiji responded to it with enthusiasm."[14]

But is this the same thing as "true faith" of "Hindus" in a "holy book?" In a time and place in which almost no one can read? Palpable here is not only uncertainty over facts of "Hindu" faith in Fiji, but also a structural pressure generated by the Christian holy book. This pressure was not merely for the reconfiguration of "Hinduism" as a "religion" centered on its true "holy writ," congruent in form with the particular versions of Christian religion. That dynamic was real enough, and much scholarly literature attests to the dialogic influence of Christian missions and schools on the missions and schools of the Arya Samaj, both in India and in Fiji.[15] Yet there was also pressure generated by the Bible of the courtroom itself, the holy book of truth and punishment powers.

In this light we are ready to appreciate a further puzzle of historical ethnography. What set this whole bureaucratic machine in motion was a petition delivered in 1916 to the government by Manilal Maganlal Doctor. Manilal was a barrister from Mauritius (and originally, Baroda) who came to Fiji in 1912 with Gandhi's blessing. He answered an appeal for a barrister sent to Gandhi by Sanadhya and other ex-indentured laborers in Fiji, published by Gandhi in *Indian Opinion*. The puzzle is this: Manilal's twenty-nine clients were not petitioning for the Ramayana and the Koran to be introduced in court, but rather, simply for the abolition of the required oath to God, Parameshwar, Ganga or the Koran. "Most of the Hindus and Musalmans dishonor the name of God and Parameshwar by telling lies." Instead, they requested the system used in Mauritius, where the Indians simply declared and promised to the court that they would tell the truth, and were otherwise liable for legal punishment.

The Government dismissed the petitioners' solution immediately, finding that the problem was not dishonor to God(s) by perjurers but the prevalence of perjury itself. Merely civil pledges would simply worsen the problem. Manilal, in turn, was as caustic in criticism of their solution as was the Ba D.C., but more nuanced, and public.[16] On January 4, 1917, he published his views in English, in *The Western Pacific Herald:*

> Now it is true that the majority of the northern (Calcutta) Indians look upon the Ramayana with special reverence; but there are a good few who do not look upon it with any more respect than, for example, the English would look upon Pope's Homer's Iliad . . . . The magistrates and their interpreters will not always be able to say whether the Ramayana would really affect the conscience of a particular witness or not. The analogy of the Christians swearing on the Bible is misleading.

Despite the fact that it had no impact on the change in court procedures, Manilal here put his finger on a crucial issue. The Bible could be used to swear in Europeans even of "inimical countries," Britain and Germany, Protestants, Catholics, and even "Hebrews." The Europeans were "more uniform or similar . . . than not only Indians of different provinces in India, but Indians belonging to different social grades stereotyped by their castes and creeds." As Manilal detailed in his article, India housed a vast number of deliberately distinguished groups; "All these people do not equally revere the Ramayana." The problem with his argument was that, like this sentence, it was static, yet an effort to describe a changing situation. It would take an extraordinarily transformative social crucible to reforge that deliberate, useful diversity into a sociability "more uniform or similar"—something like the reconstitution of everyone as a "coolie" fit for plantation labor.

So let us return then, to the indenture period court rooms, where the binding power of oaths was enforced, starting with the indenture contract and its penal sanctions, where the palpable pressure of Holy Books was felt, and where those books enabled plantation masters to establish truths and make real their rights and authority. Allow me to borrow from the epic stylebook, and embed another story about books to remind us of the social dynamics and stakes, and, not least, the violence here. The narrator, James Montague Kemmis, has already been sworn in on the Holy Bible, and confronts 17 accused on January 20, 1901.[17] He remembers Monday 7th January, a day he, the overseer in charge of Vuo plantation, had set the men to road and drain work. He remembered being warned, two days previous, that Jokhan Khan and two other men were planning to assault him because, the day before that, Kemmis had forced Khan to work despite a hand injury when Khan could not produce his hospital discharge. "I believed in the intention of these three + relied on assistance but never anticipated being mobbed."

Kemmis often stayed on horseback, but on 7th January he had to dismount to inspect each man's drain work. He noticed men glancing behind him, looked back and then confronted a crowd following him down the road, carrying heavy sticks and spades. "I asked what this meant. Jokhan Khan said 'We are going to beat you.'" Kemmis called for help, especially from the sardars (work bosses), but they refused and withdrew. Kemmis was badly beaten. Then came the book:

> I dropped half-senseless. I then said to them "I think you have done me enough damage now, you had better leave me alone." I could not then move for the pain. They seemed rather scared then. Some one called out "Let us put him in a bag and throw him in the big drain." Jokhan Khan said to me "You kiss this book + promise you will not summons any of us + we won't beat you up anymore on those conditions." The book he referred to was a pocket book in my belt. He saw I could not get it out as he took it out himself. He held the book up to me, kneeling beside me + made me repeat that I would not summons any of them if they let me off then. Khan Mahomed took the book from Jokhan Khan + said "You must kiss the book for me too." I did so. I could promise that I would not summons them because I knew that someone else would.

The testimony of Kemmis was corroborated by sardars and other witnesses, and by Exhibits A and B, two heavy sticks. But it was surely the testimony of Kemmis, primarily, that made the case against the accused. Only three of the seventeen asked Kemmis any questions, none of which generated any exonerating evidence. In the end, following closely the details of Kemmis's specific descriptions of the violence, six of the seventeen were found guilty of either attempted murder or wounding with intent to cause grievous bodily harm, and sentenced to four or five years of prison at hard labor. We need not presume from this that Kemmis and his supporting witnesses were telling the truth, the whole truth, and nothing but the truth. As the Ba D.C. noted in his memorandum against the Ramayana oath plan, "Perjury is frequent in local courts . . . . Fijians [Fiji's other major 'race'] commit perjury only less than Indians and Europeans are not so much more truthful as is generally supposed by those who have no intimate acquaintance with the actual working of a Fiji court." But he surely was beaten, and he was effective in court.

In Fiji, the so-called coolies came to call themselves girmitiyas, the people of the indenture contract or the *girmit*, from the English word "agreement." The girmitiyas were routinely convicted, in the so-called "coolie courts," on the word of a European planter or overseer, on the word of a man sworn in on a Holy Bible. The assault on Kemmis was unusual because the number of assailants was large, and because nothing involving women or sex was involved. But there was nothing unusual about the way the court determined truths and meted out punishment. And the girmitiyas' effort to bind by oath was not entirely unusual. In court records I have found other stories of violent girmitiya men seeking to bind behavior of others with oaths, but always the men had taken oaths themselves, promises before God of retaliation if oppressive behavior continues. Such oaths of retaliation, probably more frequently pronounced by men seeking to control "their" women than their overseers, most often appeared in court records after they had been acted upon. I have also heard stories—Sanadhya tells one—of overseers excusing and covering up assaults on them by girmitiyas. Admitting to being assaulted and beaten by a coolie would be admitting to loss of control, and might cause an overseer to lose his job and be shipped home to Australia.

Both Booth and the Ba D.C. argued that the best form of oath in court for Indians was actually one taken on their children, with a hand on their child's head. Putting the children, too, at stake seemed to have a chilling effect on witnesses that both administrators favored. When Chowdhury argued for the Ramayana and Koran oaths, he wrote that "The natural inference is that . . . defendants or witnesses *dare* not tell any lies after they have been sworn to on their sacred books . . . [or] the curse of God will fall upon them". He was in favor of relying upon what he called "the sensitive and rather superstitious nature" not, as he saw it, of the court, but of "the ordinary Indians," and advised provoking specific religious emotions: "a little Sea water (representing the holy water of the River Ganges) in their hands will give a finishing touch to the ceremony and I feel certain that the procedure will be regarded with *superstitious awe.*" [emphasis original] Chowdhury hoped to constitute "a little uncanny feeling" even in "callous" witnesses. I wonder if Jokhan Khan and Khan Mohamed induced even a slight uncanny feeling in Kemmis, as he kissed his pocket book while men surrounding him contemplated their other option, to kill him. While testifying, Kemmis sought and found a way to justify his promises: the summonses were carried out by others. But finally, there is something uncanny about Kemmis's "pocket book" itself. The court record does not further identify it. I do not know that it was a recognizably religious book. In fact, I wonder whether it was a printed book at all, or whether it was a notebook, perhaps leather-bound, in which he tallied work details in simple lists. This is because I doubt that Kemmis was an avid, competent reader. We know he could not write. Unlike many of the signatories to Manilal's petition, but like a large number of the plantation "Europeans," Kemmis did not sign his name when he certified the court papers, but simply marked them with his "x".

Manilal was clearly a fellow traveller with the more western-educated and westernizing segment of the elite Indian nationalists (and in fact, with its most anticapitalist elements). He may not have understood everything in the social lives and aspirations of his girmitiya clients in Fiji. But I think he correctly understood that many of them felt that the coercive and dangerous binding by oaths in court was itself part of their ongoing punishments. We will give him, here, the last words on holy books, also from his article criticizing the oath plan:

> in India, it was found that Hindus and Mussalmans were very unwilling to take religious oaths; . . . They said, let the Europeans, whose culture is entirely or mainly based on secularism, stake their destinies . . . upon their jeopardising their spiritual welfare . . . . But in Fiji, far away from India, the poor helots of Indian labourers had neither the spirit nor the intelligence to resist the religious oath, which is even now administered mechanically to a witness who may like to protest against it, but who is awed by the manner in which he may be dealt with by the "Babu" or the magistrate himself[.]

Despite such criticism, which required no substantive response, the Ramayana entered Fiji's court rooms, tied in red cloth, where it is still in use today.

## Sanatan Dharm

In Fiji, through the end of indenture, the Ramayana gained social salience, but on two very different vectors. It was becoming a clear candidate to be the Hindu Bible, not only in the more obvious sense of a promotable alternative in the contests with Christian missions, but also in the more subtle, and at least equally consequential, grammar of the law and rituals of the courts. It was becoming a formal as well as substantive ground for specifically Hindu truth. But meanwhile what substantive power it had actually acquired in Fiji and Empire followed down different and antagonistic instantiations of the narrative: not contained in clean books sealed and wrapped in red cloth, tied with a ribbon or even encased in an airtight box in the wetter climates, but proclaimed in loud Ramlilas, burning towers of evil. The angry invocations typified by the text of Gyani Das, the explicit comparisons of virtuous indentured women with Sita, Fiji as exile, overseers, planters, police, and other government officials as demons, the suffering, steadfast calls for the public of India to be the deus ex machina—these all sprang from the Ramayana beyond colonial ken, the Ramayana not really very comparable to the Odyssey. Down this oppositional vector, rituals of resistance connected to countercolonial initiatives, literally generating the core moral theatrics of the successful 1910s campaign in India to abolish indenture, the campaign Gandhi called India's first national satyagraha campaign (n.b. not Gandhi's first, which came much earlier, in South Africa). The Ramayana was alive in two different ways in Fiji in 1920, but its oppositional power was not fully articulated with its new, official, "holy book" reality. Not yet articulated: that synthesis came amidst a major, post-indenture social struggle over the form to be given to Hinduism in the post-indenture colonies.

In indenture days, Fiji Indian leaders appealed to all religious organizations to send teachers and missionaries, just as they called for barristers and doctors. A group called the Arya Samaj was best organized to respond. The Arya Samaj was (and still is) an effort to reform Vedic, Aryan religion to what the Arya Samaj regarded as its original pure form, focussed on an impersonal, formless *(nirguṇa)* divinity, on knowledge as the path to emancipation, and on a duty (dharma) to work on behalf of Aryan Society, to struggle to defend and to advance this superior Vedic culture for the benefit of all humanity. From its beginnings in Punjab in the late nineteenth century, Arya Samaj leaders actively engaged Christians, Muslims and others in religious controversies. A substantial portion of *Satyarth Prakash, The Light of the Truth,* the book by Arya Samaj founder Swami Dayananda Saraswati, is devoted to frank ridicule of other religious traditions, not only Christian and Muslim, Jain and Buddhist, but also Shaivite, Shakta, and Vaishnavite. From Dayananda's day onward, the Arya Samaj set out to build the institutions that would rebuild true Aryan society, notably schools, especially in competition with Christian schools, and publishing houses to spread the word. It tried various strategies for persuading people, especially those seen as corrupted ex-Aryans, to purify themselves by abandoning other religious commitments and returning to what the Samajis saw as pure Vedic (and also completely scientific) truths and practices.

These Arya Samajis, by the 1910s, had not only announced one of the first explicit, general, countercolonial visions of a vibrant Hindu and Indian future, but were veterans of struggles to make it real. Arya Samaj teachers, preachers and missionaries could meet and challenge government standards and policies for schools and presses, could extend Western education by locating it within their Vedic curriculum, and were skilled and practiced at baiting and combatting Christians, Muslims, and defenders of "Hindu" practices which they thought were corrupt. In the 1920s, many Arya Samaji teachers and preachers answered urgent calls and came to Fiji, especially to build schools. And in fact, it was largely their efforts that thwarted the Fiji Methodist Mission's plan to monopolize higher education among Fiji's Indians. Fiji's Arya Samaj monitored its competition with the Methodist Mission most acutely, but also sought to incite explicit controversy with Muslims and with defenders of Hindu texts and practices that they found corrupt. It was much to their surprise that they lost, catastrophically, in the early 1930s, in extensively publicized debates with some other missionaries recently arrived from India, pandits advancing and defending a Hindu mission they called "Sanatan Dharm."

The Arya Samaj had room in their Vedic culture for Rama and Sita, but mainly for Valmiki's version of the story; the earlier the better. And they had little use for the Ramayana narrative, but they sometimes tried to use Ramlila performances as vehicles for organizing a purely Hindu society. In both 1920s India and 1930s Fiji, Arya Samaj advocates invoked the emergent political cultures of Germany, Italy and Japan as models to emulate at least as avidly as they did Ramraj, earning the Arya Samaj the nickname, in government papers in Fiji, of "Indian fascismo."[18] Trying to work from the ground up, Arya Samajis used occasions such as Ramlila organizing to insist on restricting the event to proper Aryans. For example, in November 1930 a meeting was called of a local "Hindu Sangathan Sabha" in Samabula to pass "resolutions of disgust," (reported clerk S. Buksh[19]) against a Sanatani Pandit who maintained social relations and even conducted rituals together with "Puttu." Buksh explained:

> There is a Muslim at Samabula whose name is xxxx [illegible] Hussein otherwise known as Puttu a man well versed in Ramayan. He could expound Ramayan as good as a Pandit. This Muslim Pandit although a sincere Muslim himself used to conduct every year the Ramlila festival in the past. Now he has given it up because of the strained relations between the Hindus & Muslims.

Meetings led to counter-meetings, boycotts were launched and fizzled. The Puttus of the girmitiya world were driven out of business, but local Arya Samaj organizers met much resistance to their efforts to tighten and unify one great Hindu Sabha ("Hindu Society"). Meanwhile calls to India for aid against Arya Samaj agitation, on behalf of what was often called "orthodox" Hinduism, were answered with the arrival of "Sanatan Dharm" missionaries Murarilal Shastri and Ram Chandra Sharma in late 1930. Arya Samaj leaders frustrated by the breakdowns of their organizing efforts leaped at their chance to stage events that would be of colony-wide interest, and launched public attacks on the new Pandits. Public debates followed, on themes that astonished the British observers.

The debates focussed on the sexual morality of women and of gods. Arya Samaj spokesmen ridiculed Shaivite lingas as objects of worship, and, mixing eugenic arguments into their Vedic framework, argued that child marriage was making Hindus weak and sickly. There were good contextual reasons for debate over proprieties of marriage, in this ex-indentured society whose sex and gender relations were stressed in multiple ways. But the Samaji leaders failed to persuade Fiji's emergent Hindu public that either child marriage, or immoral mythological accretions on a pure Aryan, core Vedic dharm, were the cause of Hindu communal weakness, and problems in need of reform. Much that happened here was a consequence of contradictions in Arya Samaj doctrines and tactics, especially their fascist-inspired aggressiveness. But from here we can quite properly focus on the surprising synthesis offered by their opponents, the allegedly "orthodox" Sanatan Dharmis. Murarilal Shastri scored points in debate by criticizing Arya Samaj sex and marriage rules.[20] But these were not the telling arguments. In short, the Arya Samajis attacked the sexual morality of Shiva and of Krishna, and realities of prostitution and of children having sex in Fiji; the Sanatanis replied, Ram, Ram, Sita, Ram.

As Pierre Bourdieu among others has demonstrated, no "orthodoxy" can be a simple extension of a given way of doing things; it has to be a self-centering argument for a specific way of understanding the proper way of doing things. And certainly, the Sanatan Dharm that organized in Fiji in opposition to Arya Samaj reform simultaneously claimed for itself the sponsorship of orthodoxy, but did far more than resist religious change. Under the leadership especially of Ram Chandra Sharma, it promoted a radical centering of the Hinduism of overseas Indians, under the unique guidance and shelter provided by one specific text, Tulsi Das's *Rāmcaritmānas*. Ram Chandra Sharma's own book, *Fiji Digdarshan,* was simultaneously an overview of the life of overseas Indians in Fiji, a memoir of his time there, and a manifesto for his vision of this Sanatan Dharm:

> The great Tulsi Ramayan delivers the medicine of immortality to the foreign-dwelling men and women, teaching the true lesson of constancy; . . .
>
> Whereas in government courts in India, a priest first takes an oath to God before there is a deposition by a plaintiff or a defendant before a judge, in Fiji the mode is that the court clerk causes the oath to be given, by a Hindu with a hand on the book of the great Ramayan.
>
> The Ramayan is the fifth Veda in the colonies, teaching Hindi and doing good for people . . . .
>
> God, who protects the eternal religion [sanatan dharm] with ordinary and extraordinary powers, knew that descendants of simple devotees would spend lives in foreign countries in the indenture system. Protecting Vedic rules against this environment would be not only hard but impossible. Thus God transformed Tulsi Das from unworthy to worthy, and gave the great power to him to put the essence of the four Vedas, eighteen Puranas, and six Shastras into his Ramayan. Today it is a great blessing that the name and glory of Ram has spread from India across the seven seas. In India, even without this Ramayan there would be people who know the Sutras, and simple people would be saved because the Vedic truths would still be known. But the foreign-dwelling simple ones trapped in evil work have no other religious protection. In foreign countries the solution for the protection of Hinduism is the Ramayan.[21]

Thus Ram Chandra taught that *Rāmcaritmānas* was the fifth Veda, designed by God especially for the needs of indenture-system overseas Hindus, living in suffering and away from the supports required to maintain the ritual and literary corpus, spawned from the original four. In this image he brought together the two vectors of Ramayana salience in Fiji. The contrast between the Indian courts' willingness to employ religious specialists (not only for oaths but for interpretation of "personal law") with Fiji's restriction of the Hindu presence to a closed, bound, "holy writ," here fit seamlessly into the theological and historical story of exile. Fiji's Hindus, he taught, were not expected by God to master both science and Vedic Sanskrit in order to receive God's love and protection; their path was not to be knowledge but faith, especially faith in the form of God whose experiences so resonated with their own. The Ramayana's divine reality provided not only divinities on whom devotion could be focussed but also models for moral behavior in the devout personages of Sita and Ram. Mere emulation of Ram by Fiji Indian men, and more especially, emulation of Sita by Fiji Indian women, would solve Fiji's social problems, or so the Sanatanis believed and taught. No longer was the Ramayana simply in a competition to be the Hindu Bible. It was more than this: it was the fifth Veda, the Veda consolidating virtue in permanent exile, a coherent theological concept.

Ram Chandra Sharma, Murarilal Shastri and the other missionaries of the new Sanatan Dharm found an avid audience for their synthesis. They too condemned the evils of colonial economics, but also gave meaning to the girmitiyas' history of suffering. In their vision of the primacy of recitation and performance of the Ramayana narrative itself, they provided the Fiji Hindus with a path not just to dignity but to personally attainable *śānti*, the post-cataclysmic peace that, theoretically vital to all enmeshed in maya, was of particular value to those once enmeshed in indenture. Long before the arrival of Sharma and Sastri, clearly but variably in the indenture lines themselves, informal, egalitarian circles gathered for Ramayana readings and other *kathā*. Under Sanatan Dharm sponsorship, the circles consolidated into the primary religious institutions of the Fiji Hindus, the "tenderly egalitarian" *Rāmāyaṇ maṇḍalīs* that meet weekly to hear portions of Tulsidas.[22]

## Diaspora, Part Two

In conclusion, I want to return to the theme of exile, and the force of epic political imagination in "Indian" self-consciousness. Recall the earlier discussion of origins: has there always been an Indian diaspora? Another limit might be found not in the history of migration but in the history of self-identification. When, exactly, is there an "India" with "Indians"? And what exactly is an "Indian"? We have space here to address these questions only in connection to the indentured labor migration. As determined and taught by the British, especially in the later decades of the nineteenth century and the early decades of the twentieth, "Indians" were a race (or a congeries of races) and "India" their land of origin (or at least, their habitat of the long run, constitutive of their alleged character). By such conception, the indenture system distributed people racially "Indian" and in fact, suited by nature for hot sun agricultural and other manual labor, to other sites requiring them around the world. The history of political action against indenture in South Asia begins with growing elite consciousness—on the part of Gokhale, Gandhi, Sarojini Naidu and others—of the implications for all "Indians" of Imperial conceptions of "Indians" as natural "coolies" rather than a civilized citizenry. But it begins much earlier in plantation colonies themselves, with much more tangible, violent, interested grappling over the implications of designations such as "coolie," "Indian" and "labor unit."

Even if diaspora emanating from South Asia were not new phenomena, we can still ask when, where, how, or even whether the indentured labor migrations became a diaspora, especially in the sense of a self-conscious, permanent dispersion of a people from a homeland. My argument is that the Ramayana political imaginary has played a major role at several stages of this very real social project, and has been developed in specific ways in the course of this history. The "Indians" of indenture lived a life wherein their "race," their Indianness as a racial nature, was brutally salient to almost every quotidian detail of their lives. Not only were they "Indians" but they had to grapple with the implications of this, long before oppression of "Mother India" impelled mass public action in India itself. Of course, this doesn't mean that they were the first discoverers or inventors of binding oaths to God on holy books, of the Moharram Tazias or of giant, burning Ravana images. But I think they used such cultural materials to constitute a countercolonial symbol pool, and that they gave the Ramayana political imaginary in particular a vast countercolonial concretization, as they became not only girmitiyas but Indians who were Hindus in exile, rather than coolies by nature.

I don't mean this to become a hagiography. Any close inspection of Gyani Das's narrative, from the outset of the paper, will find that the demonization enabled by Ramayana tropes not only consolidated racial identities and differences but established self-righteous, and frankly racist, ranking of them. It produced a counterracism. And the later turn of Fiji's Ramayana, into a far more quiescent, sheltering Fifth Veda, need not be accused of moral or social innocence. No doubt, in their success the Sanatan Dharmis consolidated, also, a new patriarchy for Fiji Hindus, a staunch Sita ideal, and no doubt their antagonism to Arya Samaj ventures and their willingness to cooperate with government limited many countercolonial initiatives the Arya Samaj had launched. Rather than hagiography, I would like to finish with a sketch of a final bit of narrative vicissitude: the arrival of Ramrajya.

The Ramayana as a vehicle for self identification offers many more than one point of entry. One can be Rama, incarnate divinity fighting enemies identified as Ravana and demonic. Pollock tracks both middle-period kings and contemporary Hindutva politicians seeking such divinization. But one can also be the victim of Ravana, calling for Rama to come to your aid, as when Fiji Indians cast India's public as the fount of divine intervention and political deliverance—and did so successfully. One can be a sufferer in exile, or find Sita among the women at the crux of contradictions in the social and sexual life of the indenture lines. Or, one can be part of the audience welcoming Rama home to Ayodhya. In Fiji, as the twentieth century progressed, anxiety to establish permanence and rights of place in Fiji overtook anxiety either to understand the suffering of indenture or to maintain connection to India. And as it did, the performance of Ramlilas also shifted. Mayer's ethnography from 1951 neatly captured the attenuation of interest in the climactic immolation of Ravana.[23] None of the Ramlilas I attended in 1984 even included an outsized, or even human sized, Ravana for burning. But much vigor—in independent Fiji before the coups—attended on Rama's triumphant return to Ayodhya, an event also tightly associated, in Fiji, with Diwali night. On the night of Diwali, Fiji's single official Hindu national holiday, brightly lit houses and yards not only invited Lakshmi, but played out a homecoming, an end to Ram's exile.

If the tropes of exile and struggle make trying to bring Ramrajya into existence irresistible to so many, it is equally overwhelming how much failure and strife has actually attended the efforts, not only

Advani's, and even Gandhi's, but in Fiji. In Fiji, the coups of 1987 overturned Fiji's only Indian-elected government ever, and undercut the Diwali Ramraj symbolism and much of the celebrating. In 1991, Diwali celebrations were actually officially canceled by the Sanatan Dharm leadership, after an indigenous Fijian Methodist Youth group destroyed by firebomb the four leading Indian centers of worship in Lautoka, Fiji's biggest city. In postcolonial Fiji, there has been a dangerous dialogic of demonization, but that is another story.[24] Here let us simply ask whether Fiji's Tulsi devotees, and perhaps many of India's as well, find the most resonance in the imagery of exile and struggle, not triumph. Embrace of their fifth and only Veda, this Veda for the alienated, can provide *śānti* (peace) in many circumstances of strife, imposition, unfairness and suffering, even the *śānti* of permanent exile.

# Appendix

LINDA HESS

The following answers to the list of questions on the first page of Chapter Two give only a taste of what is actually in the collections. I have selected and summarized from answers that sometimes go on at great length.

## Fourteen Years of Exile

(a) Manthara advised Kaikeyi only to demand forest exile for Ram and the throne for her own son. Kaikeyi added the particulars—the fourteen-year term and the dress and attitude of a renunciant—on the inspiration of Sarasvati, who was carrying out the gods' will. Ravan's allotted earthly life had fourteen more years to run. Therefore, the exile needed to be that long, not more or less (Din: 48–50).

(b) The king came to Kaikeyi's apartments in the night at 2 *ghari* [a time unit]. Fourteen *ghari* remained until sunrise, the moment of Ram's installation. In her anger, Kaikeyi said fourteen years in place of fourteen *ghari*. Another view: *Shrī Vālmīki Tilak Bhūshan* says that Manthara first told Kaikeyi of Ram's upcoming installation fourteen days in advance. On hearing that, Kaikeyi decided to demand fourteen years (Pathak: 47–8).

(c) Sinha begins with Pathak's two explanations, then gives a third and says that many more are possible (Sinha 1919:13–14).

## Where Would Lakshman Stand?

This speech occurs at the Bow Contest. The answer to the question is found later in the same scene, as Ram is about to lift the bow. Lakshman, seeing the great event about to happen, addresses the elephants of the directions, the tortoise, the snake, and the boar (all of which animals are known in myth for supporting or lifting the earth). "Heed my command, hold fast, don't let the earth shake as Ram lifts the bow of Shiva." Who is Lakshman to give orders to these mighty beings? Is he just a young man? No, he is the incarnation of the thousand-headed serpent Shesh, on whom Lord Vishnu-Narayan reclines in the Milky Ocean. In fact, Vishnu-Narayan and Shesh are one. To mighty Shesh, the whole universe is no more than a speck of dust on one of his hoods. So what trouble should he have in tossing it? Does he to whom the universe is a dust-speck need a rock to dash it against? Lakshman is out of the system. He does not need a ground to stand on. He is the ground of grounds (Din: 33–5).

## Women Entrancing Women

(a) *Mohanā*—to entrance, fascinate—has more than one meaning; 1) when one sees something beautiful and suddenly bliss and elation arise in the heart; 2) when delusion invades the intelligence; 3) when, on seeing the beauty of a woman or man, one becomes contaminated by lust and defilement. Das illustrates each of the three meanings with *Mānas* verses. The scene in Janakpur where men and women are entranced by Sita's beauty has the first meaning; the general statement that women are not entranced by women's beauty has the third (Das 1962: 192–4).

(b) First, we must note the context of each verse. In Janakpur the poet shows that Sita's beauty is divine, incomparable, beyond any beauty one sees in worldly women. Thus women as well as men are entranced. Second, there are several kinds of *moha*; when he says, "Women are not entranced by women," he is speaking of the lustful kind of *moha*. The verb "to see" is not used here, because this kind of lust is born in the mind, not the eye. With Sita the entrancement is born from the vision of pure beauty—as when at the sight of a beautiful baby, even a bird or animal baby, the minds of all men and women are fixed; more than that, on seeing the beauty of a vine, a leaf, or a flower, they become entranced, they begin to stare. . .(Din 144–6).

(c) When this is said of Sita in *Bālkānd*, it is because everyone is in the *rasa* of love. They are entranced by Sita's beauty and Ram's beauty and the beauty of the pair. Further, the women of Janakpur are not ordinary women. They are the women of Brahma's world, the hymns of the Vedas, *shaktis* of the first mothers who have manifested in Janakpur for the *darshan* of Ram (Sinha 1918: 73–5).

## Did Vibhishan Rule for a Kalpa?

(a) Din's answer discusses the vast cycles of time in a kalpa as calculated in manvantaras (14), mahayugas (71), and years (4,003,200,000), quoting the *Gita* about God's avatars, listing further questions—how could Vibhishan live that long, why is he no longer king in Lanka, how could the English ships that go everywhere have failed to find his kingdom, etc. The answers include: if God wants to keep someone alive that long, he can (the crow Bhushundi is an example); no one knows where Lanka really is, but it isn't necessarily the modern island we know by that name (pp. 133–7).

(b) Das's ten-page answer begins: "Most of the so-called pre-eminent scholars of the colleges and universities, on the basis of their hollow knowledge, half-learned geography, and fantasized history that doesn't go back farther than 3000 or 4000 BC, trying to demonstrate that the facts in India's holy books—*shruti, smriti, itihāsa, Purāṇas*, etc.—are false, squander all their powers of argument and succeed in emptying their existence. Count yourself among those fallen minds. The solution is that the Ceylon of today is not the Lanka of Ravan . . . ." He gives a long history and geography lesson, citing copiously from Sanskrit texts (1987: 191–201).

## Why didn't Dasharath Adopt a Son?

Quoting the Rigveda and other weighty sources, Das lists the limited number of relatives permitted to be adopted and says that no proper candidate was available (1962: 148–51).

Worshiping Ganapati before he is Born?

If you put the question this way, you haven't correctly understood the reality. In our world, a position is filled by a series of individuals one after another. The position remains the same and is called by one name—king, president, minister, priest, general, head of temple, head of village, judge, collector, revenue officer, superintendent, sweeper, etc. So in one kalpa there are fourteen Manus, fourteen Indras, fourteen Kartikeyas, fourteen Seven-Sages, etc. Different individuals fill those positions. The honored holders of those positions are said to be endless. Thus the Ganapati positon is endless. Whoever holds it is worshiped. In the *Ganesh Purāṇa* at one point it is Kashyap and Aditi's son Mahotkut, at another Shiva and Parvati's son Mayuresh, at another Virupaksha, born of Shiva, abandoned by King Barenya and raised by Parashar. . . . [Das summarizes these three stories in the next six pages] (1962: 88–95).

Dasharath's Wives not *Pativratā*?

The questioner identifies himself as an educator. Das says: Savitri had special status; in the Puranic world among countless descriptions of *satīs* and *pativratās*, there is no other example like hers. I don't know what kind of half-baked (*adhyapake*) educator (*adhyāpak*) you are if you don't know this. You may be a schoolmaster but not an educator. Savitri had no offspring. If she'd had any, Yama would never have given Satyavan back. Dasharath couldn't have been restored because he had sons. In the Raghu lineage, the purpose of marriage was to produce progeny. Further, special dharma takes precedence over ordinary dharma. To become *satī* along with one's husband is ordinary dharma; to adore the Lord is special dharma. Following ordinary dharma, Dasharath's queens intended to become *satī*. But Bharat, explaining the importance of special dharma, didn't let them: "grasping their feet, Bharat stopped all the mothers: There is still hope of Ram's *darshan*." Read this solution, applying your mind fully. It will be clear that Dasharath's wives were supreme *pativratās* (Das 1972: 98–100).

## A Barley Worm?

Barley is not a common grain but the finest among grains used for *yajña*. In the shastras it is forbidden to eat a grain that has a worm in it. In nearly all grains, you can know if there is a worm because a black spot appears, and you can remove that grain. Worms take hold on the side or the edge in most cases. But with barley they are exactly in the middle and can't be seen from outside. Thus the worm is ground up with the barley. "The worm ground up with the barley" is a folk saying. Das now compares the worm at the center of the barley to the life breath or *prāṇ* at the center of the body. As Ram has told Vibhishan he will protect him like his own *prāṇ*, Ravan will kill Vibhishan, the worm at the center, by killing Ram, the *prāṇ* at the center (Das 1987: 90–1).

## Drum, Rustic, Shudra, Animal, Woman

Din advances a series of arguments not necessarily consistent with each other. (1) An 1895 publication of the *Mānas* based on Tulsidas's manuscript has "kshudra" (wicked person) instead of "Shudra." (2) The character who says this line, Ocean, is an offender asking for forgiveness. He is not authoritative and does not speak for Tulsidas. (3) The "right" (*adhikār*) to beat drums, rustics, Shudras, animals, and women does not suggest the duty to beat them. Only if it is necessary to set them on the right path is it permitted. Many rustics and Shudras are of a saintly and truthful nature, many animals are peaceful and disciplined, many women are goddesses to be worshiped. Should they be beaten? Certainly not! One should not tighten and hammer that drum whose voice is already fine. (4) The word often taken as "beating" (*tāṛnā*) means educating and disciplining, not beating up physically. It means teaching for their good, not with anger or enmity. Further details represent the ethos of "benevolent" high-caste male domination that yokes reverence for exemplary women with control of women as well as of lower castes and classes (Din: 162–6).

Das, in a fascinating (though, to me, disturbing) ten-page disquisition on this line, also takes several different interpretive directions not necessarily related to each other. First, he lists diverse dictionary meanings and Sanskrit precedents for usage of the verb *tāṛnā*, denying that it means physical beating in this context and suggesting that "discipline" is more fitting. Then he devotes a paragraph to each class of objects/creatures in the line—drum, rustic, Shudra, animal, woman. While ostensibly appreciating each of them for their wonderful qualities and services, he reveals a degrading and superior attitude toward them on the part of the only class of beings assumed to have consciousness and agency: upper-caste men.

The "drum, rustic" line occurs in a speech in which Ocean begs Ram to pardon a transgression. The previous line in that speech describes the five elements (including water/ocean) as inanimate or unconscious. Das expands *tāṛnā* to embrace the dual concepts of understanding and controlling; he expatiates on the great things humans can achieve when they know and control the five inanimate elements. In a triumphant climax to this section, he claims:

> In Tulsi's word "drum" all the arts are embraced; in his word "rustic," all humans in the world who give food and clothing; in the word "animal," all nonhuman creatures who give service; in the word "woman," all those tender females who give service, including all the conscious and unconscious mothers who give birth from their wombs. To understand, serve, and keep disciplined all these—that is the great cosmic mantra that Gosvami has given in his line about *tāṛnā*. This verse of the *Mānas* holds the secret of establishing a supremely auspicious friendship (*maitrī*) among all conscious and unconscious beings.

Taking another tack, Das shows how the list can be regrouped to make a series of three: drum, rustic Shudra, and animal woman. He recaps several episodes of the *Mānas* to show how this list is meant to recall them. In a final flourish, typical of the etymological playfulness for which Indian exegetes are famous, Das finds a way to derive "ocean" from *nārī* (woman) (Das 1987: 95–105).

# Notes

*Chapter One*

1. For an English translation of this telling, see E. B. Cowell, ed., *The Jataka; or Stories of the Buddha's Former Births*, 7 vols. (1895–1913; repr. London: Luzac and Co., for the Pali Text Society, 1956), vol. 4, 78–2.

2. See "Sahmat Performance for Cultural Understanding Results in Criminal Charges: A Selection of Accounts," abridged and reprinted in *Bulletin of Concerned Asian Scholars* 25. 4 (October–December 1993): 69–71 for an analysis of this incident. For a historical interpretation of the *jātaka*, see Romila Thapar, *Exile and the Kingdom: Some Thoughts on the Ramayana* (Bangalore: The Mythic Society, 1978), 7.

3. For a full statement of the implications of this view, see *Many Rāmāyaṇas: The Diversity of a Narrative Tradition in South Asia* [henceforth *MR*], ed. Paula Richman (Berkeley: University of California Press, and Delhi: Oxford University Press, 1991).

4. Scholars disagree about whether Valmiki wrote all seven *kāṇḍas* of the *Rāmāyaṇa*, and whether he composed all the verses in the Sanskrit critical edition. Nonetheless, throughout this essay I call the *Rāmāyaṇa* attributed to Valmiki "Valmiki's *Rāmāyaṇa*." In his *Poems to the Child-God: Structures and Strategies in the Poetry of Sūrdās* (Berkeley: University of California Press, 1978), x, Kenneth Bryant made a similar decision to refer to "Sūrdās" rather than "poems from the tradition associated with the name Sūrdās." The latter implies that Sūrdās was "a fictive character, and he is not; he is a *mythic* character, bigger than life, not smaller." The statement is even more true of Valmiki, as Naryana Rao demonstrates in his essay herein.

5. For a discussion of the popularity of the series see, for example, Philip Lutgendorf, "Ramayan: The Video," *The Drama Review* 34. 2 (summer 1990).

6. See Camille Bulcke, *Rāmkathā: Utpatti aur Vikās* (Prayag: Hindi Parishad, Prakashan, 1950). For an English piece that discusses succinctly the stages by which Bulcke believes that the text developed, see his "The Rāmāyaṇa: Its History and Character," *The Poona Orientalist XXV Silver Jubilee Volume,* ed. M. M. Patkar (Poona: Oriental Book Agency, 1960), 36–60.

7. The notion of "*ur*" text comes from scholarship on Western classical texts. See L.D. Reynolds and N. G. Wilson, *Scribes and Scholars: A Guide to the Transmission of Greek and Latin Literature* (London: Oxford University Press, 1968).

8. For Sanskrit views of Valmiki, see V. Raghavan, "The Ramayana in Sanskrit Literature," in his edited volume, *The Ramayana Tradition in Asia* (New Delhi: Sahitya Akademi, 1980), 1–10.

9. Frank Whaling, *The Rise of the Religious Significance of Rama* (Delhi: Motilal Banarsidass, 1980).

10. Frank Reynolds, "Ramayana, Rama Jataka, and Ramakien," in *MR*, 61, n. 8 and, for a bibliography and overview of the controversy about the *Mahābhārata*, see Robert P. Goldman, *The Rāmāyaṇa of Vālmīki,* vol. I: *Bālakāṇḍa* (Princeton: Princeton University Press, 1984), 32–4 and J.A.B. van Buitenen, *The Mahābhārata*, v. 2 (Chicago: University of Chicago Press, 1975), 207–14.

11. A.K. Ramanujan, "Three Hundred Ramayanas: Five Examples and Three Thoughts on Translation" in *MR*, 46.

12. See David Shulman, "Divine Order and Divine Evil in the Tamil Tale of Rama," *Journal of Asian Studies* 38. 4 (August 1979): 651–69.

13. Such tellings have also been called "classical" or "dominant" tellings. The first term works for Valmiki, Tulsidas, and Kamban but not Sagar.

14. Philip Lutgendorf, *The Life of a Text: Performing the* Rāmcaritmānas *of Tulsidas* (Berkeley: University of California Press, 1991), 1–3, characterizes the ways that the *Rāmcaritmānas*' popularity has been described over the years. This phrase betrays its missionary origins. See also Kelly's essay in this volume, 3.

15. For Baba Ramchandra, see Kapil Kumar, "The *Ramcharitmanas* as a Radical Text: Baba Ram Chandra in Oudh, 1920–1950," in *Social Transformation and Creative Imagination*, ed. Sudhir Chandra (New Delhi: Allied Publishers, 1984), and Gyanendra Pandey, "Peasant Revolt and Indian Nationalism: The Peasant Movement in Awadh, 1919–22," in *Subaltern Studies*, I, ed. Ranajit Guha (Delhi: Oxford University Press 1982), 166–78.

16. Paula Richman, "E.V. Ramasami's Reading of the Ramayana," *MR*, 175–201.

17. For a rich analysis of self-reflexivity in Indian texts, see A.K.

Ramanujan, "Where Mirrors are Windows: Toward an Anthology of Reflections," *History of Religions* 23. 3 (February 1989): 187–216.

18. Goldman expands on a point discussed briefly by Sheldon Pollock, who argues that one of the two pre-eminent imaginative resources of Valmiki's text is its semiotic slot for demons, which he describes as "a conceptual instrument for the utter dichotomization of the enemy." See "Rāmāyaṇa and Political Imagination in India," *The Journal of Asian Studies*, 52. 2 (May 1993): 283, where he touches upon the different diets of humans and demons.

19. Pollock.

*Chapter Two*

Many people and institutions have helped me to carry out this research and writing. The American Institute of Indian Studies and the University of California provided generous financial and other support. Vibhuti Narain Singh, the Maharaja of Banaras, in a relationship extending over twenty years, has been constantly courteous and supportive. Specifically, he arranged to have the multiple locks of his precious library opened so I could retrieve and photocopy the 1853 manuscript of Vandan Pathak's *Shankāvalī*. C.N. Singh gave unstintingly of his time and knowledge even though he had entirely justified doubts about whether I would be able to understand correctly. Special thanks are due to Philip Lutgendorf, who first told me about Ramkumar Das's four-volume *Shankāvalī* and then provided me with his own copy of it. This set has turned out to be my richest source of information on the genre. Paula Richman, Philip Lutgendorf, and Aditya Behl gave detailed comments that resulted in much improvement. Many individuals in India helped me take steps that were necessary for this work to proceed.

1. References and brief, partial answers to these questions are provided in the Appendix.

2. For a story illustrating this view, see Linda Hess and Shukdev Singh, *The Bijak of Kabir* (San Francisco: North Point Press, 1983), 37.

3. After the resurgence of Hindu nationalism in the last two decades—largely organized around narratives, images, and geographic sites associated with Ram—some readers may find my emphasis on love incongruous. The 1993 meeting of the Association of Asian Studies, where the original "Questioning Ramayanas" panel was presented, took place less than four months after a mob demolished the Babri mosque at Ayodhya. It was suggested during the panel discussion that all uses of the Ramayana at the present time are tainted with this widespread political mobilization and fomenting of hatred. One scholar commented that if the bhakti Ramayanas had ever opened a more multivocal space around the epic (which he doubted), that space was foreclosed by this univocal political appropriation by the VHP, BJP, Shiv Sena, etc.

At such a historical moment, is it sentimental, foolish, even dangerous to continue discussing the text in terms of love and devotion? I contend that several realities exist at once with regard to this text. It is as foolish to think that politics is the only reality as to think that devotion is the only reality. Without the devotion, there would be no political appropriation. To understand the text's political power, we need to understand its devotional power—and not just in order to "know the enemy." The world of bhakti is a world in itself, with its own heart, yet—like all such imagined worlds—having indistinct boundaries, interpenetrating with social and political worlds. The sincere practice of bhakti involves emotional vulnerability and strong commitment. These characteristics are exploited by political movements that seek to channel the energy of Ram-bhakti into violent forms of religious nationalism. But the same characteristics can open the way to profound experiences of compassion, fearlessness, illumination. The way to counteract the misuse of bhakti is neither to debunk bhakti nor to encourage the disconnection of religious devotion and sociopolitical realities.

4. Ramkumar Das, *Shrī Mānas Samādhān Ratnāvalī,* 4 vols. The publication information for each volume is as follows: vol. 1 (Allahabad: Shri Tulsi Sahitya Pracharak Samiti, 1962); vol. 2 (Ayodhya: published by the Author, 1972); vol. 3 (Garadih, Madhya Pradesh: Ramsharan Singh Bhuval, 1981); vol. 4 (Ayodhya: Sachchidanand Das, 1987). Since Das will be quoted frequently in the remainder of this article, henceforth citation will occur in the body of the article immediately after the quote and will provide the year (thereby indicating the volume) and page number.

5. Jay Ramdas (who writes under the name "Din"), *Mānas Shankā Samādhān,* ed. Hanuman Prasad Poddar (Gorakhpur: Gita Press, 1942), 156–7. "Din" is the sort of pen name often taken by Hindi writers and sometimes by other public figures. The short, self-chosen moniker presents a quality or image that the individual wishes to project. "Din" means humble or lowly.

6. At the beginning of his poem, Tulsidas offers a long series of *vandana*s (reverent obeisances), to all gods, all beings, finally everything in the universe, including those normally thought of as evil. The word *sīyarāmamaya,* cited above, appears in a famous line in this section:

*ākara cāri lākha caurāsī / jāti jīva jala thala nabha bāsī//*
*sīyarāmamaya saba jaga jānī / karau pranāma jori juga pānī*

*Four classes, eight million four hundred thousand / species who dwell on earth, in sea and sky—/*
*knowing all to be filled with Sita-Ram, / I bow, my two hands joined. (Mānas 1.7.1–2)*

7. I first obtained a manuscript copy of this text, dated 1853, from the library of the Maharaja of Banaras. Afterwards I found a printed version

dated 1847 at the Nagari Pracharini Sabha library in Banaras. I am very grateful to the Director of NPS and to his staff for helping me to find and photocopy this work, as well as the *Mānas Shankā Mochan* of Jang Bahadur Sinha.

8. This text seems to have been strongly influenced by Pathak's work: many doubts are nearly identical. The title page, which declares that Sinha composed and published the work for devotees and lovers of Ram, is partly in English: "MANAS SHANKA MOCHAN/OR/ Model Questions on Tulsi Krit Ramayana/BY/Babu Jang Bahadur Sinha/(Of Kothiyan, P.O. Sheohar, Dt. Muzaffarpur)/Ramnagar, Dist. Champaran." (This Ramnagar is in Bihar, unrelated to the Ramnagar of Banaras.)

9. On the importance of Gita Press and the role of Poddar, see Philip Lutgendorf, *The Life of a Text: Performing the* Rāmcaritmānas *of Tulsidas* (Berkeley: University of California Press, 1991), 61–2 and Monika Hortsmann, "Towards a Universal Dharma: *Kalyāṇ* and The Tracts of the Gītā Press" in *Representing Hinduism: The Construction of Religious Traditions and National Identity,* ed. Vasudha Dalmia and H. von Stietencron (New Delhi: Sage Publications, 1995), 294–305.

10. The preface writer is Pandit Shri Janakinath Sharma Shastri, Editorial Department, *Kalyāṇ.*

11. He must not have found many good ones, given the great number that he published.

12. The serial went on for over two years, including the "afterthought" *Uttar Ramayan*, which began after a break of several months; these letters belong to a two-month period near the end.

13. Lutgendorf, 142.

14. Ibid., 126.

15. Thus Din has *sīyāvar rāmchandra kī jay!* at the end of each solution.

16. See seven questions of Garuda, *Mānas* 7.120 ff., and questions of Parvati, 7.53 ff. On the frame structure of the *Mānas*, see Linda Hess, "Staring at Frames Till They Turn into Loops: An Excursion Through Some Worlds of Tulsidas" in *Living Banaras: Hindu Religion in Cultural Context,* ed. Bradley R. Hertel and Cynthia Ann Humes (Albany: State University of New York Press, 1933), 73–101 and Philip Lutgendorf, "The View from the Ghats: Traditional Exegesis of a Hindu Epic," *Journal of Asian Studies* 48: 272–88.

17. Charlotte Vaudeville notes in *Etude sur les sources et la composition du Rāmāyaṇa de Tulsīdās* (Paris: Libraire d'Amerique et d'Orient 1955, 15): "One can . . . suppose that Tulsi borrowed from the Tantras the idea of presenting his narrative as a dialog between Shiva and Parvati, but this presentation had already been adopted by the *Ādhyātma Rāmāyaṇa* and other sectarian works from which Tulsi could have borrowed it" (my translation). Vaudeville discusses the Shiva-Parvati frame at length in chaps. 1–3.

18. See Lutgendorf, *Life of a Text,* 10. "Reconciliation and synthesis are

. . . underlying themes of Tulsi's epic: the reconcilation of Vaishnavism and Shaivism through a henotheisitic vision that advocates worshiping Shiva as Father of the Universe while making him the archetypal devotee of Ram."

19. Dr R. Sharma, M.A., D.Litt., Hindi Department, Patna University, in Das 1972: 2.

20. One is editor of *Marutī Sanjīvan*, another of *Dharmaguru*.

21. See below for discussion of Kripalidevi Shrivastav's question on women's offering sacrifices to the goddess.

22. Even in this, the difference may not be so complete: Most EuroAmerican academic specialists in Judaism and Christianity are also members of these religions. The salient difference may be that academic norms don't usually permit EuroAmerican scholars to express enthusiastic piety in their scholarly writing.

23. See, for example, David L. Haberman, *Acting as a Way of Salvation: A Study of Rāgānugā Bhakti Sādhanā* (New York: Oxford University Press, 1988); Linda Hess, "Ramlila: The Audience Experience" in *Bhakti in Current Research, 1979–1982,* ed. Monika Thiel-Horstmann (Berlin: Dietrich Reimer Verlag, 1983), 171–94; John Stratton Hawley, *At Play with Krishna* (Princeton: Princeton University Press, 1981); Lutgendorf, *Life of a Text.*

24. Din, 22–7; Das 1962: 163–7. The relevant episode in the *Mānas* occurs in the story of King Pratapabhanu, part of an elaborate set of framing materials in Book 1.

25. The text says 54—surely a misprint, as each number in the series is half of the previous one.

26. I use "Brahminization" here for a process frequently called "Sanskritization," following the famous work of M.N. Srinivas.

27. The writer is Kripalidevi Shrivastav.

28. Those who have seen the film *Altar of Fire*, recording the performance of an ancient Vedic ritual under the patronage of European and American scholars, will remember the controversy about the goats. The texts, as preserved in the memories of brahmin priests, clearly called for goat sacrifice. But such killing was no longer acceptable in the community to which the priests belonged. After deliberation they decided to substitute packets of cooked grain for the animals. One priest found what he felt to be a textual precedent for such substitution.

29. See Sheldon Pollock, *The Rāmāyaṇa of Vālmīki: An Epic of Ancient India, vol. II: Ayodhyākaṇḍa* (Princeton, Princeton University Press, University Press, 1986), 64–73.

30. Ibid., 183v.79. One commentator says that during the exile they gave up fine meat but not plain meat. Another says they gave up meat except at ceremonial *shraddha* feasts. Still others try "to obliterate the signification of 'meat' altogether" (358). Further informative verses and notes are found on 261v.49; 262vv.62–3, 65; 411n.79; 482n.65.

31. "Calling his brothers and friends, he would always go out to hunt deer in the forest. Knowing in his heart that they were pure, he would kill the deer and show them every day to the king. The deer Ram killed with his own arrow dropped their bodies and went straight to heaven." *Mānas* 1.204.1–6. Discussed in Din, 28–9, Das 1962: 163–7.

32. At the end of a month of performance, there is a touching private ceremony in which the crowns are removed for the last time. I have seen the youngsters who play the gods weeping unabashedly during this ritual.

33. Peter Van der Veer, *Gods on Earth* (London: Athlone Press, 1988), 131–7ff.

34. On the ubiquitous image, invented and disseminated by the VHP and its allies, of sadhu Ram with weapon raised, see Anuradha Kapur, "Deity to Crusader: The Changing Iconography of Ram" in *Hindus and Others: The Question of Identity in India Today,* ed. Gyanendra Pandey (New Delhi: Penguin India, 1993), 74–109. On Hindu nationalist appropriations of Tulsidas, see Linda Hess, "Martialing Sacred Texts: Ram's Name and Story in Late Twentieth-Century Indian Politics," *Journal of Vaiṣṇava Studies* 2.4 (Fall): 175–206. On recent uses of "Ram's chariot" by politicians, see Richard Davis, "The Iconography of Ram's Chariot," *Contesting the Nation: Religion, Community, and the Politics of Democracy in India,* ed. David Ludden (Philadelphia: University of Pennsylvania Press, 1996).

35. Some of these activities directly benefit brahmins, especially offerings and Vedic rituals.

36. *Desh, kāl, pātra, avasthā*—these four contextualizing factors were first introduced to me by C.N. Singh, and their importance was illuminated for me in our many conversations in Banaras.

37. "Uma, your questions are naturally lovely, delightful, in accord with the saints and pleasing to me. But one thing didn't please me, though you said it in the grip of delusion. That's when you said that Ram was someone other than the one the Vedas sing and the sages contemplate on. Such words are spoken only by vile people possessed by an enchanting demon, hypocrites, turning away from Ram, not knowing the difference between truth and lies. They are ignorant, stupid and blind wretches, their minds clouded by sensuality, lecherous, deceitful, extremely perverse, who have never even in a dream seen a holy gathering. They speak against the Vedas, can't see the difference between benefit and harm, their inner mirror is filthy, they have no eyes. How could such lowdown creatures see Ram's beauty? They can't distinguish between *nirguṇ* and *saguṇ*, they jabber all kinds of fantastic words and roam the world in the grip of Hari's *māyā*. Nothing's too absurd for them to say. Delirious, possessed by ghosts, drunk, they don't talk sense. No one should listen to those who have drunk the wine of supreme delusion. Thus reflecting in your heart, abandon all doubt, worship Ram's feet. Oh daughter of the mountain king, listen to my words,

which are sunlight to the darkness of delusion." *Mānas* 1.113.6–115.

38. See *Mānas* 7.113.7ff. for Bhushundi's joyous fulfilment; 7.124 ff. for Garuda's; 7.128.7ff. for Parvati's.

39. Examples can be seen in a number of Ramayana-related articles and poems over the years in *Manushi: A Journal about Women and Society*. For these and other examples, see my "Rejecting Sita: Indians Respond to the Ideal Man's Cruel Treatment of His Ideal Wife" in *Journal of the American Academy of Religion* 67.1(1999): 1–35.

*Chapter Three*

1. See Ch. Malamoud, *Cuire le monde: Rite et pensée dans l' inde ancienne* (Paris: Editions La Decouverte, 1989), 295–306.

2. On Bhavabhūti's date and location, see M. Coulson, *Three Sanskrit Plays* (Harmondsworth: Penguin Books, 1981), 295; Shripad Krishna Belvalkar, *Rama's Later History* (Cambridge, Mass.: Harvard University Press, 1915), vol. 1, xxxv–xlvi.

3. *advaitam sukha-duḥkhayor anugataṃ sarvāsv avasthāsu yad*
*viśrāmo hṛdayasya yatra jarasā yasminn ahāryo rasaḥ/*
*kālenâvaraṇâtyayāt pariṇate yat sneha-sāre sthitam*
*bhadraṃ tasya sumānuṣasya katham apy ekaṃ hi tat prāpyate//*

This verse was translated together with Velcheru Narayana Rao. I cite the edition of the *Uttara-rāma-carita* edited by P.V. Kane (Delhi: Motilal Banarasidass, 1971).

4. I read *tasya sumānuṣasya* as correlative to *yad, yatra, yasmin, yat-* in the first three lines. For *bhadra* with genitive, see Pāṇini 2.3.73.

5. *kim api kim api mandaṃ mandam āsakti-yogād/*
*a-viralita-kapolaṃ jalpator akrameṇa/*
*a-śithila-parirambha-vyāpṛtaikaika-doṣṇor/*
*a-vidita-gata-yāmā rātrir eva vyaraṃsīt//.*

On the story connected to this verse (and its inferior variant reading in the final line, *evam* for *eva),* see V. Narayana Rao and D. Shulman, *A Poem at the Right Moment: Remembered Verses from Premodern South India* (Berkeley: University of California Press, and Delhi: Oxford University Press, 1998): When Bhavabhūti had composed the *Uttara-rāma-carita,* he sent a version to be recited before the great poet Kālidāsa, to win his approval; Kālidāsa listened to the work while playing chess. In the middle of the game, and the recitation, he sent for betel from the market. When the recitation was finished, Bhavabhūti's servant returned to report. "What did Kālidāsa say?" asked Bhavabhūti. "Nothing," said the servant. "Nothing at all?" asked Bhavabhūti. "He said there was a little too much *sunnam,"* replied the servant. *Sunnam* is Telugu for lime-paste, to be eaten with the betel; but it also means a nasal consonant. Bhavabhūti understood that Kālidāsa was telling him that there was one nasal too many in the play, and removed the *m* from *evam* in this verse.

6. The technical term for this device of unconscious double entendre is *patākā-sthānaka.*

7. On Vālmīki and the *krauñca* birds, see J. L. Masson, "Who Killed Cock Krauñca," *Journal of the Oriental Institute of Baroda* 18 (1969): 207–24.

8. See *Rāmāyaṇa* 2.46. [I cite the edition edited by K. Chinnaswami Sastrigal and V. H. Subrahmanya Sastri (Madras: Ramaratnam, 1958)].

9. In combat with the demon Khara, Rāma is said, by Vālmīki, to have given way at one point by two or three steps (*Rāmāyaṇa* 3.30.23). He killed Vālin unfairly, from an ambush: see D. Shulman, "Divine Order and Divine Evil in the Tamil Tale of Rama," *Journal of Asian Studies* 38 (1979): 651–69.

10. Reading *kṣaṇam avêkṣasva.*

11. The indefinites *kim-api* and its analogues, in this play, tend to point to "something" remarkable, wondrous, transcendent—as in 1.27 (see above).

12. Perhaps including a version like that of *Padma-purāṇa* (Ānandâśrama Sanskrit Series, 1894) 4.1–68; see Belvalkar, lvi–lviii.

13. "Fire and Flood: The Testing of Sītā in Kampaṉ's *Irāmāvatāram,*" in *Many Rāmāyaṇas: The Diversity of a Narrative Tradition in South Asia*, ed. Paula Richman (Berkeley: University of California Press and Delhi: Oxford University Press,1991), ed. 89–113; and see S. Pollock, *The Rāmāyaṇa of Vālmīki, Vol. III, Āraṇya Kāṇḍa* (Princeton: Princeton University Press, 1991), 15–21, 63.

14. On these names, both attested in the manuscripts, see the sources cited in n. 2.

15. Perhaps in Padmapura, Bhavabhūti's own place; but possibly Ujjayinī, the site of the great Mahākāleśvara-Śiva shrine.

16. In a similar way, the goddess Bhagavatī is the primary audience for the shadow-puppet performers of the Kerala Ramayana tradition of *tol-pāva-kūttu*: see S. Blackburn, *Inside the Drama-House: Rāma Stories and Shadow Puppets in South India* (Berkeley: University of California Press, 1996).

17. D. Shulman, "Toward a Historical Poetics of the Sanskrit Epics," *International Folklore Review* 1991: 9–17.

18. D. Winnicott, *Psychoanalytical Explorations*, ed. Clare Winnicott, Ray Shepherd, and Madeleine Davis (Cambridge, Mass.: Harvard University Press, 1989), 181.

19. Thus, for example, 2.19 = 6.5.

20. This *śloka* is missing from our Ramayana text; see note by Nadine Stchoupak in her fine annotation to the text, *Uttararāmacarita (La Derniere Adventure de Rama)* (Paris: Societé d'edition "Les Belles Lettres," 1935), 126.

21. Discussion in V. V. Mirashi, *Bhavabhuti* (Delhi: Motilal Banarasidass, 1974), 253.

22. See 3.7ff. ; 3.8ff. ; Act VI is known in the colophons as *kumāra-pratyabhijñāna*, "Recognizing the Boys."

23. See example discussed above, 1.33; discussion of this pattern by Stchoupak, xli, and see Narayana Rao and Shulman on *para-pūrita* verses.

24. On the theme of tautological self-identification, see D. Shulman, "Embracing the Subject: Harṣa's Play within a Play," *Journal of Indian Philosophy* 25 (1997): 69–89.

25. See, e.g. 1. 27 and 1.35 (both translated above); 3.36; 6.38 etc. This stylistic trait is also noted by Stchoupak, xlvi–xlviii. The oral (*cāṭu*) tradition parodies this distinctive "signature" of Bhavabhūti's, ascribing to him the following verse in which he challenges Kālidāsa: *Kālidāsa-kaver vāṇī kadā-cin mad-girā saha / kalayaty adya sāmyaṃ ced bhītā bhītā pade pade. //* "If Kālidāsa's words ever compete with mine, they'll be afraid, very afraid, step by step, word by word . . . ." *Bhoja-caritra* of Ballala, edited by Ko. Subrahmaṇya Śāstrī (Madras: Prabhākara mudrâkṣara-śālā, 1895) [= *Bhoja-prabandha* ], verse 249.

26. v.l. *parivarta*; cf. *vivarta* in 6.6.

27. See *Śatapatha Brāhmaṇa* [Banaras: Kashi Sanskrit Series 127, n.d.] 1.1.1.6.

28. On the liar's paradox and allied forms of self-referential riddles, see Ilan Amit, "Squaring the Circle," in *Untying the Knot: On Riddles and Other Enigmatic Modes,* ed. Galit Hasan-Rokem and D. Shulman (New York: Oxford University Press, 1996), 284–93. I thank Yohanan Grinshpon for discussions of this point.

29. *na hi tad avakalpate yad brūyād idaṃ aham satyād anṛtam apaîmîti tad u khalu punar manuṣo bhavati tasmād idam aham ya evâsmi so 'smîty eva vrataṃ visṛjate* (ibid.). "It is not right for him to say, 'I have come from truth into untruth.' Since he becomes human again, let him release himself from the ritual by saying, 'I am just who I am.'" See J. Heesterman, "'I am who I am': Truth and Identity in Vedic Ritual," in *Beiträge zur Hermeneutik indischer und abendlandischer Religionstraditionen,* ed. G. Oberhammer (Vienna: Österreischichen Akademie der Wissenschaften, 1991), 147–77.

30. See Pollock, *Rāmāyaṇa of Vālmīki*; Shulman, "Fire and Flood."

31. E.g. 1.24–30; 1.35–8; 5.13–16 (with intervening *śārdūla-vikrīḍita*); 6.26–30 (with intervening *indravajrā*); the subtle variation and transition from one meter to another, often via a third, merits attention and careful study. Bhavabhūti is the great master, in the classical tradition, of both these meters, which again comprise a kind of "signature." *Śikhariṇī* has the highest distribution in this play (30 examples).

32. I wish to thank Nita Shochet for suggesting this link with the theme of healing, so deeply relevant to this text.

33. There, however, the dominant meter is the epic *śloka*, in line with Vālmīki's text.

34. *smarasi sutanu tasmin parvate lakṣmaṇena*
*prati-vihita-saparyā-susthayos tāny ahāni/*
*smarasi sārasa-nīrāṃ tatra godāvarīṃ vā*
*smarasi ca tad-upânteṣv āvayor vartanāni//*
This is the immediate prelude to the verse of whispered nights (1.27)

35. *eṣo 'smi karyavaśād āyodhyakas tadānīṃtanaś ca saṃvṛttaḥ.*

36. Cf. Malamoud, 297: ". . . le verbe [*smṛ*] lui-même ne signifie pas purement et simplement 'se rappeler', mais plutot 'fixer avec intensité son esprit sur un objet (qui n'est pas materiellement présent).'"

37. I have argued this at some length in "The Prospects of Memory," *Journal of Indian Philosophy* 26 (1998).

38. See Bimal Krishna Matilal, *Perception: An Essay on Classical Indian Theories of Knowledge* (Oxford: Clarendon Press, 1986), 141–79.

39. I wish to thank V. Narayana Rao for discussions of this term.

40. 3. 30; weeping here is a vital sign that Rāma is still capable of breathing. For *drava*, "flux," as the state of the emotion-laden heart, cf. 3.25.

41. These themes are discussed at length in Don Handelman and David Shulman, *God Inside Out: Śiva's Game of Dice* (New York: Oxford University Press, 1997), in the light of the original insights by Margaret [Trawick] Egnor, *The Sacred Spell and Other Conceptions of Life in Tamil Culture* (Ph.D. diss., University of Chicago, 1978), 32–64, 82–7.

42. *anirbhinno gabhīratvād antar-gūḍha-ghana-vyathaḥ/*
*puṭa-pāka-pratīkāśo rāmasya karuṇo rasaḥ//*

43. Kane, 78, on this verse.

44. See, e.g. R. D. Karmarkar, *Bhavabhuti* (Dharwar: Karnatak University, 1971), 64; also the recent essay by Lalita Pandit, "Patriarchy and Paranoia: Imaginary Infidelity in *Uttararāmacarita* and *The Winter's Tale,*" in *Literary India: Comparative Studies in Aesthetics, Colonialism, and Culture*, ed. Patrick Colm Hogan and Lalita Pandit (Albany: SUNY Press, 1995), 129, offering a very different perspective on this issue.

45. 1.40, 1.46 (both connected to images of poisoning), 7 (following verse 2).

46. E.g. 3.3; but cf. 4.6.

47. See "Embracing the Subject" (on *Priyadarśikā*); and Act VI of the *Nala-vilāsa-nāṭaka* of Rāmacandrasūri, where Nala watches a troupe of actors playing his own story.

48. See D. Shulman, "On Being Human in the Sanskrit Epic: The Riddle of Nala," *Journal of Indian Philosophy* 22 (1994): 21–4.

49. *Jaiminīya Upaniṣad Brāhmaṇa* 89.

50. Shulman, "Embracing the Subject."

51. *athavā snehaś ca nimitta-savyapekṣaś cêti vipratiṣiddham etat.*

52. See, e.g. 3.13 with its preceding prose passage.

53. E.g. 3.34 [leading up to 3.47]; cf. prose following 3.25. The juxtaposition of these terms is particularly compelling in Act III, which begins with the powerful statement of Rama's *karuṇā* but then proceeds through various accusations and reproaches relating to his *dāruṇa* acts.

54. *yad vā sarva-sādhāraṇo hy eṣa manaso moha-granthir āntaraś ca cetanāvatām upaplavaḥ (v.l. anuplavaḥ) saṃsāra-tantuḥ*: 7, before verse 4 (spoken by the Ganges to the Earth).

*Chapter Four*

1. *Ānanda-Rāmāyaṇam,* ed. Pandit Yugal Kishor Dvivedi with commentary "Jyotsnā" by Pandey Ramtej Shastri (Vārāṇasī: Pandita Pustakālaya, 1977). *Yātrā kāṇḍa* 2: 73–4. Henceforth, references to *Ā.R.* appear in the body of the text in parentheses.

2. The processes of questioning, othering and localizing continue to result in new Ramayanas even now. After the production of the T. V. Ramayana in 1987, some scholars worried that it might put an end to further creativity, but that is not the case. New Ramayanas are being written, sung, and performed. A recent feminist interpretation of the Rāma myth tries to combine grass roots social concerns with science fiction. See Shaila Belle, *Dakṣiṇāyana* (Bombay: Granthali Publication, 1994).

3. The date ascribed to *Ā.R.* by Camille Bulcke, *Rām-kathā: Utpatti aur Vikās*, rev. edn. (Allahabad: Allahabad University, 1971), 168, is between the fourteenth and the fifteenth century AD. The upper limit is furnished by *Adhyātma-Rāmāyaṇa* (fourteenth century AD) which is mentioned in *Ā.R.* The lower limit is set by the two vernacular Ramayanas that draw upon some incidents found only in *Ā.R.*, namely *Torave-Rāmāyaṇa* of Narahari (c. AD 1500–90; cf. Bulcke, 224) in Kannada, and *Bhāvārtha-Rāmāyāṇa* of Eknāth (AD 1533–99) in Marathi.

4. This list gives at least twenty-five names or descriptions of Ramayanas and claims that they all originated from the original *Rāmāyaṇa* by Vālmīki, extending over a billion verses.

5. There is a lengthy account here of a fight among residents of the triple worlds, the gods, the mortals, and the Nāgas, over who is to possess the *Rāmāyaṇa* created by Vālmīki. The fight is resolved by Viṣṇu by dividing the original into three equal portions, for the benefit of the triple world, with a remainder which also gets divided equally, with a remainder, and so on. Lastly one letter/syllable remains which is Śree, which Viṣṇu scatters over the nine continents. Elsewhere, a similar division occurs where the last two syllables remaining are the name "Rāma" which are given to Śiva.

6. *Ā.R. Sāra kāṇḍa* 3: 22 offers two versions of the Ahalyā myth. *Ā.R. Sāra kāṇḍa* 13: 163 offers two birthdates of Hanumān, whereas *Ā.R. Sāra*

*kāṇḍa* 11: 277 offers two versions of the death of Rāvaṇa. *Ā.R. Yātrā kāṇḍa* 4: 85–8 offers two myths explaining the etymology of the name Śarayu or Sarayu.

7. Theoretically, the composer could have been one or many, male or female. The identity of the composer is unknown. It was believed by some to be the *sant* poet Rāmdās of Maharashtra, but Rāmdās lived in the seventeeth century, and could not have been the composer of a fifteenth-century text. Since the identity (gender or number) of the composer is secret, wherever I use the habitual masculine singular it does not imply anything more than my being conventional for the sake of brevity. At present, all I can say is that the entire *Ā.R.* reads like a carefully integrated composition, with definite goals and a meticulously self-reflexive texture. For more on the integrated nature of its composition, see Vidyut Aklujkar, "Battle as Banquet: A Metaphor in Sūradāsa," *Journal of the American Oriental Society* 111.2 (April–June 1991): 353–61.

8. For example, *Ā.R. Manohara kāṇḍa* 8: 60–72 lists among others *Yoga Vāsiṣṭha* and *Adhyātma-Rāmāyaṇa*.

9. On the topic of sacralization of alternative variants of myths, see Vidyut Aklujkar, "Why Build A Bridge Over The Ocean: Propriety in The *Ānanda Rāmāyaṇa*" in *Siting Sita,* ed. Mary McGee (forthcoming).

10. There is no complete translation into English of the text. I have provided partial translations as needed in articles written on the text. My complete translation and an edition of the text, in progress, are based on 1) an early printed edition published from Bombay, by Govardhandas Lakhmidas, in *pothi* form with no date of publication and some pages of earlier chapters missing, 2) a Marathi translation by Pundit Vishnushastri Bapat published by Dā. Sāṁ. Yande, in 1900 (I have secured two pages of the "prastāvanā" or preface to this edition, but not the translation), and 3) a Hindi commentary called "Jyotsnā" written by Pandey Ramtej Shastri and included in *Ā.R.* published by Pandit Yugal Kishor Dvivedi (Varanasi: Pandita Pustakālaya, 1977). Also see Aruna Gupta, *Ānanda-Rāmāyaṇa: A Cultural Study* (Delhi: Eastern Book Linkers, 1984).

11. Vālmīki. *The Vālmīki-Rāmāyaṇa* critical edition, vols. 1–6 (Baroda: Oriental Institute, 1960–75). [*The Uttarakāṇḍa: The Seventh Book of the Vālmīki Rāmāyaṇa,* critically ed. Umakant Premchand Shah. Critical edn., vol. VII]

12. Notably the *Rasik saṁpradāya*. See Shridhar Bhaskar Varnekar, *Sanskrit Vāñmaya Kośa* (Encyclopedia of Sanskrit Literature), vols. 1–2 (Calcutta: Bharatiya Bhasha Parishad. 1988), 27.

13. For his influence on Sūrdās, see Vidyut Aklujkar, "Battle as Banquet." For Eknāth, see *Bhāvārtha Rāmāyaṇa by Śrī Santa Ekanātha,* ed. Narahari Viśṇuśāstri Paṇaśīkar, vols. 1–2 (Pune: Yashwant Prakashan,1968).

14. See C. R. Sharma, "The Rāmāyaṇa Tradition in Telugu and Tamil:

A Comparative Study" in *Folk Rāmāyaṇas in Telugu and Kannada*, ed. T. Gopala Krishna Rao (Nellore: Saroja Publications, 1984).

15. For more information on this topic, see Vidyut Aklujkar, "Rāmāvatāra Recycled," *Annals of the Bhandarkar Oriental Research Institute,* vol. LXXVI (Pune: Bhandarkar Oriental Research Institute, 1995), 107–18.

16. This refers to a conventional account of the extent of *Rāma-carita. Caritaṁ raghunāthasya śata-koṭi-pravistaraṁ/ Rāma-rakṣā stotra. Ā.R.* often refers to *V. R.* by using the term *śata-koṭi-pravistaraṁ* which means "extending over a billion (verses)."

17. This is a clever reference to the wrapper-story of *V. R.*, which centers on the sorrow of the surviving bird whose mate was killed by a hunter's arrow, and the sorrow of the sage who cursed the hunter moved by the misery of the bird. A famous dictum describes how Vālmīki's sorrow took the form of a meter of even letters and four parts, called *śloka: Śokaḥ ślokatvaṁ āgataḥ, V. R. Bāla kāṇḍa* 2: 39.

18. Since Brahmā was born of the lotus, born of the navel of Viṣṇu, and since Rāma is the incarnation of Viṣṇu, Brahmā becomes Rāma's offspring.

19. In Maharashtra, the temple priests used this text for their daily recitation and story-telling sessions. I have seen on *Ā.R. pothis* hand-written notes by the priests of Nasik to the effect, "These cantos were lent to such and such priest to use at the *kathā-purāṇa* session at such and such temple."

20. For example, one of the stories of Birbal relates Akbar's decree to put to the stake all sons-in-law. Birbal points out the folly to the king by ordering a stake of silver for himself, and a golden one for the king. The very theme of the ban on laughter is also found in a children's comic book, called *Tinkle*, no. 205 from the *Amar Chitra Kathā* series (Bombay: India Book House Pvt. Ltd., 1990), where the king who bans first crying and then laughter from his kingdom is appropriately called Murakh Singh, which means Mr Idiot.

21. Stith Thompson lists this as: CA60—Laughing Taboo. Type 451; BPI 71—India-Thompson-Balys. It may also fall under C600: Unique prohibition. See Stith Thompson, *Motif Index of Folk Literature,* vols. 1–6, rev. edn. (Bloomington: Indiana University Press, 1975).

22. *dukkha-saṁvedanāyaiva rāme caitanyamāhitam,* act 1 v 47 in *The Uttara-rāma-carita of Bhavabhūti*, ed. with commentary of Vīrarāghava and English translation by M. R. Kale (Bombay: Gopal Narayan and Co., 4th edn., 1934).

23. For more on why this incarnation is more joyous, see Vidyut Aklujkar, "Rāmāvatāra Recycled."

24. *Ā.R. Rājya kāṇḍa* 16. The placement of these two *sargas* with the order being "practice before precept" reflects a popular Marathi proverb about commendable behavior which says, "*ādhī keleṁ, maga sāṅgitaleṁ*" (First practiced, then preached).

25. The *Ā.R.* choice of the word to denote a monk here is ironic, since a *yati* (n. from the root *yam*, to control) is supposed to be in control of his emotions.

26. By using the word *Sārameya* which invokes the Vedic dog Saramā, who was sent by Indra to locate his lost cows, and who succeeded in locating them in the land of Paṇis, perhaps *Ā.R.* is trying to elevate the dog by citing his lofty pedigree. Rāma's addressing the dog thus perhaps echoes the courteous, formal speech prevalent in courtly circles.

27. The adjective used here is *Ramā-pati*, which is in fact Viṣṇu's adjective, but since Ramā means Lakṣmī, and Sītā is an incarnation of Lakṣmi, just as Rāma is of Viṣṇu, the adjective is applied to Rāma.

28. For example, there is the story of Sant Nāmdev, who is eating ghee and *bhākrīs* when a dog steals one from his lunch, and runs away with it. Nāmdev gets up with a bowl of ghee in his hand, and runs after the dog to offer the ghee to the dog, so that the dog may not suffer the belly-ache that will surely result from digesting a dry *bhākrī*. Of course, the dog turns out to be God, and Nāmdev is celebrated for the clarity of his vision which does not differentiate between himself and the dog.

29. The critical edition of *V. R.* does not include this incident, but it is narrated in two *sargas* (in the *Uttara kāṇḍa* 60–61, or 61–2) in *V. R.* editions based on the Southern and the North-eastern recensions. [*The Vālmīki Rāmāyaṇa* according to Southern Recension, ed. T. R. Krishnacharya. (1st edn.: Kumbakonam: Sri Garibdas Oriental Series 3, 1905; rpt., Delhi: Sri Satguru Publications, 1982) and *The Vālmīki Rāmāyaṇa* edition based on the North-eastern recension, ed. Gasparo Gorresia (1843; rep. edn. by V. Raghavan, Madras: Indian Heritage Trust,1981–2).] The respective editors call the two *sargas* devoted to the tale of the crying dog interpolated *sargas*, and Sanskrit commentators do not comment on them. *The Rāmāyaṇa of Vālmīki* with the commentary Tilaka by Rāma, ed. Wāsudev Laxman Śāstrī Paṇaśikar (Delhi, Varanasi: Indological Book House, 1983).

The *V. R.* and the *Ā.R.* differ in the actual verses as well as certain details. In *V. R.*, for example, Rāma orders the dog to come to his assembly, and the dog complies, whereas in *Ā.R.* Rāma goes to the dog to hear his complaint. More important, in *V. R.*, these *sargas* appear rather out of place in the *Uttara kāṇḍa*, after the myth of Yayāti, and bear no connection to it, whereas in *Ā.R.* the very placement of the incident is of crucial importance and makes it an integral part of its overall scheme.

30. *Ā.R. Manohara kāṇḍa* 12: 35–6. All these conciliatory statements support the claim of *Ā.R.*'s origin in Maharashtra. The *Bhāgavata Dharma,* which was popular in Maharashtra in the medieval period, was actively concerned with the reconciliation of the Śaiva and Vaiṣṇava ideologies.

31. This is why I have included the full translation of the entire speech of the wise dog.

32. Vyāsa and not Vālmīki here is linked with *Rāma-kathā*, but this is not problematic to the author of *Ā.R.* who believes in the ultimate unity of God, and perhaps follows the *paurānika* tradition of thought which regards Vyāsa as another form of Vālmīki in a different *yuga*. Besides, as we saw earlier, the author of *Ā.R.* has already assumed both Vālmīki and Vyāsa are engaged in the enterprise of narrating the same divine comedy.

33. Kālidāsa in *Mālavikāgnimitram*, act 1, *Kālidāsa Granthāvalī: Complete Works of Kālidāsa,* ed. Revāprasāda Dwivedi (Varanasi: Banaras Hindu University, 1976), and Rājaśekhara in *Bāla Rāmāyaṇam,* 1: 16, ed. Pundit Govinda Deva Shastri (Benaras: Medical Hall Press, 1869).

*Chapter Five*

1. With apologies to Ramchandra Gandhi. See his *Sita's Kitchen: A Testimony of Faith and Inquiry* (Albany: State University of New York Press, 1992).

2. Such stories are widely distributed throughout the tradition. Thus it is a point of doctrine among Digambara Jains that once a Tirthankara attains perfect spiritual enlightenment (*kevalajñāna*), he no longer requires physical nourishment. See Padmanabh S. Jaini, *Gender and Salvation: Jaina Debates on the Spiritual Liberation of Women* (Berkeley: University of California Press, 1979), 4, 24, 36. Similarly the Hindu epics are full of stories of sages so spiritually adept and so fully in control of their sensual apparatus that they subsist only on air (*vāyubhakṣa*) or fast for thousands of years. That the notion was in general circulation among intellectuals in ancient India is further suggested by Patañjali's use of the terms *vāyubhakṣa* (subsisting on air) and *abbhakṣa* (subsisting on water) as illustrations in his discussion of the eternal relation of word to meaning (*siddhaśabdārthasaṃbandha*). See *The Vyākaraṇamahābhāṣya of Patañjali, Vyākaraṇa-Mahābhāṣya,* ed. Franz Kielhorn (Poona: Bhandarkar Oriental Research Institute, 1962), vol. 1, 6, lines 23–4. A modern literary example is Paramahamsa Yogananda's account of his meeting with Giri Bala, whom he terms "the woman yogi who never eats" in Paramahamsa Yogananda, *Autobiography of a Yogi* (New York: Philosophical Library, 1946), 460–71. Then too, like most people who have worked in India with members of various religious communities, I have been told about, and even met, men and women whose spiritual advancement, so it was said, enabled them to transcend the otherwise universal need for food.

3. As at *Manusmṛti* 3.45, 9.4, 70, etc. See Nārāyaṇa Rāma Ācārya, ed., *The Manusmṛti with the Commentary Manvarthamuktāvali of Kullūka*, 10th edn. (Bombay: The Nirṇaya Sāgar Press, 1946).

4. Cf. for example the discussion of Rāma's anorexia in Goldman and Goldman's notes to *Sundarakāṇḍa* 5.34.39 in R. P. Goldman and S. J. Goldman, *The Rāmāyaṇa of Vālmīki: An Epic of Ancient India, Vol. V, Sundarakāṇḍa* (Princeton: Princeton University Press, 1996), 550–1.

5. The pervasiveness of this preoccupation can perhaps be judged from the great grammarian Patañjali's selecting the issue of permitted and forbidden foods as an illustration of the nature of rules themselves. Kielhorn, vol. I, 5, lines 14–17.

6. Thus one of Carstairs's informants, the Rajput Rajendra Singh, argued that, at least in his case, "drink does not interfere with 'spiritual rise.'" On the contrary he argued that in moderation it may help one attain it. The same man clearly articulates the South Asian bi-polar tradition of indulgence and abstention when he argues that "the two greatest things life has to offer are, to take one's ease in the pleasures of the bed with one or two girls of sixteen, or else to devote oneself to prayer and spiritual rise." He also closely associates indulgence of the appetite and the passions when he states, "one should taste experience to the full—if one eats, one should eat until one is replete, and the same with making love." G. Morris Carstairs, *The Twice-Born: A Study of a Community of High-Caste Hindus* (Bloomington: Indiana University Press, 1961), 194. A similar idea is expressed by a clearly inebriated, *soi disant* Rajput in Anand Patwardhan's documentary film on the Ayodhya controversy, *Rām ke Nām*, who claims that his liquor is "*somras*" and that it is therefore appropriate for a Kshatriya to drink it, even in connection with what is represented as a religious undertaking.

7. Consider the anecdote related by Verrier Elwin in his autobiography, according to which the British Gandhian Mirabehn (Madeleine Slade) once closed the windows of her sea-front apartment while serving him food. When Elwin protested because of the heat, she replied, "No Verrier, the sea-breeze carries particles of salt. These will fall on our food and it will make it more difficult for you to control your passions." Verrier Elwin, *The Tribal World of Verrier Elwin* (Calcutta: Oxford University Press, 1964), 55–6. Compare the quote (n. 9) from Gandhi, for whom the control of diet and, consequently, of sexuality, amounted virtually to an obsession.

8. *Mahābhārata* 1.182. *The Mahābhārata Text as Constituted in its Critical Edition* (Poona: Bhandarkar Oriental Research Institute, 1971).

9. One such explicit association can be seen in some remarks of Gandhi quoted by Paramahamsa Yogananda, *Autobiography,* 443: Gandhi told him, "Yes, diet is important in the *Satyagraha* movement . . . Because I advocate complete continence for the *satyagrahis,* I am always trying to find out the best diet for the celibate. One must conquer the palate before he can control the procreative instinct . . . . By inward and outward wisdom in regard to eating, the *satyagrahi's* sexual fluid is easily turned into vital energy for the whole body."

10. The association of these two domains of desire is widely experienced in many cultures.

11. The well-known story of how Śaṅkara took yogic possession of the body of the dead king Amaruka in order to equip himself for a scholarly

debate on the science of erotics with the wife of Maṇḍanamiśra is narrated in the ninth and tenth chapters of Mādhavācārya's poem the *Śaṅkaradigvijaya* (*Śṛīśaṅkaradigvijaya Mādhavācāryaviracita*), 2nd edn., Sri Śravaṇanātha Jñānamandiragranthamālā, *Saṃvat* 2024 (=1967–68) puṣpa 1. Hardvar: Śrī Śravaṇanātha Jñāna Mandir. vss. 9.44–10.18, 314–35.

12. Sheldon I. Pollock, *The Rāmāyaṇa of Vālmīki: An Epic of Ancient India, Vol. III: The Araṇyakāṇḍa* (Princeton: Princeton University Press, 1991), 68–84.

13. Ibid., 82.

14. Ibid., 83–4.

15. Rām 5.7.30–59 (excerpted). All references are to the critical edition of the *Vālmīki Rāmāyaṇa* ed. G. H Bhatt, et al. (Baroda: Oriental Institute,1960–75). The translations are taken from R. Goldman and S. Goldman, *Rāmāyaṇa of Vālmīki.* Henceforth, verse numbers follow the translations in the body of the text.

16. Note here the even more pointed contrast between Śūrpaṇakhā's ugliness and the masculine beauty of Rāma.

17. The actual identities of the creatures included in Rāvaṇa's banquet whose Sanskrit names are used are not entirely clear and form a subject of debate among the text's commentators. For a detailed discussion see the notes to this passage in R. Goldman and S. Goldman, 377–8.

18. The identity of this organ is not entirely clear. The Sanskrit commentators on the *Rāmāyaṇa,* when they accept this reading, differ as to the meaning of the term. Thus the author of the *Amarakataka* commentary and the author of the popular *Tilakaṭīkā* (the latter taking the term as an alternate reading) takes *utpīḍa* to mean "a fleshy ligature situated above the heart." Govindarāja defines it as "a fleshy mass located on top of the spleen." See R. Goldman and S. Goldman, 417.

19. Mysore Narasimhachar Srinivas, *The Cohesive Role of Sanskritization and Other Essays* (Delhi: Oxford University Press, 1989).

*Chapter Six*

1. From a song about Shabari, presumably by a folk poet, quoted (without further identification) in *Kalyāṇ: Bhakta Caritrāṇk*, ed. Hanumanprasad Poddar (Gorakhpur, U.P.: Gita Press, 1952), 294.

2. Unless otherwise specified, I cite the Baroda critical edition, in Sheldon Pollock's translation, *The Rāmāyaṇa of Vālmīki, Volume III: Araṇyakāṇḍa* (Princeton: Princeton University Press, 1991).

3. A.K. Ramanujan, "Three Hundred *Rāmāyaṇas:* Five Examples and Three Thoughts on Translations," in *Many Rāmāyaṇas: The Diversity of a Narrative Tradition in South Asia,* ed. Paula Richman (Berkeley: University of California Press and Delhi: Oxford University Press, 1991), 46.

4. On the usage of such labels as *śabara, kirāta, pulinda, niṣādha,* etc. in ancient Sanskrit texts, see Aloka Parasher, *Mlecchas in Early India* (Delhi: Munshiram Manoharlal, 1991), especially 179–221. In general, Parasher's comprehensive study documents the use of such terms to denote *mlecchajātis*—people born into communities outside the geographical limits and sphere of influence of Brahmanical *varṇa*-based ideology—and (increasingly over time) of *śabara* and *pulinda* as "generic names for barbarous tribes," often associated with the Vindhya region, but sometimes located elsewhere (ibid., 187, 191). *Śabara* and its variants (e.g. *sabara, savara, saora*) have been applied in modern times to "tribal" ethnic groups found from Tamil Nadu [see Edgar Thurston, *Castes and Tribes of Southern India,* 7 vols. (Madras: Government Press, 1909), vol. 6, 305] to Orissa [see Frédérique Apffel Marglin, "Death and Regeneration: Brahmin and Non-Brahmin Narratives," in *Devotion Divine,* ed. Diana L. Eck and Françoise Mallison. (Groningen: Egbert Forsten,1991), 221]; note the comments of one of Marglin's *śabara* interviewees: "In all the *yugas* the *śabaras* are the most devoted to Bhagavan. In the *treta yuga,* the age of Rāma, the *śabaras* were good friends with Rāma and they helped him cross rivers in their boats . . . ." Indeed, Guha, the tribal chief who first befriends Rama in the forest and escorts him across the Ganges, is identified as a *śabara* in some texts, especially in Ramayana narratives from north-eastern India. That he and his followers are "outsiders" of a decidedly base and impure sort is also occasionally emphasized, e.g. in Balaramadasa's (early sixteenth century) Oriya *Jagamohana Rāmāyaṇa*: "The hair on their bodies was frightening to see, the languages they spoke impossible to understand. Some wore their hair in heavy locks. One chewed on chunks of meat scorched in a fire. The bodies of some were smeared with ashes, castor-seed oil oozed down from the hair of the heads of others . . . ." [quoted in W. L. Smith, *Rāmāyaṇa Traditions in Eastern India* (Stockholm: University of Stockholm, Department of Indology, 1988; reprint, Delhi: Munshiram Manoharlal, 1995), 68–9].

5. *Śrīmad Vālmīki Rāmāyaṇa,* 2 vols. (Gorakhpur, U.P.: Gita Press, 1976), 1: 665, 3.74.11 and 1: 666, 3.74.31.

6. Cited in Pollock, 354.

7. George Hart and Hank Heifetz (trans.), *The Forest Book of the Rāmāyaṇa of Kampaṉ* (Berkeley and Los Angeles: University of California Press, 1988), 298–9.

8. C. R. Sarma, *The Ramayana in Telugu and Tamil* (Madras: Lakshminarayana Granthamala, 1973), 93.

9. Swami Tapasyananda, trans., *Adhyātma Rāmāyaṇa* (Madras: Sri Ramakrishna Math, 1985), 166.

10. Ibid., 167.

11. Ibid., 169–70.

12. Other examples could be added; thus neither Madhava Kandali's (*c.*

1350) Assamese telling nor Krittibasa's fifteenth-century Bengali epic mention the offering of *ucchiṣṭa* fruit, and W. L. Smith observes that the episode generally "is not at all well represented in our eastern vernacular *Rāmāyaṇas*" (49–50, 125). Of the two references to the tainted food offering that Smith cites, the earliest is found in Balaramadasa's *Jagamohana Rāmāyaṇa*, in which Shabari serves Rama mangoes, concerning which he remarks, "If they were good, why didn't you mark them with your teeth?" (ibid., 125)—which (like other examples cited above) seems to allude to an untold story, even as it makes the Lord himself, rather than his devotee, the instigator of the implied transgression. Not until the late-eighteenth-century *Jagadrāma Rāmāyaṇa* in Bengali is the offering of pre-tasted fruit explicitly mentioned, and it prompts Rama to think, "If I feel disgust and do not eat this fruit, my name as one who is obligated to his devotees will be gone at once. [Therefore] I must eat the leavings of Shabari" (ibid., 111). These references support the conclusion that the matter of the *ucchiṣṭa* food is either avoided by the authors of literary Ramayanas, or that it developed at a comparatively late date.

13. Monier Monier-Williams, *A Sanskrit-English Dictionary* (rev. edn., Oxford: Clarendon Press, 1956), 1052.

14. George A. Grierson, "Gleanings from the *Bhaktamāla*," *Journal of the Royal Asiatic Society*, 1909: 607–44, 608.

15. Sitaramsharan Bhagvanprasad Rupkala, ed., *Gosvāmī Śrī Nābhā-jī Kṛt Śrī Bhaktmāl, Śrī Priyā Dās-jī praṇita ṭīkā-kavitta* (rep. edn., Lucknow: Tejkumar Press, 1962), 82.

16. E.g. in Poddar, *Kalyāṇ*, and in Dayashankar Avasthi, "Devesh," *Śabarī Caritra, Khaṇḍ Kāvya* (Lucknow: Ramdev Avasthi, 1975).

17. Poddar, 292.

18. Ibid., 293–6.

19. Anjaninandan Sharan, *Mānas-pīyūṣ*, 12 vols. (1925–56), vol. 8, *Araṇya Kāṇḍ* (Ayodhya: Mānas-Pīyūṣ Kāryālay, 1952), 324.

20. Poddar, 294.

21. Sharan, 326.

22. Ibid.

23. For the metaphor of the Vedic corpus as oceanic but "salty" see Vasudha Narayanan, *The Vernacular Veda* (Columbia, South Carolina: University of South Carolina Press, 1994), 26–7. Pollock's phrase occurs in his article "From Discourse of Ritual to Discourse of Power in Sanskrit Culture," *Journal of Ritual Studies* 4. 2 (1990): 315–45; 342, n. 49.

24. See Philip Lutgendorf, "Ramayan: The Video" in *The Drama Review* 34. 2 (1990): 127–76, esp. 141–57.

25. In a modern oral telling of the Shabari story recorded by Ann Gold in the village of Ghatiyali in Ajmer District, Rajasthan, the "Bhil woman" likewise serves the brothers berries that she has previously tasted herself.

Rama eats them, saying, "These are great!" but Lakshmana (here less submissive to his elder brother than in written or televised versions) protests "They are polluted and bad," and throws his away. Rama is so pleased with Shabari that he gives the boon that, each year during the spring harvest festivals of Holi, hail will fall on the grain crops, so that the fallen grain left in the fields after harvest—customarily allotted to local tribals—will be abundant. Thus Shabari's "polluted" food, accepted by God, expands into an annually renewed food supply for her community. But the food rejected by Lakshmana also bears (ironic) fruit in this tale, for his discarded berries grow into the life-restoring *sañjīvanī* herb which Hanuman will later fetch in order to save Lakshmana's life when the latter lies mortally wounded during the battle in Lanka. (Ann Gold, personal communication, 11/30/97.)

*Chapter Seven*

The Research Committee of the University of Wisconsin–Madison (1996) and American Institute of Indian Studies (1996–7) supported research for this project. I thank Paula Richman for her comments on earlier drafts of this paper.

1. See Tulsīdās, *Rāmcaritmānas* (Gōrakhpur: Gītā Press, 1940), *Araṇya Kāṇḍa*, 736. Also well-known is the verse "Old, sickly, fool, or poor,/blind, deaf, illtempered or undignified,/a woman who shows disrespect to such a husband/undergoes untold torture in hell. This is the only dharma, only vow and only course of action/to serve with body, speech and heart, your husband's feet lovingly." See *Sundara Kāṇḍa*, 601.

2. See Santrām Anil, *Kanauji Lōk Sāhitya* (New Delhi: Abhinav Prakāshan, 1977), 99

3. Kayasthas are a visible and powerful group in Uttar Pradesh, Madhya Pradesh, Bihar, and Bengal. Many claim that Kayasthas belong to a Kshatriya splinter group. Although some identify them with Shudras or call them "half-Muslims" due to their food and speech practices, the government does not recognize the Kayasthas as Scheduled or Other Backward Castes.

4. Most younger (high-caste and low-caste) women disdained old songs in favor of new film songs.

5. Two songs I heard in childhood mentioned this occupation: "Four Kahar carry my wedding palanquin" (Kabir) and "Rest my palanquin under the lemon tree, O Kahar" (anonymous).

6. In the privacy of their home, an older grandfather or grandmother might ask a granddaughter or a daughter-in-law to recite from the *Mānas*, but seldom in front of outside males. See Philip Lutgendorf, *The Life of a Text: Rāmcaritmānas of Tulsidas* (Berkeley and Los Angeles: University of California Press, 1991), 171, for a discussion of women singers.

7. I recorded this song from Anusuya Devi, a Kayastha woman literate in Hindi, English, and Sanskrit. In my translations of the songs, I have used the singers' version of Ramayana names without correcting them. Thus Kausalya sometimes is Kosila or Kaushalya, Sita is sometimes Sital or Siya, Lakshman becomes Lachchman in places, and Dashrath turns into Dasrath.

8. Hanskumār Tiwāri and Radhāvallbha Sharmā, *Bhojpurī Samskārgēt* (Patna, Bihar: Rāshtrabhāsha Parishad, 1977), 107.

9. In another song Kaushalya tells us that in the cold season she awoke early, when the stars were still out, to bathe in cold water and in the hot season denied herself even breeze from a fan.

10. This song appears in both Anil's collection of Kanauji songs and Kiran Marālī, *Lok Gēton Men Rāma* (Allahabad: Sāhitya Bhavan, 1986), 72, which shows its wide currency and the fluid geographical boundaries in women's folksongs. Tiwāri and Sharmā include a similar song, p. 113. This song mixes Rama and Krishna stories. Instead of killing demons during exile, Rama plays his flute and sports with a hunchback woman, behavior from the Krishna corpus. Since Rama's time on earth preceded that of Krishna, reference to Rama makes sense there, but not vice versa.

11. This song was sung by an illiterate Kahar woman named Lilavati. For a variant, see Sarojinī Rohatagī, *Awadhī kā Lok Sāhitya* (New Delhi: National Publishing House, 1971), 267.

12. For a study of *maṅgal* songs, see Edward C. Dimock, "The Goddess of Snakes in Medieval Bengali Literature," *History of Religions* (Winter 1962), 307–21.

13. In 1950 I heard this song performed by Saubhagyavati Devi, a Kayastha woman literate in Hindi and English. In 1997, her daughter-in-law, Sudha Shankar, a retired principal of a higher secondary school, performed it for me. In the 3rd and 7th lines, Kayastha women call Rama "prince," *kunwar.* Kaharins substitute *Kahar,* "man from the Watercarrier *jāti,*" identifying Rama with the traditional function of drawing wellwater, exalting their *jāti* by claiming Rama as one of their own.

14. From Anusuya Devi's songbook.

15. Marālī, 132

16. Many Kayastha and Kahar women knew parts of this song, also found in Marālī, 182–3. In it Dashrath is still alive, whereas in the *Mānas* Dashrath dies after Rama's exile. Sita lives in Brindavan, a place associated with Krishna. Two women sang the first part of this song while grinding wheat together, but women usually sang of Sita's pregnancy when doing housework alone. In groups women joined in when they remembered verses, falling silent otherwise. The main singer sang the whole song, occasionally taking a short pause when others joined in.

17. In a North Indian wedding, Barber women carry out Tel and Haldī,

two premarriage rituals, for the bride and groom. An auspicious number (5 or 7) of married kinswomen anoint with tumeric and oil the person to wed. Later, the bride gets an oil and turmeric massage. A popular folktale which explains both the tensions and resentment between these high- and low-caste women, as well as the auspiciousness of Washerwomen in marriage ritual, recounts that once Shiva and Parvati came to visit this world and camped outside a city. Women heard that Parvati was distributing *suhāg* (long life for one's husband). High-caste Hindu women got ready to receive *suhāg* by bathing, adorning themselves, and decorously proceeding to Parvati. Women of lower social groups, however, rushed there as they were, unbathed and dishevelled. First to arrive, a washerwoman took *suhāg* by the basketful. By the time the caste Hindu women arrived, lower-caste women had taken most of the *suhāg* so each high-caste woman just received a small pinch. Therefore, high-caste women marry only once but low-caste women can divorce and remarry.

18. This song came from the songbook of Asha Lata, a Kayastha college graduate literate in Hindi and English.

19. See Marālī, 99 and Anil, 61. These items used in childbirth become impure, and are given away to the midwife. When a woman delivers a child at home, the midwife breaks a new pitcher in half and collects the placenta in the bottom round, which she buries elsewhere. In this song, the midwife cleverly gets much more than she would in ordinary circumstances.

20. This came from the songbook of Anusuya Devi.

21. See Marālī, 99.

22. Rām Naresh Tripathi, *Grām Sāhitya* ( Sultanpur: Hindi Mandir, 1951), 93–5. Seeing an auspicious face first thing in the morning is thought to bring good luck, whereas an inauspicious faces brings bad luck. People are often heard to comment "I don't know whom I saw first thing in the morning, I didn't get even a grain of food in my mouth."

23. This song was sung for me by Asha Lata, a high-caste woman. She recalled fondly that her high-caste version of this was the first song she sang as a bride in 1954. The sixth-day celebration (*chhathhi*), the first ritual after childbirth, is celebrated with feasts, especially for a male child.

24. This version of the Doe Song was sung by Lilavati and her friends, all Kahar women. A variant of this song is also quoted in the appendix to A.G. Shirreff, *Hindi Folksongs* (Allahabad, 1936). In his preface he mentions that he attended a recital of folksongs by Ahir (dairy caste) women in 1934 in Koeripur, when he was the Collector at Jaunpur. Ahirs consider themselves higher than Kahars and Barbers, since they provide a service, selling milk and curds. They also link themselves to Krishna, who grew up in a cowherd village. Parts of this song, available both in oral and written versions, were also collected by Tripathi from a Chamar woman in 1925.

25. From the version sung by Asha Lata.

*Chapter Eight*

1. Tripurāṇeni Rāmasvāmi Chaudari, *Śambuka Vadha,* 1920, rept. in vol. 2 of *Kavirāju Sāhitya Sarvasvaṁ* (Complete Works of Ramasvami Chaudari) 2 vols. (Gunturu: Kaviraju Sahiti Samiti,1996), 1–79. Each text in these volumes is independently numbered.

2. For the Valmiki telling, see 7.73–5 and 76. 1–16, *Rāmāyaṇa of Vālmīki,* ed. Katti Srinivāsa-shāstri (Delhi: Parimal Publications, 1983).

3. *Raghuvaṁśa,* 15. 42–53, especially verse 53,

4. *Uttararāmacarita,* 2.10–13, ed. S.K. Belvalkar (Poona: Oriental Book Supplying Agency, 1921).

5. Sheldon Pollock, "*Rāmāyaṇa* and Political Imagination in India," *Journal of Asian Studies* 52. 2 (May 1993): 263.

6. This is the story told by King Raghunāthanāyaka of Tanjore in his *Vālmīki Caritramu.*

7. Narayana Rao, "A *Rāmāyaṇa* of One's Own: Women's Oral Tradition in Telugu" in *Many Rāmāyaṇas: The Diversity of Narrative Tradition in South Asia,* ed. Paula Richman,(Berkeley: University of California Press, and Delhi: Oxford University Press, 1991), 114–36.

8. Sheldon I. Pollock, *The Rāmāyaṇa of Vālmīki: An Epic of Ancient India,* vol. 2, *Ayodhyākāṇḍa* (Princeton, NJ: Princeton University Press, 1986), 10.

9. Velcheru Naryana Rao, unpublished remarks for panel on "Audiences and Indian Literature," presented at the Association for Asian Studies, 1982.

10. There was, however, no lack of Ramayanas that presented events from the perspective of Sita. For example, a number of women's songs and tales did so.

11. Rāvūri Dorasāmi Śarma, *Telugu Sāhityamu: Rāma-kathā* (Machilipatnam: Triveni Publishers, 1972), 71–6.

12. From *Visvanātha Madhyākkaralu,* cited by Śarma, *Telugu Sāhityamu,* 247. Bhadradri, or Bhadracalam, is a famous Rama shrine in West Godavari District.

13. Tāṇḍra Subrahmanyam, *Śrī Rāmāñjanēya Yuddham* (Tenali: Śrī Venkaṭaramaṇa Book Depot, 1979). This play, which does not have a source in any purana, has been performed widely in Andhra Pradesh and was also produced for radio. A phonograph album of this play sold well; a movie was also made.

14. Kāsula Puruṣottamakavi, *Āndhranāyaka-śatakamu,* ed. Yārlagaḍḍa Bālagāngādhara Rāvu (Visakhapatnam: Nirmala Publications, 1975), verse 88.

15. Professor Ravvā Śrīhari says Kāmasamudram Appalācāryulu led a five-scholar team for this project, including Kānādam Peddana Sōmayāji, a great Sanskrit scholar of his time, preface to Kānādam Peddana Sōmayāji, *Mukundavilāsamu* (Hyderabad: Telugu Vijñāna Pītham, 1985), 9–10.

16. *samskṛtaṁ rāmacaritaṁ parityajya narādhamah*
*paṭhan bhāṣāntara-kṛtam mṛgatṛṣṇā jalam pibet*

17. Two such books, for instance, are: *Sakala-kārya-siddiki Śrīmadrāmāyaṇa-pārāyaṇamu* (Reading Ramayana for success in all efforts) (Madras: Little Flower Company, 1967), reprinted several times, and *Sundara-hanumad-vaibhavamu* (*Sundara-kanda* with rules for reading) by Śiṣṭlā Candramouli Śāstri (Pedapadu, Andhra Pradesh: Author, N.D).

18. Chaudari presents "linguistic evidence" to suggest that Ravana's name was derived from the Koya language. See *Sūta Purāṇamu,* 2 vols. (Gunturu: Kaviraju Sahiti Samiti, 1996), vol. 1, 224–5.

19. *Sūta Purāṇamu,* 3.210, 210.

20. Richman, "E.V. Ramasami's Reading of the Rāmāyaṇa," 175–201.

21. Chaudari clearly anticipates E.V. Ramasami of Tamil Nadu. The chronology of their ideas has not received attention since Ramasvami Chaudari is not as well known as E.V. Ramasami in the West. Ramasvami Chaudari wrote *Śambuka Vadha* during 1914–17; however, he published it, along with a long preface, only in 1920. His *Sūta Purāṇamu,* with several detailed prefatory essays for each of its chapters, was published in 1924, whereas E.V. Ramasami's anti-Ramayana pamphlet *Irāmāyaṇappāttiraṇkaḷ* made its first appearance in 1930, a full decade after Chaudari's *Śambuka Vadha.* Their ideas bear very close resemblance, yet significant differences as well. No work has yet been done to determine whether there were any contacts between the two leaders.

22. Introduction to *Śambuka Vadha,* 17–18.

23. Guḍipāṭi Veṅkaṭa Calam, *Sīta Agnipravēśam* (Vijayawada: Aruna Publishing House, 3rd edn., 1976), 45.

24. Satyanārāyaṇa began writing the first volume of his six-volume *Śrīmad Rāmāyaṇa Kalpavṛkṣamu,* popularly known as *Rāmāyaṇa Kalpavṛkṣamu,* in 1934 and concluded the sixth volume in 1962. The first volume was not published until 1944. The other volumes were published during the following years, ending with the sixth volume in 1963. Satyanārāyaṇa gave readings from his book long before the first volume was published. The six volumes have been reprinted several times.

25. Viśvanātha Satyanārāyaṇa, *Rāmāyaṇa Kalpavṛkṣamu* (Vijayawada: Viśvanātha Publications, 1992; 1st edn, 1944), 1.5. Translation in collaboration with David Shulman.

26. Nārla Venkateśvara Rao, *Sīta Jōsyam* (Vijayawada: Navodaya Publishers, 1979), 131.

27. Muppāḷa Raṅganāyakamma. *Rāmāyaṇaviṣavṛkṣam,* 3 vols. (Hyderabad: Sweet Home Publications, 1974–6). The title parodies *Rāmayaṇa Kalpavṛkṣamu* (Ramayana, The Giving Tree), written a few years earlier by Viśvanātha Satyanārāyaṇa (see n. 24).

28. Two such books are Suravaram Pratāpa Reḍḍi, *Rāmāyaṇa Viśeṣamulu* (Hyderabad: Āndhra Racayitala Saṅgham, 1957), and Kotta Satyanārāyaṇa

Chaudari, *Rāmāyaṇa Rahasyālu* (Nidubrolu: Bhaśapōṣakagranthamaṇḍali, 1968).

*Chapter Nine*

I wish to acknowledge debts of gratitude to Paula Richman and Sumathi Ramaswamy for their close readings of this work in its various stages and for their numerous suggestions for its improvement. In Kerala, special thanks are due to my long-time friend and field-assistant, A. Tamban of Cherumoola, to the learned Kunhiraman Vaidyar of Pilikkode, and to the many performers and devotees of teyyam who gave me so unstintingly of their time and knowledge.

1. The Kerala tradition is historically continuous with that of Tamil Nadu, from which it diverged some thousand years ago. Before this, both traditions shared the religious and political culture documented in the Caṅkam literature from the early centuries of the Common Era, regarding which, see George Hart, *The Poems of Ancient Tamil: Their Milieu and Their Sanskrit Counterparts* (Berkeley: University of California Press, 1975), 21–50.

2. Some sources on *teyyāṭṭam* performance and myth include K. K. N. Kurup, *The Cult of Teyyam and Hero Worship in Kerala,* Indian Folklore Series, no. 21 (Calcutta: Indian Publications, 1973); Wayne Ashley, "The Teyyam Kettu of Northern Kerala," *The Drama Review* 23 (June 1979): 99–112; Rich Freeman, "Purity and Violence: Sacred Power in the Teyyam Worship of Malabar" (Ph.D. Dissertation, Department of Anthropology, University of Pennsylvania, 1991); Freeman, "Performing Possession: Ritual and Consciousness in the Teyyam Complex of Northern Kerala," in *Flags of Fame: Studies in South Asian Folk Culture,* Heidelberg University South Asia Studies, no. 27, ed. H. Brückner, L. Lutz, and A. Malik (New Delhi: Manohar, 1993), 109–38; and Balan Nambiar, "Tāi Paradēvata: Ritual Impersonation in the Teyyam Tradition of Kerala," in ibid., 139–62.

3. On the antiquity of this conceptualization of divine powers as immanent in the Tamil country, including Kerala, see Hart, 81–137.

4. Kerala castes were traditionally reckoned in the dominant Brahmin ideology as having only three macro-grades: Brahmins and Shudras, constituting those of caste-grade (*savarṇa*) who were permitted entry within the temple walls and upper-caste households, and Untouchables (*avarṇa*), those literally without "caste" (*varṇa*), who were banned from temple entry and whose very approach within certain graded distances polluted the higher castes. Thus the Kshatriya and Vaishya grades that usually intervene between Brahmin and Shudra were elided in Kerala, reserving the "twice-born" status usually granted to these other castes elsewhere in India to Brahmins alone. This elision was also prominent in Tamil Nadu and other parts of South India as well.

5. When performing their shrine rituals, Āśāri priests temporarily wear sacred threads and mock *uttarīyams*. Both are normally worn only by Brahmins in Kerala, the latter being a twisted top-cloth, donned only by priests who are actually engaged in worship. In the case of the Āśāris, however, these *uttarīyams* are in a conspicuous red cloth, instead of the usual unbleached white. In response to whether they followed the usual custom of other Non-Brahmin priests in having a change of cloth (*māṟṟu*) supplied by the Washerman caste following the requisite bath before they enter the shrine, I was told, "We never require this change at any time. There is no pollution for Viśvakarmas!"

6. For an analogous case in Tamil Nadu, with a general discussion, see Stuart Blackburn, *Singing of Birth and Death: Texts in Performance* (Philadelphia: University of Pennsylvania Press, 1988), 214–21.

7. Some pieces are sung solo, by the dancer himself; others are sung with accompaniment by his supporting drummers and assistants. After possession, he reverts to speech only, of a hoarse stylized variety, and in the first-person, as the deity.

8. All citations here are from the version of Bāli's teyyam collected by M. V. Viṣṇunambūtiri, ed., *Uttarakēraḷattile Tōṟṟampāṭṭukaḷ* (Trichur: Kerala Sahitya Akademi, 1981), 13–82, supplemented by my own notes and recordings from the field. I have kept as much of the line-by-line syntax of the original as possible, in order to retain something of their elliptical cohesion.

9. I have discussed the semantics of the word *tōṟṟam* at some length in Freeman, "Purity and Violence," 316–17, 340, n. 11; "Performing Possession," 121–3; and in my forthcoming article on this term in *South Asian Folklore: An Encyclopedia*, ed. Peter Claus and Margaret Mills (New York: Garland Publishing).

10. Blackburn, *Singing of Birth and Death.*

11. Following his death (or *mōkṣam*), Bāli is said to have "descended into the *kuṇḍam* of Mālyavān (mountain), then performed his rituals of worshiping the god through bathing and putting on his sacred marks." Mālyavān is the name of the mountains where Bāli ruled and died (in the Kerala context, the Western Ghats), and *kuṇḍam* means any hole or pit, but usually refers to the fire pit into which oblations are offered. In another song in this corpus this slot of the "descent" is filled by Bāli's cremation rites on Mālyavān, so this may allude to his cremation as a sacrificial offering into the fire. On the other hand, this "descent" into a hole also suggests entry into the underworld (which Bāli enacted in life to battle with the demon, Māyāvi), which a number of other teyyams reportedly undergo, to pop up into the world elsewhere. Finally, this word for descent also suggests that of the god into the world, which is enacted as the entrance of the teyyam into the shrine compound as well. This convergence of ideas is strengthened by the fact that teyyams also mime the very bathing and worshiping

rites alluded to here (*kuḷi-kuṟi-tēvāram*) as part of their rituals. Mythically, these last rites seem to have archetypically purified Bāli after his death-transformation, and to have inceptively empowered him as a god himself.

12. Vaṭuva is a usual variant for Vaṭuka, literally the "Northerners" who are also the dominant tribal group settled now in the Nilgiri mountains, just over the Kerala border. It is quite possible that the ancestors of these or some other such Tulu or Coorgi mountain folk are referred to here. On the origins and migrant identity of the Vaṭuka (or Badaga), see Paul Hockings, *Ancient Hindu Refugees: Badaga Social History, 1550–1975* (New Delhi: Vikas Publishing House, 1980), 11–39.

13. Rich Freeman, "Gods, Groves, and the Culture of Nature in Kerala." *Modern Asian Studies* 33.2 (April 1999): 257–303.

14. My reference to "the Keralas and other Tamils," odd though it may sound to contemporary ears, is historically informed and deliberate. As late as the close of the fourteenth century, intellectuals in Kerala were advancing arguments that the *Kēraḷas* (to use their own chosen ethnonym) partook of a political, religious and linguistic heritage that gave them as equal a claim to the name *Tamiḻ* as the separate *Pāṇḍya* or *Cōḻa* peoples more centrally located in what we today consider the Tamil land. See Freeman, "Rubies and Coral: The Lapidary Crafting of Language in Kerala," *Journal of Asian Studies* 57.1 (February 1998): 38–65.

15. While the motif of the gods churning the milk-sea is prevalent in early Sanskrit works, its narrative reworking around Bāli seems characteristically southern, as discussed later in this paper.

16. K. S. Mathew, *Society in Medieval Malabar: A Study Based on Vadakkan Pāṭṭukaḷ* (Kurichy, Kottayam: Jaffe Books, 1979), 27–33.

17. T. Gaṅgādharan, ed., *Puttariyaṅkam (Vaṭakkan Pāṭṭu)* (Bhagavati Naṭa P.O., Kerala: Kairali Sāhitya Publications, 1984), 119ff.

18. Cf. David Shulman, "Battle as Metaphor in Tamil Folk and Classical Traditions," in *Another Harmony: New Essays on the Folklore of India,* ed. S. Blackburn and A. K. Ramanujan (Delhi: Oxford University Press, 1986), 105–30.

19. Freeman, "Purity and Violence," e.g. 368–71, 546–7. My mapping of mythical roles onto social ones is supported in recent work by a scholar of the 18th-century work of Kuñcan Nambyār; see K. N. Ganesh, *Kuñcan Nambyār: Vākkum Samūhavum* (Sukapuram, Kerala: Vaḷḷattōḷ Vidyā Pīṭham, 1996), 26–39.

20. Bāli complains bitterly at his death of collusion between Sugrīva and Rāma since they are both of the Solar lineage. In Rāma's case, this is regarding his royal lineage as a member of the *Sūryavaṃśa*, or solar dynastic line, while in Sugrīva's case, this is through his rather bastardized, but more direct, siring by the Sun.

21. Compare here the monkey as the quintessential symbol of dubious

social identity for Japan's "special-status people" so persuasively delineated by E. Ohnuki-Tierney, *The Monkey as Mirror: Symbolic Transformations in Japanese History and Ritual* (Princeton: Princeton University Press, 1987).

22. Kuñcan Nambyār, *Eḻuppattañcu Tuḷḷal Kathakaḷ*, ed. V. S. Śarma (Kottayam, Kerala: D.C. Books, 1976), 617.

23. Ibid.

24. Ibid.: *Bāli ennuḷḷoru pērum labhikkum/Mēlil parākramam pāram bhavikkum.*

25. M. Monier-Williams, *Sanskrit-English Dictionary* (1899; rept. New Delhi: Munshiram Manoharlal, 1991), 946.

26. T. Burrow and M. B. Emeneau, *A Dravidian Etymological Dictionary* (Oxford: Clarendon Press, 1961), 367.

27. Ibid., 359–60.

28. J. L. Brockington, *Righteous Rāma: The Evolution of an Epic* (Delhi: Oxford University Press, 1984), 310.

29. The twelve-year period assigned to Rāvaṇa's bondage is significant; known as a *Vyāḻa-vaṭṭam* in Malayalam, the "circuit of Jupiter" through the zodiac, it is the traditional period of reckoning for great vows and certain religious festivals.

30. This role of Pulastyan is a plot innovation of the *tōṟṟams,* transposed from the similar episode of Rāvaṇa's binding by Kārttavīryārjuṇa.

31. In this tradition, Rāvaṇa has apparently the requisite number of arms to go with his ten heads.

32. *vanpanām Rāvaṇan pantirāṇḍennuṭe/*
*vanpeḷum vālmēl kiṭannu valaññavan*
In this context his tail is also called his *paraśu-vāl,* the "axe-tail."

33. *vāl koṇḍu bhūmiyil/ antarīkṣam ñeṭṭumār onnu aṭikkayum.*

34. This figure of speech may also be taken as an allusion to the Vāli myth itself, "a wounded Vāli," used for one whose might has been vanquished, though such an allusion within this myth, when Vāli yet lives, would seem a jarring anachronism. My more literal reading of the figure is discussed later in the paper.

35. These lines are taken from the performance notebooks of Malayan performers of Poṭṭan. A printed variant of these lines can be found in C.T. Bālakṛṣṇan Nāyar, ed., *Kēraḷabhāṣāgānaṅṅaḷ: Nāṭan Pāṭṭukaḷ*, vol. 1 (Trichur, Kerala: Kerala Sahitya Akademi, 1979), 431–2.

36. This was indeed a concern of pre-modern Sanskrit commentators on the Rāmāyaṇa as well; see Rosaland Lefeber, "Introduction" in *The Rāmāyaṇa of Vālmīki: An Epic of Ancient India,* vol. IV, *Kiṣkindhākāṇḍa,* trans. Lefeber, ed. R. Goldman (Princeton: Princeton University Press, 1994), 45–50.

37. The implication here is that since the polity bears the name of Kiṣkindha, Bāli's capital, he is its king and is responsible for the state of affairs throughout the region.

38. I have been alerted to these issues through recent literature on the anthropology of emotion, and particularly in going back through my videotapes of Bāli's teyyam and attending to the mournful expression running through much of the performance. As examples of this literature, see Catherine Lutz and L. Abu-Lughod, eds., *Language and the Politics of Emotion* (Cambridge: Cambridge University Press, 1987); and Owen Lynch, ed., *Divine Passions: The Social Construction of Emotion in India* (Delhi: Oxford University Press, 1990).

39. The interpolated text from the Critical Edition of Vālmīki is in U. P. Shah, *The Vālmīki-Rāmāyaṇa: Critical Edition,* vol. 7, *Uttarakāṇḍa* (Baroda: Oriental Research Institute, 1975), appendix I, no.3, 573–6. A general discussion of the interpolations, including this one, and the manuscripts on which it is based can found in vol. 7's introduction (8–25). The chapter telling this episode from the *Adhyātma Rāmāyaṇa* is just a *verbatim* excerpt from this interpolation, as the footnotes in that critically edited text attest; see N. Siddhantaratna, ed., *Adhyātma-Rāmāyaṇam,* Part II, Calcutta Sanskrit Series, vol. XI (Calcutta: Metropolitan Printing and Publishing House, 1932), 942–54.

40. On the Rāmānanda sectarian affiliation of the Sanskrit *Adhyātma Rāmāyaṇa,* see Brockington, 252, n. 51; and on the links of this to South India, Brockington, *The Sacred Thread: Hinduism in its Continuity and Diversity* (Edinburgh: Edinburgh University Press, 1981), 154. The *Adhyātma Rāmāyaṇa* was adapted into Malayalam by Eḻuttachan in the sixteenth century.

41. G. Venu, *Production of a Play in Kūṭiyāṭṭam: Abhiṣekanāṭakam* (Trichur: Natankairali, 1989), 71ff.

42. Kuñcan Nambyār, 609–19.

43. Apparently this origin myth is related in the Tamil *Tiruvānmiyūr* and *Tiruvottūr sthalapurāṇams* according, respectively, to David Shulman, *The King and the Clown in South Indian Myth and Poetry* (Princeton: Princeton University Press, 1985), 219, n. 16 and S. Mutaliyār, *Apitāṉa Cintāmaṇi* (New Delhi: Asian Educational Services, 1983), 93; I have not, however, managed to trace either of these works.

44. Modern commentators adduce this myth behind the vulgate Kampaṉ's allusions to Vāli's origins from Indra; see Kopālakiruṣṇamācāriyar, ed., *Kamparāmāyaṇam,* vol. 1 (Chennai: Kōpālakiruṣṇamācāriyar Co, 1964), 153; Ibid., vol. 5 (1963), 410. I discuss this narrative variant later in my main text, regarding the deviant method of Vāli's conception. There is a Malayalam translation of another version of Kampaṉ known as *Nāṭakakāvyam* in which this same myth is retold in its entirety as part of the main text in J. Śivakumar, trans., *Kamparāmāyaṇam (Gadyaparibhāṣa)* (Ālappuḻa: Vidyāraṃbham Publishers, 1995), 80–3. This myth further occurs in a fifteenth-century prose Malayalam version of the *Uttararāmāyaṇam* from the performance area of *teyyāṭṭam;* see C. T. Bālakṛṣṇan Nāyar, *Uttararāmāyaṇam*

(1938; reprint, Trichur: Kerala Sahitya Akademi, 1990), 103–6.

45. Clifford R. Jones, ed., *The Wonderous Crest-Jewel in Performance* (Delhi: Oxford University Press, 1984), 61.

46. E.g. Kōpālakiruṣṇamācāriyar, *Kamparāmāyaṇam,* vol. 4 (1967), 109, where the commentary fleshes out the episode.

47 Kuñcan Nambyār, 367–89 and 609–19.

48. V. S. Rangachar, trans., *Abhiṣekanāṭakam: A Play in Six Acts* (Mysore: Samskrita Sahitya Sadana, 1966), 38.

49. This motif of reading the arrow continues down to contemporary adaptations of Kampaṉ in the Kerala tradition of shadow puppet theater; see Stuart Blackburn, *Inside the Drama-House: Rāma Stories and Shadow Puppets in South India* (Berkeley: University of California Press, 1996), 83.

50. Examples from the vulgate text of Kampaṉ are in Kōpālakiruṣṇamācāriyar, *Kamparāmāyaṇam,*vol. IV, 111; 301; and vol. V, 410. A complete telling of this binding of Rāvaṇa in Bāil's tail occurs in the *Uttarakāṇḍam* of Kampaṉ, though this last book is usually considered a spurious and later addition by contemporary Kampaṉ scholarship; see U.V.T.K. Irāmānujaiyaṅkār, ed., *Kamparāmāyaṇam: Uttarakāṇṭam,* Tiruñāṉamuttirai Kovai, no. 30 (Āḻvārtirunakari: Tiruñāṉamuttiraip-pirasurālayam, 1968), 69–71. Regarding the likely pre-Kampaṉ attestation of this episode in Kerala, recall the clear allusion to Rāvaṇa's binding in Bāli's tail from a ninth-century playwright, Śaktibhadran (n. 45, above).

51. The sources are given in n. 44, above.

52. This version of the growth of Hanuman's tail and the means of its arresting comes from the text of Kampaṉ known in Kerala as the *Nāṭakakāvyam,* in n. 44, above (Śivakumar, 121–2).

53. Karuṇākaran Nāyar, ed., *Adhyātma Rāmāyaṇam* (Trichur: Kerala Sahitya Akademi, 1977), 355.

54 See Hart, *The Poems of Ancient Tamil*; Friedhelm Hardy, *Viraha Bhakti: The Early History of Kṛṣṇa Devotion in South India* (Delhi: Oxford University Press, 1983), 131ff; and David Shulman, *Tamil Temple Myths: Sacrifice and Divine Marriage in the South Indian Tradition* (Princeton: Princeton University Press), 1–17.

55. Though earlier attributed to the famous Sanskrit dramatist, Bhāsa, the whole corpus of these plays is attested only from Kerala, and seems rather to represent the local dramatic tradition, perhaps drawing inspiration from Bhāsa's works; see N. P. Unni, *New Problems in Bhasa Plays* (Trivandrum: New College Book House, 1978).

56. These works are discussed in one of the best treatments of kathakaḷi literature and its development, Aymanam Kṛṣṇakkaimaḷ, *Āṭṭakkathāsāhityam* (Trivandrum, Kerala: State Institute of Languages, 1989).

57. An interesting testament to the attraction of the familial revenge theme is found in the Kerala *Rāmāyaṇa Campu.* Though following the

Sanskrit motif of Rāvaṇa's capture in Bāli's armpit, the text reflects the later kathakaḷi frame of filial vengeance as the motivating impetus. See *Bhāṣārāmāyaṇa Campu*, ed. V. Vēṅkiṭṭarāma Śarma (Trichur: Kerala Sahitya, 1982), 571–2. There Rāma praises Bāli:

What Indrajit, using all his might,
Did to humiliate Indra
(Whose force of strength was curbed by the curse of Gautama),
That your wakefulness to filial duty wiped away,
Removing its pain when Rāvaṇa
Was brought to the crab-like vise of your armpit!

[See Bhaṣārāmāyaṇa, Campu (V. Vēṅkiṭṭarāma Śarma) Trichur: Kerala Sahitya, 1982), 571–2.]

58. Gaṅgādharan, 106.

*Chapter 10*

1. See Sally J. Sutherland, "Draupadī and Sītā: Aggressive Behavior and Female Role-Models," *Journal of the American Oriental Society* 109.1 (1989): 63–79. Sītā's aggressive behavior and even her somewhat abusive language in this instance are socially acceptable as carried out within the context of *pātivratyam*, "devotion to her husband." See n. 2 below.

2. Literally the word means, "she whose husband is her religious vow," i.e., a woman who is devoted, faithful, and loyal to her husband.

3. *Rām* 2.110–11. All references are to the critical edition of the *Vālmīki Rāmāyaṇa* unless otherwise indicated [*The Vālmīki Rāmāyaṇa: Critical Edition*, 7 vols., general editors: G. H. Bhatt and U. P. Shah (Baroda: Oriental Institute, 1960–75)]. The translations of the *Sundarakāṇḍa* are taken from Robert P. Goldman and Sally J. Sutherland Goldman, *The Rāmāyaṇa of Vālmīki: An Epic of Ancient India, Vol. V, Sundarakāṇḍa* (Princeton: Princeton University Press, 1996). Henceforth citations for translations appear in parentheses in the text, immediately after the quote.

4. *Rām* 3.8.

5. It is not merely an issue of gender, but of class and status as well. See A. Berriedale Keith, *The Sanskrit Drama in its Origin, Development, Theory and Practice* (Oxford: The Clarendon Press, 1924), 308–10 and 2.15–42ab in *Daśarūpaka of Dhanañjaya with the Commentary of Avaloka by Dhanika and the Sub-commentary Laghuṭīkā by Bhaṭṭanṛsiṃha*, ed. T. Venkatacharya (Madras, India: Adyar Library and Research Centre, 1969).

6. The *Vālmīki Rāmāyaṇa*, as we know it, views the world through eyes of male royal and Brahmanical figures, or of their representatives. Even throughout the *Sundarakāṇḍa*, where the realm of the lord of the *rākṣasas* is graphically

depicted, the narrative is told through the voice of the Sanskrit-speaking monkey messenger of Rāma, Hanumān. Vālmīki has crafted this book largely as a meditation on Rāma. See R. Goldman and S. Goldman, 13–20.

Here I define "women" as a biological sexual identification. "Women's voices" are women speaking of their own individual experiences. "Woman," on the other hand, is a social construction. The "feminine voice" is defined as the construction of "Woman" as produced by patriarchal control over language, culture, texts, and the like. See Theresa de Lauretis, *Alice Doesn't: Feminism, Semiotics, Cinema* (Bloomington: Indiana University Press, 1984), 5–6 and Barbara Gold, "'But Ariadne was Never There in the First Place': Finding the Female in Roman Poetry" in *Feminist Theory and the Classics,* ed. Nancy Sorkin Rabinowitz and Amy Richlin (New York, London: Routledge, 1993), 82–3.

If R. Goldman is right in his reading of the Sanskrit epics, the obsessive, yet ambivalent, attention given to women, stems, in part, from an ambivalent relationship with an authoritative, paternal figure. In this formulation, while women have no voice, "Woman" and the feminine are represented from a variety of positions. We have no means of determining or recovering from other sources what a women's voice might sound like. See Robert P. Goldman's "Fathers, Sons, and Gurus: Oedipal Conflict in the Sanskrit Epics," *Journal of Indian Philosophy* 6 (1978): 325–92; "Rāmaḥ Sahalakṣmaṇaḥ: Psychological and Literary Aspects of the Composite Hero of Vālimīki's Rāmāyaṇa," *Journal of Indian Philosophy* 8 (1980): 149–89; and "Transexualism, Gender, and Anxiety in Traditional India," *Journal of the American Oriental Society* 113.3 (1993): 374–401.

7. Although perhaps the most well known, Sītā is by no means the only heroine to be placed in such a situation. Draupadī, Sāvitrī, Damayantī, Vāsavadattā, to name but a few, are placed in similar situations where, separated from their husbands, they must make independent decisions.

8. It is not unusual for the male audience to identify with the sexual aggressor. See, for example, Sudhir Kakar's discussion of male reaction to rape in modern Hindi films: *Intimate Relations: Exploring Indian Sexuality* (New Delhi: Penguin Books, 1989), 32–5.

9. Sītā's culpability is at issue. Some would argue that Sītā played a part in initiating her abduction. Rāma jests with Śūrpaṇakhā and thereby initiates the sequence of events leading up to the abduction (3.16–17). Sītā, however, insists that Rāma catch the golden deer (3.41) and exhorts Lakṣmaṇa to go to Rāma's aid despite the former's reluctance to do so (3.43).

10. 9.15 in *Manusmṛti,* 10th edn. (Bombay: Nirṇayasāgar Press, 1946), With the commentary *Manvarthamuktāvali* of Kullūka, ed. N. R. Acharya and *Manu Smṛti*, 5 vols. (Bombay: Bharatiya Vidya Bhavan, 1972–82), with nine commentaries by Medhātithi, Sarvajñanārāyaṇa, Kullūka, Nandana, Rāmacandra, Maṇirāma, Govindarāja, and Bhāruci, ed. Jayantakrishna Harikrishna Dave:

*paumścalyāc calacittāc ca naisnehyāc ca svabhāvataḥ/*
*rakṣitā yatnato 'pīha bhartṛṣv etā vikurvate//*
"Since inherently [*svabhavataḥ*] women are attracted to different men, are fickle of heart, and lack affection, even when guarded with effort, they will be unfaithful to their husbands."

11. The garden location is important. For not only is it culturally coded as a Woman's space, it is marked as a location of sexual activity.

12. See *Sundarakāṇḍa* 13.18–46 and 15.20–1, and *sarga* 17, where Vālmīki carefully crafts his passages to both intensify Sītā's beauty and to remind the audience of her chastity and devotion to her lord.

13. Compare *Rām* 2.30.8 where even the birds are said never to have seen Sītā:
*yā na śakyā purā draṣṭuṃ bhūtair ākāśagair api/*
*tām adya sītāṃ paśyanti rājamārgagatā janāḥ//*
"People on the royal highway can now look at Sītā, a woman whom even creatures of the sky have never had a glimpse of before."
[Translation taken from Sheldon I. Pollock, trans., *The Rāmāyaṇa of Vālmīki: An Epic of Ancient India, Vol. II, Ayodhyākāṇḍa,* ed. Robert P. Goldman (1986), 146.]

14. See R. P. Goldman's essay in this volume, where he discusses this very issue.

15. 5.47.2–14.

16. But compare 7.24.3 where Rāvaṇa abducts the daughters of the *pannagas*, *yakṣas*, mortals, *rākṣasas*, *daityas*, and *dānavas*, and 7.24.14–15 where the abducted women curse him to be destroyed on account of a woman. Although I feel that the *Uttarakāṇḍa* has portions that are much closer to the original texts than many scholars have been willing to allow, one still must consider the *kāṇḍa* as composed later and by a different hand than the central books, and reflecting a more monovalent and demonic image of Rāvaṇa than that crafted by Vālmīki. See S. Sutherland Goldman, "A Tale of Two Tales: The Episode of Hanumān's Childhood in the Critical Edition," *Journal of the Oriental Institute of Baroda* (in press).

17. See R. Goldman and S. Goldman, 71–4, for a more detailed discussion of the similarities among these three characters.

18. 5.18.3ab reads:
*kāmaye tvāṃ viśālākṣi bahu manyasva māṃ priye/*

19. Abductions are not unusual outside of the *rākṣasa* realm and are, in some situations, considered an expected mode of behavior. For example, in the *Mahābhārata* Bhīṣma abducts the three daughters of the king of Kāśi, Ambā, Ambālikā, and Ambikā, to be the wives of Vicitravīrya (*MBh* 1.96). But these women are all unmarried. [All *Mahābhārata* references are to the critical edition, *Mahābhārata: Critical Edition,* 24 vols. (Poona: Bhandarkar

Oriental Research Institute, 1933–70), With *Harivaṃśa* (1969–71), critically ed. V. S. Sukthankar et al.]

20. The *Uttarakāṇḍa* rationalizes that Rāvaṇa's downfall at the hands of a woman arises in part from his earlier treatment of women (7.24.14–15). See n. 15 above.

21. The style is worn by women who are separated from their husbands.

22. This is particularly true of women prior to marriage. Epic heroines, such as Damayantī and Draupadī, are given little voice before marriage, however, after marriage, and in situations where they, like Sītā, must defend their virtue and, by extension the patriarchy, are quite articulate.

23. See 3.54.1, where Sītā first encounters Rāvaṇa and places a piece of straw between them prior to speaking.

24. See 5.19.2–3. The commentators are in general agreement that the interposition of the straw is done to avoid the impropriety on Sītā's part of speaking directly to a man other than her husband. Evidently it is symbolic of the screening of women from the gaze of unrelated men. Nāgeśabhaṭṭa (Tilakaṭīkā) and Yogīndra Mādhava (Katakaṭīkā) compare the practice to a similar one which they say is done during urination, etc. According to Paṇḍit Śrīnivāsa Śāstri this is the practice of some people who place straw on the ground so as not to urinate directly upon the earth, i.e., the goddess Earth. At *Rām*. 3.54.1, the gesture is also seen, but the commentators are not as exercised about it. See R. Goldman and S. Goldman, notes to 5.19.2–3, for a detailed account of the commentator's interpretations of the passage.

25. *Sarga*s 15.20–31 and 17 provide similar lists of similes to the one found at *sarga* 13, in part, further intensifying the audience's pathos of the forlorn heroine.

26. 5.17.3 ab, 8a. Here the action is understood as akin to a child rocking itself for comfort.

27. The scene is reminiscent of that in the *Ayodhyākāṇḍa* between Kaikeyī and Daśaratha. See 2.10–12.

28. Additionally, these women might possibly be understood as markers of resistance and/or feminine solidarity (despite the fact that she constitutes a real threat to them) in a text which offers little. Perhaps, the women were not all as grateful to be in Rāvaṇa's harem as we were led to believe earlier.

29. Compare *Mahābhārata* 3.60.26–38, where Damayantī, abandoned in the forest by her husband, Nala, is assaulted by a hunter. She defends her virtue on the basis of her *pātivratya*, "Just as I have never thought of another man . . . " (37).

30. Pollock has argued convincingly that the divinity of Rāma is fundamental to the epic narrative, *The Rāmāyaṇa of Vālmīki: An Epic of Ancient India, Vol. III, Araṇyakāṇḍa* (1991), 51–2 and "The Divine King in the Indian Epic," *Journal of the American Oriental Society* 104 (1984): 505–28. I, along with Robert P. Goldman, have argued similarly for the divinity of Hanumān

in Vālmīki's text in R. Goldman and S. Goldman, 39–57 and Robert Goldman and Sally Sutherland Goldman, "Vālmīki's Hanumān: Characterization and Occluded Divinity in the *Rāmāyaṇa*," *Journal of Vaiṣṇava Studies* 2.4 (1994): 31–54. Sītā is explicitly connected with the mother goddess in Vālmīki's text: at her birth, she is born from the Earth as her father, Janka, is plowing the sacrificial field (1.65.16–18) and at the close of the epic, she takes final refuge with her (7.88.12–14). See too 5.14.16 where her birth from the earth is again referred to, as well as Sally J. Sutherland, "Draupadī and Sītā," 63–79, esp. 77–8.

31. 5.35.

32. See Janet Walker, "Couching Resistance: Women, Film, and Postwar Psychoanalytic Psychiatry" in *Psychoanalysis and Cinema,* ed. Ann E. Kaplan, (New York: Routledge, 1990), 143 for discussion on the rhetoric of resistance.

33. See R. Goldman and S. Goldman, 1996, note to 5.13.22; *Araṇyakāṇḍa* Appendix 1, no. 12; and Pollock, 1991, 332.

34. William Ryan, *Blaming the Victim* (New York: Vintage Books, 1972).

35. 5.23.20:

*dhig astu khalu mānuṣyaṃ dhig astu paravaśyatām /*
*na śakyaṃ yat parityaktum ātmacchandena jīvitam //*

36. Two commentators, Nāgeśa (Tilakaṭīkā) and Yogīndra Mādhava (Katakaṭīkā), see Sītā as bemoaning her captivity by the *rākṣasīs*, etc., but given the use of the phrase later in the *kāṇḍa,* this does not seem as plausible. Rāmānuja understands that without both of these conditions—*mānuṣyam,* "humanity," and *paravaśyatām,* "dependence"—such misery would have never come about. Tilaka and Kataka think that Sītā curses her humanity (*mānuṣyam*) as it prevents her from honorably committing suicide. These same commentators understand the *rākṣasīs* alone to be the referent of *para,* neither of them mentioning Rāvaṇa. Later, at 24.49, Sītā uses a different expression, *rāvaṇasya vaśaṃ gatām* to indicate that she is in "Rāvaṇa's clutches." For Sītā's dependence on her husband Rāma, see 5.34.9 and 5.26.5.

37. See n. 9 above and *Rām* 3.16–17.

38. The reference here is to when Lakṣmaṇa, although specifically told to guard Sītā (3.41.47cd–48), at her importuning (3.44.1–34), leaves her alone and goes to Rāma's aid (3.44.37).

39. When Sītā refers to being in "Rāvaṇa's clutches," the phrase she uses is *rāvaṇasya gatā vaśam,* rather than the earlier phrase *paravaśyātām* used at 5.23.30.

40. Simone de Beauvoir, *The Second Sex,* trans. H. M. Parshley (New York: Vintage, 1974), 739.

41. The increased pathos reflected in the *sarga* is enhanced by a change in meter. The entire *sarga* is composed in *upajāti.*

42. The commentators Satyatīrtha and Maheśvaratītha in their comments on this verse place the blame for the abandonment of these little girls on

"heartless mothers," whereas modern evidence of female infanticide in India demonstrates that while the mother is usually directly responsible for ending the girl's life, it is generally under pressure from the father or mother-in-law. See Barbara D. Miller, *The Endangered Sex: Neglect of Female Children in Rural North India* (Ithaca: Cornell University Press, 1981).

43. The equation is attested elsewhere in the Sanskrit literature. The early Sanskrit playwright Bhāsa similarly equates abandonment and death. Compare, for example, Vāsavadattā's words at the opening to Act 3, of the *Svapnavāsavadattam: "dhaññā khu cakkavāavahū jā aṇṇoṇṇavirahidā a jīvai, ṇa khu ahaṃ pāṇāṇi parittajāmi. ayyauttaṃ pekkhāmi tti ediṇā maṇorahena jīvāmi mandabhāā.* [*dhanyā khalu cakravākavadhūḥ yānyonyavirahitā na jīvati. na khalv ahaṃ prāṇān parityajāmi. āryaputraṃ paśyāmīty anena monorathena jīvāmi mandabhāgā.*] "Indeed, the fortunate *cakravāka* female—separated from her mate [lit., "mutually separated"]—does not live. But I do not abandon life. Wretched, I will continue to live with the hope of seeing my lord." *Svapnavāsavadattam* Act 3, lines 5–13 in *Bhāsanāṭakacakram: Plays Ascribed to Bhāsa*, edited by C. R. Devadhar (1932; rept., Poona: Oriental Book Agency, 1962).

44. See 3.42.12–27ab where the demon Mārīca takes on the form of a golden deer.

45. Sally J. Sutherland Goldman, "Poetic Constructions of Gendered Space in the *Sundarakāṇḍa* of *Vālmīki's Rāmāyaṇa,*" paper presented at "Spaces: The Representation and Use of Space In South Asia," the Ninth Annual South Asia Conference University of California, Berkeley, March 1995.

*Chapter Twelve*

1. Kṛttibāsa, *Rāmāyaṇa,* ed. Subodhacandra Majumdāra, new edn., West Bengal Education Department (Calcutta: Aruṇacandra Majumdāra at Deva Sāhitya Kuṭīra Pvt. Ltd., 1985); *Kṛttibāśī Rāmāyaṇa,* ed. Āśutoṣa Bhaṭṭācārya (Calcutta: Akhila Bhārata Janaśikśā Pracāra Samiti, n.d. [1970?]); and the similarly titled work edited by Harekṛṣṇa Mukhopādhyāya, with an introduction by Sunitikumāra Caṭṭopādhyāya (Calcutta: Sāhitya Saṃsad, 1979). Because the sections are clearly marked in all the printed editions, usually every few pages, the headers for the accompanying translations will serve for the citation.

2. Personal communication to Stewart.

3. D. C. Sen, *History of Bengali Language and Literature,* 2nd rev. edn. (Calcutta: Calcutta University Press, 1954), 162–75, 485–8; similar statements are made in passing in the Bengali literary histories by Sukumar Sen and Asit Kumāra Bandyopādhyāya.

4. Jatindra Mohan Bhattacharjee, *Catalogus Catalogorum of Bengali Manuscripts,* vol. 1 (Calcutta: The Asiatic Society, 1978).

5. Ghanarāma Cakravartī, *Dharma Maṅgala,* ed. Pīyūṣa Kānti Mahāpatra (Calcutta: Calcutta University, 1962).

6. Vṛndāvana Dāsa, *Caitanya Bhāgavata*, ed. with the commentary *Nitāikaruṇakallolinī ṭīkā* by Rādhāgovinda Nātha, 6 vols. (Calcutta: Sādhanā Prakāśanī, 1373 BS).

7. Kavi Sañjaya, *Mahābhārata*, ed. Munīndrakumāra Ghoṣa (Calcutta: Calcutta University, 1969).

8. W. L. Smith, *Rāmāyaṇa Traditions in Eastern India: Assam, Bengal, Orissa*, 2nd rev. edn., Stockholm Studies in Indian Languages and Culture (New Delhi: Munshiram Manoharlal Publishers Pvt. Ltd., 1994), 30.

9. It is perhaps germane that the most popular Bengali *Mahābhārata*, that of Kāśīrāma Dāsa, which is two and one-half times the length of Kṛttibāsa's *Rāmāyaṇa*, is reproduced in much the same manner as the latter, suggesting for the contemporary edition a group assembly rather than single authorship; see Kāśīrāma Dāsa, *Mahābhārata*, originally ed. Maṇilāla Bandhyopādhyāya and re-ed. Dhīrenda Ṭhākura (Calcutta: Tārācānda Dāsa and Sons, n.d. [1988?]).

10. Bhattacharjee lists more than 160 MSS of Kṛttibāsa's *uttara kāṇḍa*, most of which are complete; and another 18 anonymous *uttara kāṇḍa*s, many of which are likely to be Kṛttibāsa's (anonymity in this publication most often being attributed primarily from incomplete cataloging information), this number representing an extremely popular and widespread circulation; see Bhattacharjee, 243, 252, 354.

11. Smith, 29.

12. "A Vālmīkian skeleton is fleshed out with apocryphal stories." Ibid., 46.

13. This position is found in the historical criticism of many of the regional traditions, and is one that has been partially corrected by the stimulating volume of essays conceived and edited by Paula Richman, *Many Rāmāyaṇas: The Diversity of a Narrative Tradition in South Asia* (Berkeley: The University of California Press, and Delhi: Oxford University Press, 1991). Richman briefly notes the problem with the concept of apocrypha and the implied standard on pp. 8-9 of the introduction.

14. Gerard Gennette, *Paratexts: Thresholds of Interpretation*, trans. Jane E. Lewin and Richard Macksey (Cambridge: Cambridge University Press, 1997) from the French original (1987).

15. Kermode's work on the "classic" is germane here; see Frank Kermode in *The Classic: Literary Images of Permanence and Change* (Cambridge, MA: , and London: Harvard University Press, 1983).

16. See Michel Foucault, "What is an Author?" in *Critical Theory Since 1965*, ed. Hazard Adams and Leroy Searle (Tallahassee: Florida State University Press, 1986), 138–48.

17. *Dasarathi rāya pāñcālī*, ed. Haripada Cakravartī (Calcutta: University of Calcutta, 1962), 523.

18. Vettam Mani, *Purāṇic Encyclopedia* (Varanasi: Motilal Banarasidass, n.d. [1975?]).

19. This is according to the Mukhopādhyāya text. Others give the name of the kingdom as Kalinga, which is not infrequently depicted as a region full of vagaries and difficult to rule.

20. *Dasarathi rāya pāñcālī*, 510.

21. Śaṣṭhī is the goddess of child–bearing and children. The ambiguity of the phrase is in the Bengali.

22. Tripurásundarī is a name of Durgā. The "three cities" were built in heaven, the air, and on the earth for the *asuras* by Māyā; they were destroyed by Śiva. The *tulasī* is the basil plant sacred to Vaiṣṇavas, and perhaps this line suggests that the translation "hatred" is a little strong.

23. Presumably the reference is to the son of Vyāsa, named after a particularly enchanting parrot, who was tempted by celestially beautiful women in the gardens of the royal palace of Mithilā, whom he shunned in order to meditate; *Devī Bhāgavata* 1, according to Mani.

24. I.e. Śiva, Dakṣa's son–in–law, who offended Dakṣa by not rising when he entered the room; Dakṣa returned the insult by not inviting Śiva to a sacrifice, and Śiva, in fury, created two monsters who cut off Dakṣa's head (along with the heads of everybody else they saw); *Devī Bhāgavata* 7.

25. Goddess of snakes.

26. Bhagavatī is a generic name for the goddess; "orthodox" is the way we have translated *gõṛā*, which Jñendramohana Dāsa defines as "one who does not deviate from traditional dharma," *Bāṅglāra Bhāṣāra Abhidhāna* [Calcutta: Indian Publishing House, n.d. [1323 BS]), but which also has the connotative overtone of following blindly, i.e. being bigoted.

27. I.e. Kāmadeva, who tried to tempt Śiva from his meditation.

28. In some *Rāmāyaṇas* this Shudra is identified as Śambūka, but the text of Kṛttibāsa leaves him unnamed.

29. *Akṣauhiṇī,* a division consisting of 109,350 infantry, 65,610 cavalrymen, 21,870 elephant-borne warriors and an equal number of horse-drawn charioteers.

30. Smith, 47.

31. Michael's correspondence, quoted by Clinton B. Seely, "Homeric Similes, Occidental and Oriental: Tasso, Milton, and Bengal's Michael Madhusudan Dutt" in *Comparative Literature Studies* 25. 1 (1988), as well as in idem, "The Rājā's New Clothes: Redressing Rāvaṇa in *Meghanādhavadha Kāvya*" in Richman, 137.

32. The poem has been translated, but not yet published, in a stunning metrical English, a mirror of the original, by Seely.

33. Seely, "Homeric Similes," 40, quoting a letter by Michael cited in *Kavimadhusūdana o tāra patrāvalī*, ed. Kṣetra Gupta, (Calcutta: Granta Nilava, 1963), 246.

34. *The Autobiography of an Unknown Indian* (New York: Macmillan, 1951), 183, quoted in Seely, "The Rājā's New Clothes," 152.

35. See for example, D. C. Sen, 485–8;

36. A maund is about 82 pounds av.

37. *Daśarathi rāya pāñcālī*, 523–4.

38. Ironically, the disruption (*bandha*) of both meter (*chandaḥ*) and intention or desire (*chanda*) is pronounced exactly the same way in spoken Bengali.

*Chapter Thirteen*

1. Mangala Murugesan, *Sangam Age* (Madras, Thendral Pathippakam: 1982), 254. For a discussion on this topic see Champakalaksmi, *Vaiṣṇava Iconography in the Tamil Country* (New Delhi: Orient Longman, 1981), 44–5 and 117–18. She notes that "inscriptional evidence . . . comes only from a record of about the seventh-eighth centuries A.D. and definite evolution of a Rama cult dates from the tenth century A.D . . . . (p. 117).

2. See my article "The Rāmāyaṇa in the Theology and Experience of the Śrīvaiṣṇava Community: The Poetry of the Ālvārs and the Commentaries of Periyavāccān Piḷḷai" in *The Journal of Vaiṣṇava Studies*, 2.4 (Fall 1994): 55–91.

3. M.M. Ismail, "Kavicakravarti" in *Kavicakravartiyum kaviyaracarum* (Madras: Vānati Patippakam, 1993), 15.

4. Arabs were associated with the horse trade in South India.

5. I have discussed Umaru Pulavar's life and the *Cīṟā Purāṇam* in my paper "Religious Vocabulary and Regional Identity: A Study of the Tamil *Cīṟāppurāṇam* ('Life of the Prophet')" in *Beyond Turk and Hindu: Rethinking Religious Identities in Islamicate South Asia,* ed. David Gilmartin and Bruce Lawrence (Gainesville: University of Florida Press, forthcoming).

6. *Vilāttatu Kāṇṭam, Nāṭṭu Paṭalam* (The Chapter on the Countryside), v. 2. Umaru Pulavar's *Cīṟāppurāṇam,* ed. M. Itrīs Maraikkāyar (Chennai: Maraikkāyair Patippakam, 1987). All references to the *Cīṟāppurāṇam* will be to this edition.

7. *Kamparāmāyaṇam pālakāṇṭam, Āṟruppaṭalam,* 7. *Śrī Kamparāmāyaṇam, pālakāṇṭām,* ed. Vai.Mu. Kopālakiruṣṇamācāryar (Chennai: Vai. Mu. Kopālakiruṣṇamācāriyar Kampeni, 1964). All references to Kamban's Ramayana will be to this edition.

8. *Cīṟāppurāṇam, Vilāttattu Kāṇṭam, Nāṭṭu Paṭalam,* 12.

9. *Kamparāmāyaṇam, pālakāṇṭam, Āṟruppaṭalam,* 6.

10. *Cīṟāppurāṇam, Vilāttattu Kāṇṭam, Nāṭṭu Paṭalam,* 9.

11. To these five situations of love two more are added: *peruntiṇai* (mismatched love) and *kaikkilai* (unrequited love) which have no corresponding landscape. For discussions of the landscapes, see A.K. Ramanujan, *The Interior Landscape* (Bloomington: Indiana University Press, 1975), 104–12 and K. Zvelebil, *Tamil Literature* (Leiden: E.J. Brill, 1975), 98–9.

12. The line may also be translated as "a galaxy of splendorous stars."

13. *Kamparāmāyaṇam pālakāṇṭam, Ulāviyar Paṭalam,* 1 and 2.

14. *Cīṟāppurāṇam, Kicurattukāṇṭam, Pāttima Tirumaṇappaṭalam,* 132 (*Cīṟāppurāṇam,* Canto of the Hijrat; the Chapter on Fatima's Wedding).

15. Ibid., 134.

16. This account of his life is based on interviews in summer 1993 and 1994, as well as his autobiographical narrative in "My childhood" ("Eṉ kuḻantai paruvam"), *Untum Uvakai* (Madras: Vanati Patippakam, 1987). Henceforth, I have placed page numbers from this narrative directly after the quote or reference in the body of the text.

17. Apart from these books, Justice Ismail has also written a legal text on the powers of the president and governors according to the Indian constitution, and a work on the names of God in Islam.

18. *Kavicakravartiyum kaviyaracarum,* 28.

19. M.M.Ismail, "Mūṉṟu Pēccuṭaiyāḷ" in *Paḻaiya Maṉṟāṭi* (Madras: Vānati Patippakam, 1980), 27–69.

20. M.M. Ismail, "Nāṟpēccuṭaiyāḷ" in *Kampaṉ Kaṇṭa Camaracam* (Madras: Vānati Patippakam, 1985), 59–80.

21. M.M. Ismail, "Iṛupēccuṭaiyāṉ" in *Mummaṭaṅku Polintaṉa* (Madras: Vānati Patippakam, 1992), 17–36.

22. M.M. Ismail, "Aruntavattu araci" in ibid., 47–60.

23. M.M. Ismail, "Aintu pēcuṭaiyāḷ" in *Tāyiṉum* (Madras: Vānati Patippakam, 1986), 139–58.

24. M.M. Ismail, *Ilakkiya Malarkaḷ* (Madras: Vānati Patippakam, 1990).

25. "Śaṅkara, the teacher," a title given to the abbot of five monastic institutions in India.

26. M.M. Ismail, *Oru Maṛakkamuṭiyāta Anupavam* (Madras: Vānati Patippakam, 1992).

27. In a similar structural manner, argues Justice Ismail, the positions of Surya and Indra are reversed in the *Mahābhārata*: Surya's son Karna fights on the side of adharma and is sacrificed on the battlefield by Indra's son Arjuna.

28. M.M. Ismail, *Oru Maṛakkamuṭiyāta Anupavam,* 16. Reprinted from *Kalki,* December 8, 1985. Justice Ismail called my attention to this episode and also narrated the incident to me in July 1993.

29. Interview with Justice Ismail, July 1993. He voiced similar sentiments in an interview with a newspaper reporter the same month. See Rasheeda Bhagat, "M.M. Ismail: A Multi-faceted Personality," *The Indian Express,* Sunday, July 11, 1993.

30. For a full account of this incident, see J.B.P. More, "Tamil Muslims and Non-Brahmin Atheists, 1925–1940," *Contributions to Indian Sociology (new series)* 27.1 (January–June 1993): 83–104.

31. I have discussed this in "The Strains of Hindu-Muslim Relations: Babri Masjid, Music, and Other Areas Where the Traditions Cleave" in *After Babri Masjid,* ed. Arvind Sharma (Macmillan Press, forthcoming).

*Chapter Fourteen*

1. I wish to clarify two points at the outset. First, I focus primarily on the Sita of popular imagination rather than the Sita of Tulsi, Valmiki, or any other literary (or oral) version of *Rāmkathā*. Therefore, I eschew detailed textual analysis, concentrating on how Sita's life is interpreted and seen as paradigmatic in today's context. Second, the interviews from which I quote form a small but representative sample from scores of interviews that I have collected during the last decade. Although many of the quotes come from the Delhi area, they echo words I have heard in discussions from other regions of India where *Rāmkathā* has taken root and people have acquired familiarity with the story's characters.

2. Buddhināth Miśra, "Ek din Urvījā kī bhūmi par" in *Jan Janak Jānakī*, ed. Saccidānand Vatsyāyan (New Delhi: Vatsal Foundation, 1986), 25.

3. Rām Manohar Lohiā, "Draupadī yā Sāvitrī" in a collecton of his essays and speeches, *Jātī prathā* (Hyderabad: Rām Manohar Lohiā Samtā Vidyālay Nyās, 1964), 124–5.

4. Ibid., 125.

5. Pandurang Shastri Athavale, *Vālmīki Rāmāyaṇ, A Study* (Bombay: Sat Vichar Darshan Trust, 1976).

6. Ibid.

7. "Jānakī jīvan yātrā vrttānt," in *Jan Janak Jānakī*.

8. Uṣā Kiraṇ Khān, "Sītā janam biroge gail," *Jan Janak Jānakī*, 119.

9. Ibid., 119–20.

10. Ilā Dālmia, *Jan Janak Jānakī*, 32.

11. Uṣā Kiraṇ Khān, *Jan Janak Jānakī*, 120.

12. Ibid., 121.

13. Vidyā Bindu Siṃha, *Jan Janak Jānakī*, 122.

14. Śankar Dayāl Siṃha, "Ek gudgudi, ek vyathagīt" in *Jan Janak Jānakī*, 56.

15. Saccidānand Vatsyāyan, "Vanāshram Nagar," *Jan Janak Jānakī*, 61–2.

16. Lakshmī Kānt Varmā, "Kabīr kī do samādhiyoṃ ke bīc," *Jan Janak Jānakī*, 73.

17. M. K. Gandhi, Speech at a prayer meeting, October 18, 1946, *The Collected Works of Mahatma Gandhi* (Ahmedabad: Navajivan Trust, 1982), vol. 85, 491.

18. Gandhi, *Harijan*, March 1, 1942, *Collected Works*, vol. 75, 338.

19. Gandhi, *Young India*, October 21, 1926, *Collected Works*, vol. 31, 511.

20. Gandhi, *Collected Works*, vol. 20, 411.

21. Gandhi, *Harijan*, January 25, 1936, *Collected Works*, vol.62, 158.

22. Gandhi, *The Searchlight*, October 11, 1925, *Collected Works*, vol. 28, 295.

23. Ibid.

24. Gandhi, *Young India,* February 21, 1929, *Collected Works,* vol. 134, 447.

25. Gandhi, February 1940, *Collected Works* vol. 71, 209.

26. Cited in D.G.Tendulkar, *Mahatma* (New Delhi: Government of India, Publications Division, 1960), vol. 3, 60.

27. Gandhi, *Harijan,* August 4, 1940, *Collected Works,* vol. 72, 326.

28. Makhanlal Sen, trans. and abridged, *Valmiki Ramayana* (Delhi: Rupa and Co., 1989), 193.

29. This attitude contrasts sharply with the popular western view that assumes people in bygone ages were less knowledgeable, less aware of their rights and dignity, had fewer options, and therefore were less evolved as human beings. This linear view of human society makes the past something to be studied, but not a source of superior wisdom for the present generation.

30. See the citation of P. Pratap's unpublished thesis in Sudhir Kakar, *The Inner World* (New Delhi: Oxford University Press, 1978), 194.

31. Meenakshi Mukherjee, "The Deadweight of Tradition," *Manushi* 2 (March–April 1979): 8–9 and Sally Sutherland, "Aggressive Behavior and Female Role Models in the Sanskrit Epics," *Journal of the American Oriental Society* 109.1 (1989): 79.

32. Kalidasa, *Raghuvaṃśa,* 14.61.

*Chapter Fifteen*

Avtar Brah, Perminder Dhillon, Parita Mukta, and several other members of the original Southall Black Sisters graciously shared their time and memories with me. Arjun Kashyap made available two photographs of the production. I benefitted from questions about an earlier draft of this paper in Wendy Doniger's seminar at the University of Chicago and at the Annual Conference on South Asia (1996) in Madison, Wisconsin. Thanks also go to Leela Fernandes, Michael H. Fisher, and Lakshmi Holmström for comments that improved this paper. I alone am responsible for any errors.

1. The original group of "Southall Black Sisters" was formed in 1978–9. More recently a new group has adopted the name "Southhall Black Sisters." Throughout this article, I refer exclusively to the original Southall Black Sisters.

2. The complex socio-economic developments in Southall's post-WWII South Asian immigrant community lie beyond the scope of this paper. Instead, my analysis deals only with specific factors that shaped the SBS Ramlila. For perspectives on South Asian immigration to the United Kingdom, see Avtar Brah, *Cartographies of Diaspora: Contesting Identities* (London: Routledge Press, 1996), 17–48; Peter Fryer, *Staying Power: The History of Black People in Britain* (London: Pluto Press, 1984); Rozina Visram, *Ayahs, Lascars and Princes: Indians in Britain 1700–1947* (London: Pluto Press 1987).

3. Several community associations were active in Southall, including the Indian Workers Association (IWA), composed mainly of older men who came to Southall in the 1950s and '60s. Many looked to the IWA as community leaders since they dealt not only with employment issues, but also provided information about social welfare rights and mediated family conflicts. The Pakistani Workers Association played a similar role for Pakistanis. For a history of Asian women's labor activism, especially in factories near Southall, see Amrit Wilson, ed., *Finding a Voice: Asian Women in Britain* (London: Virago Press, 1978), 48–70 and Beryl Dhanjal, "Sikh Women in Southall," *New Community* (henceforth *NC*) 5.1–2 (summer 1976): 109–14.

4. Beryl Dhanjal, "Asian Housing in Southall," *NC* 6.1–2 (winter 1977–8): 88–93; *Southall: The Birth of a Black Community* (London: Institute of Race Relations, 1981), 23–38, and Trevor R. Lee, "Immigrants in London: Trends in Distribution and Concentration, 1961–71," *NC* 2.2 (spring 1972): 145–58.

5. See Parminder Bhachu, *Twice Migrants: East African Sikh Settlers in Britain* (London: Tavistock Publications, 1985) and Brah, *Cartographies.*

6. *Southall,* 31

7. Even though other political parties did not express their views in as crude a manner as the NF did, as Brah notes in *Cartographies,* 37: "When the 'mainstream' politicians resort to using language which has the ring of that of the extreme right-wing groups, the rhetoric and the political position of the latter acquires increasing credibility and respectibility." See also Robert Miles and Annie Phizacklea, *Racism and Political Action in Britain* (London: Routledge, 1978), 124–46.

8. On April 21 (two days before the NF meeting in Southall), John Tyndall said at a St George Day March in Leicester, another city with a sizable South Asian community, that the National Front must emulate the heroes of H.G. Wells' *The Time Machine* and defeat "dark-skinned, hook-nosed dwarfs." Quoted on p. 190 of *Southall 23 April 1979: The Report of the Unoffical Committee of Enquiry,* ed. Michael Dummett (Published for the Committee by the National Council for Civil Liberties, 1980), in discussing why Southall residents were reluctant to have the National Front meet in their Town Hall.

9. Headline from *Punjab Times* as quoted in *Southall, Birth of Black Community,* 36. See also Perminder Dhillon's article about why feminists are concerned with police brutality, "They're Killing Us in Here," *Spare Rib,* 1979.

10. *The Report of the Unofficial Committee of Enquiry,* 9–10. Equivalent to the American Civil Liberties Union in the United States, this group felt that so much information had been withheld during official police investigations that they undertook their own investigation.

11. Ibid. 10.

12. The sense of Black identity as a unifying force developed in the

later 1970s and remained strong in the 1980s. For writings on the topic, see A. Sivanandan, *A Different Hunger: Writings on Black Resistance* (London: Pluto Press, 1982) and Shabnam Grewal et al., *Charting the Journey: Writings by Black and Third World Women* (London: Sheba Feminist Publishers, 1988). The term "Asian" had been used to describe South Asian immigrants in Kenya and Uganda. Although the term "Asian" is more limited than the term "Black," it still involves unity across boundaries, since it includes people of different nationalities (Indians, Pakistanis), religions (Hindus, Muslims, and Sikhs primarily), and classes (mostly lower class and middle class).

13. A.C.W. Peggie, "Minority Youth Politics in Southall" in *NC* 7.2 (1979): 170–7 and Avtar Brah, "South Asian Teenagers in Southall: Their Perceptions of Marriage, Family, and Ethnic Identity," *NC* 7.3 (Summer 1978): 197–206.

14. See *Festivals in India* (Madras: Vivekananda Prakashan Kendra, 1977), 69–75. Diwali lasts for 4–5 days, depending upon the lunar calendar, and falls in October or November each year. Until fairly recently Sikhs in the U.K. shared the celebration of Diwali with Hindus, since Guru Amar Das had approved of it for Sikh congregations. According to tradition Guru Hargobind was freed from the Gwalior jail during Diwali. In the years of South Asian immigration under discussion in this paper, Sikhs and Hindus in Southall did celebrate Diwali together. After Indira Gandhi ordered the destruction of the Golden Temple in Amritsar, and then was assassinated by two Sikh bodyguards, the situation changed in Southall and elsewhere. Today, Hindus celebrate Diwali and Sikhs celebrate the holiday as the day of Guru Hargobind's release. See Eleanor Nesbitt, "Panjabis in Britain: Cultural History and Cultural Choices," *South Asia Research* 15.2 (Autumn 1995): 234.

15. For a different view of Sita's character, see Madhu Kishwar's essay in this volume.

16. Many Indians in the Caribbean did, however, celebrate Diwali and perform Ramlilas. For ethnography and photographs of Ramlila performances in Trinidad, see Arthur and Jaunita Niehoff, *East Indians in the West Indies,* Publications in Anthropology, no. 6 (Milwaukee: Milwaukee Public Museum, 1960), 124–5.

17. The IWA's loan of their meeting room for the event suggests not only recognition of the contribution that the SBS Ramlila would make to the community, but makes them part of a lineage of community activism in this space.

18. In many genres of traditional Indian drama, male actors play both female and male roles. Examples include Terukkuttu performances in Tamil Nadu, Kathakali plays in Kerala, and the *svarūps* (Brahmin boys believed to incarnate a deity) of the Ramnagar Ramlila performance of Benaras.

19. Within the Ramayana tradition, such framing has an extensive history. See, for example, Linda Hess, "Staring at Frames Till They Turn into Loops"

in *Living Banaras: Hindu Religion in Cultural Context*, ed. Cynthia Humes and B. Hertel, (Albany: SUNY Press, 1993), 73–101, for analysis of frames in the Hindi *Rāmcaritmānas.*

20. *The Southall Gazette,* October 19, 1979, 5.

21. Brah, "Journey to Nairobi," in Grewal, 86.

22. Parita Mukta, *Upholding the Common Life: The Community of Mirabai* (Delhi: Oxford University Press, 1994).

23. According to the recollections of those whom I interviewed, in absolute numbers fewer audience members came from the Southall African Caribbean community than the South Asian community. Since African Caribbeans formed a smaller percentage of the Southall population and SBS membership, that partially explains their smaller presence in the audience. Equally if not more important, however, the Ramlila did not have the same long-standing cultural relevance for them. Nonetheless, because several African Caribbean women played major roles in the performance, families and friends showed up to applaud their efforts. While several South Asian women in the group had either kept in touch with each other or heard of each others' whereabouts during the twenty years that had passed since the performance, this proved less true of the African Caribbean members. I could only interview one African Caribbean member, who said that the play took place so long ago that she barely remembered it. Since the Ramlila was not an annual celebration in her family, it had less personal resonance for her. Thus, the evidence is too limited to generalize about the long-term effect of the performance on the African Caribbean women involved.

24. Some of these rifts have developed at least partly in response to political events in India, Pakistan, and Bangladesh. For example, Indira Gandhi's decision to bring troops into the Sikh Golden Temple in Amritsar (1984), her subsequent assassination, and the rioting that took the lives of hundreds of Sikhs, affected Hindu/Sikh relationships in Britain. Events surrounding the media coverage of Salman Rushdie's publication of *Satanic Verses* also affected relations within the South Asian community. See Talal Asad, *Genealogies of Religion: Discipline, and Reasons of Power in Christianity and Islam* (Baltimore and London: Johns Hopkins University Press, 1993).

25. Gerd Baumann, *Contesting Culture: Discourses of Identity in Multi-Ethnic London* (Cambridge: Cambridge University Press, 1996), 60–71, discusses how borough politics enhances competition between South Asians and African Caribbeans in Southall.

26. Paula Richman, *Many Rāmāyaṇas: The Diversity of a Narrative Tradition in South Asia* (Berkeley: University of California Press and Delhi: Oxford University Press, 1991), 7–10.

27. Velcheru Narayana Rao, "A Ramayana of Their Own: Women's Oral Tradition in Telugu" in Richman, 114–36. Also Joyce Flueckiger, "Literacy

and the Changing Concept of Text: Women's Ramayana *Maṇḍalī* in Central India," in *Boundaries of the Text,* ed. Joyce Flueckiger and Laurie Sears (Ann Arbor: South and Southeast Asian Studies, University of Michigan, 1991), 43–60.

28. For example, see Joanna Williams, *The Two-Headed Deer: Illustrations of the Ramayana in Orissa* (Berkeley: University of California Press, 1996).

29. Philip Lutgendorf, *The Life of a Text: Performing the* Rāmcaritmānas *of Tulsidas* (Berkeley: University of California Press, 1991), 254–94.

30. See Jonathan GoldbergBelle, "Clowns in Control: Performances in a Shadow Puppet Tradition in South India" in *Oral Epics in India,* ed. Stuart Blackburn et al. (Berkeley: University of California Press, 1989), 118–39.

31. Romila Thapar, "The Ramayana Syndrome," *Seminar* 353 (January 1989): 72–4.

32. Sheldon Pollock, "Rāmāyaṇa and Political Imagination in India," *Journal of Asian Studies* 52.2 (May 1993): 261–97.

33. Paula Richman's "Epic and State: Contesting Interpretations of the Ramayana," *Public Culture* 7.3 (1995): 631–54, shows how a key moment in the Dravidian protests against dominant tellings of Rama's story had been the burning of pictures of Rama.

34. Bhikkhu Parekh's six-part series on the Indian Diaspora in *The Asian Age,* March 28 to April 2, 1994, suggests that Rama's story possesses a particular resonance for diaspora Hindus.

*Chapter Sixteen*

This essay is based upon archival and field research in the Fiji Islands in 1982, 1984–5, 1991 and 1998. I owe thanks to the governments of Fiji for permission for research, and to the Fiji National Archives for permission and assistance over the years. Ms Margaret Patel, librarian, and later head archivist at the National Archives, has provided invaluable information, insight and guidance at many stages in my research. I owe thanks also to Ramayan mandalis in Samabula, in Narere seven and eight miles, and in Coboni, which have allowed me to attend their functions over the years. For their forebearance and many explanations I would like to mention, in particular, Shiu Sharan Sardar, "Moce" Prasad, Bas Deo and Ambika Prasad Maharaj of Narere. Special thanks also to the gracious and knowledgable Pandit Devakar Prasad. This essay has benefited from Paula Richman's editing advice at several stages, and also from the comments of Subramaniam, Francis Mugler, Vijay Naidu, Doug Munro and others at the University of the South Pacific in Suva Fiji, where I read the middle sections in July of 1998. As always Martha Kaplan has improved every draft.

1. I have not seen the Hindi original, and quote here from Gyani Das, "Fiji—An Indian Colony" (manuscript, Mitchell Library, Sydney, Australia).

This is a translation and summary, in English, of "Bharatiye Upnivesh Fiji," published in *Tara* 1 (Delhi: Arjun Press, New Bazaar, 1948).

2. I have written elsewhere about sex, gender and violence in indenture period Fiji, and about the crucial role of devotionally-troped protest about sexual abuse in the abolition of indenture. See (1) *A Politics of Virtue: Hinduism, Sexuality, and Countercolonial Discourse in Fiji* (Chicago: University of Chicago Press, 1991); (2) "Gaze and Grasp: Plantations, Desires, Indentured Indians, and Colonial Law in Fiji," in *Sites of Desire, Economies of Pleasure: Sexualities in Asia and the Pacific*, ed. Lenore Manderson and Margaret Jolly (Chicago: University of Chicago Press, 1997); and (3) Totaram Sanadhya, *My Twenty-One Years in the Fiji Islands,* trans. and ed. John D. Kelly and Uttra Kumari Singh (Suva: Fiji Museum, 1991), and especially the research appendix therein, "Fiji Indians and the Law, 1912." When Das denied that each woman served three men, he refers to a claim in a medical report on syphilis in Fiji that C.F. Andrews found, publicized, and brought to India's Viceroy in 1918, a crucial moment in the abolition of indenture. See Kelly, 55–6. The best general history of Fiji is Brij Lal's *Broken Waves: A History of the Fiji Islands in the Twentieth Century* (Honolulu: University of Hawaii Press, 1992).

3. See Paula Richman, ed., *Many Rāmāyaṇas* (Berkeley: University of California Press and Delhi: Oxford University Press, 1991) and Sheldon Pollock, "Rāmāyaṇa and Political Imagination in India," *The Journal of Asian Studies* 52.2: 261–97. Quotation is from p. 264.

4. Gandhi deliberately framed his own political acts in epic devotional terms, and made clear his commitment to the epics as and against history: "I was determined to read Gibbon in the jail this time. I was glad of it. For me even history has a spiritual significance . . . . I believe in the saying that a nation is happy that has no history. It is my pet theory that our Hindu ancestors solved the question for us by ignoring history as it is understood today and by building on slight events their philosophical structure. Such is the *Mahabharata.* And I look upon Gibbon and Motley as inferior editions of the *Mahabharata* . . . . The substance of all these stories is: Names and forms matter little, they come and go. That which is permanent and therefore necessary eludes the historian of events. Truth transcends history" [from M.K. Gandhi, "Islam, English History, and the *Mahabharata*" in *The Moral and Political Writings of Mahatma Gandhi, Vol. I, Civilization, Politics and Religion* (Oxford University Press, 1986), 187–8. Gandhi originally published this in *Young India,* September 11, 1924, "My Jail Experiences—XI."] In contrast Pollock juxtaposed political deployments of the Ramayana, past and present, with Marx's famous discussion, opening the *Eighteenth Brumaire,* of the Roman togas on the French Revolutionaries. This juxtaposition is also central to my book about the politics of Hinduism in post-indenture Fiji (Kelly, 24–5, 241–7). Pollock raises questions about historical imitation as a kind of politics with consequences for historical research generally; my interest

was the dilemmas posed by colonial history for political uses of the past (which past? colonizer's or colonized's? with what consequences in combination, as when the Arya Samaj attempts to be the Hindu Enlightenment, the Hindu Reformation, the Hindu Great Awakening, and Scientific Hinduism?). Epic political imagination, Gandhi's truth transcending history, offers to erase these dilemmas, part of its attractiveness in postcolonial as well as anticolonial situations.

5. Pollock, 288. Thus, it is all the more interesting that research now underway among members of the South Asian Labor Studies Group is beginning to show how closely intertwined is the history of indentured labor emigration from South Asia with the development both of plantation labor in South Asia, and with the emergence of urban industrial centers. Here I can merely raise the proposition with Fiji's tiny fragment of the necessary data: in addition to Jain Ramayanas, high and low caste Ramayanas, regional Ramayanas, gendered Ramayanas, etc., won't we find, if we look, some very important wage laborers' Ramayanas, especially migrant wage laborers' Ramayanas?

6. Sources: On military service migration, Dirk H.A. Kolff, *Naukar, Rajput and Sepoy: The Ethnohistory of the Military Labour Market in Hindustan, 1450–1850* (Cambridge: Cambridge University Press, 1990). On indenture, Hugh Tinker, *A New System of Slavery* (London, Oxford University Press, 1974), Jan Breman, *Taming the Coolie Beast* (Delhi, Oxford University Press, 1989), E. Valentine Daniel, Henry Bernstein, and Tom Brass, *Plantations, Proletarians and Peasants in Colonial Asia* (London: Frank Cass, 1992), *Journal of Peasant Studies* 19.3&4 (1992). On Indian Ocean merchant capitalism, Janet Abu-Lughod, *Before European Hegemony: The World System A.D. 1250–1350* (New York: Oxford University Press, 1989) and M.N. Pearson, *Merchants and Rulers in Gujarat: The Response to the Portuguese in the Sixteenth Century* (Berkeley: University of California Press, 1976). As far as I know, no historian has yet done justice to the whole scope and pattern of Gujarati commercial migration.

7. In keeping with the style customary for users of the National Archives of Fiji, where this and all other extant Colonial Secretary's Office minute papers reside, this quotation is from C.S.O. m.p. 2057/16. Further minute papers concerning holy books and oaths in court include 4202/16, 8504/16. 9958/16, 671/17, 1037/17, and 1706/17.

8. Sanadhya, 34.

9. C.S.O. m.p.1037/17.

10. C.S.O. m.p. 9958/16.

11. This quotation and all quotations from Buksh can also be found in C.S.O. m.p. 9958/16.

12. For material on Ramlilas in the 1910s, see Sanadhya, 66; also Ram Chandra Sharma, *Fiji Digdarshan* (Mandawar U.P.: Shree Ram Chandra

Pustkalaya, 1937), J. W. Burton, *The Fiji of To-Day* (London: Charles H. Kelly, 1910), esp. 327–9 and photo opposite p. 308, and Ahmed Ali, ed., *The Indenture Experience in Fiji* (Suva: Fiji Museum, 1979), a book of interviews with surviving indentured laborers, esp. 25, 31, 34–5, 38–9, 41, 55. For information on the plantation where no one could read the Ramayana, see 35.

13. For more details and a fuller analysis see also John D. Kelly, "From Holi to Diwali in Fiji: An Essay on Ritual and History," *Man* (n.s.) 23 (1988): 40–55.

14. Vijay Misra, "Epilogue: Rama Returns" in *Rama's Banishment: A Centenary Tribute to the Fiji Indians 1879–1979*, ed. Vijay Misra, (Auckland: Heinemann Educational Books, 1979), 139–43. In the course of reflecting on V.S. Naipaul and the emergence of Indo-Fijian fiction writers, Misra emphasized the dilemmas and restrictions constituted by the exile mythos, not only for Fiji but for all the indenture colonies. See also his "Introduction," 1–11.

15. For India see Kenneth W. Jones, *Arya Dharm: Hindu Consciousness in Nineteenth Century Punjab* (Berkeley: University of California Press, 1976), and G.R. Thursby, *Hindu-Muslim Relations in British India: A Study of Controversy, Conflict, and Communal Movements in Northern India 1923–1928* (Leiden: Brill, 1975) and for Fiji, my *A Politics of Virtue.*

16. Not only this, but he was clearly aware of the Ba Commissioner's reference to Veda and Shaster, and heaped public scorn on it: "Some one from the country districts suggests that the "Shasters" (correctly "Shastras") should be sworn on and not the Ramayana. Now . . . the average European, having a smattering of Hindi or Hindustani, only reflects the ignorance of his clients when he glibly begins to speak of the "Shasters" of the Hindus, and looks very grave and solemn as if he has got the real secret . . . . "Shastra" means . . . a body of rules pertaining to any science or art. There is a "Shastra" for poetry, grammar, rhetoric, love-making, and even on thieving. Now, on which of these "Shastras" is a Hindu to be sworn? . . . the Veda? The masses only repeat the name and pronounce it "Beda." The learned Brahmans of the orthodox school consider it a sin and a sacrilege even to scan the verses of the Vedas with a view to guessing their meaning . . . German scholars like Max Müller, Grassman and several others have not yet definitively established the meanings of the Vedic hymns." After this the Ba D.C., the last holdout within the officialdom, turned from internal minutes protesting against oaths on Ramayanas to internal minutes protesting against Manilal. Smarting from this publicly delivered humiliation, more acutely painful, as Manilal well knew, across the colonial color bar, the D.C. Ba (futilely) requested return of his earlier papers and demanded to know who had showed them to Manilal. The cover notes on the final minute paper on the oath issue trails off in this chain of denials. (See C.S.O.

m.p. 671/17, which also includes a copy of Manilal's newspaper article, and the D.C. Ba's protest about it.)

17. All quotations here are from the records of the Fiji Supreme Court, Criminal case 6 of 1901, which are housed in the National Archives of Fiji.

18. For references to Indian fascismo, see, e.g., C.S.O. m.p. 2600/30. For an example of this kind of Arya Samaj rhetoric, see the June 6, 1931 *Fiji Samachar,* a leading Hindi-language newspaper of Fiji, whose editorial position was strongly pro-Arya Samaj. In that issue, an influential Samaji named K. B. Singh wrote that "just as great fishes swallow up little fishes . . . so powerful races swallow up weaker ones. As Bismarck unified the states of Germany so that, welded into a powerful whole they were able to defy the whole world and just as Japan has so organized that she is able to hold her head up in the world, so different sects of Hindus need to combine together and present a united front. Therefore organize Sangathan Sabhas in every settlement and a Hindu Sabha in every district so as to be well organized to oppose external forces." For more about this argument in the context of the debates with Ram Chandra and Murarilal, and generally for a much more elaborate narrative of this history, see Kelly, *A Politics of Virtue,* esp. 213.

19. Papers in C.S.O. m.p. 2600/30.

20. Under attack was especially *niyog,* a form of temporary sexual liaison for the purpose of begetting children, which the Arya Samaj licensed in certain circumstances. Fiji's Secretary for Indian Affairs J. R. Pearson noted with amazement (in C.S.O. m.p. 2600/30) that at one meeting, in response to a publicly posed Sanatani question, "the Arya Samaj reply was read, it ran to 100 pages! all about some rather obscure Arya Samaj tenet relating to marriage." Discussing a different meeting, Fiji's Inspector General of Constabulary minuted tersely that Pandit Murarilal spoke for three hours, and "enlarged on some unsavoury practices which are permitted by Arya Samaj doctrine."

21. Ram Chandra Sharma, 27–9.

22. The most detailed English language studies of Fiji's Ramayana mandalis I have seen are those of Ian Somerville of 464 Old South Head Rd., Rose Bay 2029 NSW, Australia, to my knowledge, unfortunately not yet published, including but not limited to his paper "The Ramayan Mandali Movement in Fiji," originally read at The Theological Club, Suva, in August 1969. See also Jim Wilson, "Text and Context in Fijian Hinduism: Uses of Religion" and "Text and Context in Fijian Hinduism: Ritual as a Framework for Life," *Religion* 5 (Spring 1975): 53–68, 101–16, Jim Wilson, "Fijian Hinduism" in Vijay Misra, *Rama's Banishment* and Adrian Mayer, *Peasants in the Pacific: A Study of Fiji Indian Rural Society* (Berkeley: University of California Press, 1973, 2nd edn.). For the Ramayana and *kathā* in the indenture lines see Ahmed Ali, *The Indenture Experience in Fiji.* The phrase

"tender egalitarianism" is Donald Brenneis' description of Indo-Fijian social ethics and etiquette; see, e.g. "Performing Passions: Aesthetics and Politics in an Occasionally Egalitarian Society," *American Ethnologist* 14: 236–50.

23. "Almost everyone in the settlements of the town's hinterland came to the last day, and spent the time meeting friends, taking children round the stalls, and only incidentally watching the enactment of the battle and the burning of the enormous straw-filled guy of Ravan. Indeed, at a Ramlila in Mba, the burning took place at sunset, and most people had either gone or were too busy preparing to leave to watch the proceedings." Mayer, 94.

24. See John D. Kelly "*Bhakti* and Post-Colonial Politics: Hindu Missions to Fiji" in *Nation and Migration: The Politics of Space in the South Asian Diaspora*, ed. Peter van der Veer, (Philadelphia: University of Pennsylvania Press, 1995), 43–72. Recent political developments are more hopeful.

# Contributors

BINA AGARWAL, Professor of Economics at the Institute of Economic Growth at Delhi University, has authored three books, including *A Field of One's Own: Gender and Land Rights in South Asia* (Cambridge University Press, 1994), which won the Ananda Coomaraswamy Prize of the Association for Asian Studies (USA), the Edgar Graham Book Prize, (SOAS, University of London), and the H.K. Batheja Award (Bombay) in 1996. Notable articles include "The Gender and Environmental Debate: Lessons from India" in *Feminist Studies* (1992); "Gender and Command Over Property: A Critical Gap in Economic Analysis and Policy in South Asia," *World Development* (1994); "Gender and Resistance: Interlinked Struggles Over Resources and Meanings in South Asia," *Journal of Peasant Studies* (1994). She has also served on the editorial board of several academic journals, and is Vice-President of the International Association for Feminist Economics. Her poems have appeared in a number of American literary journals, including *Ploughshares, The Kenyon Review* and *Agni Review.*

VIDYUT AKLUJKAR taught for several years in the Department of Asian Studies at the University of British Columbia and is presently a research associate there. Her academic publications include *Primacy of Linguistic Units* (Pune: Indian Philosophical Quarterly Publications, University of Poona, 1987), as well as a number of scholarly articles, among which three on *Ānanda Rāmāyaṇa* are most relevant to Ramayana studies: "Battle as Banquet: A Metaphor in Sūradāsa," *Journal of the American Oriental Society* (1991); "Rāmāvatāra Recycled," *Annals of the Bhandarkar Oriental Research Institute* (1995); and "Why Build a Bridge over the Ocean? Propriety in the *Ānanda*

*Rāmāyaṇa*" in *Siting Sita*, ed. M. McGee (forthcoming). Co-editor of *Ekata*, a Marathi literary journal, she has also written several volumes of short stories, essays, and poetry.

EDWARD C. DIMOCK, Professor Emeritus at the University of Chicago, has played a major role in the development of South Asian Studies in the United States over the last forty years. His works on Bengali language, religion, and literature include, with Denise Levertov, *In Praise of Krishna* (Doubleday, 1966); *The Sound of Silent Guns and Other Essays* (Oxford University Press, 1989); "A Theology of the Repulsive: The Myth of the Goddess Śītalā" in *The Divine Consort*, ed. J. Hawley and D. Wulff (Berkeley Religious Studies Series, 1982); "Sacred Biography in India: The Case of the Caitanya-Caritāmṛta," in *The Biographical Process*, ed. F. Reynolds and D. Capp (Mouton, 1976); "The Bauls and the Islamic Tradition," in *The Sant Tradition*, ed. K. Schomer (Berkeley Religious Studies Series, 1982). Due out shortly is his translation of *The Caitanya-Caritāmṛta of Kṛṣṇadāsa Kavirāja*, ed. Tony K. Stewart (Harvard University Press, forthcoming).

[JOHN] RICH[ARDSON] FREEMAN teaches in the Department of Anthropology and Program for Studies in Religion at the University of Michigan. A specialist in Kerala's culture, he has conducted ethnographic projects for the French Institute of Pondicherry on Kerala's Tantric tradition and on forest life in the region's highlands. Recent publications include "Gods, Groves, and the Culture of Nature in Northern Kerala," *Modern Asian Studies* (1998); "Formalised Possession among the Tantris and Teyyams of Malabar," *South Asia Research* (1998); and "Rubies and Coral: A Lapidary Language for Kerala," *Journal of Asian Studies* (1998). His current research concerns the development of Malayalam literature and Kerala's regional identity, as part of a collaborative study titled "Literary Cultures in History: Reconstructions from South Asia," funded by the National Endowment for the Humanities.

ROBERT GOLDMAN is the Sarah Kailath Professor of Indian Studies and Chairman of the Center for South Asian Studies at the University of California at Berkeley. He serves as general editor for the multi-volume translation, *The Rāmāyaṇa of Vālmīki: An Epic of Ancient India* (Princeton University Press, 1985-2000). In addition he translated, co-annotated, and wrote the introduction for vol. 1 (*Bālakāṇḍa*) and co-translated, annotated, and wrote the introduction with S. Sutherland Goldman for vol. 5 (*Sundarakāṇḍa*). Currently he is at work on vol. 6 (*Yuddhakāṇḍa*). Recent articles include "Transsexualism, Gender and Anxiety in Traditional India," *Journal of the American Oriental Society* (1993); "Gods in Hiding: The *Mahābhārata's Virāṭa Parvan* and the Divinity of the Indian Epic Hero," in *Modern Evaluation of the Mahābhārata* (Nag Publishers, 1995); and "*Eṣa Dharmaḥ*

*Sanātanaḥ*: Situational Ethics in the Epic Age" in *Relativism, Suffering and Beyond,* ed. P. Bilmoria and J.N. Mohanty (Oxford University Press, 1997).

SALLY SUTHERLAND GOLDMAN, Lecturer in Sanskrit at the Department of South and Southeast Asian Studies at the University of California, Berkeley, has served as associate editor of the Valmiki Ramayana Translation Project since 1980. She is co-annotator, with R. Goldman of vol. 1 (*Balakāṇḍa*) and vol. 5 (*Sundarakāṇḍa*) of *The Rāmāyaṇa of Vālmīki*. In addition, she has published a number of articles, including "The Bad Seed: Senior Wives and Elder Sons" in *Bridging Worlds: Studies on Women in South Asia* (Center for South and Southeast Asia Studies, University of California, Berkeley, 1991), a volume she edited, as well as "The Text Which is No Text: Critical Edition as Text" in *Translation East and West: A Cross-Cultural Approach,* ed. C. N. Moore and L. Lower (University of Hawaii at Manoa, 1992), and "Seduction and Counter-Seduction: Bedroom Politics in the Ancient Epics" in *Journal of Indian Philosophy* (1992); and "A Tale of Two Tales: The Episode of Hanumān's Childhood" in the *Critical Edition Journal of the Oriental Institute of Baroda* (1995).

LINDA HESS, who teaches in the Religious Studies Department at Stanford University, began her scholarly career with publications on Kabir. In the last decade, she has published a number of articles on the Hindi Ramayana tradition, including "Staring at Frames Till They Turn into Loops: An Excursion through Some Worlds of Tulsidas" in *Living Banaras: Hindu Religion in Cultural Context,* ed. C.A. Humes and B. Hertel (State University of New York Press, 1993); "The Ram Legend as Theatre" in *The Legend of Rama,* ed. V. Dehejia (Marg Publications, 1994); "Martialing Sacred Texts: Ram's Name and Story in Late Twentieth-Century Indian Politics," *Journal of Vaiṣṇava Studies* (1994); and "Rejecting Sita: Indians Respond to the Ideal Man's Cruel Treatment of his Ideal Wife," *Journal of the American Academy of Religion* (1999).

JOHN KELLY, who writes on linguistic and political systems of ancient India as well as on colonialism and postcolonialism in Fiji, is Associate Professor in the Department of Anthropology at the University of Chicago. He has published *A Politics of Virtue: Hinduism, Sexuality, and Counter-Colonial Discourse in Fiji* (University of Chicago Press, 1991) and translated, with Uttra Singh, *My Twenty-One Years in the Fiji Islands* by Totaram Sanadhya (The Fiji Museum, 1991). Recent articles include "Diaspora and World War, Blood and Nation in Fiji and Hawai'i," *Public Culture* (1995); "Bhakti and Post-Colonial Politics: Hindu Missions to Fiji" in *Nation and Migration,* ed. P. van der Veer (University of Pennsylvania Press, 1995); and "What Was Sanskrit For? Metadiscursive Strategies in Ancient India" in *Ideology and Status of Sanskrit,* ed. J. E.M.

Houben (Brill, 1996). Together with Martha Kaplan, he is currently writing a book titled *Nation and Decolonization*.

MADHU KISHWAR, a Fellow at the Center for the Study of Developing Societies, is a founding editor of *Manushi: A Journal about Women and Society.* Since 1979 *Manushi* has brought issues of social justice into academic and popular debate. In addition to teaching at Satyawati College, Delhi University, Kishwar has edited several volumes, including *The Dilemma and Other Stories* by Vijaydan Detha (Manushi Prakashan, 1997), *Women Bhakta Poets* (Manushi Prakashan, 1989), and *Collected Stories from Manushi* (Penguin, 1999). Her books include *Gandhi and Women* (Manushi Prakashan, 1986); *Off the Beaten Track: Rethinking Gender Justice for Indian Women,* and *Religion in the Service of Nationalism and Other Essays* (both Oxford University Press). She has also published more than forty essays on issues of politics, gender, and history and has lectured throughout the world in academic conferences and activist venues.

PHILIP LUTGENDORF, Associate Professor of Hindi and Modern Indian Studies at the University of Iowa, writes on literary, political, and performance aspects of the Ramayana tradition. In addition to *The Life of a Text: Performing the* Rāmcaritmānas *of Tulsidas* (University of California Press, 1992), and *Rāmcaritmānas Word Index* (Manohar 1997), co-authored with W. Callewaert, he has written "The Secret Life of Rāmcandra of Ayodhya," in *Many Rāmāyaṇas;* "My Hanuman is Bigger than Yours," *History of Religions* (1994); "Interpreting Rāmrāj" in *Bhakti Religion in North India,* ed. D. Lorenzen (SUNY Press, 1995); "All in the (Raghu) Family" in *Media and the Transformation of Religions in South Asia* (University of Pennsylvania Press, 1995), and "Monkey in the Middle: the Status of Hanuman in Popular Hinduism," *Religion* (1997). He is presently finishing a book on Hanuman and researching the global impact of Hindi cinema.

VASUDHA NARAYANAN, University of Florida Research Foundation Professor in the Department of Religion at the University of Florida, served as project director and co-translator for Nammalvar's *"Sacred Utterance:" A Complete Translation* (Harvard University Press, forthcoming). She published *The Vernacular Veda: Revelation, Recitation, and Ritual* (University of South Carolina Press, 1994) and, with John B. Carman, *The Tamil Veda: Piḷḷāṉ's Interpretation of the Tiruvāymoḻi* (University of Chicago, Press, 1989). Her wide-ranging articles include "The Rāmāyaṇa in the Theology and Experience of the Śrīvaiṣṇava Community," *Journal of Vaiṣṇava Studies* (1993), "'One Tree is Equal to Ten Sons': Some Hindu Responses to the Problems of Ecology, Population and Consumption," *Journal of the American Academy of Religion* (1997), and "Religious Vocabulary and Regional Identity" in *Beyond Hindu and Turk: Shaping Religious Identities in Islamicate South Asia,* ed. D. Gilmartin and B. Lawrence (University of Florida Press, forthcoming).

VELCHERU NARAYANA RAO holds the Krishnadevaraya Chair in the Department of Languages and Cultures of Asia at the University of Wisconsin, Madison. One of the foremost scholars of Telugu literature in the world, he has translated recently, with D. Shulman and A.K. Ramanujan, *When God is a Customer: Telugu Courtesan Songs by Kṣetrayya and Others* (University of California Press and Oxford University Press, 1993) and, with D. Shulman, *A Poem at the Right Moment: Remembered Verses from Premodern South India* (University of California Press and Oxford University Press, 1997). With D. Shulman and S. Subrahmanyam, he wrote *Symbols of Substance: Court and State in Nāyaka-Period South India* (Oxford University Press, 1991). Among his many articles are "A Rāmāyaṇa of Their Own: Women's Oral Tradition in Telugu" in *Many Rāmāyaṇas,* and "Texture and Authority: Telugu Riddles and Enigmas" in *Untying the Knot: Riddles and Other Enigmas,* ed. G. Hasan-Rokem and D. Shulman (Oxford University Press, 1996).

USHA NILSSON, Professor of Indian Literature in the Department of Languages and Cultures of Asia at the University of Wisconsin, Madison, is a literary scholar, translator, and writer of novels and short stories. Her articles on Hindi literature include "Women in Contemporary Indian Literature," in *Bridging Worlds: Studies on Women in South Asia,* ed. S. Sutherland Goldman (1991); "Modernization and South Asian Literary Traditions: The Case of the Hindi Novel," in *Dimensions of Sociolinguistics in South Asia,* ed. E. Dimock, et al. (Oxford Publishing Company, 1992); and "Construction of Self: Autobiographies of Three Women Writers from India," *Journal of Asian Studies* (Hong Kong, 1994). She has published three Hindi novels and six volumes of short stories. Her English translation of her Hindi story appeared as "What a Big Lie" in *Living in America: Poetry and Fiction by South Asian American Writers* (Westview Press, 1995).

PAULA RICHMAN, Irvin E. Houck Professor in the Humanities at Oberlin College, specializes in Tamil religious literature. Her anthology of translations and critical essays, *Extraordinary Child: Poems from a South Indian Devotional Genre* (University of Hawai'i Press) came out in 1997. Recent articles include "E.V. Ramasami's Reading of the Rāmāyaṇa" in *Many Rāmāyaṇas: The Diversity of a Narrative Tradition in South Asia* (University of California Press and Oxford University Press, 1991), a volume which she edited; "Veneration of the Prophet Muhammad in an Islamic Piḷḷaittamiḻ," *Journal of the American Oriental Society* (1993); "Epic and State: Interpretations of the Ramayana" in *Public Culture,* (1995); and, with Norman Cutler, "A Gift of Tamil: On Compiling an Anthology of Translations from Tamil Literature" in *Translations*

*Across Cultures,* ed. A. Needham Dingwaney and C. Maier (University of Pittsburgh Press and Oxford University Press, Delhi?, 1996). She recently completed a monograph on Tamil tellings of the Ramayana in Madras from 1929 to 1973, and is now working on a study of Ramayana performances in South Asian diaspora communities.

DAVID SHULMAN, Professor in the Department of Indian, Iranian, and Armenian Studies at The Hebrew University, has published widely on Tamil, Sanskrit, and Telugu literature and religion. Author of *The Hungry God: Hindu Tales of Filicide and Devotion* (University of Chicago Press, 1993); with V. Narayana Rao, *A Poem at the Right Moment: Remembered Verses from Premodern South India* (University of California Press and Oxford University Press, 1997); and, with D. Handelman, *God Inside Out: Śiva's Game of Dice* (Oxford University Press, 1997), Shulman has also written a number of articles dealing with South Indian Ramayanas, including "Divine Order and Divine Evil in the Tamil Tale of Rāma," *Journal of Asian Studies* (1979); "Battle As Metaphor in Tamil Folk and Classical Traditions" in *Another Harmony: New Essays on the Folklore of India,* ed. S. Blackburn and A.K. Ramanujan (University of California and Oxford University Press, 1986); and "Fire and Flood: The Testing of Sītā in Kampaṉ's *Irāmāvatāram*" in *Many Rāmāyaṇas.* At present, he is engaged in a study of the literature and ritual of the Tirupati Temple in Andhra Pradesh.

TONY K. STEWART, Associate Professor of South Asian Religions at North Carolina State University and Director of the North Carolina Center for South Asia Studies of the Triangle South Asia Consortium, specializes in religions and literatures of pre-modern Bengal. Along with *The Caitanya Caritāmṛta of Kṛṣṇadāsa Kavirāja,* for which he and Edward C. Dimock have provided an introduction and commentary (Harvard University Press, forthcoming), he has written "Alternate Structures of Authority: Satya Pīr on the Frontiers of Bengal" in *Beyond Hindu and Turk* (University of Florida Press, forthcoming); "When Rāhu Devours the Moon: the Myth of the Birth of Kṛṣṇa Caitanya," *International Journal of Hindu Studies* (1997); and "In the Name of Devotion: Acyutacarana Caudhuri and the Hagiographies of Advaitacarya," *Journal of Vaiṣṇava Studies* (1996-97). He is completing a study of theological, rhetorical, and political strategies used in the sixteenth-seventeenth centuries to create the Gaudiya Vaishnava movement.

ROMILA THAPAR, one of the foremost scholars of Indian history in the world, has published extensively in the areas of ancient Indian culture as well as the political uses of history in modern India. Currently Emeritus Professor at Jawaharlal Nehru University, she is also Honorary Fellow at Oxford University. Among her many books and articles, some that shed light on interpretation of Rama's story in controversies about religion and India's past include *Exile and the Kingdom: Some Thoughts on the Rāmāyaṇa* (The Mythic Society, 1978); "Society and Historical Consciousness: the Itihāsa-Purāṇa Tradition" in *Situating Indian History,* ed. S. Bhattacharya and R. Thapar (Oxford University Press, 1986); "The Ramayana Syndrome," *Seminar* (1989); "Epic and History: Tradition, Dissent and Politics in India," *Past and Present* (1989); "Imagined Religious Communities? Ancient History and the Modern Search for a Hindu Identity," *Modern Asian Studies* (1989); and "A Historical Perspective on the Story of Rama" in *Anatomy of a Confrontation: The Babri Masjid–Ramjanmabhumi Issue,* ed. S. Gopal (Penguin, 1991).

# Copyright Statement

"Sita Speak," published in a slightly different form, appeared in *Indian Express,* 17 November 1985, copyright 1985 by Bina Agarwal.
"Beyond Captivity," copyright 1985 by Bina Agarwal.

Several sections of "Yes to Sita, No to Ram: The Continuing Hold of Sita on Popular Imagination in India" appeared in *Manushi* 98 (January-February 1997), pp. 20–31, and have been reprinted with the permission of Madhu Kishwar.

A longer version of "The Ramlila Migrates to Southall" was published as "A Diaspora Ramayana in Southall, Greater London" in the *Journal Of The American Academy Of Religion* 67/1 (winter 1999), pp. 33–57 and has been reprinted with permission.

# Index

*Abbreviations:*

| | |
|---|---|
| A/B | Awadhi/ Bhojpuri |
| *ĀR* | *Ānanda Rāmāyaṇa* |
| *DJ* | *Dasaratha Jātaka* |
| *IR* | Kamban's *Irāmāvatāram* |
| *KR* | Krittibasa's *Rāmāyaṇa* |
| *Mānas* | *Rāmcaritmānas* |
| SBS | Southall Black Sisters |
| UK | United Kingdom |
| *URC* | *Uttararāmacarita* |
| *VR* | Valmiki's *Rāmāyaṇa* |

Note: Except for the titles of texts, names are given without diacritical marks or italics. This policy means, for example, that Shambuka appears somewhat later in the text than the Telugu play titled *Śambuka Vadha*.

Antahpuram (inner apartments of the palace), 224–26
Apophasis, 17, 244, 252
April 23 (conflict in Southall), 19, 312–17, 321–22, 328, 402n8–n10
Arabia: 267–70; Arabic, 267, 274, 280–81; Arabs, 398n4
*Araṇya-kāṇḍa*: of Valmiki, 111, 119–20, 122, 224, 229; of Kamban, 124
Aruna, 195, 201–02, 207
Arundhati, 55, 58, 60, 75–76
Arya Samaj, 344–48, 407n4, 409nn18, 20
Aryan: 37, 159, 175–77, 208: Rama's ministers as, 159–61
Asceticism: 112, 128, 251, 253, 256; and high caste, 128–30, 136, 159–61; and low birth, 124, 127–28, 134–35, 160; Lava and Kusha and, 262; Sita and, 214, 231, 263; Rama and, 170, 294
Ashari (Carpenter) caste, 190, 194, 196, 207, 219
Ashoka grove (in Ravana's compound), 178–79, 224, 238, 323, 392n11
Ashram: 130; of Rsyasrnga, 51; of Valmiki, 53, 55, 254; of Agastya, 54; of Matanga, 122, 127
Ashvamedha (horse sacrifice), 40, 54, 56, 60, 67, 247, 254–57, 262, 294
Athavale, Shastri Pandurang V., 294–95
Audience: for *Mānas* doubts, 31–33, 35–37, 46–47; for and within *URC*, 59–61, 71, 77, 79; for Shabari story, 122, 126–27; for Sagar Ramayan, 9, 132–33; and rakshasa behavior, 107, 109, 113; for *KR*, 244–47, 261; for *IR*, 16, 277–79; for SBS Ramlila, 318–21, 324, 327
Authority: of Vedas, 40; of *Mānas*, 45–46; authoritative tellings of Ramkatha, vii–viii, x–xi, 3, 8–13, 16, 20–21, 327; Valmiki as, 8, 13, 90–97, 103
Authorship: 10, 174; *ĀR*; 14, 83–85, 90–91, 100–02; *VR*, 162–64; *KR*, 246
Awadhi/Bhojpuri, 15, 137–85
Ayodhya: in Ramkatha, 3, 28, 51, 70, 79, 85, 94, 100, 146–47, 151, 153, 256, 281, 295, 297, 301; modern, vii, xi, xiii, 1, 3, 18, 329, 332, 352, 359nn1–2, 361n3, 375n6
*Ayodhyā-kāṇḍa*, 40, 165, 183, 223–24, 393n27

Baba Ramchandra, 12, 360n15
Babri Masjid, vii–ix, xii–xiii, 265, 279, 281, 361n3
*Bāla-kāṇḍa*, 62, 91, 355
Bali, 34, 187–220, 252–54, 259, 385nn8, 11, 386n20, 387n37, 389n50, 390n57. See also Vali
*Bāli Vijayam*, 214–15
Banaras: 28, 37, 42–43, 251, 326, 403n18; Maharaja of, 31, 37, 42–43
Bangladesh, 17, 244, 404n25
Banishment of Sita, 6, 13, 19, 254, 287, 293–94, 297, 300–03
Barber: 137, 140, 145–46, 151; Barber's wife and ritual roles, 153–55, 380n17
Bengal: 7, 17, 32, 244, 247–48, 264, 398n38; literature of, 243–64, 378n12, 379n3, 396n10
Ber (jujube), 119, 123, 126, 129–30, 135
*Bhāgavata Purāṇa*: in Sanskrit, 88, 91, 97; in Telugu, 171
Bhagavati, 251, 335, 397n26
Bhajans: 293; to Rama, 169–70; by

Tyagaraja, 169; by Ramadasu (Kancarla Gopanna), 169
*Bhakta Caritrāṅk*, 123, 129
Bhakti: viii, 95–96, 125, 130–31, 170, 362n3; chanting Rama's name, 96–97, 99, 125, 170, 288; in *Mānas*, 27, 34–6, 39, 43, 45, 125–35. See also Devotion
*Bhaktirasabodhinī*, 127
Bharata (Rama's brother), 34–5, 37–39, 41, 255–58, 276, 294, 356
Bharatiya Janata Parishad [BJP], 2, 21, 361n3
Bhavabhuti, 3, 12–13, 49–82, 160, 366nn2, 5, 368nn25, 31. See also *Uttararāmacarita*, Drama
Bhils, 126, 133, 135, 378n25
Bhojpuri, see Awadhi/Bhojpuri
Bhushundi, 25, 31, 45, 366n38
Bihar, 32, 286, 334, 379n3
Blacks: in UK, 311–12, 314, 323–24, 328, 403n12; as an activist term, 314–15, 324, 403n12
Booth, R.M. (Inspector-General of Immigration, Fiji), 335–36, 342
Bourdieu, Pierre, 246, 347
Bow Contest, 25, 35, 41, 51, 354
Brah, Avtar, 323, 402n7
Brahma, 87–90, 100, 103, 164, 249, 355, 372
Brahmins: viii, 32, 34, 38–42, 46–47, 95–97, 403nn16, 18; in Malabar, 201–03, 210, 219, 384n4, 385n5; in Andhra, 159–62, 166–68, 170–84, 325; in *KR*, 259, in Tamilnadu, 274, 278, 365n35, 403n18; Brahmanical tradition, xi, 10, 14, 16, 39, 41, 45, 109, 111, 124, 131–33, 364n26; anti-Brahminism, xii, 159–62, 173–81
Buddhism: 40, 344; in Bengal, 264; and Tamil texts, 279; Buddhist Ramayanas, xii, 1–2, 21
Buksh, S., 336–38, 345
Bulcke, Camille, 370n3

Cakyars, 201–202, 213, 217, 219
Calcutta, 243, 335, 337, 340
Caribbean, See African Caribbeans
Caste hierarchy: ix–x, 5–6, 10–11, 14–16, 407n5; and *Mānas*, 38–39, 47; in *ĀR*, 84, 94–97; and Shabari, 119–36; in Malabar, 16, 188, 194, 200–03, 208–11, 217–20; in A/B songs, 137–73; varna mobility, 166–67. See also High Caste, Low Caste
Central Asia, 41, 129, 331, 334
Chalam, Gudipati Venkata, 179–80
Chandraketu, (Lakshmana's son) 54, 56–57, 72, 78
Chandravati, (singer), 140
Chaudari, Tripuraneni Ramasvami, 159–61, 169, 173–78, 383n21
Chaudhuri, Nirad, 261
Childbirth: 319, 325, 381nn9, 23; childlessness, 142, 155–56, 251, 319
Chitrakuta, 262, 295, 297
Chowdhury, J., 336–37, 342
Christians, 41, 336, 338–40, 343–45
*Cīṟā Purāṇam*, 267–73, 398n5. See also Umaru Pulavar
Colonialism, 167–68, 173, 182, 264, 311–14, 324, 327, 330–36, 340–42, 346, 349, 407n4, 408n16
Commentary: on Ramkatha, 6–7, 10, 12, 21, 52, 325; on *Bhaktamāl*, 127; on *Mānas*, 12–13, 25–47, 130–31; on *Adhyātma Rāmāyaṇa*, 169; on *IR*, 18, 276–79; on *VR*, 387n36
Communalism: in India, 299, 316, 346; in UK, 316; and coalitional politics, 324–25
Compassion: 161, 292; in *URC*, 12, 59–60, 69, 72–74, 78, 81, 370n53; in *ĀR*, 7, 13, 84, 95–96

Congress, Indian National, 132, 264, 275, 332

*Daily Telegraph*, 313
Daksha, 251, 397n24
Dandaka forest, 53, 177, 234, 339
Darshan: of Rama, 43, 96, 129, 143, 327, 355–56; and televised Ramayan, 132
Das, Pandit Ramkumar, 27–33, 36–39, 41, 354–58, 362n4
Dasaratha, 25, 46, 142, 151, 153–54, 156, 227, 229, 253, 255–56, 355–56, 380n16, 393n27
*Dasaratha Jātaka*, xi–xii, 1, 4, 20
Dasarathi Raya, 247, 248, 251–52, 261
Dayanand Saraswati, Swami, 344
Delhi, 287, 329, 400n1
Demons, 13–14, 35, 105–16, 261, 330–32, 338, 344, 361n18, 365n37. See also Rakshasas
Devi (goddess), 41, 139, 146–47
Devi, Anusuya (singer), 138, 146, 380nn7, 14, 380n1, 381n20
Devotion: and *Mānas*, 13, 27, 39, 42–45, 362n3; of Shabari, 15, 120–22, 134, 136; through enmity, 169; sentiment in Fiji, 329–31, 406n2; and Gandhi, 406n4. See also Bhakti
Dhagrin (midwife), 153–55, 381n19
Dharma: 6, 10, 33–34, 40, 44, 80, 120, 249, 303, 344, 356; of Rama, 6, 244, 253–55, 258, 278–79, 293–94, 301; of Sita, 304–05; of wife, 137, 379n1; of husband, 287, 306–07; of king, 56, 92, 159–61, 287, 293–94, 301; of kshatriya, 40–41, 257
Dharma shastras, 6, 95, 166, 181, 250, 258, 294
Dhillon, Perminder, 317–18, 323, 402n9
Dhobi (washerman): 148, 169, 287, 293, 295, 301, 385n5; wife of, 153
Diaspora: 327, 333–34, 348–50; South Asian, 329, 333–35, 348–51, 405n34; Ramlilas, 19, 309–10
Din, Jayram Das, 27–29, 31, 36–39, 43–45, 353–55, 357, 362n5
Diwali, 316, 320, 322, 328, 403nn14, 16
Doe song, 15, 139, 156–58, 381n24
Dog: (as polluting), 126, 258, 373nn28–29, in *ĀR*, 13, 92–98, 373n29; in *KR*, 248–51; *VR*, 373n29
Domestic servants: female, 5, 10, 14–15, 137–73, 287, 290; and wedding songs on Sita, 145–46
Doubts: 7, 83; about *Mānas* 12–13, 25–47, 353–58
Drama: 50–81, 369n47; play within play, 13, 51, 63, 69, 75, 77–78, 80; regional, 213–19, 318, 326
Draupadi, 107, 304, 306, 391n7, 393n22
Dravidian, 18, 159, 175–77, 383n18, 405n33
Durga, x, 100, 267, 397n22

Ealing, 321–22
Earth: as mother of Sita, 53, 55, 59–60, 80, 263, 289, 293; support of, 357
Education: 356; in Tamil literature, 274–75; English-language in Andhra, 174, 177, 181
Eknath, 83–84, 86, 371n13
English language, 34, 174, 177, 181, 380n7
Exile: in Ramkatha, 3, 25, 42–43, 49, 51, 55, 71, 325, 353; and Fiji, 20, 329, 332, 339, 344, 408n14

Fate: 17, 34, 43, 45, 75, 254; in *KR*, 244, 254, 259

85, 88, 95, 247–48, 254–62, 292–93, 295, 307
Lilavati (A/B singer), 380nn11, 381n24
Lohia, Ram Manohar, 293
Low caste: ix–x, 39, 53–54, 96, 202, 384n4; female servants, 15, 137–40, 145–48, 152–55, 158, 381n17. See also Caste Hierarchy or caste name
Lutgendorf, Philip, 30

Madhusudana Datta, Michael, ix, 260
Madhya Pradesh, 28, 31, 379n3
*Mahābhārata*, xi, 4, 88, 91, 97, 107, 173, 245, 300, 337, 360n10, 392n19, 393n29, 396n9, 399n27, 406n4
Maharashtra: 86, 94, 96, 370n3, 371nn7, 10, 372nn19, 24, 30; Marathi, 86
Malabar, 16, 187–220, 384nn1, 4. See also Kerala
Malayalam, 205, 213–19, 387n29, 388n44
Malyavant, Mount, 52, 70, 385n11
*Mānas: Mānas Pīyūsh*, 30, 37, 130; *Mānas Shankā Mochan*, 28; *Mānas Shankā Samādhān Ratnāvalī*, 27, 31; *Mānas Shankā Samādhān*, 27–28, 31, 45; *Mānas Shankāvalī*, 28. See also *Rāmcaritmānas*
Manasa, 251, 397n25
Manilal Maganlal, Doctor, 339–40, 343
*Manohara-kāṇḍa*, 84, 97, 101–02
*Manushi*, 19, 366n39
Marxism: 16, 317, 327; Communist Party (Marxist), 264
Maryada Purushottama, x, 6, 33–34, 130, 244, 285, 287, 304
Matanga, 120, 124, 127–29, 133–34, 209
Matha (monastery), 94, 97–98, 278, 399n25
Mauritius, 333, 339
Meat eating, 36, 38–41, 112–13, 175, 364–65nn28–31. See also Animals
Medina, 271
Meghanadha (son of Ravana): 30; *Meghanādhvadha Kāvya*, ix, 260–61
Mishra, Buddhinath Pandit, 292
Misra, Vijay, 339
Mithila, 19, 51, 138, 271, 295–97, 397n23
Moharram, 338
Monkeys: 3, 11, 44, 177, 252–53, 260–61; in Kerala temples, 16, 187, 206–07, 209, 216, 386n21
Muhammad, Prophet, 266–68, 277
Mukta, Parita, 323
*Mūn̲ru Vin̲ākkaḷ*, 276, 278
Murarilal Shastri, 346, 348
Muslims: x, xii, 37, 41–43, 265–81; in Fiji, 335–39, 343, 345–46, 379n3; and *IR*, 16, 18, 265–67, 273–75, 279–81; and SBS Ramlila, 317, 324.

Nabhdas, 127
Nambyars, 217, 219
Narayana Rao, Velcheru, 325, 359n4
Narayandasu, Ajjada Adibhatla, 169–70
National Front [NF] Party, 19, 312–14, 321–22, 402nn7–8
Nayars, 167, 201, 217, 219
Nirguna, 46, 344, 365n37
Non-Brahmins: in Andhra, 15, 166–69, 173–82; in Malabar, 217, 385n5

Orissa, 377n4, 378n12

Pampa, Lake, 120, 128–29, 136
Panchavati forest, 51, 54–55, 57, 59–60, 65, 67, 69–70, 72
Partition (of India and Pakistan), 280, 310–11, 404n24

Parvati, 25, 31, 44, 47, 60; 83, 288–89, 304–06, 363n17, 366n38, 381n17
Patanjali, 375n2, n5
Pathak, Vandan, 28–31, 36–37, 41, 353
Pativrata, 25, 111, 137, 223, 225, 231–32, 237, 258, 356, 390nn1–2, 393n29
Patriarchy, 17, 107, 224, 229–34, 238, 317, 323, 327, 393n22
Pavanna Dawoodsha Sahib, Pa., 275
Persian, 37, 280
Phala-shruti, 99–100
Pilgrimage, 43, 98, 274, 292
Poddar, Hanuman Prasad, 28–9, 363n9
Pollock, Sheldon, 18, 109, 111, 132, 162, 165, 331–32, 361n18, 378n23, 406n4
Pollution, 15, 39–40, 53, 98, 109, 126, 128–31, 135–36, 142, 381n19, 384n4
Possession, in teyyattam, 16, 187–94, 198–203, 208, 213–16
Powell, Enoch, 309, 313, 321
Print Culture, 7, 10, 161, 168, 173–74, 177–78, 243, 245
Priyadas, 126–29, 131, 135–36
Pulayan, 208–12
Punjab: 286, 310, 319–22, 324, 333, 344; *Punjab Times*, 313, 402n9
Puranas: 88–89, 267, 305, 355–56, 374n32; criticized by Chaudari, 173
Purushottam Kavi, Kasula, 170–71

Queen mothers: of Ayodhya, 51, 55, 58; of Janakpur, 34, 38
Questioning Ramayanas, vii–viii, 2, 5–21, 25–28, 31–47, 50, 57, 83, 85–86, 94–95, 130–31, 152–56, 161, 177–78, 207–20, 244, 247–55, 258–64, 276–77, 287–308, 314–22, 325–28, 348–51, 370n2

Racism, 18–19, 309–10, 312–17, 322–24, 326–28, 334
Raghunathanayaka, Gona Buddharaju, 166, 382n6
*Raghuvaṃśa,* 160, 307
Rajasthan: 32; Rajputs, 106, 375n6
Rajasuja, 255
*Rājya-kāṇḍa*, 85–86, 88, 92, 94, 97–98
Rakshasas, x, xii, 6, 14, 105–16, 229, 232–33, 235, 237, 260–61, 390n6, 392n19. See also Ravana, Demons
Rama: in Ramkatha, xi, xiii, 1–17, 20–21, 287–89, 292–95, 306–08, 365n34; in *Mānas* doubts, 23, 25, 33–5, 37–46, 353–58, 364n18; in *URC*, 49–82; in *ĀR*, 84–98; in Shabari story, 119, 122–28, 134–35; A/B songs, 141, 143–52, 156–58; in modern Telugu, 159–61, 168–69, 171, 175, 178–81, 405n33; in Malabar, 194–95, 209–11, 218, 220, 386n20; in *VR*, 228–31, 237, 393n30, 394n36; in *KR*, 17, 243–44, 249–64; in *IR*, 265–66, 276–80; in Mithila, 296–97; and Gandhi, 298; and Sharad Joshi, 300–03; SBS Ramlila, 316, 318–20, 324–25; in Fiji, 345–46, 348, 350
Ramalinga Reddi, Cattamanci, 173, 177–78
Ramanandi, 43, 130, 388n40
Ramanavami (Rama's birth and wedding day), 169–70
*Rāmāñjanēya Yuddham* (Battle of Rama and Hanuman), 170
Ramanujan, A.K., 4
Ramaswami, E.V., 12, 18, 176–77, 383n21

Saguna, 42, 46, 365n37
Sahmat Exhibit, xi, 1, 359n2
Samabula, Fiji: 345–46; "Puttu" Hussein of, 346
*Śambuka Vadha*, 159–61, 173, 178, 383n21. See also Shambuka
*Sampūrṇa Rāmāyaṇ*, 295
Sanadhya, Totaram, 338–39, 342
Sanatan Dharm, 118, 129, 345–48
Sanskrit: xi, 3–4, 9, 13–14, 33, 50, 61, 67, 69, 102, 106, 213, 217–18, 266–67, 276, 338, 358, 380n7, 382n15, 387n36, 389n55, 395n43;
Sanskritization, 115, 364n26
Sarayu River, 268, 371n6
Sastrulu, Vavilla Ramasvami (Telugu publisher), 172–73
Sati, 25, 44, 46–47, 356
Satsang, 27–8, 30, 46
Satyagraha, 298–99, 329, 332, 344
Satyanarayana, Viswanatha, 170, 181–82, 383nn24, 27
*Satyārth Prakāsh*, 344
Savitri, 25, 356, 391n7
Self-Reflexivity, 84–86, 91–92, 94, 100, 103, 360n17
Sexism, 309, 316, 324, 327
Sexuality, 17, 105–11, 115–16, 144–45, 179–80, 202, 210, 215–16, 225–29, 231, 305, 331, 348, 406n2, 409n20
Shabari, 6, 15, 119–36, 276, 376n1
Shaivism, 133, 277, 280, 344–46, 364n18, 373n30
Shambuka, x, 6–7, 54, 60, 94–97, 124, 159–61, 169, 397n28. See also *Śambuka Vadha*
Shankara, 375n11
Shankaracharya (of Kanchi Kamakoti Pitham), 278–79
Sharma, Ram Chandra, 346–47
Shastras, 224, 229, 337, 357, 408n15. See also Dharma shastras
Shatrughna, 34, 100, 256–58, 276
Shetkari Sangathana, 300–01, 307
Shiva, 25, 31, 34, 44, 46, 61, 79, 83, 94, 97, 100, 102, 249–52, 267, 278–80, 288–89, 297, 304–06, 354, 381n17, 363–64n17, 370n5, 397nn22, 24, 27
Shudra, x, 6, 26, 34–8, 49, 54, 94–97, 124, 137, 159, 173, 175–77, 201, 217–19, 255–58, 379n3, 384n4
Shurpanakha: 6, 34, 111, 175, 276–77, 391n9, in *IR*, 124; in Sagar, 132
Sikhs, 310, 317, 324, 327, 403nn12, 14, 404n24
Singers (in Awadhi and Bhojpuri) 138–40, 145–46, 380nn7, 14, 380n1, 381nn18, 20, 23, 25
Singh, Shankar Dayal, 297
Singh, Shri Vibhuti Narain Singh (Maharaja of Banaras), 37
Sinha, Babu Jang Bahadur, 28, 37, 42, 353, 355
Sita: 1–3, 6–7, 11, 17, 19, 239–42, 285, 287–92, 303–08; in *Mānas* doubts, 25, 27, 34–5, 41–42, 46, 354–55; in *URC*, 49–60, 62–63, 67–73; in *ĀR*, 76, 78, 80, 85, 95; in A/B songs, 20, 139, 141–52, 158, 380n16; in modern Telugu, 166, 169, 178–80, 183; in Malabar, 211, 216, 218; in *VR*, 113–14, 223–38, 390n1, 391n9, 393nn22–24, 394n30; in *KR*, 254–58, 261–64; in *IR*, 276; and reformers, 292–95, 298–303; in SBS Ramlila, 316, 318–23, 325–27; in Fiji, 330–31, 345–46, 348, 350; as Sita Mata, 291–93, 297, 306; Sita Marhi, 292, 295; *Sīta Agnipravēśam*, 180; *Sīta Josyam*, 182–84
Smith, William, 245, 260
*Śoka Rāmāyaṇa*, 88, 91, 95
South Asians in UK, 19, 309–14,

character in *Mānas*, 34; character in *URC*, 55–59, 71; character in *ĀR*, 13–14, 83–91, 95–97, 100–02, 370nn4–5; and Telugu Ramayanas, 162–64, 174–75, 178, 182; character in *KR*, 254, 262–64; in ashram, 290, 295, 297
Valmiki's Ramayana. See *Rāmāyaṇa* of Valmiki
Van der Veer, Peter, 43
Varma, Lakshmi Kant, 297
Vasanti (goddess of forest), 53–55, 65–66, 68, 78
Vasistha, 55, 58, 87, 160–61
Vatsyayan, Sachidanand, 295, 278
Vedic texts and rituals, xi, 37–40, 44, 68, 74, 85, 88, 94, 133, 142–5, 167, 181, 256–57, 268, 337–38, 344–46, 355, 364n28, 365n35, 373n26, 378n23, 408n16
Venkateswara Rao, Narla, 182–83
Vettam Mani, 247
Vibhishana, 25–26, 35, 176, 276, 294, 355, 357
Vidushaka, 217
Vindhya Mountains, 95–96
Viradha, 111–12, 234
Vishnu, 31, 42, 86, 90, 96–97, 249, 267, 280, 354, 370n5, 372n18, 373n27
Vishva Hindu Parishad [VHP], viii, 1–2, 361n3, 365n34
Vishvakarma, 190, 196, 199
Vishvamitra, 51, 57, 175, 183
Voice: silenced or marginalized, 16; Sita's voice, 16–17, 223–38
Vyajokti (censure which implies praise), 98
Vyasa, 88–89, 101–02, 374n32, 397n23

Water: swearing upon, 148; and Sita 150, 297; reviving dead warriors, 262; and penance, 380n9
Weapons, 43, 51, 57–59, 77; of rakshasis, 111, 115, 257, 259
Wedding: 66, 380–381n17; songs, 145–48
*Western Pacific Herald*, 339
Wine and liquor: 38; and rakshasas, 109–13, 115
Women: 6, 17–19, 101–11, 203, 286–92, 298–308, 391n6, 393nn21–24; in *Mānas* doubts, 25–6, 32, 34, 37–41, 47, 357–58; songs of, xi, 15, 137–58, 293, 296–97, 379n6, 382n9; in modern Telugu, 179–80, 183–84; in *VR*, 109–11, 223–38; in *KR*, 251, 263; in SBS Ramlila, 309–10, 314–28; in Fiji, 330–31, 335, 344, 350, 357

Yajna, 294, 302, 357
Yamuna River, 53, 262
Yati (monk), 93–94, 96–98, 373n25
*Yātrā-kāṇḍa*, 84, 102, 371n6